Reading STREET

Program Authors

Peter Afflerbach

Camille Blachowicz

Candy Dawson Boyd

Elena Izquierdo

Connie Juel

Edward Kame'enui

Donald Leu

Jeanne R. Paratore

P. David Pearson

Sam Sebesta

Deborah Simmons

Alfred Tatum

Sharon Vaughn

Susan Watts Taffe

Karen Kring Wixson

PEARSON

Glenview, Illinois • Boston, Massachusetts
Chandler, Arizona • Upper Saddle River, New Jersey

We dedicate Reading Street to
Peter Jovanovich.

His wisdom, courage,
and passion for education
are an inspiration to us all.

Accelerated Reader

PEARSON

ISBN-13: 978-0-328-46984-0
ISBN-10: 0-328-46984-X
2 3 4 5 6 7 8 9 10 V064 14 13 12 11 10
CC1

Any Path, Any Pace

Reading Street

CALLE de la Lectura

"Welcome to Reading Street! Bienvenidos too."

PEARSON

Find Your Place on Reading Street!

Who said so?

The Leading Researchers,

Program Authors

Peter Afflerbach, Ph.D.
Professor
Department of Curriculum and
Instruction
University of Maryland at
College Park

**Camille L. Z. Blachowicz,
Ph.D.**
Professor of Education
National-Louis University

Candy Dawson Boyd, Ph.D.
Professor
School of Education
Saint Mary's College of California

Elena Izquierdo, Ph.D.
Associate Professor
University of Texas at El Paso

Connie Juel, Ph.D.
Professor of Education
School of Education
Stanford University

Edward J. Kame'enui, Ph.D.
*Dean-Knight Professor of
Education and Director*
Institute for the Development of
Educational Achievement and
the Center on Teaching and Learning
College of Education
University of Oregon

Donald J. Leu, Ph.D.
*John and Maria Neag Endowed
Chair in Literacy and Technology
Director, The New Literacies
Research Lab*
University of Connecticut

Jeanne R. Paratore, Ed.D.
Associate Professor of Education
Department of Literacy and
Language Development
Boston University

P. David Pearson, Ph.D.
Professor and Dean
Graduate School of Education
University of California, Berkeley

Sam L. Sebesta, Ed.D.
Professor Emeritus
College of Education
University of Washington, Seattle

Deborah Simmons, Ph.D
Professor
College of Education and
Human Development
Texas A&M University

Alfred W. Tatum, Ph.D.
*Associate Professor and Director
of the UIC Reading Clinic*
University of Illinois at Chicago

Sharon Vaughn, Ph.D.
*H. E. Hartfelder/Southland
Corporation Regents Professor
Director, Meadows Center for
Preventing Educational Risk*
University of Texas

Susan Watts Taffe, Ph.D.
Associate Professor in Literacy
Division of Teacher Education
University of Cincinnati

Karen Kring Wixson, Ph.D.
Professor of Education
University of Michigan

Consulting Authors

Jeff Anderson, M.Ed.
Author and Consultant
San Antonio, Texas

Jim Cummins, Ph.D.
Professor
Department of Curriculum,
Teaching and Learning
University of Toronto

Lily Wong Fillmore, Ph.D.
Professor Emerita
Graduate School of Education
University of California, Berkeley

Georgia Earnest García, Ph.D.
Professor
Language and Literacy Division
Department of Curriculum
and Instruction
University of Illinois at
Urbana-Champaign

George A. González, Ph.D.
Professor (Retired)
School of Education
University of Texas-Pan American,
Edinburg

Valerie Ooka Pang, Ph.D.
Professor
School of Teacher Education
San Diego State University

Sally M. Reis, Ph.D.
*Board of Trustees Distinguished
Professor*
Department of Educational
Psychology
University of Connecticut

Jon Scieszka, M.F.A.
*Children's Book Author
Founder of GUYS READ
Named First National Ambassador
for Young People's Literature 2008*

Grant Wiggins, Ed.D.
Educational Consultant
Authentic Education
Concept Development

Lee Wright, M.Ed.
Pearland, Texas

Practitioners, and Authors.

Consultant

Sharroky Hollie, Ph.D.
Assistant Professor
California State University
Dominguez Hills, CA

Teacher Reviewers

Dr. Bettyann Brugger
*Educational Support Coordinator–
Reading Office*
Milwaukee Public Schools
Milwaukee, WI

Kathleen Burke
K–12 Reading Coordinator
Peoria Public Schools, Peoria, IL

Darci Burns, M.S.Ed.
University of Oregon

Bridget Cantrell
District Intervention Specialist
Blackburn Elementary School
Independence, MO

**Tahira DuPree Chase,
M.A., M.S.Ed.**
*Administrator of Elementary
English Language Arts*
Mount Vernon City School District
Mount Vernon, NY

Michele Conner
Director, Elementary Education
Aiken County School District
Aiken, SC

Georgia Coulombe
*K–6 Regional Trainer/
Literacy Specialist*
Regional Center for Training and
Learning (RCTL), Reno, NV

Kelly Dalmas
Third Grade Teacher
Avery's Creek Elementary, Arden, NC

Seely Dillard
First Grade Teacher
Laurel Hill Primary School
Mt. Pleasant, SC

Jodi Dodds-Kinner
Director of Elementary Reading
Chicago Public Schools, Chicago, IL

Dr. Ann Wild Evenson
District Instructional Coach
Osseo Area Schools, Maple Grove, MN

Stephanie Fascitelli
Principal
Apache Elementary, Albuquerque
Public Schools, Albuquerque, NM

Alice Franklin
*Elementary Coordinator, Language
Arts & Reading*
Spokane Public Schools, Spokane, WA

Laureen Fromberg
Assistant Principal
PS100 Queens, NY

Kimberly Gibson
First Grade Teacher
Edgar B. Davis Community School
Brockton, MA

Kristen Gray
Lead Teacher
A.T. Allen Elementary School
Concord, NC

Mary Ellen Hazen
State Pre-K Teacher
Rockford Public Schools #205
Rockford, IL

Patrick M. Johnson
Elementary Instructional Director
Seattle Public Schools, Seattle, WA

Theresa Jaramillo Jones
Principal
Highland Elementary School
Las Cruces, NM

Sophie Kowzun
*Program Supervisor, Reading/
Language Arts, PreK–5*
Montgomery County Public Schools
Rockville, MD

David W. Matthews
Sixth Grade Teacher
Easton Area Middle School
Easton, PA

Ana Nuncio
Editor and Independent Publisher
Salem, MA

Joseph Peila
Principal
Chappell Elementary School
Chicago, IL

Ivana Reimer
Literacy Coordinator
PS100 Queens, NY

Sally Riley
Curriculum Coordinator
Rochester Public Schools
Rochester, NH

Dyan M. Smiley
Independent Educational Consultant

Michael J. Swiatowiec
Lead Literacy Teacher
Graham Elementary School
Chicago, IL

Dr. Helen Taylor
Director of English Education
Portsmouth City Public Schools
Portsmouth, VA

Carol Thompson
Teaching and Learning Coach
Independence School District
Independence, MO

Erinn Zeitlin
Kindergarten Teacher
Carderock Springs Elementary School
Bethesda, MD

Any Path, Any Pace

Look at Us!

In this Teacher's Edition Unit 2, Volume 2

WEEK 4 · **Bear Snores On**

Differentiated Instruction **SI** **OL** **A** **ELL**

WEEK 5 · **A Bed for the Winter**

Differentiated Instruction **SI** **OL** **A** **ELL**

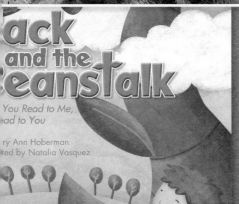

WEEK 6 · **Jack and the Beanstalk**

Differentiated Instruction **SI** **OL** **A** **ELL**

In the **First Stop** on Reading Street

 GO Digital!

See It!

- **Big Question Video**

- **Concept Talk Video**

- **Envision It! Animations**

- **Sing With Me Animations**

Hear It!

- **Sing With Me Animations**

- **eReaders**

- **Grammar Jammer**

- **Leveled Reader Database**

Do It!

- **Story Sort**

- **Letter Tile Drag and Drop**

UNIT 1

All Together Now

Volume 1

Volume 2

UNIT 2

Look at Us!

Volume 1

Volume 2

UNIT 3

Changes All Around Us

Volume 1

Volume 2

Let's Go Exploring

Volume 1

WEEK 1 • Rooster's Off to See the World
Animal Fantasy...7–102

Differentiated Instruction SI OL A ELL ....DI•1–DI•17

WEEK 2 • My Lucky Day Animal Fantasy 103–204

Differentiated Instruction SI OL A ELL ....DI•18–DI•34

WEEK 3 • One Little Mouse Animal Fantasy...............205–304

Differentiated Instruction SI OL A ELL ....DI•35–DI•51

Volume 2

WEEK 4 • Goldilocks and the Three Bears
Classic Fairy Tale...305–406

Differentiated Instruction SI OL A ELL ....DI•52–DI•68

WEEK 5 • If You Could Go to Antarctica
Nonfiction 407–502

Differentiated Instruction SI OL A ELL ....DI•69–DI•85

WEEK 6 • Abuela Fantasy 503–605

Differentiated Instruction SI OL A ELL ....DI•86–DI•102

Customize Literacy...CL•1–CL•31

Going Places

Key
- **SI** Strategic Intervention
- **OL** On-Level
- **A** Advanced
- **ELL** ELL

Volume 1

Volume 2

UNIT 6

Putting It Together

Volume 1

Volume 2

Skills Overview

Key

T Tested

 Target Skill

	WEEK 1	WEEK 2
	 **Flowers** Nonfiction pp. 60–71	**Nature Spy** Nonfiction pp. 158–171

Get Ready to Read

Question of the Week	How are flowers unique?	What can we learn about nature when we look closely?
Amazing Words	*seeds, fruits, buds, stem, bloom, petals*	*discover, nature, spy, acorn, pod, pattern*
Phonemic Awareness	T  /a/	T  /s/
Phonics	T  /a/ Spelled *Aa* Review /t/ Spelled *Tt*	T  /s/ Spelled *Ss* Review /a/ Spelled *Aa*
High-Frequency Words	T *have, is*	T *have, is*

Read and Comprehend

Comprehension	 **Skill** Compare and Contrast Review Classify and Categorize	T  **Skill** Setting Review Sequence

Language Arts

Writing	Label	List
Conventions	Nouns for More Than One	Proper Nouns
Vocabulary	Color Words	Nature Words
Speaking/Listening	Listen for Sequence	Listen for Directions

The Big Question

How are animals and plants unique?

WEEK 3	WEEK 4	WEEK 5	WEEK 6
Animal Babies in Grasslands Nonfiction pp. 258–271	**Bear Snores On** Animal Fantasy pp. 358–373	**A Bed for the Winter** Nonfiction pp. 459–473	**Jack and the Beanstalk** Fairy Tale pp. 560–571
What special animals live in the grasslands?	What unique thing does a bear do in the winter?	What kind of home does an animal need?	How are real and make-believe plants alike and different?
calf, grassland, cub, pup, joey, foal	*sleep, winter, cave, woods, storm, blustery*	*nest, meadow, stump, tree trunk, hive, den*	*beanstalk, lad, ogre, magic, naughty, lend*
T /p/	T /k/	T /i/	T /i/
T /p/ Spelled *Pp* Review /s/ Spelled *Ss*	T /k/ Spelled *Cc* Review /p/ Spelled *Pp*	T /i/ Spelled *Ii* Review /k/ Spelled *Cc*	T /i/ Spelled *Ii* Review Sound-Spellings *Cc, Pp, Ss, Tt, Mm, Aa*
T *we, my, like*	T *we, my, like*	T *he, for*	T *he, for*
T **Skill** Main Idea Review Compare and Contrast	T **Skill** Realism and Fantasy Review Setting	T **Skill** Sequence Review Classify and Categorize	T **Skill** Realism and Fantasy Review Sequence
Notes	Poem	Caption	Writing Process: Story
Adjectives for Colors/Shapes	Adjectives for Sizes/Numbers	Adjectives for Opposites	Adjectives
Words for Animal Babies	Words for Seasons	Sequence Words	Direction Words
Discussions: Who Am I? Who Are You?	Listen for Setting	Give a Description	Listen for Plot

UNIT 2

Monitor Progress
Make Data-Driven Decisions

Data Management
- Assess
- Diagnose
- Prescribe
- Disaggregate

Classroom Management
- Monitor Progress
- Group
- Differentiate Instruction
- Inform Parents

Don't Wait Until Friday

SUCCESS PREDICTOR	WEEK 1	WEEK 2	WEEK 3	WEEK 4
Phonemic Awareness	T ⏱ /a/	T ⏱ /s/	T ⏱ /p/	T ⏱ /k/
Phonics	T ⏱ /a/ Spelled *Aa*	T ⏱ /s/ Spelled *Ss*	T ⏱ /p/ Spelled *Pp*	T ⏱ /k/ Spelled *Cc*
High-Frequency Words	T have T is	T have T is	T we T my T like	T we T my T like
Oral Vocabulary/ Concept Development (assessed informally)	seeds fruits buds stem bloom petals	discover nature spy acorn pod pattern	calf grassland cub pup joey foal	sleep winter cave woods storm blustery
Comprehension	T ⏱ **Skill** Compare and Contrast **Strategies** Preview and Predict; Retell	T ⏱ **Skill** Setting **Strategies** Preview and Predict; Retell	T ⏱ **Skill** Main Idea **Strategies** Preview and Predict; Retell	T ⏱ **Skill** Realism and Fantasy **Strategies** Preview and Predict; Retell

WEEK 5	WEEK 6
T /i/	T /i/
T /i/ Spelled *Ii*	T /i/ Spelled *Ii*
T he T for	T he T for
nest meadow stump tree trunk hive den	beanstalk lad ogre magic naughty lend
T **Skill** Sequence **Strategies** Preview and Predict; Retell	T **Skill** Realism and Fantasy **Strategies** Preview and Predict; Retell

GO Digital!

See It!

- **Big Question Video**
- **Concept Talk Video**
- **Envision It! Animations**
- **Sing with Me Animations**

Hear It!

- **Sing with Me Animations**
- **eReaders**
- **Grammar Jammer**
- **Leveled Reader Database**

Do It!

- **Story Sort**
- **Letter Tile Drag and Drop**

UNIT 2

Assessment and Grouping
for Data-Driven Instruction

4-Step Plan for Assessment
1 Diagnose and Differentiate
2 Monitor Progress
3 Assess and Regroup
4 Summative Assessment

STEP 1 Diagnose and Differentiate

Scott Foresman
Baseline Group Tests
- Assess phonemic awareness, phonics, high-frequency words, listening comprehension, and fluency
- Guidelines for grouping—strategic intervention, on-level, and advanced
- Guidelines for taking the Early Reading Intervention program placement test

Baseline Group Tests

Diagnose

To make initial grouping decisions, use the Baseline Group Test, the Texas Primary Reading Inventory (TPRI), or another initial placement test. Depending on students' ability levels, you may have more than one of each group.

Differentiate

If... student performance is **(SI)** **then...** use the regular instruction and the daily **Strategic Intervention** small group lessons.

If... student performance is **(OL)** **then...** use the regular instruction and the daily **On-Level** small group lessons.

If... student performance is **(A)** **then...** use the regular instruction and the daily **Advanced** learners small group lessons.

Small Group Time

(SI) Strategic Intervention

- Daily small group lessons provide more intensive instruction, more scaffolding, more practice, and more opportunities to respond.
- Reteach lessons in the *First Stop* provide more instruction of target skills.
- Leveled readers, decodable readers, and other weekly texts build background and practice target skills and vocabulary.

(OL) On-Level

- Explicit instructional routines teach core skills and strategies.
- Daily On-Level lessons provide more practice and more opportunities to respond.
- Independent activities provide practice for core skills.
- Student Readers and Get Set, Roll! Readers provide additional reading and practice for core skills and vocabulary.

(A) Advanced

- Daily Advanced lessons provide instruction for accelerated learning.
- Independent Leveled Readers provide additional reading tied to lesson concepts and skills.

Additional Differentiated Learning Options

Reading Street Response to Intervention Kit
- Focused intervention lessons on the five critical areas of reading: phonemic awareness, phonics, vocabulary, comprehension, and fluency

My Sidewalks on Reading Street
- Early Reading Intervention

STEP 2 Monitor Progress

Use these tools during lesson teaching to **monitor student progress.**

- **Skill and Strategy** instruction during reading

- **Don't Wait Until Friday** boxes to check letter and sound fluency, word reading, retelling, and oral vocabulary

- **Weekly Assessment** on Day 5 to check phonics, high-frequency words, and comprehension

- **Reader's and Writer's Notebook** pages at point of use

Weekly Phonics and High-Frequency Words Assessment

Weekly Comprehension Assessment

STEP 3 Assess and Regroup

Use these tools during lesson teaching to **assess and regroup.**

- **Weekly Assessments** Record results of weekly assessments for phonics and high-frequency words to track student progress.

- **Unit Benchmark Assessment** Administer this assessment to check progress of unit skills.

- **Regroup** We recommend the first regrouping to be at the end of Unit 2. Use weekly assessment information and Unit Benchmark Assessment performance to inform regrouping decisions. Then regroup at the end of each subsequent unit.

Unit 1 Reading Chart in First Stop

Group

Baseline Group Test → Regroup Units 1 and 2 → Regroup Unit 3 → Regroup Unit 4 → Regroup Unit 5 → End of Year

| Unit 1 Weeks 1–6 | Unit 2 Weeks 7–12 | Unit 3 Weeks 13–18 | Unit 4 Weeks 19–24 | Unit 5 Weeks 25–30 | Unit 6 Weeks 31–36 |

Outside assessments, such as DRA, TPRI, and DIBELS, may recommend regrouping at other times during the year.

STEP 4 Summative Assessment

Use these tools after lesson teaching to **assess students.**

- **Unit Benchmark Assessments** Use to measure a student's mastery of each unit's skills.

- **End-of-Year Benchmark Assessment** Use to measure a student's mastery of program skills covered in all six units.

Unit and End-of-Year Benchmark Assessment

Understanding By Design

*Grant Wiggins, Ed. D.
Reading Street Author*

"We need to go beyond questions answerable by unit facts to questions that burst through the boundaries of the topic. Deep and transferable understandings depend upon framing work around such questions."

Look at Us!

Reading Street Online

www.ReadingStreet.com

• Big Question Video
• Envision It! Animations
• Story Sort

THE BIG ?

How are animals and plants unique?

UNIT **2**

Small Group Time
Flexible Pacing Plans

Small Group Time

Sometimes you have holidays, programs, assemblies, or other interruptions to the school week. This plan can help you make Small Group Time decisions if you have less time during the week.

5 Day Plan

DAY 1	• Phonemic Awareness • Phonics • Reading Practice
DAY 2	• Phonemic Awareness • Phonics • Reading Practice
DAY 3	• Phonemic Awareness/ Phonics • Leveled Reader
DAY 4	• Phonemic Awareness • Reading Practice
DAY 5	• Phonics • Reading Practice

4 Day Plan

DAY 1	• Phonemic Awareness • Phonics • Reading Practice
DAY 2	• Phonemic Awareness • Phonics • Reading Practice
DAY 3	• Phonemic Awareness/ Phonics • Leveled Reader
DAY 4	• Phonemic Awareness • Reading Practice

3 Day Plan

DAY 1	• Phonemic Awareness • Phonics • Reading Practice
DAY 2	• Phonemic Awareness/ Phonics • Leveled Reader
DAY 3	• Phonemic Awareness • Reading Practice

ELL

5 Day Plan

DAY 1	• Frontload Concept • Phonemic Awareness/ Phonics • Comprehension
DAY 2	• Comprehension • Vocabulary
DAY 3	• Phonemic Awareness/ Phonics • Conventions
DAY 4	• Phonemic Awareness/ Phonics • Concepts and Oral Language
DAY 5	• Language Workshop • Writing

4 Day Plan

DAY 1	• Frontload Concept • Phonemic Awareness/ Phonics • Comprehension
DAY 2	• Comprehension • Vocabulary
DAY 3	• Phonemic Awareness/ Phonics • Conventions
DAY 4	• Language Workshop • Writing

3 Day Plan

DAY 1	• Frontload Concept • Phonemic Awareness/ Phonics • Comprehension
DAY 2	• Phonemic Awareness/ Phonics • Conventions
DAY 3	• Language Workshop • Writing

This Week's ELL Overview

ELL Handbook

- Maximize Literacy and Cognitive Engagement
- Research Into Practice
- Full Weekly Support for Every Selection

  ### Bear Snores On
  - Routines to Support Instruction

- Transfer Activities
- Professional Development

Daily Leveled ELL Notes

ELL notes appear throughout this week's instruction and ELL Support is on the DI pages of your Teacher's Edition. The following is a sample of an ELL note from this week.

English Language Learners

Beginning Build Background English learners will benefit from additional visual support to understand words in the song. For example, point to the *cave* in the art to scaffold meaning.

Intermediate High-Frequency Words After the Team Talk activity, have children continue to work in pairs to check understanding. Have one child read one of the sentences aloud while another child makes a simple drawing to illustrate the sentence.

Advanced Support High-Frequency Words To help children understand what *my* means and how to use it in a sentence, have children practice saying *This is my ____.* and filling in a word that tells about something they are wearing, such as *shoe.*

Advanced High Language Transfer In languages such as Spanish and Vietnamese, adjectives may follow nouns, as in the name *Rio Grande* ("big river"). If children say *insect small* instead of *small insect,* provide additional practice saying adjectives before nouns.

ELL by Strand

The ELL lessons on this week's Support for English Language Learners pages are organized by strand. They offer additional scaffolding for the core curriculum. Leveled support notes on these pages address the different proficiency levels in your class. See pages DI•63–DI•68.

ELL Guy
Dr. Jim Cummins

The Three Pillars of ELL Instruction

ELL Strands	Activate Prior Knowledge	Access Content	Extend Language
Vocabulary p. DI•65	Frontload Vocabulary	Provide Scaffolding	Practice
Reading Comprehension p. DI•65	Provide Scaffolding	Set the Scene	Frontload Vocabulary
Phonics, Spelling, and Word Analysis pp. DI•63, DI•66–DI•67	Frontload Words with /k/	Isolate Initial and Final /k/	Review /p/
Listening Comprehension p. DI•64	Prepare for the Read Aloud	First Listening	Second Listening
Conventions and Writing pp. DI•66, DI•68	Provide Scaffolding/ Introduce and Model	Practice	Leveled Practice Activities/ Leveled Writing Activities
Concept Development p. DI•63	Read the Concept Literacy Reader	Read the Concept Literacy Reader	Develop Oral Language

This Week's Practice Stations Overview

Six Weekly Practice Stations with Leveled Activities can be found at the beginning of each week of instruction. For this week's Practice Stations, see pp. 312–313.

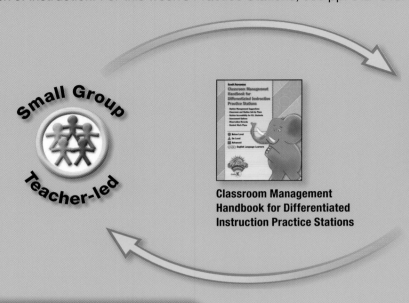

Small Group Teacher-led

Classroom Management Handbook for Differentiated Instruction Practice Stations

Practice Stations

Daily Leveled Center Activities

⬤ Below   ▢ Advanced

△ On-Level   ⒺⓁⓁ

Practice Stations Flip Charts

	Listen Up	**Word Work**	**Words to Know**	**Let's Write**	**Read for Meaning**	**Let's Make Art**
Objectives	• Identify and say words with /p/.	• Identify and build words with /p/.	• Identify and use words for animal babies.	• Write notes.	• Identify the main idea.	• Create a picture of a grasslands animal.
Materials	• *Listen Up* Flip Chart Activity 10 • *cup, cap, map, pig, pail, pan, tent, yarn* Picture Cards	• *Word Work* Flip Chart Activity 10 • *Pp, Tt, Ee, Zz* Alphabet Cards • *green, mop, nut, pen, pillow, roof, soap* Picture Cards • Letter Tiles	• *Words to Know* Flip Chart Activity 10 • magazines or book with pictures of a puppy, kitten, calf, chick • Teacher-made Word Cards: *puppy, kitten, calf, chick* • paper, pencils, crayons	• *Let's Write* Flip Chart Activity 10 • Little Book *Animal Babies in Grasslands* • crayons, paper, pencil	• *Read for Meaning* Flip Chart Activity 10 • Little Book *Animal Babies in Grasslands* • pencil, crayons, paper	• *Let's Make Art* Flip Chart Activity 10 • Little Book *Animal Babies in Grasslands* • pencil, paper, crayons, glue

This Week on Reading Street!

Look at Us!

Question of the Week

What unique thing does a bear do in the winter?

Daily Plan

Don't Wait Until Friday

Whole Group

- ◉ /k/ Spelled *Cc*
- ◉ Realism and Fantasy
- • Vocabulary

MONITOR PROGRESS | **Success Predictor**

Day 1	Day 2	Day 3	Day 4	Day 5
Check Phonemic Awareness	Check Sound Spelling/ Retelling	Check Word Reading	Check Phonemic Awareness	Check Oral Vocabulary

Small Group

Teacher-Led

- • Reading Support
- • Skill Support
- • Fluency Practice

Practice Stations

Independent Activities

Customize Literacy More support for a Balanced Literacy approach, see pp. CL•1–CL•31.

Whole Group

- • Writing
- • Conventions: Adjectives for Sizes and Numbers
- • Listening and Speaking

Assessment

- • Day 5 Assessment for Phonics
- • Day 5 Assessment for Comprehension

You Are Here! Unit 2 Week 4

This Week's Reading Selections

Bear Snores On

Big Book
Genre: **Animal Fantasy**

Decodable Reader 10

Leveled Readers

Get Set Roll! Reader 10

Resources on Reading Street!

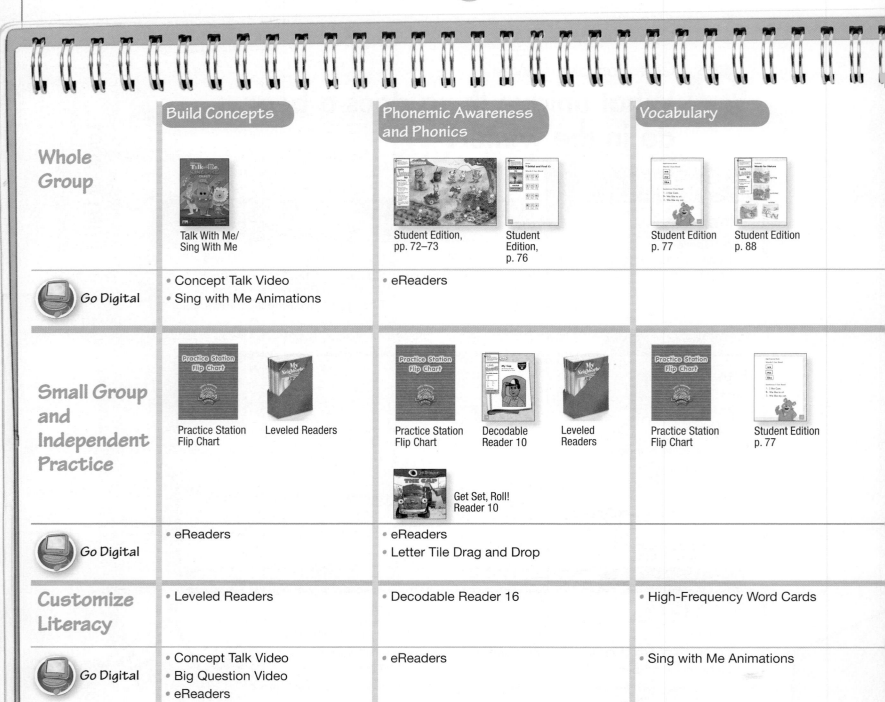

	Build Concepts	Phonemic Awareness and Phonics	Vocabulary
Whole Group	Talk With Me/ Sing With Me	Student Edition, pp. 72–73 — Student Edition, p. 76	Student Edition p. 77 — Student Edition p. 88
Go Digital	• Concept Talk Video • Sing with Me Animations	• eReaders	
Small Group and Independent Practice	Practice Station Flip Chart — Leveled Readers	Practice Station Flip Chart — Decodable Reader 10 — Leveled Readers — Get Set, Roll! Reader 10	Practice Station Flip Chart — Student Edition p. 77
Go Digital	• eReaders	• eReaders • Letter Tile Drag and Drop	
Customize Literacy	• Leveled Readers	• Decodable Reader 16	• High-Frequency Word Cards
Go Digital	• Concept Talk Video • Big Question Video • eReaders	• eReaders	• Sing with Me Animations

What unique thing does a bear do in the winter?

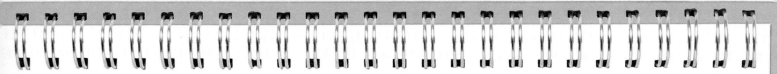

Comprehension

Student Edition
pp. 74–75

Big Book

- Envision It! Animations

Fluency

Decodable
Reader 10

Kdg. Student
Reader K.2.4

Get Set, Roll!
Reader 10

- eReaders

Conventions and Writing

Reader's and
Writer's Notebook

- Grammar Jammer

Practice Station
Flip Chart

Leveled
Readers

Get Set, Roll!
Reader 10

Practice Station
Flip Chart

Leveled Readers

Practice Station
Flip Chart

Reader's and
Writer's Notebook

- Envision It! Animations
- eReaders

- eReaders

- Grammar Jammer

- Leveled Readers

- Leveled Readers

- *Reader's and Writer's Notebook*

- Envision It! Aminations
- eReaders

- eReaders

- Grammar Jammer

You Are Here!
Unit 2
Week 4

My 5-Day Planner for Reading Street!

MONITOR PROGRESS
Don't Wait Until Friday

	Check Phonemic Awareness **Day 1** pages 314–329	Check Sound-Spelling Check Retelling **Day 2** pages 330–347
Get Ready to Read	**Concept Talk,** 314 **Oral Vocabulary,** 315 *sleep, winter, cave, woods, storm, blustery* **Phonemic Awareness,** 316–317 ◉ Initial /k/ **Phonics,** 318–319 ◉ /k/ Spelled *Cc* **Handwriting,** 320 Letters *C* and *c* **High-Frequency Words,** 321 *we, my, like* **READ Decodable Story 10,** 322–323	**Concept Talk,** 330 **Oral Vocabulary,** 331 *sleep, winter* **Phonemic Awareness,** 332–333 ◉ Initial and Final /k/ **Phonics,** 334–335 ◉ /k/ Spelled *Cc* **Handwriting,** 336 Words with *Cc* **High-Frequency Words,** 337 *we, my, like* **READ Decodable Reader 10,** 338–339
Read and Comprehend	**Listening Comprehension,** 324–325 ◉ Realism and Fantasy	**Listening Comprehension,** 340 ◉ Realism and Fantasy **READ Big Book—First Read,** 340 *Bear Snores On* **Retell,** 341 **Think, Talk, and Write,** 342
Language Arts	**Conventions,** 326 Adjectives for Sizes **Writing,** 327 Wonderful, Marvelous Me! **Daily Handwriting,** 327 Letters *C* and *c* **Listening and Speaking,** 328 Listen for Setting **Wrap Up Your Day,** 328 **Extend Your Day!,** 329	**Conventions,** 343 Adjectives for Numbers **Writing,** 344 Respond to Literature **Daily Handwriting,** 344 Letters *C* and *c* **Vocabulary,** 345 Words for Seasons **Wrap Up Your Day,** 346 **Extend Your Day!,** 347

You Are Here!
Unit 2 Week 4

What unique thing does a bear do in the winter?

Check Word Reading	Check Phonemic Awareness	Check Oral Vocabulary
Day 3 pages 348–379	**Day 4** pages 380–391	**Day 5** pages 392–405
Concept Talk, 348 **Oral Vocabulary,** 349 *cave, woods* **Phonemic Awareness,** 350–351 ⊚ Final /k/ **Phonics,** 352–353 ⊚ /k/ Spelled *Cc* **READ Kindergarten Student Reader K.2.4,** 354–355	**Concept Talk,** 380 **Oral Vocabulary,** 381 *storm, blustery* Review **Phonemic Awareness,** 382 /p/ Review **Phonics,** 383 /p/ Spelled *Pp* **Spelling,** 384 ⊚ /k/ Spelled *Cc* **READ Get Set, Roll! Reader 10,** 385	**Concept Wrap Up,** 392 **Oral Vocabulary,** 393 *sleep, winter, cave, woods, storm, blustery* Review **Phonemic Awareness,** 394 ⊚ /k/ Review **Phonics,** 395 ⊚ /k/ Spelled *Cc* **Assessment,** 396–397 Monitor Progress
Comprehension, 356–357 ⊚ Realism and Fantasy **READ Big Book—Second Read,** 358–373 *Bear Snores On*	**Comprehension,** 386 ⊚ Realism and Fantasy Review Setting **READ Big Book—Third Read,** 387 *Bear Snores On*	**Let's Practice It!,** 398–399 Lullaby **Assessment,** 400–401 Monitor Progress
Conventions, 374 Adjectives for Colors and Shapes **Writing,** 375 Poem **Daily Handwriting,** 375 Letters *C* and *c* **Listening and Speaking,** 376–377 Listen for Setting **Wrap Up Your Day,** 378 **Extend Your Day!,** 379	**Conventions,** 388 Adjectives for Sizes **Writing,** 389 Extend the Concept **Daily Handwriting,** 389 Letters *C* and *c* **Vocabulary,** 390 Words for Seasons **Wrap Up Your Day,** 390 **Extend Your Day!,** 391	Review **Conventions,** 402 Adjectives for Numbers **Writing,** 403 This Week We… **Daily Handwriting,** 403 Letters *C* and *c* **Wrap Up Your Week,** 404 What unique thing does a bear do in the winter? **Extend Your Day!,** 405

Week 4

Grouping Options for Differentiated Instruction
Turn the page for the small group time lesson plan.

Planning Small Group Time on Reading Street!

SMALL GROUP TIME RESOURCES

DAY 1

Look for this Small Group Time box each day to help meet the individual needs of all your children. Differentiated instruction lessons appear on the DI pages at the end of each week.

Teacher-Led

SI Strategic Intervention	**OL** On-Level	**A** Advanced
Teacher-Led	Teacher-Led	Teacher-Led
• Phonemic Awareness and Phonics	• Phonemic Awareness and Phonics	• Phonemic Awareness and Phonics
Reread Decodable Story	**Reread** Decodable Story	**Reread** Decodable Story for Fluency

ELL Place English language learners in the groups that correspond to their reading abilities in English.

Practice Stations
• Listen Up
• Word Work

Independent Activities
• Read Independently
• *Reader's and Writer's Notebook*
• Concept Talk Video

ELL Poster 10

Day 1

SI Strategic Intervention	**Phonemic Awareness and Phonics,** DI•52 **Reread** Decodable Story 10, DI•52
OL On-Level	**Phonemic Awareness and Phonics,** DI•57 **Reread** Decodable Story 10, DI•57
A Advanced	**Phonemic Awareness and Phonics,** DI•60 **Reread** Decodable Story 10 for Fluency, DI•60
ELL English Language Learners	DI•63–DI•64 Frontload Concept Phonemic Awareness and Phonics Comprehension Skill

Reading Street Response
to Intervention Kit

Reading Street Leveled
Practice Stations Kit

Question of the Week
What unique thing does a bear do in the winter?

SI Strategic Intervention

Decodable Reader

Listen to Me Reader

Concept Literacy Reader

Get Set, Roll! Reader

OL On-Level

Kindergarten
Student Reader

Get Set, Roll! Reader

Decodable Reader

A Advanced

Independent
Reader

Decodable Reader

Week 4

Small Group Weekly Plan

Day 2	Day 3	Day 4	Day 5
Phonemic Awareness and Phonics, DI•53	**Phonemic Awareness and Phonics,** DI•54	**Phonemic Awareness and Phonics,** DI•55	**Phonics Review,** DI•56
Reread Decodable Reader 10, DI•53	**Read** Concept Literacy Reader K.2.4, DI•54	**Read** Get Set, Roll! Reader 10, DI•55	**Read** Listen to Me Reader K.2.4, DI•56
Phonemic Awareness and Phonics, DI•57	**Phonemic Awareness and Phonics,** DI•58	Review Phonics and High-Frequency Words	**Phonics Review,** DI•59
Reread Decodable Reader 10, DI•57	**Read** Kindergarten Student Reader K.2.4, DI•58	**Read** Get Set, Roll! Reader 10, DI•59	**Reread** Leveled Books
Phonics and Spelling, DI•60	**Read** Independent Reader K.2.4 or Kindergarten Student Reader K.2.4, DI•61	**Read** Get Set, Roll! Reader 10 or **Reread** Kindergarten Student Reader K.2.4, DI•62	Fluency and Comprehension, DI•62
Reread Decodable Reader 10 for Fluency, DI•60			**Reread** Independent Reader for Fluency, DI•62
DI•65	DI•66	DI•67	DI•68
Comprehension Skill Frontload Vocabulary	Review Phonemic Awareness and Phonics Scaffold Conventions	Review Phonemic Awareness and Phonics Revisit Concept and Oral Language	Language Workshop Writing

Practice Stations for Everyone on Reading Street!

Listen Up!
/p/

Objectives
• Identify and say words with /p/.

Materials
• *Listen Up!* Flip Chart Activity 10
• *cup, cap, map, pig, pail, pan, tent, yarn* Picture Cards

Differentiated Activities

🔵 Find the *pig* Picture Card. Say the sound you hear at the beginning. Find another Picture Card with the same beginning sound.

🔺 Find the *pig* Picture Card. Say the sound you hear at the beginning. Point to a Picture Card with the same beginning sound. Find the *cup* Picture Card. Point to a Picture Card with the same end sound.

🟥 Find the *pig* Picture Card. Say the beginning sound. Point to all Picture Cards with the same beginning sound. Find the *cup* Picture Card. Point to all Picture Cards with the same end sound.

Word Work
/p/ Spelled *Pp*

Objectives
• Identify and build words with /p/.

Materials
• *Word Work* Flip Chart Activity 10
• *Pp, Tt, Ee, Zz* Alphabet Cards
• *green, mop, nut, pen, pillow, roof, soap* Picture Cards
• Letter Tiles

Differentiated Activities

🔵 Find the Alphabet Card for the letter *Pp*. Look for Picture Cards that begin with /p/.

🔺 Find the *Pp* Alphabet Card. Find Picture Cards that begin with /p/. Find Picture Cards with /p/ at the end. Find objects in the room that have /p/ at the beginning or at the end.

🟥 Find the Alphabet Card for the letter *Pp*. Find Picture Cards with the beginning sound of /p/. Find Picture Cards with the sound of /p/ at the end. Use the Letter Tiles to spell other words that begin with /p/ or end with /p/.

Technology
• Letter Tile Drag and Drop

Words To Know
Words for animal babies

Objectives
• Identify and use words for animal babies.

Materials
• *Words to Know* Flip Chart Activity 10
• Magazine or book with pictures of a puppy, kitten, calf, chick
• Teacher-made Word Cards: *puppy, kitten, calf, chick*
• paper, pencils, crayons

Differentiated Activities

🔵 Find pictures of a *puppy, kitten, calf*, and *chick*. Say the name for each picture.

🔺 Match the Word Cards with pictures that show a *puppy, kitten, calf*, and *chick*.

🟥 Match Word Cards and pictures that show a *puppy, kitten, calf*, and *chick*. Draw a picture of a farm with a *puppy, kitten, calf*, and *chick*. Label your picture.

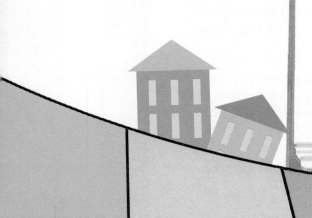

You Are Here! Unit 2 Week 4

Use this week's materials from the Reading Street Leveled Practice Stations Kit to organize this week's stations.

Key
● Below-Level Activities
▲ On-Level Activities
■ Advanced Activities

Practice Station Flip Chart

Practice Station Flip Chart

Let's Write!
Notes

Objectives
• Write notes.

Materials
• *Let's Write!* Flip Chart Activity 10
• Little Book *Animal Babies in Grasslands*
• crayons, paper, pencil

Differentiated Activities

● Look at the Little Book. Use pictures and words to write notes about what you read.

▲ Look at the Little Book. Think about what is important. Use pictures and words to write notes about what you read.

■ Look at the Little Book. Use words and sentences to write notes about what is important.

Read For Meaning
Main idea

Objectives
• Identify the main idea.

Materials
• *Read for Meaning* Flip Chart Activity 10
• Little Book *Animal Babies in Grasslands*
• pencil, crayons, paper

Differentiated Activities

● Look at the Little Book. Think about the main idea. Point to pictures and words that tell about the main idea.

▲ Look at the Little Book. Point to pictures and words that tell about the main idea. Draw a picture that tells the main idea.

■ Look at the Little Book. Think about the most important part. Write a sentence that tells the main idea.

Let's Make Art!

Objectives
• Create a picture of a grasslands animal.

Materials
• *Let's Make Art!* Flip Chart Activity 10
• Little Book *Animal Babies in Grasslands*
• pencil, paper, crayons, glue

Differentiated Activities

● Look at the Little Book. Choose an animal that lives in the grasslands. Draw a picture that shows what it looks like.

▲ Look at the Little Book. Find the animals that live in the grasslands. Draw a picture that shows your favorite animal and where it lives.

■ Look at the Little Book. Make a picture that shows what you learned about animals in the grasslands. Write a sentence about your picture.

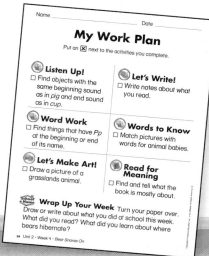

Name _____ Date _____

My Work Plan
Put an ☒ next to the activities you complete.

🎧 **Listen Up!**
☐ Find objects with the same beginning sound as in *pig* and end sound as in *cup*.

✏️ **Let's Write!**
☐ Write notes about what you read.

Word Work
☐ Find things that have *Pp* at the beginning or end of its name.

Words to Know
☐ Match pictures with words for animal babies.

Let's Make Art!
☐ Draw a picture of a grasslands animal.

Read for Meaning
☐ Find and tell what the book is mostly about.

🏠 **Wrap Up Your Week** Turn your paper over. Draw or write about what you did at school this week. What did you read? What did you learn about where bears hibernate?

Unit 2 • Week 4 • Bear Snores On

My Weekly Work Plan

Objective

- Share information and ideas about the concept.

Today at a Glance

Oral Vocabulary
sleep, winter, cave, woods, storm, blustery

Phonemic Awareness
◉ Initial /k/

Phonics
◉ /k/ Spelled *Cc*

Handwriting
C and *c*

High-Frequency Words
we, my, like

Comprehension
◉ Realism and Fantasy

Conventions
Adjectives for Sizes

Writing
Wonderful, Marvelous Me!

Listening and Speaking
Listen for Setting

TRUCKTOWN on Reading Street

Start your engines! Display p. 14 of *Truckery Rhymes.*

- Read aloud "Jack and Kat" and track the print.
- Reread the rhyme and have children say it with you.
- Ask children to identify the rhyming words. (*down, Trucktown*)

Truckery Rhymes

Concept Talk

Question of the Week

 What unique thing does a bear do in the winter?

Introduce the concept

To build concepts and to focus their attention, tell children that this week they will talk, sing, read, and write about **a sleeping bear.** Write the question of the week on the board and track the print as you read it.

Play the CD that features the sounds of snoring, a dog barking, fire crackling, and a car. The little brown bear snores when he sleeps. Do you snore? Can you hear some of the sounds? What are they?

🔘 Background Building Audio

ROUTINE — Activate Prior Knowledge — Team Talk

1. **Think** Have children think for a minute about what they know about what bears do during the winter.

2. **Pair** Have pairs of children discuss the question of the week. Remind them to take turns speaking and to use complete sentences.

3. **Share** Call on a few children to share their ideas with the group. Guide discussion and encourage elaboration with prompts such as: Where do bears find a safe place to live?

Routines Flip Chart

Anchored Talk

Develop oral language

Display Talk with Me Chart 10A. This week we will be talking about where a bear hibernates, or sleeps for the winter. What do you see in the pictures? Point to the bear. This picture shows a bear sleeping. What else do you see in these pictures? What is a snowy, windy day like?

We are going to learn six new Amazing Words this week. Listen as I say the words: *sleep, winter, cave, woods, storm, blustery.* Have children say each word as you point to the picture.

Display Sing with Me Chart 10B. Tell children they are going to sing a song about a bear hibernating. Read the title. Have children describe the picture. What are the bears doing? Where are they? Sing the song several times to the tune of "Hush, Little Baby." Listen for the Amazing Words: *sleep, winter, cave, woods, storm, blustery.* Have children stand up and sing with you.

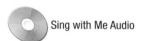 Sing with Me Audio

Talk with Me/Sing with Me Chart 10A

Talk with Me/Sing with Me Chart 10B

ELL **Preteach Concepts** Use the Day 1 instruction on ELL Poster 10 to assess and build background knowledge, develop concepts, and build oral vocabulary.

ELL Poster 10

Amazing Words

sleep	winter
cave	woods
storm	blustery

Differentiated Instruction

A **Advanced**

Activate Prior Knowledge Have children share what they know about animal shelters. Where do birds find shelter? Where do squirrels find shelter?

ELL

English Language Learners

Build Background English learners will benefit from additional visual support to understand words in the song. For example, point to the *cave* in the art to scaffold meaning.

ELL Support Additional ELL support and modified instruction is provided in the *ELL Handbook* and in the ELL Support Lessons on pp. DI•63–68.

Bear Snores On • 315

Objectives

◎ Introduce initial /k/.
• Identify words with initial /k/.
• Discriminate words with initial /k/.

Check Phonemic Awareness
SUCCESS PREDICTOR

My Skills Buddy, pp. 72–73

Phonemic Awareness
Initial /k/

Introduce   Today we will learn a new sound. Listen carefully: /k/ /k/ /k/. Say it with me: /k/ /k/ /k/. Display the *cat* Picture Card. *Cat begins with /k/: /k/, cat.* What sound does *cat* begin with? Continue with the *can, cap,* and *carrot* Picture Cards.

Model   Have children look at the picture on pp. 72–73 of *My Skills Buddy.* Tell them that they will be listening for a new sound—/k/. *I see coloring pages. What sound do you hear at the beginning of coloring? I hear /k/ at the beginning of coloring. The first sound in coloring is /k/.* What other things do you see that begin with that sound?

Picture Card

Guide practice   As children name example words from the picture, guide them in stating that /k/ is the beginning sound. Discuss with children some of the bulleted items on p. 72 of *My Skills Buddy.* Save the other bulleted items for discussion on Day 2.

Corrective feedback   **If...** children have difficulty naming words with /k/,
then... say the /k/ words in the picture and ask them: What is the first sound in *carrots?*

Discriminate sounds

I am going to say a word. If it begins with /k/, I want you to clap your hands. If it does not begin with /k/, fold your hands. Listen carefully. The first word is *can*. (clap hands) The next word is *carrot*. (clap hands) The third word is *mouse*. (fold hands) Continue with the following words: *carry, hay, cut, bite, corn, cook, love, silly, cold, me, find.*

Corrective feedback

If... children cannot discriminate initial /k/,
then... have them enunciate /k/ as they say *can*.

Demonstrate how to produce this sound with the back of your tongue humped and touching the top of your mouth. When you say /k/, does the back of your tongue touch the top of your mouth? Feel where your tongue is. Say /k/ with me: /k/. Repeat the discrimination activity.

Blend

Review blending sounds. Listen to these sounds: /k/ /a/ /p/. Say these sounds with me: /k/ /a/ /p/. Now blend the sounds to say the word *cap*. Continue the blending practice with *pat, cat, tap,* and *map*.

Don't Wait Until Friday

MONITOR PROGRESS ⟳ Check Phonemic Awareness Words with Initial /k/

Say *cup* and *pan*. Have children identify the word that begins with /k/. Continue with these words: *cow, duck; dog, cap; can, fish; nine, coin.*

If... children cannot discriminate /k/,

then... use the small-group Strategic Intervention lesson, p. DI•52, to reteach /k/.

Day 1	**Day 2**	**Day 3**	**Day 4**	**Day 5**
Check Phonemic Awareness	Check Sound-Spelling/ Retelling	Check Word Reading	Check Phonemic Awareness	Check Oral Vocabulary

Success Predictor

Differentiated Instruction

 Advanced

Access Content Ask children to find /k/ words. Have them use each /k/ word in a sentence.

Teacher Tip

Be aware that pronouncing /k/ is very much like pronouncing /g/, with the back part of the tongue raised and pressed against the front of the soft palate. The difference between /g/ and /k/ is that the vocal cords are not vibrating when /k/ is pronounced.

English Language Learners
Phonemic Awareness The sound /k/ exists in many languages. To introduce this sound, you could point out words in the home languages that begin with /k/. For example, these words for *cat* begin with /k/: *kat* (Afrikaans, Dutch), *kot* (Polish, Russian), and *kedi* (Turkish).

Phonemic Awareness **Success Predictor**

Objectives

- Recognize uppercase *C* and lowercase *c*.
- Associate the sound /k/ with the spelling *c*.
- Blend and read words with /k/.

Skills Trace

- **/k/ Spelled *Cc***
  Introduce U2W4D1
  Practice U2W4D2; U2W4D3
  Reteach/Review U2W4D5; U2W5D4; U2W6D
  Assess/Test Benchmark Assessment U2

KEY:
U=Unit   W=Week   D=Day

Phonics—Teach/Model
 /k/ Spelled Cc

Introduce

Display the *Cc* Alphabet Card. Point to the *cactus* on the Alphabet Card. *Cactus* begins with /k/. Say the word with me: *cactus.* What sound does *cactus* begin with? Write the word *cactus* on the board and point to the *c*. *Cactus* begins with /k/ spelled *c*. Now point to the letters *Cc* on the card. The sound we are learning for this letter is /k/. The names of these letters are uppercase *C* and lowercase *c*. What is the sound for this letter? What are the names of these letters?

Alphabet Card

Model

Write "Can Cat Come to Captain's Cave?" on the board. Point to the first *C*. When I see this letter I think of the sound /k/. The first word is *Can*—/k/, *Can*. I know that when I see a *c* the sound may be /k/. The second word is /k/, *Cat*. Repeat the routine for the rest of the /k/ words in the title. The song we will sing is "Can Cat Come to Captain's Cave?"

Guide practice

Display Phonics Songs and Rhymes Chart 10. Teach children the song "Can Cat Come to Captain's Cave?" sung to the tune of "London Bridge Is Falling Down." Play the CD and sing the song several times. I hear many words that begin with /k/. When you hear a word that begins with /k/, clap your hands. As you sing the song, point to words that begin with *c*.

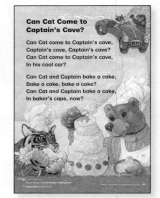

Can Cat Come to Captain's Cave?

Can Cat come to Captain's cave,
Captain's cave, Captain's cave?
Can Cat come to Captain's cave,
In his cool car?

Can Cat and Captain bake a cake,
Bake a cake, bake a cake?
Can Cat and Captain bake a cake,
In baker's caps, now?

🔘 Phonics Songs and Rhymes Audio

On their own

Look around the room. Find something that begins with /k/. What do you see that begins with /k/?

Children may point out *cans, cups, cars, cases, coins, collars,* and *curtains.*

Phonics Songs and Rhymes Chart 10

Blend Words

Review

To review sound-spellings, use Alphabet Cards *Aa, Mm, Pp, Ss,* and *Tt* and the *apple, mop, pig, sock,* and *tent* Picture Cards. Then use this routine for sound-by-sound blending to have children blend new words.

ROUTINE **Sound-by-Sound Blending**

1. **Connect** Write the letter *c*. What sound are we learning for this letter? The sound is /k/. Say it with me: /k/ /k/ /k/. When you see this letter in a word, what sound will you try?

2. **Model** Write *cap* on the board.

   • Touch under the letter *c:* What is a sound for this letter? Say it with me: /k/ /k/ /k/. Repeat the routine touching under *a* and *p*.

   • Let's blend the sounds together. Listen as I blend the sounds: /k/ /a/ /p/. Say it with me: *cap*. Now say it without me.

   • Listen as I use *cap* in a sentence. *I like my red cap.* Say it with me. Then have children use *cap* in their own sentences.

3. **Guide Practice** Continue the routine established in step 2 with the words below:

   cat   Cam

   Children should successfully read these words before reading Decodable Story 10 on p. 119 of *Reader's and Writer's Notebook.*

   Corrective Feedback If children have trouble reading a word, model blending the sounds to read the word. Then have children say it with you.

Routines Flip Chart

Differentiated Instruction

 Strategic Intervention

Connect Sound-Spelling Help children remember the new letter sound by having them write the letters *Cc* on a card and drawing a picture of a cat by the letters. Have them refer to the card when they practice the letter-sound activities.

Teacher Tip

If children have difficulty blending sounds, have them blend the initial sound and the rest of the word, and then try breaking the word into separate sounds again.

Objectives
• Write *C* and *c.*
• Learn high-frequency words.

Handwriting

Introduce

Write *Cc* on the board. Some words that begin with /k/ are written with an uppercase *C* or a lowercase *c*. Which letter is uppercase *C*? Which letter is lowercase *c*?

Model uppercase *C*

Write the word *Cam* on the board. Point to the uppercase *C*. This is the uppercase *C*. We use uppercase letters to begin sentences and for the first letter in a person's name. Watch as I trace the uppercase *C* with my finger. Follow the stroke instructions pictured below.

Guide practice

Have children write the uppercase *C* in the air. Use your finger to make an uppercase *C* in the air. Now write it on the palm of your hand.

Model lowercase *c*

Write the word *cat* on the board. Point to the lowercase *c*. This is a lowercase *c*. Watch as I trace a lowercase *c* with my finger. Write another lowercase *c* on the board following the stroke instructions. Again, have children write *c* in the air and on their hands.

Guide practice

Have children use their Write-On Boards to write a row of uppercase *C* and a row of lowercase *c*.

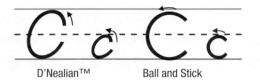

D'Nealian™   Ball and Stick

More practice

Use *Reader's and Writer's Notebook,* pp. 117, 118, for additional practice with initial *c*.

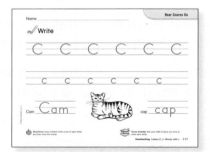

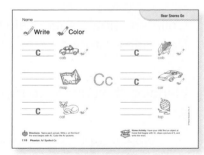

Reader's and Writer's Notebook, p. 117   Reader's and Writer's Notebook, p. 118

High-Frequency Words

Introduce Use the routine below to teach high-frequency words *we, my,* and *like*.

ROUTINE **Nondecodable Words**

1. **Say and Spell** Some words we have to learn by remembering the letters rather than saying the sounds. We will say and spell the words to help learn them. Write the word *we* on the board. This is the word *we*. It has two letters. The letters in *we* are *w* and *e*. Have children say and spell the word, first with you and then without you.

2. **Demonstrate Meaning** I can use the word *we* in lots of sentences. Here is one sentence: *We played a game.* Now you use the word in a sentence.

Repeat the routine with the words *my* and *like*.

Routines Flip Chart

Academic Vocabulary

Write the following words on the board:

realism	poem
fantasy	lullaby
setting	animal fantasy

Point to the list. This week we are going to learn these important words. They are tools for learning. As we work this week you will hear them many times. Read the words. Preteach the Academic Vocabulary at point-of-use by providing a child-friendly description, explanation, or example that clarifies the meaning of each term. Then ask children to restate the meaning of the Academic Vocabulary in their own words.

Differentiated Instruction

 Advanced

High-Frequency Words Have children practice writing the high-frequency words in the air with their fingers. Have children say the letters as they "write" them in the air.

ELL

English Language Learners

Support High-Frequency Words To help children understand what *my* means and how to use it in a sentence, have children practice saying *This is my _____* and filling in a word that tells about something they are wearing, such as *shoes*.

Decodable Story 10
/k/ Spelled Cc and High-Frequency Words

Review

Review the following high-frequency words. Have children read each word as you point to it on the Word Wall.

I	the	a	have
is	we	my	like

Read Decodable Story 10

Display Decodable Story 10. Today we will read a story about a girl who has a cap. What is the title of the story? Point to the title of the story. The title of the story is *The Cap*. What sound do you hear at the beginning of *cap*? We will read words that begin with /k/ in this story. Have children read Decodable Story 10 on pp. 119–120 in *Reader's and Writer's Notebook.*

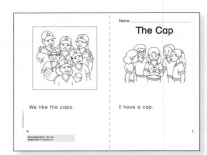

Reader's and Writer's Notebook, pp. 119–120

Use the routine for reading decodable books to read Decodable Story 10.

ROUTINE **Reading Decodable Books**

1. **Read Silently** Have children whisper read the story page by page as you listen in.

2. **Model Fluent Reading** Have children finger point as you read a page. Then have children reread the page without you.

3. **Read Chorally** Have children finger point as they chorally read the page. Continue reading page by page, repeating steps 1 and 2.

4. **Read Individually** Have children take turns reading aloud a page.

5. **Reread and Monitor Progress** As you listen to individual children reread, monitor progress and provide support.

6. **Reread with a Partner** Have children reread the story page by page with a partner.

Routines Flip Chart

Differentiated Instruction

 Strategic Intervention

Support Phonemic Awareness
Before children read *The Cap*, review /k/ words with the following Picture Cards: *can, cap, carrot, cat, caterpillar.*

A **Advanced**

Connect Sound Spelling
Display the *Cc* Alphabet Card. Have children say the sound they are learning and then the letter name. Then have children name other /k/ words.

Small Group Time

 DAY 1 **Break into small groups after reading the Decodable Story and before the comprehension lesson.**

Teacher-Led

SI Strategic Intervention	**OL** On-Level	**A** Advanced
Teacher-Led Page DI•52	**Teacher-Led** Page DI•57	**Teacher-Led** Page DI•60
• Phonemic Awareness and Phonics	• Phonemic Awareness and Phonics	• Phonemic Awareness and Phonics
• **Reread** Decodable Story 10	• **Reread** Decodable Story 10	• **Reread** Decodable Story 10 for Fluency

ELL Place English language learners in the groups that correspond to their reading abilities in English.

Practice Stations
• Visit the Listen Up! Station
• Visit the Word Work Station

Independent Activities
• Read independently
• Concept Talk Video
• *Reader's and Writer's Notebook*

Objectives
◉ Identify and distinguish realism and fantasy.
• Respond to questions about a text read aloud.

Skills Trace
◉ **Realism and Fantasy**
Introduce U2W4D1; U2W6D1; U5W1D1
Practice U2W4D2; U2W4D3; U2W4D4; U2W6D2; U2W6D3; U2W6D4; U5W1D2; U5W1D3; U5W1D4
Reteach/Review U2W4D5; U2W6D5; U3W2D4; U4W6D4; U5W1D5; U6W5D4v

KEY:
U=Unit   W=Week   D=Day

My Skills Buddy, pp. 74–75

Listening Comprehension
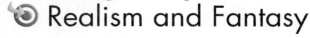 Realism and Fantasy

Introduce

Envision It!

Some stories are about things that could happen in real life. These are **realistic stories**. Other stories could not happen in real life. These make-believe stories are called **fantasies**. Good readers look for details that tell them if a story is real or make-believe.

Have children turn to pp. 74–75 in *My Skills Buddy* and look at the two pictures.

• Which picture is make-believe? How do you know? (The fish are in a classroom with a teacher and are sitting at desks. Fish don't go to school and sit at desks.)

• Which picture shows real things, people, or animals? How do you know? (The fish is swimming in the water like fish really do.)

Model

Tell children that you will read a story about a bear. Read "**Bolie's First Winter**" and model how to distinguish fantasy and realism.

Think Aloud
When I read, I look at what characters do and say. I ask myself whether they could do and say these things in real life. In "Bolie's First Winter," the bears talk like people. In real life, bears do not talk, so this story is a fantasy.

Guide practice

Have children tell something that happens in the story that could not happen in real life. Bolie asks lots of questions. A human child can ask questions, but a bear cannot. What else does Bolie do or say that is not realistic? (He whispers that he is not afraid.)

More practice

Display Big Book *Animal Babies in Grasslands.* Page through the book. Do the pictures of animals look real or make-believe? What does the baby elephant do with its trunk? Is this real or make-believe? Have children recall actions of other animals in the book and tell if they are real or make-believe.

Connect to everyday life

Think about cartoons you know. What happens in the cartoons that tell you they are made up? Think about stories you know. What happens in the stories that tell you they are real?

Differentiated Instruction

 Advanced

Access Content Have children think of real-life things animals can do and make-believe things animals can do. Make a two-column chart on the board and record children's responses. Discuss which make-believe things that animals can do are things that people can really do.

Academic Vocabulary

realistic story a story about something that could really happen

fantasy a make-believe story that and could not really happen

English Language Learners
Oral Comprehension To prepare English learners for the Read Aloud, use the modified Read Aloud in the ELL Support lesson p. DI•64.

Bolie's First Winter

"What's that white stuff, Ma?" asked Bolie Bear. He caught a flake in his paws and sniffed it.

"Snow!" cried Ma. "Those are snowflakes, Bolie. Goodness. Is winter here already? Finish eating your roots and nuts. We have to go!"

Ma hurried Bolie along. She knew winter. Winter meant cold and little food. It was time for the big sleep. This was Bolie's first winter. As they walked deep into the woods, he asked a million questions.

Halfway up a hill, Bolie saw a cave. He peeked inside. The cave was dark but warm. Bolie decided to be brave. "I'm not afraid," he whispered. Then he and Ma fell fast asleep.

Objectives
- Identify and use adjectives for sizes.
- Write a story.

Conventions
Adjectives for Sizes

Teach adjectives

Remind children that adjectives are words that tell about people, animals, places, and things. One way we use adjectives is to tell about the way something looks. Today we are going to use adjectives to tell about the size of animals.

Model

Display the *insect* and *elephant* Picture Cards. This is an insect. What size is an insect? An insect is small. *Small* describes the size of the insect. This is an elephant. What size is an elephant? An elephant is big. *Big* describes the size of the elephant.

Write these sentences on the board and complete them with children:

> **An insect is _____.** (small)
>
> **An elephant is _____.** (big)

When the sentences are complete, read the sentences together with children, pointing to the adjective for size as you read it.

Guide practice

Display a variety of pictures of animals of different body sizes and body part sizes, such as eyes and tails. Then discuss adjectives for sizes with children, such as *large, small, tall, short, narrow, wide, enormous, tiny, thick, thin, big, little.* Have children identify adjectives to describe the sizes of the animals.

Team Talk Pair children and have them each choose an adjective that describes a size. Have the other child use that adjective in a complete sentence to describe something.

Daily Fix-It

Use the Daily Fix-It for more conventions practice.

Writing
Wonderful, Marvelous Me!
I'll Tell You a Story...

Introduce

Talk with children about what kinds of stories they can tell. *I always have a story to tell. Sometimes things happen around me that make good stories. Sometimes I make up stories. When I make up a story, I can make the characters do anything I want. That's what makes storytelling so much fun.* Encourage children to share their thoughts and ideas about what kinds of stories they like.

Model

Today we are going to write a make-believe story about a bear. I'm going to close my eyes and use my imagination. I have a story in my mind about a bear named Buddy. One day Buddy looked out the window. It looked cold outside. It was even snowing! Draw a picture of a bear looking out a window. Label the bear *Buddy*. *I wonder why I'm still awake,* he thought. *Buddy knew when the weather gets cold it was time for him to eat lots of food and then sleep through winter. Buddy asked his friend Pat why he was still awake.* Draw a picture of a bear and a penguin. Label it *Pat and Buddy*. *"You are right Buddy,"* Pat said. *"Bears sleep during winter, but you are not a real bear. You are a stuffed animal!"*

Guide practice

List children's suggestions about other things that Buddy can do.

Independent writing

Now you are going to tell a story about a bear. Close your eyes and use your wonderful, marvelous imagination. What is the bear's name? What is the bear doing? Have children write or dictate their stories and then illustrate their ideas.

Write Guy
Jeff Anderson

Conferencing Is Listening

Conferring about children's writing is more about teachers *listening* than teachers speaking. What is the child thinking trying to say? What help does he need? We can ask questions to keep children speaking. "What do you want your reader to know? Wow, how did you think of this vivid phrase?"

Academic Vocabulary

adjective a word that describes a person, animal, place, or thing

Daily Fix-It

the little cat sat
The little cat sat.

This week's practice sentences appear on Teacher Resources DVD-ROM.

Writing Routine

Day 1 Wonderful, Marvelous Me!

Day 2 Respond to Literature

Day 3 Genre Writing

Day 4 Extend the Concept

Day 5 This Week We...

Daily Handwriting

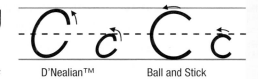

D'Nealian™   Ball and Stick

Write *Cam* and *cap* on the board. Review correct letter formation of uppercase *C* and lowercase *c*.

Have children write *Cam* and *cap* on their Write-On Boards. Remind them to use proper left-to-right and top-to-bottom progression and proper spacing between letters when writing *C* and *c*.

Listening and Speaking
Listen for Setting

Teach

When I listen to a story, I pay attention to the setting: when and where the story takes place. When I listen, I face the speaker and ask questions if I don't understand something.

Model

I am going to tell a very short story. Then I am going to tell the setting. *Mrs. Thomas sat at her desk. She was waiting for all of her students to get to school. She had a very busy day planned with math, science, and reading.*

This story takes place at school at the beginning of the school day.

Guide practice

Have children listen to a few short stories you tell and identify the setting. For example: Tommy and his dad had fun looking at the elephants, monkeys, zebras, and many other animals. What is the setting? (zoo) Refer children to the Rules for Listening and Speaking on p. 1 of the *Reader's and Writer's Notebook*. Remind them to face the speaker when listening, and to ask questions if they don't understand.

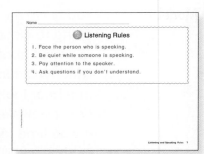

Name _____

Listening Rules
1. Face the person who is speaking.
2. Be quiet while someone is speaking.
3. Pay attention to the speaker.
4. Ask questions if you don't understand.

Reader's and Writer's Notebook, p. 1

Wrap Up Your Day

✔ **Oral Language** Today we talked about where a bear lives for the winter. Let's say our new Amazing Words: *sleep, winter, cave, woods, storm, blustery.*

✔ **Conventions** Have children use adjectives that describe the size of something. What size is each animal? Use an adjective to finish each sentence: *A whale is _____.*
An ant is _____.
A snake is _____.
A bumble bee is _____.

✔ **Homework Idea**
Send home the Family Times Newsletter on Let's Practice It! TR DVD•10.

Preview DAY 2

Tomorrow we will read about a hibernating bear and his visitors.

Science
The Four Seasons
Materials: construction paper, magazines, glue, crayons or markers

Make a Seasonal Chart Discuss the four seasons with children. Create a chart with four columns: *Spring, Summer, Fall, Winter*. Have children dictate adjectives and events that show their understanding of seasonal changes. Details could include weather (in your local area and nationally), holidays, clothing, and sports.

Make a Book of Seasons Have children create a book of seasons using their own artwork or pictures clipped from magazines. Their book can include animals in their habitat, clothing, events and holidays, trees and plants, and weather. Put books on display for other children to read.

The Four Seasons

Spring	Summer	Fall	Winter
rainy	hot	cool	cold
windy	sunny	cloudy	snowy
raincoat	shorts	jacket	mittens
umbrella	sandals	Leaves fall off	scarf
Plants start to grow.	Fourth of July	plants.	boots
		Thanksgiving	Animals hibernate.
			New Year's Day
			Valentine's Day

Phonics
Words with /k/Cc
Materials: paper, crayons

Write /k/Cc Words Help children brainstorm words that start with /k/. Write the words on the board and have children repeat the words with you. Words might include *cans, cap, cups, cart, carrots, cartoons, cat, coat, couch, curtains,* and *cushions*. If children suggest a word that starts with /k/Kk instead of /k/Cc, create a separate list on the board and tell them that they will learn about those words later. Have children create sentences using the words on the board. As children dictate sentences, write them on the board. Have children copy a sentence on a sheet of paper and illustrate it.

Comprehension
Realism and Fantasy
Materials: variety of trade books, fiction and nonfiction

Describe Realism and Fantasy Review with children the difference between fantasy and realism by giving a concrete example of something that is real and something that is not real, such as a cartoon mouse and a field mouse.

Display familiar books. Divide children into groups. Give groups of children several books to sort into *Real* or *Make-believe*. Tell the groups to choose one book from each category and explain why they think each book is real or make-believe.

Objectives
- Discuss the concepts to develop oral language.
- Build oral vocabulary.

Today at a Glance

Oral Vocabulary
sleep, winter

Phonemic Awareness
◉ Initial and Final /k/

Phonics
◉ /k/ Spelled *Cc*

Handwriting
Words with *Cc*

Comprehension
◉ Realism and Fantasy

Conventions
Adjectives for Numbers

Writing
Respond to Literature

Vocabulary
Words for Seasons

TRUCKTOWN on Reading Street

Start your engines! Display p. 14 of *Truckery Rhymes.* Point to "Jack and Kat." What do Jack and Kat do in this rhyme? Yes, they race up a hill. Let's read the rhyme together. Now have children point to the rhyming words as the class says the rhyme again.

Truckery Rhymes

Concept Talk

Question of the Week
What unique thing does a bear do in the winter?

Build concepts

Write the question of the week on the board and track the print as you read it aloud. Have children answer the question in complete sentences. To reinforce the concept and focus children's attention, display Talk with Me/Sing with Me Chart 10B. We are going to sing a song about a little bear that is hibernating.

🔘 Sing with Me Audio

Hush, Little Brown Bear

Hush, little brown bear in the woods,
You'd sleep through the winter if you could.

And if the winter continues to storm,
Stay in your cave, all safe and warm,

And if it's still blustery and cold,
You'll always have your mama's
hand to hold.

Hush, little brown bear in the woods,
You'd sleep through the winter if you could.

Talk with Me/Sing with Me Chart 10B

Listen for Amazing Words

Listen carefully for the Amazing Words *sleep* and *winter* in the song "Hush, Little Brown Bear." Read the title and have children describe the picture. Sing the song several times to the tune of "Hush, Little Baby." Have children sing with you. Have them clap when they hear the Amazing Words *sleep* and *winter*.

ELL **Reinforce Vocabulary** Use the Day 2 instruction on ELL Poster 10 to reinforce the meanings of high-frequency words.

ELL Poster 10

Oral Vocabulary
Amazing Words

Amazing Words

sleep	winter
cave	woods
storm	blustery

Amazing Words **Oral Vocabulary Routine**

Teach Amazing Words

1. **Introduce the Word** People and animals need to *sleep* every night. We need *sleep* to be healthy and strong. What's our new Amazing Word for the rest our body needs? Say it with me: *sleep.*

2. **Demonstrate** Provide examples to show meaning. *When we are tired, it means our body needs sleep.*

   Repeat steps 1 and 2.

   Introduce the Word The coldest season of the year is *winter.* During the *winter* we dress warmly. What's our new Amazing Word for the coldest season? Say it with me: *winter.*

   Demonstrate *Many animals find a warmer place or sleep for the winter.*

3. **Apply** Tell children to use *sleep* and *winter* in complete sentences. Have them draw a picture of a bear sleeping in winter.

Routines Flip Chart

Use Amazing Words

To reinforce the concept and the Amazing Words, have children supply the appropriate Amazing Word for each sentence.

The weather is cold in _____. (winter)

You feel good in the morning after a good night's _____. (sleep)

Differentiated Instruction

 Strategic Intervention

Sentence Production If children have difficulty completing the sentences with an Amazing Word, model saying the complete sentence and then have them repeat you.

ELL

English Language Learners
Vocabulary Have children say *sleep* and *winter* in their home languages. Have children say what the weather is like during the *winter.*

Phonemic Awareness
Initial and Final /k/

Picture Card

Isolate /k/

Display the *cap* Picture Card. This is a *cap*. *Cap* begins with /k/. What is this? What sound does it begin with? Continue the routine with the *can*, *cat*, and *carrot* Picture Cards.

Model

Display the *rock* Picture Card. This is a *rock*. Listen as I say the sounds in *rock*: /r/ /o/ /k/. I hear /k/ at the end of the word *rock*. Say it with me: /r/ /o/ /k/. Continue with the following words: *cook, peck, take, hike, pick*.

Picture Card

Guide practice

Have children look at the picture on *My Skills Buddy* pp. 72–73. Remember that we saw *coloring* pages in the picture. *Coloring* begins with /k/. What things that end with /k/ can we find in the picture? Name other things that end like *rock*. Discuss with children those bulleted items on p. 72 not discussed on Day 1.

Corrective feedback

If... children cannot discriminate /k/,

then... have them enunciate /k/ as they segment words that contain /k/.

Listen as I segment a word: /k/ /a/ /t/, *cat*. What sound do you hear at the beginning of *cat*? I hear /k/ at the beginning of *cat*. Continue with the following words: *can, cap, cab*. Segment the following words with the class: *pack, Mac, yak*.

My Skills Buddy, pp. 72–73

On their own Display Phonics Songs and Rhymes Chart 10, "Can Cat Come to Captain's Cave?" Remind children of the tune "London Bridge Is Falling Down." Have them sing the song with you several times. This time I want you to clap when you hear a word that ends with /k/. Children should clap when they hear the words *bake* and *cake*.

Review **Blending Sounds** Listen to the sounds in this word: /k/ /a/ /t/. Say the sounds with me: /k/ /a/ /t/. Now I am going to blend the sounds together to say the word: /k/ /a/ /t/, *cat*. Continue the blending routine with the following words: *cap, can, mat, tap, pat, pan, tan.*

Can Cat Come to Captain's Cave?

Can Cat come to Captain's cave,
Captain's cave, Captain's cave?
Can Cat come to Captain's cave,
In his cool car?

Can Cat and Captain bake a cake,
Bake a cake, bake a cake?
Can Cat and Captain bake a cake,
In baker's caps, now?

Phonics Songs and
Rhymes Chart 10

Differentiated Instruction

SI Strategic Intervention
Support Phonemic Awareness
Display the *caterpillar* and *garden* Picture Cards. Have children identify which picture shows a word that begins with /k/. Have them draw a picture of it.

English Language Learners
Phonemic Awareness Point to images in the pictures on pages 72–73 of *My Skills Buddy* as you say their corresponding words. To clarify understanding, have children point to the images as you say the words.

Phonics — Teach/Model
/k/ Spelled Cc

Alphabet Card

Teach /k/ Cc

Point to the *cactus* on the Alphabet Card. What is this? What sound does *cactus* begin with? *Cactus* begins with /k/. Write the word *cactus* on the board and point to the first letter *c*. A letter we are learning for /k/ is *c*.

Model

Display the *cat* Picture Card. What is this? Say the sounds in *cat* with me: /k/ /a/ /t/, *cat*. Where do you hear /k/ in *cat*? I hear /k/ at the beginning, do you?

Write the word *cat* on the board. Point to each letter as you say the sounds: /k/ /a/ /t/, *cat*. Continue the routine with the following words: *cap, Cam*.

Picture Card

Guide practice

Have children open *My Skills Buddy* to p. 76. Demonstrate using the blending arrows on *My Skills Buddy* p. 76 as you model blending the first word.

Put your finger on the red arrow below the *c*. Say a sound that *c* stands for: /k/. Continue with the letters *a* and *p*. Now I run my finger along the blue arrow as I blend the letters quickly to read *cap*. Have children work with a partner to blend the rest of the words on the page.

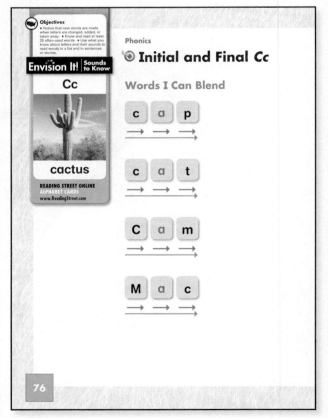

My Skills Buddy, p. 76

Blend Use the following routine to review blending *c* words.

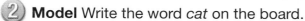

ROUTINE Sound-by-Sound Blending

1 **Connect** Write the letter *c*. What is the sound we learned for this letter? The sound is /k/. Say it with me: /k/ /k/ /k/. When you see this letter in a word, what sound will you say?

2 **Model** Write the word *cat* on the board.

- Point to the *c* and ask: What is the sound we learned for this letter? Say it with me: /k/ /k/ /k/. Repeat the routine with *a* and *t*.

- Let's blend the sounds together. Listen as I blend the sounds: /k/ /a/ /t/. Say it with me: /k/ /a/ /t/ *cat*. Now say it without me.

- Listen as I use *cat* in a sentence. *My cat is big.* Say it with me. Have children use *cat* in a sentence.

3 **Guide Practice** Continue the routine established in step 2 with these words:

| can | cap | Cam | Mac |

Have children successfully read all the words before reading Decodable Reader 10 on pp. 78–85 of *My Skills Buddy*.

Corrective Feedback Model blending the sounds to read the word. Then have children say it with you.

Routines Flip Chart

MONITOR PROGRESS 🔁 Check Sound-Spelling /k/ Spelled *Cc*

Give each child a blank card. Have children write the letters *Cc* on the card. I am going to read some words. When you hear a word that begins with /k/, hold up your *Cc* card. Say: *canary, lemon, canoe, carry, apple, cob, baby, come, concrete, turtle.*

If... children cannot discriminate initial /k/,

then... use the small-group Strategic Intervention lesson, p. DI•53, to reteach /k/.

Continue to monitor children's progress using other instructional opportunities during the week so that children can be successful with the Day 5 Assessment.

Day 1	Day 2	Day 3	Day 4	Day 5
Check Phonemic Awareness	**Check Sound-Spelling/ Retelling**	Check Word Reading	Check Phonemic Awareness	Check Oral Vocabulary

Differentiated Instruction

SI **Strategic Intervention**

Blend Words Before children blend sounds, have them say the sound for each letter in the word. Then have them blend the words in chunks, such as /k/ -at, /k/ -an, /k/ -ap, /k/ -am, and ma- /k/.

Success Predictor

Sound-Spelling

Objectives
- Write *C* and *c*.
- Read high-frequency words.

Handwriting
Write Words with Cc

Review

Write the word *Cam* on the board. This is the word *Cam*. I use an uppercase *C* for the first letter in *Cam's* name. Watch me make an uppercase *C*. Write another uppercase *C* on the board using the strokes indicated in the model.

Write the word *cap* on the board. This is the word *cap*. I use a lowercase *c* at the beginning of *cap*. Watch me make a lowercase *c*. Write another lowercase *c* on the board using the proper strokes.

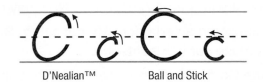

D'Nealian™   Ball and Stick

Guide practice

Have children use their Write-On Boards to make a row of uppercase *C* and a row of lowercase *c*. Circulate around the room, assisting children as necessary. Have children then write the following words: *cat, cab, Cam*.

High-Frequency Words

Model reading

Have children turn to p. 77 of *My Skills Buddy*. Read the high-frequency words *we, my,* and *like* together. Then have children point to each word and read it themselves. Read the sentences on the *My Skills Buddy* page together to read the new high-frequency words in context.

Team Talk Pair children and have them take turns reading each of the sentences aloud.

High-Frequency Words

Words I Can Read

we

my

like

Sentences I Can Read

1. I like Cam.
2. We like to sit.
3. We like my cat.

77

My Skills Buddy, p. 77

On their own

Use *Reader's and Writer's Notebook,* p. 121, for additional practice with this week's high-frequency words.

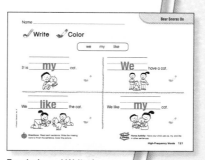

Reader's and Writer's Notebook, p. 121

 **Advanced**

High-Frequency Words Have children use the high-frequency words *we, my,* and *like* in sentences.

ELL

English Language Learners

High-Frequency Words After the Team Talk activity, have children continue to work in pairs to check understanding. Have one child read one of the sentences aloud while another child makes a simple drawing to illustrate the sentence.

Objectives
- Read decodable text.
- Read high-frequency words.

Decodable Reader 10
/k/ Spelled Cc and High-Frequency Words

Review Review the previously taught high-frequency words. Have children read each word as you point to it on the Word Wall.

I	am	the	have	is	a	my	we	like

Have children turn to Decodable Reader 10, *My Cap,* on p. 78 of *My Skills Buddy.* Today we will read a story about a boy and a girl who have a cap. What is the title of the story? **Point to the title.** The title of the story is *My Cap.* **Point to the name of the author.** The author's name is Sue Bear. What does the author do? We will be able to read lots of words in this story.

Use the routine for reading decodable books to read Decodable Reader 10.

My Skills Buddy pp. 78–85

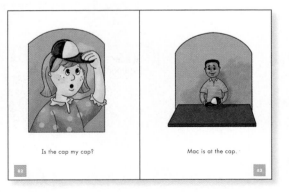

ROUTINE Reading Decodable Books

1. **Read Silently** Have children whisper read the book page by page as you listen in.

2. **Model Fluent Reading** Have children finger point as you read a page. Then have children reread the book without you.

3. **Read Chorally** Have children finger point as they chorally read the page. Continue reading page by page, repeating steps 1 and 2.

4. **Read Individually** Have children take turns reading aloud a page.

5. **Reread and Monitor Progress** As you listen to individual children reread, monitor progress and provide support.

6. **Reread with a Partner** Have children reread the book page by page with a partner.

Routines Flip Chart

Differentiated Instruction

 Strategic Intervention

Develop Vocabulary Before reading the book, have children page through the book and tell about the pictures and talk about the words that will be used in the story.

Small Group Time

 DAY 2 Break into small groups after reading the Decodable Reader and before the comprehension lesson.

Teacher-Led

Strategic Intervention	OL On-Level	A Advanced
Teacher-Led Page DI•53	Teacher-Led Page DI•57	Teacher-Led Page DI•60
• Phonemic Awareness and Phonics	• Phonemic Awareness and Phonics	• Phonics and Spelling
• Reread Decodable Reader 10	• Reread Decodable Reader 10	• Reread Decodable Reader 10 for Fluency

 Place English language learners in the groups that correspond to their reading abilities in English.

Practice Stations
- Visit the Word Work Station
- Visit the Words to Know Station

Independent Activities
- Read independently
- Background Building Audio
- *Reader's and Writer's Notebook*

Objectives
- ◎ Practice realism and fantasy.
- • Preview and predict.
- • Retell a story.

Check Retelling
SUCCESS PREDICTOR

Listening Comprehension
↻ Realism and Fantasy

Review

Envision It!

Have children turn to pp. 74–75 of *My Skills Buddy*. Remind children that some stories are about things that could not happen in real life. These stories are fantasies. Other stories could really happen. These stories are realistic. Good readers look at the details of a story to decide whether it is a fantasy or a realistic story.

My Skills Buddy, pp. 74–75

First Read—Big Book
Bear Snores On

Concepts of print

Display a page of *Bear Snores On*. Explain that the words tell that part of the story. The pictures show what the words say.

Preview and predict

Display *Bear Snores On*. I see a bear sleeping and many animals all around him. The title of this book is *Bear Snores On*. What do you think a book with the title *Bear Snores On* will be about?

Use illustrations

Take children on a picture walk through the book. Have children tell about what they see in each picture.

Introduce genre

An animal fantasy has animal characters that act like people. In this story, we will read about a bear and his friends.

Set purpose

Remind children of the question of the week: *What unique thing does a bear do in the winter?* Have children listen for what bears do in winter.

Model

Read *Bear Snores On* with expression for enjoyment.

Read for enjoyment

Reread using Develop Vocabulary notes

Reread using Guide Comprehension notes

Retell

Check retelling

Envision It!

Have children turn to p. 86 of *My Skills Buddy*. Walk through the retelling boxes as children retell *Bear Snores On*. Let's retell what happens in the first box—the beginning of the story. The bear is sleeping in the cave for the winter. Let's retell what happens in the next box. Continue with the rest of the boxes. After children retell the story as a group, have them draw pictures to retell a favorite part of the story. Have them write or dictate a word or sentence to go with each picture.

My Skills Buddy, p. 86

Top-Score Response A top-score response describes events in sequence with details.

Don't Wait Until Friday

MONITOR PROGRESS **Check Retelling**

If... children have difficulty retelling the story,

then... go through the story one page at a time, and ask children to tell what happens in their own words.

Day 1	Day 2	Day 3	Day 4	Day 5
Check Phonemic Awareness	Check Sound-Spelling/ Retelling	Check Word Reading	Check Phonemic Awareness	Check Oral Vocabulary

Differentiated Instruction

SI **Strategic Intervention**

Access Content To reinforce the concept of retelling, have children retell the events of the day, or of a previously read story.

Academic Vocabulary

animal fantasy a story about animals that talk and act like people

retell to share the most important events of a story in one's own words

Retelling Plan

☑ **Week 1** Assess Advanced students.

☑ **Week 2** Assess On-Level students.

☑ **Week 3** Assess Strategic Intervention students.

☑ **This week assess Advanced students.**

☐ **Week 5** Assess On-Level students.

☐ **Week 6** Assess Strategic Intervention students.

ELL

English Language Learners

Cognates Spanish speakers may recognize that *fantasia* is a cognate for *fantasy* and *realismo* is a cognate for *realism*.

341

Success Predictor

Retelling

Objectives

- ◎ Practice realism and fantasy.
- • Confirm predictions.
- • Practice adjectives for numbers.

Think, Talk, and Write

Discuss concept

We're learning about what a bear does during winter. Think about what you do when it's winter.

- • What activities do you do during winter?
- • How do you stay warm?

Confirm predictions

Have children recall their predictions before you read *Bear Snores On.*

- • What did you think the story would be about?
- • Was your prediction correct?

Have children turn to p. 87 of *My Skills Buddy.* Read the questions and directives and have children respond.

Text to world

1. What does a bear do in the winter?

◎ Realism and Fantasy

2. Which story is about real animals? *(Animal Babies in Grasslands)* How do you know these are real animals? (They do things animals really do.) Which story is about make-believe animals? *(Bear Snores On)* How do you know these are make-believe animals? (The rabbit is drinking from a mug.)

Look back and write

3. Let's look back at our story and write about it. We remember that Bear is sleeping when the other animals have a party in the cave. Listen for how Bear acts like a make-believe bear when he wakes up. Read pp. 30–31 of *Bear Snores On.* Now let's write our ideas. Discuss with children how Bear acts like a make-believe bear. (Possible answers: He cries. He whimpers. He feels sad. Real animals don't do these things.)

Think, Talk, and Write

1. What does a bear do in the winter? Text to World

2. Which story is about real animals? Which is about make-believe animals?

◎ Realism and Fantasy

3. Look back and write.

87

My Skills Buddy, p. 87

Conventions
Adjectives for Numbers

Review

Remind children of what they learned about adjectives. Adjectives are words that describe people, animals, places, and things. Today we will learn about adjectives for numbers.

Display p. 5 of *Bear Snores On*. In *Bear Snores On* there are many things we can count. On this page there is one cave and one bear. Display pp. 10–11. On these pages there is one mouse and one bear. Together, there are two animals. *One* and *two* are adjectives for numbers. They tell how many things are in the pictures.

Guide practice

Display p. 9. Count the number of leaves shown on the page. Then write this sentence on the board and read it with children:

> **There are four leaves on the ground.**

Guide children to count how many things they see on other pages of *Bear Snores On*. Remind children that each number word is an adjective that tells how many objects are in the picture.

Write these sentences on the board:

> **I have _____ nose.**
>
> **I have _____ ears.**

With children, complete each sentence with the appropriate adjectives for a number.

On their own

Use *Reader's and Writer's Notebook,* p. 122, for more practice reading, writing, and saying adjectives for numbers.

Daily Fix-It

Use the Daily Fix-It exercise for more conventions practice.

Reader's and Writer's Notebook, p. 122

Daily Fix-It

the bear will sleep all winter
The bear will sleep all winter.

This week's practice sentences appear on Teacher Resources DVD-ROM.

ELL

English Language Learners

Cognates English learners may recognize some number words have cognates: the Spanish word for *three* is *tres,* the Russian word for *three* sounds like *tree,* and the Haitian Creole word for *six* is *sis* (pronounced like *cease*).

Language Transfer In languages such as Spanish and Vietnamese, adjectives may follow nouns, as in the name *Río Grande* ("big river"). If children say *insect small* instead of *small insect,* provide additional practice saying adjectives before nouns.

ELL Support for additional support for language transfer see Linguistic Contrastive Analysis in the *ELL Handbook*.

Objectives
- Respond to literature.
- Identify and use words for seasons.
- Write *C* and *c*.

Writing
Respond to Literature

Discuss

Display *Bear Snores On.* Discuss with children about what bears do during the winter. Be sure to talk about the weather, the season, why the bear is sleeping, and when he will wake up.

Model

In the story, Bear sleeps while his friends have fun in his cave. What do you think Bear will do when he wakes up in spring? Some bears wake up very hungry in the spring. If you were a bear, what would you do? I am going to write:

> **I would look for food.**

Guide practice

Have children help you write more sentences about what bears would do in spring once they wake up.

> **I would yawn and stretch.**
> **I would smell some flowers.**

Independent writing

Have children write or dictate their own sentences about *Bear Snores On.* Some children may wish to use this sentence frame:

> ***If I were a bear in spring,
> I would _____.***

Then have them illustrate their sentences.

I would play.

Daily Handwriting

Write *Cam* and *cab* on the board. Review correct letter formation of uppercase *C* and lowercase *c*.

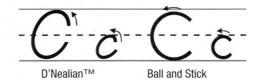

D'Nealian™   Ball and Stick

Have children write *Cam* and *cab* on their Write-On Boards. Remind children to use proper left-to-right and top-to-bottom progression when writing *C* and *c*.

Vocabulary
Words for Seasons

Model
Have children turn to p. 88 of *My Skills Buddy*. Use the first Vocabulary bullet on the page to guide the discussion. Direct them to the picture for *spring*. This picture shows the *spring* season. The flowers start to bloom and people wear light jackets. Direct children to the picture for *summer*. We wear shorts in the summer. What is the weather like in the summer? Direct children to the picture for *fall*. This picture shows the *fall* season. The leaves on the trees have changed colors, and the fallen leaves need to be raked. It starts to get cooler outside. Direct children to the picture for *winter*. Snow falls during the *winter*. What do we wear during the *winter* season? Read and discuss the first Vocabulary bullet on p. 88 of *My Skills Buddy*.

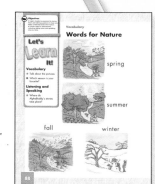

My Skills Buddy, p. 88

Guide practice
Write the words *spring, summer, fall,* and *winter* on the board. Point to each word as you read it.

| spring | summer | fall | winter |

Let's practice our new words. I'm going to describe things that happen during a specific season. When you know what season I am describing, stand up. Listen carefully: We can swim in a pool. We wear shorts and play outside. The sun shines, and the grass is green. What season am I describing? **(summer)** Repeat the routine with fall, winter, and spring.

On their own
Have children act out things we can do during each season. Make a circle and have one child stand in the center and pretend to do an activity specific to a season, such as making a snowman in winter. Have the other children guess the season we can do that activity. Have other children act out activities while the rest of the class guesses the season.

Differentiated Instruction

A Advanced

Categorize Words Review the words for seasons and ask children to tell what kinds of clothing people wear during each season.

ELL

English Language Learners
Professional Development Support Vocabulary Be sure English learners encounter new vocabulary words in different activities. Children do not learn new vocabulary and concepts by only hearing the word and definition once. Define the new word, as well as provide an example, before it is used in an activity, in a discussion, or in the reading.

Objectives

- Review skills learned and practiced today.
- Connect literature to weekly concept.
- Identify words that begin with /k/.

Wrap Up Your Day

✔ **Concept Talk** Today we read about a bear sleeping through the winter. What kind of home does the bear need for the winter? Why does he need this home? What happens to Bear during his rest?

✔ **Phonemic Awareness** I am going to read a sentence. Clap when you hear /k/ words. *Carol and Carl carried some carrots and corn to the county fair.*

✔ **Vocabulary Skill** Write the words *fall, winter, summer,* and *spring* on the board. Point to each word as you read it with children. Then have children say the words and describe the weather for each season.

✔ **Homework Idea** Have children draw a picture of a group of things they find in their homes. Then have them label the drawing with an adjective that tells how many things are in the picture.

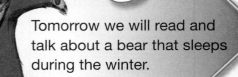

Preview DAY 3

Tomorrow we will read and talk about a bear that sleeps during the winter.

Science
Animals in Winter

Materials: construction paper, cotton balls, crayons, tape, glue, scissors

Discuss What Animals Do Discuss with children what animals do in winter. While some animals find a warm shelter, others, such as the bear, hibernate. That means they go into a very deep sleep for the whole winter. Before they hibernate, they eat extra food so that they have a layer of fat to keep them warm during the winter. What else might animals do to get ready for the cold weather? Explain that some animals grow thicker fur. Others, such as birds, fly to a warmer place until winter ends. Pretend you are an animal and winter is coming. What would you do to get ready for the cold winter weather? Have children make an art project showing their chosen way of adapting. For example, they could make a cave out of construction paper where they could hibernate; they could draw a picture of an animal and glue cotton balls to it for extra fur; or they could make wings out of construction paper to fly to a warmer place.

Math/Conventions
Adjectives for Numbers

Materials: small items such as pencils, crayons, or notebooks

Counting and Describing Have children gather materials from their desks, such as pencils and crayons. Remind them numbers can be used to describe how many objects there are. Have children pair up with someone and tell their partner the number of objects they have, such as *I have three pencils* or *I have two red crayons.*

Phonics
Letter *Cc* Hunt

Materials: classroom objects whose names begin with /k/*Cc*

See and Say /k/*Cc* On the board, list words that begin with /k/ spelled *c*. Many of these should be objects that can be found in the room, for example, *can, cap, coat, cord, cone, card,* and *calendar.* Read the words aloud, stressing the beginning /k/. Then have children say each word with you as you point to the letters. Label /k/ objects in the room with their names. Say each word and have children direct you to where the object is in the room. Have a child go to the object, point to the letter *c* on the label, and say the sound for this letter: /k/.

Objectives
- Share information and ideas about the concept.
- Build oral vocabulary.

Today at a Glance

Oral Vocabulary
cave, woods

Phonemic Awareness
◉ Initial and Final /k/

Phonics
◉ /k/ Spelled *Cc*

Comprehension
◉ Realism and Fantasy

Conventions
Adjectives for Colors and Shapes

Writing
Poem

Listening and Speaking
Listen for Setting

TRUCKTOWN on Reading Street

Start your engines! Display "Jack and Kat" on p. 14 of *Truckery Rhymes.* Have children say the rhyme with you. Do you know the rhyme about "Jack and Jill"? Recite the rhyme and then have children say it with you.

Jack and Jill went up the hill
To fetch a pail of water.
Jack fell down and broke his crown
And Jill came tumbling after.

Truckery Rhymes

Concept Talk

Question of the Week

What unique thing does a bear do in the winter?

Write the question of the week on the board. Read the question as you track the print. Talk with children about what bears do during the winter. Remind children to speak clearly and to take turns speaking.

Listen for Amazing Words

Let's Sing Display Sing with Me Chart 10B. Remind children that yesterday they sang "Hush, Little Brown Bear" and listened for the words *sleep* and *winter.* Now I want you to listen for the Amazing Words *cave* and *woods.* Sing the song several times to the tune of "Hush, Little Baby." Have children sing with you. Tell them to clap when they hear the Amazing Words *cave* and *woods.*

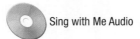 Sing with Me Audio

Hush, Little Brown Bear

Hush, little brown bear in the woods,
You'd sleep through the winter if you could.

And if the winter continues to storm,
Stay in your cave, all safe and warm,

And if it's still blustery and cold,
You'll always have your mama's
hand to hold.

Hush, little brown bear in the woods,
You'd sleep through the winter if you could.

Talk with Me/Sing with Me
Chart 10B

Oral Vocabulary
Amazing Words

Teach Amazing Words

Amazing Words — Oral Vocabulary Routine

1. **Introduce the Word** A sheltered hollowed-out place is called a *cave*. A *cave* may have an opening in the side of a hill that is underground. What's our new Amazing Word for a sheltered place under a hill? Say it with me: *cave*.

2. **Demonstrate** Provide examples to show meaning. *The brown bear sleeps in a dark cave to stay safe from winter storms.*

   Repeat steps 1 and 2.

   Introduce the Word The *woods* is an area of land covered with many trees. Bears live and find their food in the *woods*. What is our new Amazing Word for land that is covered by many trees? Say it with me: *woods*.

   Demonstrate *When winter is over, the bears will come out of the cave and walk in the woods.*

3. **Apply** Have children use *cave* and *woods* in complete sentences. Have them pretend to be bears hibernating in a *cave* in the *woods*.

Routines Flip Chart

Use Amazing Words

To reinforce the concept and the Amazing Words, have children supply the appropriate Amazing Word for each sentence.

I saw deer and many birds in the _____. (woods)

It is very dark inside the _____. (cave)

ELL Expand Vocabulary
Use the Day 3 instruction on ELL Poster 10 to help children expand vocabulary.

ELL Poster 10

Amazing Words

sleep	winter
cave	woods
storm	blustery

Differentiated Instruction

SI Strategic Intervention
Sentence Production Use Talk with Me Chart 10A to help children complete the Amazing Word sentences below.

Objectives

◎ Isolate final /k/.
• Discriminate sounds.
• Count syllables in words.
• Segment words.

Phonemic Awareness
Final /k/

Picture Card

Review

Initial /k/ Display the *carrot* Picture Card. Listen as I say this word: *carrot*. What is the first sound in *carrot*? Say it with me: /k/, *carrot*. Today we will hear /k/ at the ends of words.

Teach final /k/

Display the *duck* Picture Card. Listen to the sounds in *duck:* /d/ /u/ /k/. How many sounds do you hear? (three) Where do you hear /k/? The /k/ in duck is at the end. Continue the routine with the following words: *luck, back, black, block, rake, lake.*

Picture Card

Discriminate sounds

I am going to say some words. If you hear /k/ at the beginning of the word, hold your hands up in the air. If you hear /k/ at the end of the word, put your hands in your lap. Let's do the first few together. Listen carefully: *card.* I hear /k/ at the beginning of *card,* so I will hold my hands up. *Camp* (hands in air), *pick* (hands in lap), *lake* (hands in lap). Continue the routine with the words *cot, luck, cub, make, tack,* and *cat.*

On their own

Have children divide a sheet of paper in half. Have them draw a picture of something that begins with /k/ on one side and something that ends with /k/ on the other. Use the *cat, can, carrot, lake, rock,* and *truck* Picture Cards as examples.

Segment	Listen to the sounds in the word *back*: /b/ /a/ /k/. Say them with me: /b/ /a/ /k/. How many sounds do you hear? There are three sounds in *back*. Let's try some more words. Continue the routine with the following words: *cap, mat, sap, yak*.
Corrective feedback	**If...** children cannot segment the words into sounds, **then...** provide practice segmenting the words into chunks, such as *pi-* /g/ or /p/ *-ig*.
Count syllables	Display the *caterpillar* Picture Card. What is this? Say the word slowly with me: *caterpillar*. Clap with me for each word part, or syllable, of the word: *cat-er-pil-lar*. How many times did you clap? (4) There are four word parts, or syllables, in the word *caterpillar*. Continue the activity with the following Picture Cards: *elephant, frog, hippopotamus, iguana, kangaroo, ladybug, octopus, starfish, tiger, umbrella*.

Objectives

◎ Practice /k/ spelled *Cc*.
- Read /k/ words.
- Read high-frequency words.
- Create new words by changing letters.

Check Word Reading
SUCCESS PREDICTOR

Phonics—Teach/Model
/k/ Spelled *Cc*

Review   **/k/Cc** Display the *Cc* Alphabet Card and point to the *cactus.* What sound do you hear at the beginning of *cactus?* What letter spells that sound? Point to the letters *Cc.* What is the sound we learned for this letter? What are the names of these letters?

Review   **Letter Names and Sounds** Use Alphabet Cards to review the following letter names and sounds: *Aa, Tt, Mm, Pp, Ss.*

Alphabet Card

Blend sounds   Write the word *cat* on the board. Point to each letter as you say the sound: /k/ /a/ /t/. When I blend these sounds together, I make the word *cat.* Say the sounds with me: /k/ /a/ /t/. Now blend the sounds together: /k/ /a/ /t/, *cat.* Change the *t* to *p.* Now we have a new word. Let's blend the sounds to read this word. Say them with me: /k/ /a/ /p/, *cap.* What is the new word? The new word is *cap.*

More practice   Use *Reader's and Writer's Notebook,* p. 123, for additional practice with /k/.

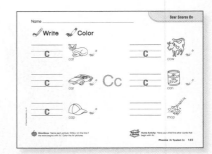

Reader's and Writer's Notebook, p. 123

Review

Sound-Spelling Display the *Ss* Alphabet Card. What sound do you hear at the beginning of *salamander?* What letter spells that sound? The letter *s* spells /s/. Review the following letters with Alphabet Cards: *Pp, Aa, Tt, Mm.*

Review

High-Frequency Words Write the word *we* on the board. This is the word *we.* What is this word? Continue the routine with *my, like, have,* and *is.*

Alphabet Card

Differentiated Instruction

SI **Strategic Intervention**

Access Content Practice high-frequency words with children by modeling the words *we, I,* and *my.* Have three children stand with you for the word *we.* Point to yourself for the words *I* and *my.* Use the words in context and have children repeat sentences with you.

Don't Wait Until Friday

MONITOR PROGRESS   Check Word Reading   High-Frequency Words

Write *we, my, like, have,* and *is* on the board. Have children take turns reading the words.

Practice reading these words from Kindergarten Student Reader K.2.4, *Winter Fun.*

| tap | Tam | cap | pat |

If... children cannot read the high-frequency words,

then... write the words on cards for them to practice at home.

If... children cannot blend sounds to read the words,

then... provide practice blending the words in chunks, /t/ -*ap.*

If... children can successfully blend sounds to read the words,

then... have them read Kindergarten Student Reader K.2.4, *Winter Fun.*

Day 1	Day 2	Day 3	Day 4	Day 5
Check Phonemic Awareness	Check Sound-Spelling/ Retelling	Check Word Reading	Check Phonemic Awareness	Check Oral Vocabulary

Success Predictor

Word Reading

Success Predictor

Kindergarten Student Reader K.2.4
↻ /k/ Spelled Cc and High-Frequency Words

Review | Review the previously taught high-frequency words. Have children read each word as you point to it on the Word Wall.

my	is	have	we	like	the

Teach rebus words

Write the word *door* on the board. This is the word *door*. Name the letters with me: *d, o, o, r, door*. Where is the *door* in our classroom? Look for the word *door* in the story we read today. Repeat the routine for the words *cold, snowballs, snowman,* and *snow*. There will be pictures above these words to help you read them.

Read Kindergarten Student Reader K.2.4

Display Kindergarten Student Reader K.2.4. Today we are going to read a new book. Point to the title of the book. The title of the book is *Winter Fun*. The author's name is Alex Jordan. The book was illustrated by David Sheldon.

Use the reading decodable books routine to read the Kindergarten Student Reader.

Small Group

ROUTINE — Reading Decodable Books

1. **Read Silently** Have children whisper read the book page by page as you listen in.

2. **Model Fluent Reading** Have children finger point as you read a page. Then have children reread the page without you.

3. **Read Chorally** Have children finger point as they chorally read the page. Continue reading page by page, repeating steps 1 and 2.

4. **Read Individually** Have children take turns reading aloud a page.

5. **Reread and Monitor Progress** As you listen to individual children reread, monitor progress and provide support.

6. **Reread with a Partner** Have children reread the book page by page with a partner.

Routines Flip Chart

Kindergarten Student Reader K.2.4

By Alex Jordan Illustrated by David Sheldon

Tap, tap, tap, tap.

Tam taps at my door.

Tam is cold.

Tam, have my cap.

We pat, pat, pat at snowballs.

We tap, tap, tap at my snowman.

We like the snow.

Differentiated Instruction

SI Strategic Intervention

Connect Sound-Spelling Use the *Tt, Pp, Aa, Ss,* and *Mm* Alphabet Cards to review sound-spellings before reading *Winter Fun.*

Small Group Time

DAY 3

Break into small groups to read the Kindergarten Student Reader before the comprehension lesson.

Teacher-Led

SI Strategic Intervention	**OL** On-Level	**A** Advanced
Teacher-Led Page DI•54 • Phonemic Awareness and Phonics • **Read** Concept Literacy Reader K.2.4 or Kindergarten Student Reader K.2.4	**Teacher-Led** Page DI•58 • Phonemic Awareness and Phonics • **Read** Kindergarten Student Reader K.2.4	**Teacher-Led** Page DI•61 • **Read** Independent Reader K.2.4 or Kindergarten Student Reader K.2.4

ELL Place English language learners in the groups that correspond to their reading abilities in English.

Practice Stations
• Visit the Words to Know Station
• Visit the Let's Write Station

Independent Activities
• Read independently
• Audio Text of Big Book
• *Reader's and Writer's Notebook*

ELL

English Language Learners

Professional Development Small Group Instruction Small group instruction is helpful to beginning English language learners. These children benefit from repeated readings of predictable texts with illustrations. When children participate in small-group read alouds, they get many opportunities to match the text they read with the words they hear.
—Dr. Georgia Earnest García

Objectives
- Recall and retell a story.
- ◎ Practice realism and fantasy.
- Develop and use vocabulary.
- Develop and use comprehension skills.

Comprehension

Retell the story

Have children turn to p. 86 of *My Skills Buddy* and use the retelling boxes to retell the story *Bear Snores On.*

Envision It!

Think Aloud

Direct children to the first retell box. This is when winter begins and Bear sleeps in the cave. Tell me what happens next.

Continue reviewing the retelling boxes and having children retell the story.

My Skills Buddy, p. 86

Review

◎ **Realism and Fantasy** Remind children that some stories are realistic and some stories are make-believe. The events in a make-believe story could not really happen. The animal characters in *Bear Snores On* do things that real animals cannot do. Display illustrations from *Bear Snores On.*

- What do the animals do in the cave? (brew tea, pop corn, make stew, have a party) Can real animals do this? (no)

- What does Bear do when he wakes up? (stomps, growls, grumbles, and cries) Why does he do these things? (He is mad and sad.) Do real bears cry and feel sad? (no)

More practice

Use *Reader's and Writer's Notebook,* p. 124, for additional practice with realism and fantasy.

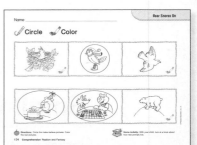
Reader's and Writer's Notebook, p. 124

Second Read—Big Book
Bear Snores On

Reread *Bear Snores On.* Follow the Day 3 arrow beginning on p. 358, and use the Develop Vocabulary notes to prompt conversations about the story.

Have children use the Amazing Words *sleep, winter, cave, woods, storm,* and *blustery* to talk about the selection.

DAY **2**
Read for enjoyment

DAY **3**
Reread using Develop Vocabulary notes

DAY **4**
Reread using Guide Comprehension notes

Differentiated Instruction

 **Strategic Intervention**

Access Content Have children use Talk with Me Chart 10A to review the Amazing Words before reading and talking about *Bear Snores On.*

English Language Learners

Access Content As you use the terms real and make-believe, act out something a bear could really do (such as roar) and something a bear could never do (such as talk).

Develop Vocabulary

DAY 3

Wh- question

Point to the bear. What do you think this is? (a bear)

- It is a sleeping bear. Bears hibernate, or sleep, during the cold winter. What is the bear doing?

Develop Vocabulary bear
Expand Vocabulary lair

*I*n a cave in the woods,
in his deep, dark lair,
through the long, cold winter
sleeps a great brown bear.

5

Big Book, pp. 4–5

Guide Comprehension

DAY 4

Inferential

Where is Bear's cave? (in the woods)
How do you know? (The text says so, and the picture shows many tree trunks.)

Wh- question

What do you see in these pictures? (a cave, snow, a bear)

• This is a cave. The bear is sleeping in the cave. There's a lot of snow. What season do you think it is?

Read page 7 aloud.

• Read the last sentence with me: *But the bear snores on.*

Develop Vocabulary snores

Cuddled in a heap,
with his eyes shut tight,
he sleeps through the day,
he sleeps through the night.

6

The cold winds howl
and the night sounds growl.
But
the bear
snores on.

7

Student Edition pp. 6–7

Recall

What season of the year is it? How do you know? (It is winter. Snow is falling, and the bear is hibernating. Bears hibernate in winter.)

Develop Vocabulary, continued

DAY 3

Distancing

Point to the mouse. What animal is this? (a mouse)

- The mouse has come in from the cold. How do you know it is cold?

An itty-bitty mouse,
pitter-pat, tip-toe,
creep-crawls in the cave
from the fluff-cold snow.

8

Mouse squeaks, "Too damp,
too dank, too dark."
So he lights wee twigs
with a small, hot spark.

9

Big Book, pp. 8–9

Guide Comprehension, continued

DAY 4

Realism and Fantasy • Inferential

Why does Mouse light a fire? (He wanted to warm up.) What does this action tell about the mouse? (He is make-believe because real mice do not light fires.)

Distancing

What does the mouse do in the cave? (builds a fire)

- A fire is one way to keep warm. What is one way you keep warm?

The coals pip-pop and the wind doesn't stop.

10

But the bear snores on.

11

Big Book, pp. 10–11

Inferential

What do you think might happen if the bear woke up and saw the mouse and fire? (I think the bear would growl.) Why? (The bear would not want another animal in his cave.)

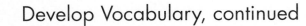

Develop Vocabulary, continued

DAY 3

Open-Ended

Some animals change color to blend in with the snow in winter. What animal in these pictures can blend in with the snow? (the hare or rabbit)

• A hare is related to a rabbit. Why can the hare blend in with the snow?

Two glowing eyes
sneak-peek in the den.
Mouse cries, "Who's there?"
and a hare hops in.

12

"Ho, Mouse!" says Hare.

"Long time, no see!"

So they pop white corn.

And they brew black tea.

13

Big Book, pp. 12–13

Guide Comprehension, continued

DAY 4

Realism and Fantasy • Inferential

What do the hare and the mouse do? (They drink tea and eat popcorn.) What do these actions tell you about the animals? (They are make-believe because real animals do not do these things.)

Completion

What is Bear doing while Hare and Mouse eat and drink? (**sleeping, snoring**)

- The bear is sleeping. When a bear hibernates, it goes into a long, deep sleep. Read the last line with me: *But the bear snores on.*

Big Book, pp. 14–15

Distancing

What does your family like to do when it is very cold outside? (Children may say their families like to sled, skate, ski, and make snowpeople outside or read books, watch TV, and play games inside.)

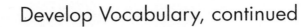
Develop Vocabulary, continued

Open-ended

DAY 3

Who comes into the cave next?
(a badger)

• A badger is a digging animal that lives in an underground burrow. Why might the badger come to the cave?

A badger scuttles by,
sniff-snuffs at the air.
"I smell yummy-yums!
Perhaps we can share?

16

"I've brought honey-nuts,"
Badger says with a grin.
"Let's divvy them up,
cozy down . . . and dig in!"

17

Big Book, pp. 16–17

Guide Comprehension, continued

DAY 4

Monitor and Recall

The badger brings more treats. What does he bring? (Badger brings honey-nuts.) If you don't remember what Badger brought, what could you do? (I could ask someone to reread that page to me.)

Wh- question

What are the hare, badger, and mouse doing?
(eating)

- The hare, badger, and mouse are eating.
  What sounds do they make?

And they nibble and they munch with a

CHEW—

CHOMP—

CRUNCH!

But
the bear
snores on.

18

19

Big Book, pp. 18–19

Wh- question

Why might the hare, badger, and mouse wake
Bear up? (They are making crunching and
chomping noises.)

Develop Vocabulary, continued

DAY 3

Wh- question

What other animals have joined the party in the bear's den? **(a gopher, mole, wren, raven)**

- Gopher, Mole, Wren, and Raven come into the cave. How many animals are there in all now?

A gopher and a mole
tunnel up through the floor.
Then a wren and a raven
flutter in through the door!

20

Mole mutters, "What a night!"
"What a storm!" twitters Wren.
And everybody clutters
in the great bear's den.

21

Big Book, pp. 20–21

Guide Comprehension, continued

DAY 4

Open-ended

Why do you think the animals are gathered close to the fire? **(The fire warms them and keeps away the winter cold.)**

Wh- question

Why isn't Bear dancing at the party? (He is sleeping.)

- Bear is sleeping in his den. What are the other animals doing?

They tweet and they titter. They chat and they chitter.

But
the bear
snores on.

22

In a cave in the woods,
a slumbering bear
sleeps through the party
in his very own lair.

23

Big Book, pp. 22–23

Wh- question

What are the visiting animals doing now?
(They are dancing. They are having a party.)

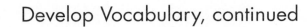

Develop Vocabulary, continued

Recall

What are the animals making? (stew)

- The animals are making stew. Name the animals.

Hare stokes the fire.
Mouse seasons stew.

Then a small pepper fleck
makes the bear . . . .

24

25

Big Book, pp. 24–25

Guide Comprehension, continued

Inferential

Who makes the stew? (Hare and Mouse make the stew.) Why are the animals making stew? (Stew is something hot to eat on a cold winter day.)

Wh- question

What is the bear doing in this picture?
(sneezing)

- The bear wakes up when he sneezes. What do the other animals do?

He blows and he sneezes,
and the whole crowd freezes . . .

RAAAAA - CHOO OOOO !!!!

26 27

Big Book, pp. 26–27

Recall

What happens to Bear? (Pepper makes him sneeze and he wakes up.)

Develop Vocabulary, continued

Open-ended

Does Bear look happy here? (No, he looks angry.)

• Bear looks grumpy. The other animals look frightened. Why are they running away?

And
the bear
WAKES UP!

BEAR GNARLS

and he SNARLS.

BEAR ROARS

and he RUMBLES!

BEAR JUMPS

and he STOMPS.

BEAR GROWLS

and he GRUMBLES!

28

29

Big Book, pp. 28–29

Guide Comprehension, continued

Inferential

Why do you think Bear is so angry when he wakes up? (I think he didn't want to wake up. He wanted to sleep until spring. Also, he doesn't like all these animals playing in his cave.)

Wh- question

Why does the bear have his head in his hands? **(He is crying.)**

● Bear is crying. Why is he upset?

"You've snuck in my lair
and you've all had fun!
But me? I was sleeping
and . . .
          I have had none!"

And he whimpers
and he moans,
he wails and he groans . . .

30   And the bear blubbers on!

Mouse squeaks, "Don't fret.
Don't fuss. Look, see?
We can pop more corn!
We can brew more tea!"

31

Big Book, pp. 30–31

Inferential

What does Mouse say they can do? Do you think that will make Bear happy? **(Mouse says they can pop more corn and brew more tea. I think Bear will be happy because the party will go on and he won't miss it this time.)**

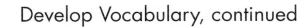

Develop Vocabulary, continued

DAY 3

Wh- question
What is Bear eating? (popcorn)

- The mouse made popcorn for Bear. What are the other animals doing?

Bear gulps. Bear gobbles.
He sighs with delight.
Then he spins tall tales
through the blustery night.

When the sun peeks up
on a crisp, clear dawn,
Bear can't sleep . . .

32

33

Big Book, pp. 32–33

Guide Comprehension, continued

DAY 4

Wh- question
What does Bear do for the other animals? (He tells them tall tales all night.)

Wh- question

What are the other animals doing now?
(sleeping)

- They are sleeping. What might happen
  next?

Continue with DAY **3**

Conventions p. 374

Big Book, p. 34

Open-ended

What is funny about the ending? (Bear is
awake and the other animals are asleep.)

Skip to DAY **4**

Conventions p. 388

Objectives
- Review adjectives for colors and shapes.
- Dictate or write a poem.

Conventions
Adjectives for Colors and Shapes

Review

Pick up AlphaBuddy. AlphaBuddy is going to help you learn about describing words, or adjectives. Words for colors and shapes are adjectives. Have AlphaBuddy point to something yellow. What color is this? This is yellow. If yellow is a color, is the word *yellow* an adjective? Yes, *yellow* is an adjective.

Shapes are describing words, or adjectives, too. Have AlphaBuddy point to a clock. What shape is this? This is round. If round is a shape, is the word *round* an adjective? Yes, *round* is an adjective.

Let's look for more adjectives for colors and shapes in the classroom. Have AlphaBuddy continue pointing to items of various colors and shapes. What adjective is in the phrase *square window*? As children identify the adjective in each phrase AlphaBuddy says, write the word on the board. Then reread the list with children, pointing to each adjective as you read it.

Guide practice

Write the following sentences on the board:

> My _____ shirt is my favorite.
>
> The _____ plate has food.

With children, complete each sentence using an adjective for a color or a shape. Then read the sentences with children

Team Talk Pair children and have them take turns telling the color of their clothing and any shapes on their clothing.

On their own

Use *Reader's and Writer's Notebook,* p. 125, for practice reading, writing, and saying adjectives for colors and shapes.

Daily Fix-It

Use the Daily Fix-It for more conventions practice.

Reader's and Writer's Notebook, p. 125

SI Strategic Intervention

Support Writing Before children copy the poem in their Reader's and Writer's Notebook, reread the lines of the poem with children, pointing to each word you read. Then have them identify the rhyming words.

Writing
Poem

Teach

Talk about poems with children. A poem is a type of writing that has short lines. Poems sometimes rhyme. We write poems to share experiences, feelings, or ideas. Poems can be about anything we want. What kinds of things can we write poems about? Write children's suggestions on the board.

Model

Display the *cat* Picture Card. Today, I'm going to write a poem about a cat. My poem will be two lines. The two lines will end with rhyming words. What is a word that rhymes with *cat?* The word *hat* rhymes with *cat,* so I will write this poem:

> **Look at the cat.**
>
> **It has a hat.**

Guide practice

Have children provide other lines for the poem. Tell them to think of words that rhyme with *cat.* Then write their sentences on the board, such as *It is fat, His name is Pat,* and *She sits on a mat.*

Independent writing

Have children turn to p. 126 of *Reader's and Writer's Notebook.* Have them copy two lines from the poem about the cat. Then tell them to draw a picture of the cat.

Daily Fix-It

brown bears live in caves
<u>B</u>rown bears live in caves<u>.</u>

This week's practice sentences appear on Teacher Resources DVD-ROM.

Reader's and Writer's Notebook, p. 126

Daily Handwriting

Write *Cam* and *cat* on the board. Review correct letter wformation of uppercase *C* and lowercase *c.*

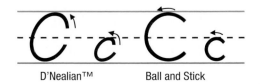

D'Nealian™   Ball and Stick

Have children write *Cam* and *cat* on their Write-On Boards. Remind children to use proper left-to-right and top-to-bottom progression and proper spacing between letters when writing *C* and *c.*

Objectives

- Identify a setting based on an oral description.
- Face the speaker when listening.
- Take turns speaking.
- Speak one at a time.

Listening and Speaking
Listen for Setting

Review Remind children that when they listen for the setting, they are listening for when and where a story takes place. Remind children to face the speaker to show they are listening attentively.

Model When we talk about when and where something happens, we are talking about the setting. What setting are we in right now? (at school, in a classroom, during the school day)

Guide practice Have children turn to p. 89 of *My Skills Buddy*. Look at these pictures. AlphaBuddy is going to describe a setting. I want you to point to the picture that shows the setting he is describing. Have AlphaBuddy say:

My Skills Buddy, p. 89

A boy is wearing a bear costume, and he is speaking. It is dark outside. The setting of this picture is a play at night. Which picture shows what AlphaBuddy is describing? Use the Listening and Speaking bullet on p. 88 of *My Skills Buddy* to guide the discussion for the rest of the pictures. Have children listen to AlphaBuddy describe the other settings. Then tell them to identify the picture that shows that setting.

Independent practice

Think about a time and place that is special to you. Think about when and where you go to that place and what you do there. Do not tell the class what the time and place are yet. How can you describe this setting?

Have children share information about their favorite place without naming it. Then have the class figure out the mystery setting from the details. Refer to the Rules for Listening and Speaking from pp. 1–2 of the *Reader's and Writer's Notebook.* Tell children that when they share their ideas, they need to speak loudly, take turns, and speak one at a time. Remind them to be good listeners by facing the speaker.

Reader's and Writer's Notebook, p. 1

Be a Good Listener

1. Face the person who is speaking.
2. Take turns and speak one at a time.
3. Pay attention to the speaker.
4. Ask questions if you don't understand.

Differentiated Instruction

 Strategic Intervention

Access Content Have children draw a picture of their special place before they describe the setting so they have an image to refer to.

English Language Learners

Access Content To explain the concept of setting to English language learners, show them pictures of familiar settings such as a schoolroom or a bedroom. Ask them: Where is this? Then show pictures of *Bear Snores On* and identify the cave as the setting.

Wrap Up Your Day

✔ **Concept Talk** Today we read a story about a bear asleep in a cave. What is it like inside a cave?

✔ **Respond to Literature** Today we read about two friends having winter fun. What do the children make out of snow?

✔ **Conventions** Ask children to look at their shoes. What adjectives can you use to describe your shoes? Write children's adjectives on the board and point to each word as you read the list with children.

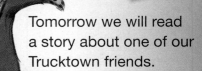

Preview DAY 4

Tomorrow we will read a story about one of our Trucktown friends.

✔ **Homework Idea** Have children draw a picture of something they find at home whose name begins with /k/ spelled *Cc*.

Extend Your Day!

Science
Animal Characteristics

Materials: red and blue construction paper cut into 4 × 4 inch squares

Discriminating Animal Traits Give each child a red square and a blue square. Tell children that you will say a sentence. The sentence may tell about real animals or make-believe animals. After they listen to each sentence, children will decide if it tells about a real or a make-believe activity.

Tell children to raise their *red* square for a real (R) activity and the *blue* square for a make-believe (MB) activity. Read these sentences:

- A gopher goes into a hole. (R)
- A chipmunk puts on a cap. (MB)
- A dog eats from a dish. (R)
- A cat eats with a fork. (MB)
- A goat talks to a friend. (MB)
- A sheep has its wool cut off. (R)
- A mouse makes tea. (MB)
- A squirrel climbs a tree. (R)
- Two monkeys play in a tree. (R)
- An ant plays bingo. (MB)
- A rat eats corn. (R)
- A fish gets a suntan. (MB)

Conventions
Adjectives for Colors and Shapes

Materials: construction paper, crayons

Illustrate Adjectives Have each child choose a shape or a color and then draw objects in the classroom, outdoors, or at home that are the shape or color they have chosen.

Write Words Beneath their pictures, have children write or dictate a label, such as *a round red clock.*

a round red clock

Comprehension
Realism and Fantasy

Materials: construction paper, crayons

Real and Make-Believe Animals Have children divide a sheet of paper in half and draw two pictures, one on each half. The first picture should be an animal as it really looks. The second picture should be the same animal but doing something that it really can't do.

Objectives

- Discuss the concept to develop oral language.
- Build oral vocabulary.

Today at a Glance

Oral Vocabulary
storm, blustery

Phonemic Awareness
Review /p/

Phonics
/p/ Spelled *Pp*
Spell Words

Comprehension
◉ Realism and Fantasy

Conventions
Adjectives for Sizes

Writing
Extend the Concept

Vocabulary
Words for Seasons

TRUCKTOWN on Reading Street

Start your engines! Display p. 14 of *Truckery Rhymes.*

- Have the group say the rhyme with you.
- Next, have children clap the rhythm as they recite the rhyme.
- Then let groups of two children act out the rhyme as the others recite it.

Truckery Rhymes

Concept Talk

 Question of the Week

What unique thing does a bear do in the winter?

Build concepts

Write the question of the week on the board. Read it as you track the print. Tell children to respond in complete sentences. Display Sing with Me Chart 10B.

Listen for Amazing Words

We are going to sing this song again. Listen for the Amazing Words *storm* and *blustery*. Sing the song several times with children. Have them hop once when they hear the words *storm* and *blustery*.

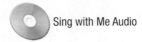 Sing with Me Audio

Hush, Little Brown Bear

Hush, little brown bear in the woods,
You'd sleep through the winter if you could,

And if the winter continues to storm,
Stay in your cave, all safe and warm,

And if it's still blustery and cold,
You'll always have your mama's
    hand to hold.

Hush, little brown bear in the woods,
You'd sleep through the winter if you could.

Talk with Me/Sing with Me Chart 10B

ELL Produce Oral Language Use the Day 4 instruction on ELL Poster 10 to extend and enrich language.

ELL Poster 10

Oral Vocabulary
Amazing Words

sleep	grassland
cave	woods
storm	blustery

Teach Amazing Words

Amazing Words — Oral Vocabulary Routine

1. **Introduce the Word** When the weather is bad and there is lightning, thunder, rain, or snow outside, we call it a *storm*. What's our new Amazing Word for bad weather? Say it with me: *storm*.

2. **Demonstrate** Provide examples to show meaning. *It is not fun to be outside during a storm.*

   Repeat steps 1 and 2.

   Introduce the Word When the wind is blowing strongly, we say it is *blustery*. What is our new Amazing Word for very windy weather? Say it with me: *blustery*.

   Demonstrate *It is not blustery if the wind is not blowing.*

3. **Apply** Have children use *storm* and *blustery* in complete sentences to describe weather they have experienced.

Routines Flip Chart

Differentiated Instruction

SI Strategic Intervention

Access Content Have children act out how they might walk if they were outside on a *blustery* day or during a *storm*.

Use Amazing Words

To reinforce the concept and the Amazing Words, have children supply the appropriate Amazing Word for each sentence.

A lot of snow fell during the _____. (storm)

My face was cold from the _____ wind. (blustery)

Phonemic Awareness
Review /p/

Picture Card

Review

Display the *pig* Picture Card. This is a *pig*. *Pig* begins with /p/. What is this? What sound does it begin with? Continue the routine with the *pan, pillow, pocket,* and *puzzle* Picture Cards. Then display the *top* Picture Card. This is a *top*. Where do you hear /p/ in the word *top*? *Top* ends with /p/. What sound does *top* end with?

I am going to say two words. Tell me which word begins like *pig*. Listen: *sun, pet*. Does *sun* begin like *pig*? (no) Does *pet* begin like *pig*? (yes) *Pet* and *pig* both begin with /p/. Continue the routine with the following pairs of words. Have children compare each word in the pair to *pig* before deciding which word begins with /p/: *puff, tall; rub, pop; pit, mop; big, pen; pat, dot; gate, pail*. Then use these word pairs to have children identify final /p/: *cap, cone; find, lip; bag, drop; cup, fan; stop, go; kite, pop.*

Picture Card

Corrective feedback

If... children cannot discriminate /p/,
then... have them say /p/ several times.

When you say /p/, your lips come together and you let out a puff of air. Have children practice saying /p/.

Phonics
/p/ Spelled *Pp*

Display the *Pp* Alphabet Card. This is a *penguin*. *Penguin* begins with /p/. What letter spells this sound? Yes, the letter *p*.

Write the word *pat* on the board. Help me blend the sounds in this word. Listen as I say each sound: /p/ /a/ /t/. Now let's blend the sounds together to read the word. Say the sounds with me: /p/ /a/ /t/, *pat*. What is the word? (*pat*) Write the word *Pam* on the board and repeat the routine.

Alphabet Card

Don't Wait Until Friday

MONITOR PROGRESS — Check Phonemic Awareness

Phoneme Segmentation Have children practice segmenting sounds with these words after you pronounce each one.

cat	Cam	cap	sat	mat

If... children cannot segment the sounds,

then... use the small-group Strategic Intervention lesson, p. DI•55, to reteach segmentation skills.

Continue to monitor children's progress using other instructional opportunities during the week so that they can be successful with the Day 5 Assessment. See the Skills Trace on p. 318.

Day 1	Day 2	Day 3	Day 4	Day 5
Check Phonemic Awareness	Check Sound-Spelling/Retelling	Check Word Reading	Check Phonemic Awareness	Check Oral Vocabulary

Success Predictor

Differentiated Instruction

A Advanced

Support Phonemic Awareness Have children say a word that begins or ends with /p/. Then have them use the word in a sentence.

Phonemic Awareness

Success Predictor

Objectives
- Spell words.
- Blend and segment words.
- Read decodable text.
- Read high-frequency words.

Spelling
/k/ Spelled *Cc*

ROUTINE **Spell Words**

Spell Words

1) Review Sound-Spellings Display the *Cc* Alphabet Card. This is a *cactus*. *Cactus* begins with /k/. What is the letter we learned for /k/? (*c*) Continue the routine with the following Alphabet Cards: *Aa, Mm, Ss, Tt, Pp.*

2) Model Today we are going to spell some words. Listen to the three sounds in *cap*: /k/ /a/ /p/.

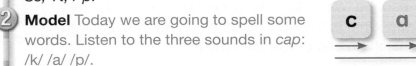

- What is the first sound in *cap*? (/k/) What is the letter we learned for /k/? (*c*) Write *c* on the board.
- What is the middle sound you hear? (/a/) What is the letter for /a/? (*a*) Write *a* on the board.
- What is the last sound you hear in *cap*? (/p/) What is the letter for /p/? (*p*) Write *p* on the board.
- Point to *cap*. Help me blend the sound of each letter together to read this word: /k/ /a/ /p/. The word is *cap*. Repeat the modeling with the word pan.

3) Guide Practice Now let's spell some words together. Listen to this word: /k/ /a/ /m/. What is the first sound in *Cam*? (/k/) What is a letter for /k/? (*C*) Write *C* on the board. Now you write *C* on your paper. What is the middle sound in *Cam*? (/a/) What is the letter for /a/? (*a*) Write *a* on the board. Now you write *a* on your paper. What is the last sound in *Cam*? (/m/) What is the letter for /m/? (*m*) Write *m* on the board. Now you write *m* on your paper. Now we can blend the sound of each letter together to read the word: /k/ /a/ /m/. What is the word? (*Cam*) Continue spell and blend practice with the following words: *tap, mat, Mac, Sam.*

4) On Your Own This time I am going to say a word. I want you to write it on your paper. Remember, first, say the word slowly in your head and then write the letter for each sound. Listen carefully. Write the word *cat*. Give children time to write the word. How do you spell the word *cat*? Listen to the sounds: /k/ /a/ /t/. The first sound is /k/. What is the letter we learned for /k/? Did you write *c* on your paper? What is the letter for /a/? Did you write *a* on your paper? What is the letter for /t/? Did you write *t* on your paper? Name the letters in *cat*. *Cat* is spelled *c, a, t.* Continue the activity with the following words: *mat, tap, pat, sat.*

Routines Flip Chart

Get Set, Roll! Reader 10
 Practice /k/ Spelled Cc

Review Review the high-frequency words *I*, *am*, *the*, *little*, *to*, *a*, *have*, and *is*. Have children find each word on the Word Wall.

Teach rebus words Write the name *Jack* on the board. This is the name *Jack*. Name the letters in *Jack* with me: *J, a, c, k, Jack*. Repeat the procedure with the word *blue*. Look for the words *Jack* and *blue* in the story today. A picture above the word will help you read it.

Read Get Set, Roll! Reader 10 Today we will read a story about our friend Jack Truck. Point to the title of the book. What is the title of the book? (*The Cap*) We will read /k/ words in this book.

Use the routine for reading decodable books found in the Routines Flip Chart to read Get Set, Roll! Reader 10.

Get Set, Roll! Reader 10

Differentiated Instruction

 Advanced

Access Content Have children use the words *Jack* and *blue* in complete sentences.

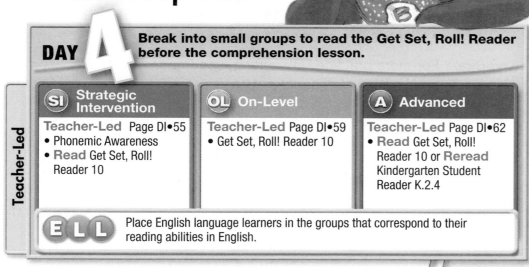

Small Group Time

DAY 4 Break into small groups to read the Get Set, Roll! Reader before the comprehension lesson.

SI Strategic Intervention	**OL On-Level**	**A Advanced**
Teacher-Led Page DI•55 • Phonemic Awareness • **Read** Get Set, Roll! Reader 10	**Teacher-Led** Page DI•59 • Get Set, Roll! Reader 10	**Teacher-Led** Page DI•62 • **Read** Get Set, Roll! Reader 10 or **Reread** Kindergarten Student Reader K.2.4

ELL Place English language learners in the groups that correspond to their reading abilities in English.

Practice Stations
• Visit the Let's Write! Station
• Visit the Read for Meaning Station

Independent Activities
• Read independently
• Audio Text of the Big Book
• *Reader's and Writer's Notebook*

English Language Learners

Frontload Reader Take a picture walk with children to preview the reader before starting the routine.

Objectives
◎ Practice realism and fantasy.
• Review and practice setting.

Comprehension
Realism and Fantasy

Practice realism and fantasy

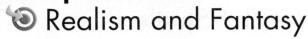

Have children turn to the Realism and Fantasy picture on pp. 74–75 *of My Skills Buddy.* As you look at the pictures, remind children that some stories are about things that could really happen and other stories are make-believe.

Team Talk Pair children and have them take turns describing things a real cat can do and things a make-believe cat can do.

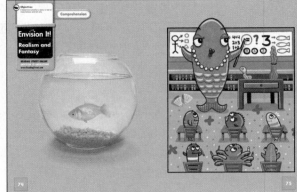

My Skills Buddy, pp. 74–75

Setting

Review

Direct children to the Literary Elements picture on pp. 34–35 of *My Skills Buddy.*

Remember, the setting of a story is when and where it takes place. Good readers pay attention to a story's setting because it helps them understand the story.

• Where is this story happening? (in a park or meadow)

• When is it happening? (during a sunny day)

More practice

For more practice with setting, use *Reader's and Writer's Notebook,* p. 127.

Reader's and Writer's Notebook, p. 127

 Triple Day Read!

Third Read—Big Book
Bear Snores On

Guide Comprehension

Display *Bear Snores On*. In this story, a bear sleeps in a cave.

- When and where does this story take place? (in a cave in the woods in winter)
- Why does the story take place in a cave? (The bear hibernates in a cave. A cave is a good place for other animals to escape the winter weather.)

Reread *Bear Snores On*. Return to p. 358. Follow the Day 4 arrow and use the Guide Comprehension notes to give children the opportunity to gain a more complete understanding of the story.

DAY **2**
Read for enjoyment

DAY **3**
Reread using Develop Vocabulary notes

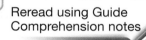

DAY **4**
Reread using Guide Comprehension notes

Differentiated Instruction

 A Advanced

Access Content Have children choose an animal and draw a picture of that animal doing something it can do in real life. Then have them draw the same animal doing something make-believe. Have pairs of children tell each other what their animal is doing in each picture.

Conventions
Adjectives for Sizes

Review Remind children of what they learned about adjectives. Adjectives are describing words. They tell more about sizes, shapes, colors, or numbers of people, animals, places, or things.

Model Some adjectives tell about sizes. Draw a large and a small circle on the board. This is a small circle. This is a large circle. *Small* and *large* are adjectives for sizes. Write *small circle* and *big circle* under the circles. With the class, read the captions.

Guide practice Have children brainstorm adjectives that describe sizes. What other adjectives can you think of that describe size? List children's responses on the board. Point to each word as you say it, and have children echo read the list with you. Then have them name things each word could describe. Use children's suggestions to write sentences on the board.

On their own Use *Reader's and Writer's Notebook*, p. 128, for more practice with adjectives for sizes.

Daily Fix-It Use the Daily Fix-It exercise for more conventions practice.

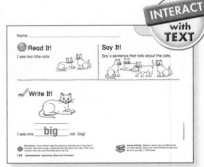

Reader's and Writer's Notebook, p. 128

Writing
Extend the Concept: Text to Self

Discuss bedtime routines

We just read a story about a bear that hibernates, or sleeps during the winter. Bears eat a lot of food and then sleep in their caves until spring. Just like a bear gets ready to sleep in a cave, we get ready to sleep in our rooms.

Have children think about how they get ready to sleep every night. Talk about what special things they do every night before they go to bed.

Guide practice

Use children's contributions to the discussion to write sentences.

Before I go to sleep,...	**I brush my teeth.**
	my dad reads me a story.
	I turn on a night-light.

Encourage children to help you write more sentences. Have them read the sentences with you.

Independent writing

Have children write or dictate their own sentences about what they do before they go to sleep, or copy one of the sentences from the board. Have children read their sentences to the class. Encourage children to act out their sentences when appropriate.

Daily Handwriting

Write uppercase *C* and lowercase *c* on the board. Review correct letter formation with children.

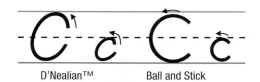

D'Nealian™   Ball and Stick

Have children write a row of uppercase *C* and a row of lowercase *c* on their Write-On Boards. Remind them to use proper left-to-right and top-to-bottom progression when writing *C* and *c*.

Differentiated Instruction

 SI Strategic Intervention

Access Content Before writing, pair children and have them share their ideas.

Daily Fix-It

the bear sleeps in winter
The bear sleeps in winter.

This week's practice sentences appear on Teacher Resources DVD-ROM.

 **ELL**

English Language Learners

ELL Support For additional support for language transfer, see Linguistic Contrastive Analysis in the *ELL Handbook.*

Objectives
- Practice using words for seasons.
- Identify words that begin with /p/.

Vocabulary
Words for Seasons

| spring | summer | fall | winter |

Teach

Write the words *spring, summer, fall,* and *winter* on the board. Point to each word as you read it. These are words that tell the seasons. Have children turn to p. 88 of *My Skills Buddy*. Direct them to the picture for winter. How can you tell this picture shows the *winter* season? Point to the fall picture. What activities do we do during the *fall?* Then direct them to the pictures for summer and spring. How can you tell the difference between the *summer* picture and the *spring picture?* Read and discuss the second Vocabulary bullet on p. 88 of *My Skills Buddy*.

Team Talk Pair children and have them take turns telling things they do each season. Have them use the season words *spring, summer, fall,* and *winter* in complete sentences.

My Skills Buddy, p. 88

Wrap Up Your Day

✔ **Oral Language** Sing "Hush, Little Brown Bear" with me. Clap when you hear an Amazing Word. The Amazing Words this week are *sleep, winter, cave, woods, storm,* and *blustery*.

✔ **Phonemic Awareness** I am going to say some words. Pat your head when you hear a word that begins with /p/: *point, sound, purse, make, push, time, pond, peach.*

✔ **Conventions** Have each child choose two objects from the class and compare them using adjectives for sizes.

✔ **Homework Idea** Have children draw a picture of a bear hibernating in a cave to take home to share with the family.

Preview DAY 5

Tell children that tomorrow they will review some of the books and stories they read this week.

Extend Your Day!

Science
Bear Goes Through Winter

Materials: chart paper, 11 × 17 paper for booklets, crayons

Sequence Steps in Hibernation Remind children that when a bear hibernates, it finds a safe place to sleep for the winter. Make a chart to tell what a bear does.

Illustrate Bear's Hibernation Have children fold a large sheet of paper in half to make a booklet and write the numbers 1, 2, 3, and 4 on the pages of the booklet. Have them draw a picture on each page to show one step in a bear's hibernation. Then, using the words on the chart, have them write a word or sentence that tells about each picture.

Bear gets ready for winter.

Conventions
Adjectives for Sizes

Materials: drawing paper, crayons, markers

Illustrate Adjectives for Sizes Help children write a list of big and small objects. Label each with an adjective for size, such as a *big* dump truck or a *small* bug. Divide a sheet of paper in half. Have children draw two objects, one big and one small. Have them label each item with an adjective that describes the object's size.

giant elephant

tiny bug

Comprehension
Realism and Fantasy

Materials: T-chart or Graphic Organizer 4

Draw on the board a T-chart with the columns labeled *Make-believe* and *Real*. Tell children to name things that are make-believe and real, and list their suggestions. Have them think of plants and animals from books, movies, or television. Then have them draw one make-believe plant or animal next to the corresponding real plant or animal.

Objectives
- Review the concepts.
- Build oral vocabulary.

Today at a Glance

Oral Vocabulary
sleep, winter, cave, woods, storm, blustery

Phonemic Awareness
◉ Initial and Final /k/

Phonics
◉ /k/ Spelled *Cc*

Comprehension
◉ Realism and Fantasy

Conventions
Adjectives for Numbers

Writing
This Week We…

Check Oral Vocabulary
SUCCESS PREDICTOR

TRUCKTOWN on Reading Street

Start your engines!

- Display "Jack and Kat" and lead children in saying the rhyme a few times.
- What do Jack and Kat do in this rhyme? Have half the group act out the rhyme while the other half recites the rhyme.
- Then have the groups change roles.

Truckery Rhymes

Concept Wrap Up

Question of the Week

What unique thing does a bear do in the winter?

Listen for Amazing Words

Write the question of the week on the board. Track the print as you read it to children. Have them use the Amazing Words in their responses (*sleep, winter, cave, woods, storm, blustery*). Display Sing with Me Chart 10B. Let's sing "Hush, Little Brown Bear." I want you to listen for the Amazing Words we learned this week. Remind children that the words *sleep, winter, cave, woods, storm,* and *blustery* are in the song. Sing the song several times to the tune of "Hush, Little Baby." Have children clap each time they hear an Amazing Word. Then discuss what a bear does during the winter. Remind children to take turns and to speak one at a time.

Hush, Little Brown Bear

Hush, little brown bear in the woods,
You'd sleep through the winter if you could.

And if the winter continues to storm,
Stay in your cave, all safe and warm,

And if it's still blustery and cold,
You'll always have your mama's
hand to hold.

Hush, little brown bear in the woods,
You'd sleep through the winter if you could.

Sing with Me Chart 10B

🔘 Sing with Me Audio

ELL **Check Concepts and Language** Use the Day 5 instruction on ELL Poster 10 to monitor children's understanding of the lesson concept.

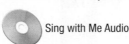
ELL Poster 10

Oral Vocabulary
Amazing Words

Let's Talk Display Talk with Me Chart 10A. We learned six new Amazing Words this week. Let's say the Amazing Words as I point to the pictures on the chart. Point to each picture and give children the chance to say the appropriate Amazing Word before offering it.

Have children supply the appropriate Amazing Word to complete each sentence.

Talk with Me/Sing with Me Chart 10A

Amazing Words

sleep	winter
cave	woods
storm	blustery

Differentiated Instruction

A Advanced

Use Amazing Words Have children use the Amazing Words in their own sentences.

The bear sleeps in a dark _____. (cave)

A cold, _____ wind blew the leaves. (blustery)

Snow fell quietly among the trees in the _____. (woods)

The snow and cold tells us the season is _____. (winter)

The _____ brought lots of snow. (storm)

The bear will _____ through the cold weather. (sleep)

It's Friday

MONITOR PROGRESS | **Check Oral Vocabulary**

Demonstrate Word Knowledge Monitor the Amazing Words by asking the following questions. Tell children to use the Amazing Word in their answer.

• **In what season does a bear hibernate?** (winter)

• **Where is a good place for a bear to sleep all winter?** (cave)

• **What do you call weather with lots of wind and snow?** (storm)

• **What do you do at night when you are tired?** (sleep)

• **What do you call land that has many trees?** (woods)

• **What word describes a loud, strong wind?** (blustery)

If... children have difficulty using the Amazing Words,

then... reteach the words using the Oral Vocabulary Routine on the Routines Flip Chart.

Day 1	Day 2	Day 3	Day 4	Day 5
Check Phonemic Awareness	Check Sound-Spelling/ Retelling	Check Word Reading	Check Phonemic Awareness	Check Oral Vocabulary

Success Predictor

Oral Vocabulary

Success Predictor

Objectives
◎ Review initial and final /k/.
◎ Review /k/ spelled *Cc*.

Phonemic Awareness **Review**
↺ /k/

Picture Card

Isolate initial and final /k/

Display the *cat* Picture Card. What is the first sound in *cat*? Say the word with me: /k/ /k/ /k/, *cat*. Review initial /k/ with the following Picture Cards: *can, cap, carrot*.

Display the *rock* Picture Card. What is the last sound in *rock*? Say it again: *rock,* /k/ /k/. Continue isolating final /k/ with these Picture Cards: *block, truck*.

Discriminate initial and final sounds

I am going to say two words. Tell me which word begins with /k/: *cup, dip*. Which word begins with /k/? Yes, *cup* begins with /k/. Continue the process with these word pairs: *cab, ten; cub, tub; cot, pot*. I am going to say two words. Tell me which word ends with /k/: *goose, yak*. Yes, *yak* ends with /k/. Continue the process with these word pairs: *back, bus; fan, lake; bug, snake; sack, sun*.

Picture Card

Phonics Review
/k/ Spelled Cc

Teach /k/Cc

Display the *Cc* Alphabet Card. This is a *cactus*. What sound do you hear at the beginning of *cactus*? What letter did we learn to spell that sound?

High-frequency words

Write the word *we* on the board. This is the word *we*. What is this word? Repeat the routine for *my* and *like*.

Apply phonics in familiar text

Let's Reread Have children reread one of the books specific to the target letter sound. You may wish to review the decodable words and high-frequency words that appear in each book prior to rereading.

Alphabet Card

Decodable Reader 10
My Skills Buddy, p. 78

Kindergarten
Student Reader K.2.4

Get Set, Roll!
Reader 10

Differentiated Instruction

 Advanced

Connect Sound-Spelling Read the following list of words and have children write the letter *c* when they hear a word that begins with /k/: *cabin, carrot, lettuce, giant, cabbage, can.*

Small Group Time

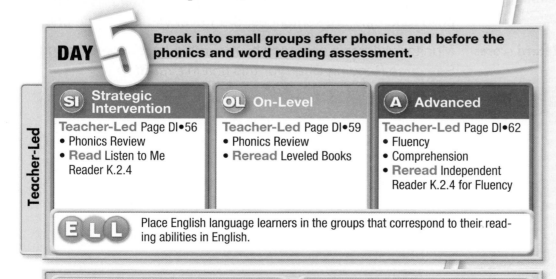

DAY 5 Break into small groups after phonics and before the phonics and word reading assessment.

Teacher-Led

SI Strategic Intervention	**OL On-Level**	**A Advanced**
Teacher-Led Page DI•56 • Phonics Review • **Read** Listen to Me Reader K.2.4	Teacher-Led Page DI•59 • Phonics Review • **Reread** Leveled Books	Teacher-Led Page DI•62 • Fluency • Comprehension • **Reread** Independent Reader K.2.4 for Fluency

ELL Place English language learners in the groups that correspond to their reading abilities in English.

Practice Stations
• Visit the Read for Meaning Station
• Visit the Let's Make Art Station

Independent Activities
• Read independently
• Story Sort
• Concept Talk Video

Assess

◎ Read words with /k/.
• Read high-frequency words.
• Read sentences.

Assessment
Monitor Progress

/k/ Spelled Cc

Whole Class Divide a paper into four equal sections for each child. Tell children to draw something whose name begins with /k/Cc in each box. Then ask children to label the picture with a word or the letter c.

MONITOR PROGRESS	Check Word and Sentence Reading

If... children cannot complete the whole-class assessment,

then... use the Reteach lesson in *First Stop*.

If... you are unsure of a child's grasp of this week's skills,

then... use the assessment below to obtain a clearer evaluation of the child's progress.

/k/ Spelled Cc and high-frequency words

One-on-One To facilitate individual progress monitoring, assess some children on Day 4 and the rest on Day 5. While individual children are being assessed, the rest of the class can reread this week's books and look for words with /k/.

Word reading

Use the word lists on reproducible p. 397 to assess a child's ability to read words that begin and end with /k/ and high-frequency words. We are going to read some words. I'll read the first word, and you read the rest. The first word is /k/ /a/ /t/, cat. For each child, record any decoding problems.

Sentence reading

Use the sentences on reproducible p. 397 to assess a child's ability to read words in sentences. Have the child read two sentences aloud. Have each child read different sentences. Start over with sentence one if necessary.

Record scores

Monitor children's accuracy by recording their scores using the Word and Sentence Reading Chart for this unit in *First Stop*.

Name _____

Read the Words

cat	☐		caps	☐
like	☐		Cam	☐
cap	☐		we	☐
my	☐		cats	☐

Read the Sentences

1. Sam is my little cat.

2. I like the little cap.

3. We have a cat.

4. Cam is at my mat.

Note to Teacher: Children read each word. Children read two sentences.

Scoring for Read the Words: Score 1 point for each correct word.

/k/ Cc (*cat, cap, caps, Cam, cats*) _____ /__5__

High-Frequency Words (*like, my, we*) _____ /__3__

MONITOR PROGRESS
- /k/ Spelled Cc
- High-frequency Words

Objectives
- Recognize a lullaby.
- Identify rhythm and rhyme.

My Skills Buddy, pp. 90–91

Let's Practice It!
Lullaby

Teach

Today we are going to read a lullaby. A lullaby is a type of song. Review features of a lullaby with children.

- A lullaby is sung to babies to help them go to sleep.

- A lullaby is often about a baby.

- A lullaby has rhyming words.

- A lullaby has a soothing rhythm. Rhythm is a beat found in songs and poems.

Have children turn to pp. 90–91 of *My Skills Buddy.* I am going to sing a lullaby called "Rock-a-Bye, Baby." Look at the pictures as I sing. Read the text of "Rock-a-Bye, Baby." As you sing, direct children to look at the appropriate picture.

Guide practice

Discuss the features of a lullaby with children and discuss the bulleted text on *My Skills Buddy* p. 90.

- A lullaby is often about a baby. Is this lullaby about a baby? How do you know? (Yes; the word *baby* is used in the lullaby, and the lullaby is being sung to a baby.)

- A lullaby has rhyming words. Which words rhyme in "Rock-a-Bye Baby"? (*fall/all; fair/chair*)

- What other words rhyme with *fair*? (*air, hair, lair, pair*)

- A lullaby is a soothing song for babies. Let's sing the lullaby as we would to a baby. Reread the lullaby with children. Have them sway to the rhythm of the lullaby.

Rock-a-Bye, Baby

Rock-a-bye, Baby,
In the treetop.
When the wind blows,
The cradle will rock.
When the bough breaks,
The cradle will fall,
And down will come Baby,
Cradle and all.

Baby is drowsing,
Cozy and fair.
Mother sits near
In her rocking chair.
Forward and back
The cradle she swings,
And though Baby sleeps,
He hears what she sings.

Differentiated Instruction

 Advanced

Context Clues After reading aloud, have children look at the picture as you reread "When the bough breaks, the cradle will fall." What do you think a bough is? (a branch)

Academic Vocabulary

lullaby a soft song sung to babies to help them go to sleep

Objectives
◎ Review realism and fantasy.

Assess
◉ Identify elements of realism and fantasy in a story.

Comprehension Assessment
Monitor Progress

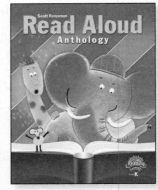

Read Aloud Anthology

Review

Realism and Fantasy Some stories are made-up. They are called fantasies. Other stories have characters and events that really could happen. They are realistic stories. What do we call make-believe stories? (fantasies)

Read "How the Bear Lost Its Tail"

Tell children that you are going to read them a story about a fox and a bear. Ask them to listen to the story and think about whether it is real or make-believe. Listen carefully while I read you the story. When I finish, I will ask you to tell me whether the story is real or make-believe. Read "How the Bear Lost Its Tail" on p. 20 of the *Read Aloud Anthology*.

Check realism and fantasy

After you read the story, have children identify elements of realism and fantasy in the story.

- How do you know this story is make-believe? (The animals talk and try to trick the otters.)
- How can you tell the difference between real and make-believe? (Make-believe things could not happen in real life.)
- Why is it important to know the difference between make-believe stories and realistic stories? (It is important to decide what actually could or could not happen.)
- What is another name for a make-believe story? (a fantasy)

Corrective feedback

If... children cannot distinguish between realism and fantasy,
then... reteach realism and fantasy using the Reteach lesson in *First Stop*.

Assess realism and fantasy

Use the blackline master found on p. 401. Make one copy for each child. Have children color the make-believe picture.

Name _____

Realism and Fantasy

Color the make-believe bear.

Note to Teacher: Have children color the make-believe bear.

Objectives
- Review adjectives for numbers.
- Write or dictate a sentence about preparing for winter.

Conventions
Adjectives for Numbers

Review Review with children what they learned about adjectives. Adjectives are describing words. Some adjectives can describe the size of a person, place, animal, or thing. Other adjectives can tell about the number of people, places, animals, or things.

Model Display *Bear Snores On*. How many animals are on this cover? I count seven animals. *Seven* tells the number of animals. *Seven* is an adjective. Display Kindergarten Student Reader K.2.4, *Winter Fun*. How many people are on the cover? I count two people. *Two* tells how many people. *Two* is an adjective.

Guide practice Continue this exercise using other pictures that show two or more people, animals, or things and asking children to give the adjective that tells how many. Write the adjectives for numbers that children say on the board. Read the list with children, pointing to each adjective as you read it.

On their own Randomly assign children a number from one to ten. Have each child draw a picture of that number of things, people, or animals. Children should write or dictate a label of the number of objects in their picture— for example, *five bears*.

Daily Fix-It Use the Daily Fix-It exercise for more conventions practice.

Writing
This Week We...

Display *Bear Snores On,* Sing with Me Chart 10B, Phonics Songs and Rhymes Chart 10, Decodable Reader 10 from *My Skills Buddy,* Kindergarten Student Reader K.2.4, and Get Set, Roll! Reader 10. This week we learned what a bear does during the winter. We read new books, and we sang new songs. Which book or song was your favorite? Let's share our ideas with each other.

Team Talk Pair children and have them take turns telling which book or song was their favorite and why.

Model writing a sentence

Today we will write about the different ways that a bear gets ready for winter. In *Bear Snores On,* Bear found a cave. I will write this sentence:

> **A bear finds a cave in winter.**

Guide practice

Continue writing sentences with children using this sentence frame:

> **A bear _____ in winter.**

On their own

Have children write or dictate more sentences about the ways animals and people get ready for winter or copy one from the board. Tell them to illustrate their sentences.

Daily Handwriting

Write uppercase *C* and lowercase *c* on the board. Review correct letter formation with children.

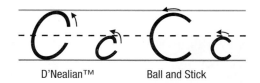

D'Nealian™   Ball and Stick

Have children write a row of uppercase *C* and a row of lowercase *c* on their Write-On Boards. Remind them to use proper left-to-right and top-to-bottom progression.

Differentiated Instruction

 Strategic Intervention

Support Writing Have pairs of children discuss what they do to get ready for winter before supplying a sentence for the group.

Daily Fix-It

there are six children singing
There are six children singing.

This week's practice sentences appear on Teacher Resources DVD-ROM.

ELL

English Language Learners

Poster Preview Prepare children for next week by using Week 5 ELL Poster number 11. Read the Poster Talk-Through to introduce the concept and vocabulary. Ask children to identify and describe objects and actions in the art.

Wrap Up Your Week!

Question of the Week

What unique thing does a bear do in the winter?

Illustrate realism and fantasy

This week we talked about the special thing bears do in the winter: They hibernate.

• Make a word web like the one shown.

• Ask children what they know about where a bear hibernates. Write key words and phrases in the *Where* circle.

• Repeat for *when* a bear hibernates and *why* a bear hibernates. Remind children to speak loudly and clearly when they share information.

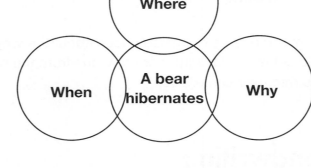
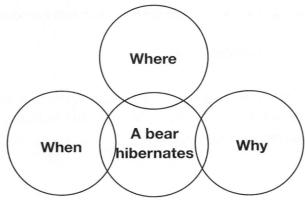

Where

When   A bear hibernates   Why

Next Week's Question

What kind of home does an animal need?

Discuss next week's question. Guide children in making connections between a bear's winter home and other animals' homes.

Preview NEXT WEEK

Tell children that next week they will read about different animal homes.

Amazing Words

You've learned
0 0 6
words this week!

You've learned
0 6 0
words this year!

Extend Your Day!

Science
Warming and Cooling
Materials: Big Book *Bear Snores On*, ice cubes

Understand Thermal Energy Explain that we use heat, or *thermal energy*, every day. We cannot see it, but we can feel it. Have children point out sources of heat in *Bear Snores On* (fire, hot tea or hot teapot, popcorn, animals). Then have children point out things that would make them cold, or take heat away from their bodies (snow, winter wind).

Have children hold an ice cube in their hands. Explain that they are using their body heat to warm the ice cube, which begins to melt. Also explain that the ice cube is cooling their hands.

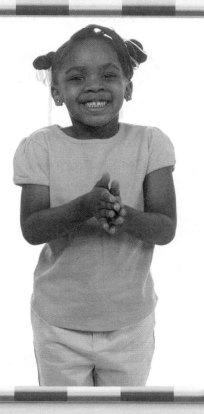

- Why does the ice cube begin to melt when you hold it in your hands? (body heat)
- What other things would make the ice cube melt? (warm air, sunlight)

Comprehension
What Am I?
Materials: construction paper, crayons, markers

Draw a Make-Believe Animal Give each child a sheet of construction paper. Have children draw a picture of a make-believe animal. If necessary, give suggestions such as *a dog with wings flying through the sky* or *a cat riding a bike.* Have children write or dictate a word or sentence that tells about their illustration.

My dog has wings.

Phonics
Word Builders
Materials: large letter cards for *a, c, m, p, s, t*

Make Words Display. Listen to this word: *map*. What sound do you hear at the beginning of *map*? The first sound is /m/. What is the letter for /m/? Yes, *m*. Have a child pick up the letter *m* and stand facing the group. Continue with the other letters, having a child pick up a letter and stand to form the word *map*. Let's blend the sound of the letters together to read the word: /m/ /a/ /p/, *map*. Continue blending the following words: *pat, cat, tap, mat, cap, sat.*

Weekly Assessment

Use the whole-class assessment on pages 396–397 and 400–401 in this Teacher's Edition to check:

✔ ◉ **/k/ Spelled *Cc***

✔ ◉ **Comprehension Skill** *Realism and Fantasy*

✔ **High-Frequency Words**   *we   my   like*

Teacher's Edition, Day 5

Managing Assessment

Use the Assessment Handbook for:

✔ **Observation Checklists**

✔ **Record-Keeping Forms**

✔ **Portfolio Assessment**

Assessment Handbook

Teacher Notes

Small Group Time

Pacing Small Group Instruction

20–30 mins.

5 Day Plan

DAY 1	• Phonemic Awareness/ Phonics • Decodable Story 10
DAY 2	• Phonemic Awareness/ Phonics • Decodable Reader 10
DAY 3	• Phonemic Awareness/ Phonics • Concept Literacy Reader K.2.4 or Kindergarten Student Reader K.2.4
DAY 4	• Phonemic Awareness/ Phonics • Get Set, Roll! Reader 10
DAY 5	• Phonics Review • Listen to Me Reader K.2.4

3 or 4 Day Plan

DAY 1	• Phonemic Awareness/ Phonics • Decodable Story 10
DAY 2	• Phonemic Awareness/ Phonics • Decodable Reader 10
DAY 3	• Phonemic Awareness/ Phonics • Concept Literacy Reader K.2.4 or Kindergarten Student Reader K.2.4
DAY 4	• Phonemic Awareness/ Phonics • Get Set, Roll! Reader 10

3 Day Plan: Eliminate the shaded box.

SI Strategic Intervention

DAY 1

Phonemic Awareness•Phonics

■ **Isolate /k/Cc** Display the *cat* Picture Card. This is a *cat*. *Cat* begins with /k/. Say it with me: /k/ /k/ /k/, *cat*. Repeat with *cap* and *can*.

■ **Discriminate /k/Cc** I am going to say two words. I want you to tell me which word begins with /k/. Listen carefully: *dog, cat*. Say the words with me: *dog, cat*. Which word begins with /k/? The letter *Cc* stands for /k/. Write the word *cat* and underline the letter *c*. *Cat* begins with /k/. *Dog* does not begin with /k/. Continue discriminating /k/ with the following sets of words: *cup, watch; carrot, bean; cap, hat*.

Decodable Story 10

■ **Review High-Frequency Words** Write the following high-frequency words on the board: *I, the, a, have, is, we, my, like*. Have children read each word as you point to it.

> **If...** children have difficulty reading the words,
> **then...** say a word and have children point to the word. Repeat several times, giving assistance as needed.

Have children read the story *The Cap* orally. Then have them reread the story several times individually.

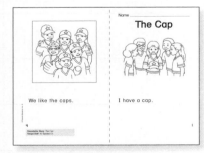

Reader's and Writer's Notebook, pp. 119–120

Objectives
• Identify the common sounds that letters represent.
• Read at least 25 high-frequency words from a commonly used list.

 Strategic Intervention

DAY 2

Phonemic Awareness•Phonics

■ **Discriminate /k/Cc** Display Phonics Songs and Rhymes Chart 10. Sing "Can Cat Come to Captain's Cave?" to the tune of "London Bridge Is Falling Down" several times with children. Show children how to salute, and ask them to salute when they hear a /k/ word.

■ **Connect /k/ to Cc** Ask children to name words that begin with Cc/k/. List the words as they say them. Have children echo read the list of words. Then ask children to take turns circling the c's on the chart. If children name a word that starts with k (e.g. kite), write it and tell them that /k/ can also be spelled k.

■ **Blend Sounds** Write cap on the board. Have children blend the sound of each letter to read the word. /k/ /a/ /p/, cap. Cap is another name for a hat. Do you wear a cap?

Decodable Reader 10

■ **Review High-Frequency Words** Review the previously taught high-frequency words. Have children read each word as you point to it on the Word Wall.

| I | am | the | have | is |
| a | my | we | like | |

If... children have difficulty reading the words,
then... say a word and have children point to the word. Repeat several times, giving assistance as needed.

Display the story *My Cap* on p. 78 of *My Skills Buddy*. The title of this story is *My Cap*. The author is Sue Bear. The illustrator is Lori Burk. Let's read the story together. What do you think the story will be about?

My Skills Buddy

More Reading
Use Leveled Readers or other text at children's instructional level.

Objectives
• Identify the common sounds that letters represent.
• Read at least 25 high-frequency words from a commonly used list.

SI *Strategic Intervention*

Phonemic Awareness•Phonics

- **Isolate /k/Cc** Display the *can* Picture Card. This is a picture of a *can. Can* begins with /k/. Say it with me: /k/ /k/ /k/, *can.* Repeat with *cap* and *cat.*

- **Connect /k/ to Cc** Display the *cactus* Alphabet Card. This is a *cactus. Cactus* begins with /k/. Say it with me: /k/ /k/ /k/, *cactus.* This is the word *cactus. Cactus* begins with /k/. The letter *c* stands for /k/. When you hear a word that begins with /k/, I want you to clap twice. Use the following words: *boat, cup, bubble, cow, carrot, dent, corn.*

- **Blend Sounds** Write *tap* on the board. Have children blend the sound of each letter to read the word. /t/ /a/ /p/, *tap. Tap* is an action. Repeat the routine with the following words: *Tam, cap.*

- **Review High-Frequency Words** Write *we* on the board. Have volunteers say the word and use it in a sentence. Continue with these words: *my, am, is, have, like, to, the, at.*

- To practice phonics and high-frequency words, have children read Kindergarten Student Reader K.2.4. Use the instruction on pp. 354–355.

For a complete lesson plan and additional practice, see the **Leveled Reader Teaching Guide**.

Concept Literacy Reader K.2.4

- **Preview and Predict** Display the cover of the Concept Literacy Reader K.2.4. Point to the title of the book. The title of the book is *The Bear.* Look at the picture. What do you think the book is about? Have children tell about the picture and what they think the book might be about.

- **Set a Purpose** We talked about the title of the book and the picture on the cover. Let's read the story to find out about the bear. Have children read the Concept Literacy Reader.

- **Read** Provide corrective feedback as children read the book orally. During reading, ask them if they were able to confirm any of the predictions they made prior to reading.

If... children have difficulty reading the book individually,

then... read a sentence aloud as children point to each word. Then have the group reread the sentences as they continue pointing to the words.

- **Retell** Have children retell the information as you page through the book. Help them identify the key information about the bear.

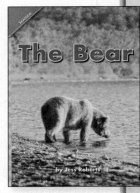

Concept Literacy Reader K.2.4

Objectives
- Identify the common sounds that letters represent.
- Predict what might happen next based on the title.
- Predict what might happen next based on the cover.
- Retell important facts in a text, heard or read.

SI Strategic Intervention

DAY 4

Phonemic Awareness•Phonics

- **Isolate /k/Cc** Display the *carrot* Picture Card. This is a *carrot. Carrot* begins with /k/. Say it with me: /k/ /k/ /k/, *carrot.* Repeat with *can, cat,* and *cap.* Then write the words on the board. Circle the *c* in each word. The letter *c* stands for /k/ in these words.

- **Discriminate /k/** Display the *caterpillar* Picture Card. This is a *caterpillar. Caterpillar* begins with /k/. Say it with me: /k/ /k/ /k/, *caterpillar.* Show children how a caterpillar moves by moving your hand and arm from one side to the other in a wave motion. When I say a word that begins like caterpillar, move your arm like a caterpillar moves. Use the following words: *egg, five, carrot, corn, brown, cow, dress, cup.*

- **Segmenting** Listen to the sounds in *cap,* /k/ /a/ /p/. Say the sounds with me: /k/ /a/ /p/. How many sounds are in *cap?* (three) Continue with *cat, pat, pass,* and *sat.*

Get Set, Roll! Reader 10

- **Review** Review the high-frequency words *I, am, the, little, to, a, have,* and *is.* Write the word *I* on the board and say the word. Have children find the word on the Word Wall. Continue with the other words.

- **Review Rebus Words** Write the word *blue* on the board. This is the word *blue.* Name the letters in blue with me: *b, l, u, e; blue.* Repeat the procedure with the word *Jack.* Look for the words *blue* and *Jack* in the story today. A picture above the word will help you read it.

Get Set, Roll! Reader 10

- **Read** Show the Get Set, Roll! Reader 10, *The Cap.* Today we will read a story about our friend Jack Truck. Point to the title of the book. What is the title of the story? (The Cap) We will read /k/ words in this story.

  If... children have difficulty reading the story individually,
  then... read a sentence aloud as children point to each word. Then have the group reread the sentences as they continue pointing to the words.

- **Reread** Use echo reading of Get Set, Roll! Reader 10 to model fluent reading. Use your oral reading to model for children where to pause, when to change pitch, and which words to stress. Then have children reread orally three to four times, or until they can read with few or no mistakes.

Objectives
- Identify the common sounds that letters represent.
- Read at least 25 high-frequency words from a commonly used list.

More Reading
Use Leveled Readers or other text at children's instructional level.

Small Group Time

More Reading

Use Leveled Readers or other text at children's instructional level.

Strategic Intervention

DAY 5

Phonics Review

■ **Recognize Cc** Write uppercase *C* on the board. Name the letter as you write it several times. Then give each child one chenille stick to bend into the shape of uppercase *C*. Then write a lowercase *c* on the board. Name the letter and ask a volunteer to write the letter on the board.

■ **Discriminate /k/Cc** Draw a row of cups on the board. Gather about ten Picture Cards, including the following /k/Cc cards: *cat, can, carrot, cap, caterpillar*. Mix the cards and display them one at a time. Have a child name the picture. If the name has /k/, have the child write a lowercase *c* in one of the cups.

Listen to Me Reader K.2.4

■ **Preview and Predict** Display the book. The title of this story is *Meet Cam the Cow*. The author is Rosa Perez. The illustrator is Amy Loeffler. Look at the book. Who is Cam? What do you think the story is about?

Listen to Me Reader K.2.4

■ **Set a Purpose** Review children's ideas. Point out that they will know more about Cam when they read the story. Tell children that you will read the story with them. Follow along with your finger as I read. Then we will take turns reading this page. Reread the book several times giving children several opportunities to read the text. Provide support with decoding as necessary.

■ **Reread for Fluency** Use echo reading of Listen to Me Reader K.2.4 to model reading fluently. Use your oral reading to model for children where to pause, when to change pitch, and which words to stress. Then have children reread orally three to four times, or until they can read with few or no mistakes.

Objectives
- Identify the common sounds that letters represent.
- Predict what might happen next based on the cover.
- Predict what might happen next based on the title.

  **eReaders**

 On-Level **DAY 1**

Phonemic Awareness•Phonics

■ **Clap for /k/Cc** Tell children you will tell them a story and they should listen for /k/. When you say a word that begins with /k/, the children should clap their hands and repeat the word. Tell a simple story, emphasizing the /k/ words and pausing to give children a chance to clap and repeat the word. *Casey colored her car using her colorful markers. Casey was good at coloring her car. When Casey was done, she showed her mom who was cutting carrots and cooking corn. Her mom said, "Your car is cool Casey!"* Repeat the activity with other simple stories, pausing and emphasizing the *c* words a little less each time.

■ **Match /k/ to Cc** Retell the story and have children take turns writing *c* or *C* on the board when they hear a word that begins with /k/.

Objectives
• Identify the common sounds that letters represent.

 On-Level **DAY 2**

Phonemic Awareness•Phonics

■ **Be a Copycat** Place the following Picture Cards in a box: *cat, cap, caterpillar, dog, duck, mop*. Have a volunteer pick a Picture Card and act out the word. If it is a /k/ Picture Card, have children be copycats and copy the volunteer's actions. If it is not, have them call out, "We can't copy you." Continue until all the Picture Cards are used.

■ **Connect /k/ to Cc** Read these words to children. If the word begins with /k/, children write a *c* on their papers: *court, ball, cool, cucumber, squash, courage*.

■ **High-Frequency Words** Write *my* on the board. This is the word *my*. What word is this? Continue with the following words: *we, am, at*.

Objectives
• Identify the common sounds that letters represent.
• Read at least 25 high-frequency words from a commonly used list.

Pacing Small Group Instruction

5 Day Plan	
DAY 1	• Phonemic Awareness/ Phonics • Decodable Story 10
DAY 2	• Phonemic Awareness/ Phonics • High-Frequency Words • Decodable Reader 10
DAY 3	• Phonemic Awareness/ Phonics • Kindergarten Student Reader K.2.4
DAY 4	• Get Set, Roll! Reader 10
DAY 5	• Phonics Review • Reread Leveled Books

3 or 4 Day Plan	
DAY 1	• Phonemic Awareness/ Phonics • Decodable Story 10
DAY 2	• Phonemic Awareness/ Phonics • High-Frequency Words • Decodable Reader 10
DAY 3	• Phonemic Awareness/ Phonics • Kindergarten Student Reader K.2.4
DAY 4	• Get Set, Roll! Reader 10

3 Day Plan: Eliminate the shaded box.

More Practice

For additional practice with this week's phonics skills, have children reread the Decodable Story (Day 1) and the Decodable Reader (Day 2).

Small Group Time

Phonemic Awareness•Phonics

■ **Listen for /k/** Teach children the following song, sung to "Are You Sleeping?" When children are familiar with the song, ask them to clap for the /k/ words.

> Little caterpillars, little caterpillars
>
> Climbing up a tree, climbing up a tree
>
> Make yourselves comfy, make yourselves comfy
>
> In your cocoons, in your cocoons.

■ **Fill the Can** Place Picture Cards across the ledge of the board including some that begin with /k/. Have volunteers take one card at a time. If it is a /k/ Picture Card, have them put it in a can. If not, have them put it in a box. Continue until all cards are correctly placed.

■ **Connect /k/ to Cc** Write the words for the picture cards in the can on the board. For each word ask: What letter stands for /k/ in this word? One letter that stands for /k/ is *Cc*.

Kindergarten Student Reader K.2.4

■ **Preview and Predict** Display Kindergarten Student Reader K.2.4. Point to the title of the book. The title of the book is *Winter Fun*. What do you think the book is about?

■ **Set a Purpose** Review the list of things that children think might happen in the story. Remind children that they want to find out about winter fun.

■ **Read** Have children follow along as they read the story with you. After reading p. 3, ask children to tell what Tam is doing. Help them conclude that Tam is very cold. Ask:

• What do the children do?

• Do the children like the snow?

Kindergarten Student
Reader K.2.4

■ **Summarize** Have children retell the story to a partner and tell what the children did at the end of the story.

■ **Text to Self** Help children make personal connections to the story as they tell about their experiences playing outside when it is very cold.

Objectives
• Read at least 25 high-frequency words from a commonly used list.
• Predict what might happen next based on the cover.
• Respond to questions about text.

OL On-Level **DAY 4**

Get Set, Roll! Reader 10

- **Review** Review the high-frequency words *I, am, the, little, to, a, have,* and *is.* Write each word and have children find the word on the Word Wall.

- **Review Rebus Words** Write the name *Jack* on the board. This is the name *Jack.* Name the letters in *Jack* with me: *J, a, c, k, Jack.* Repeat the procedure with the word *blue.* Look for the words *Jack* and *blue* in the story today. A picture above the word will help you read it.

- **Read** Today we will read a story about our friend Jack Truck. Point to the title of the book. What is the title of the book? (*The Cap*) We will read /k/ words in this book. Point to the picture. What do you think the story will be about?

Objectives
- Read at least 25 high-frequency words from a commonly used list.
- Predict what might happen next based on the title.

More Reading
Use Leveled Readers or other text at children's instructional level.

OL On-Level **DAY 5**

Phonics Review

- **Make a Letter** Show children how to make the letter *C* with your hand. Curve your fingers to make an arc with the thumb below the rest. Name the letter as you show children the handmade letter *C.* Hold up six Picture Cards, including the following /k/*Cc* cards: *cat, can, cap, caterpillar.* Display one card at a time. Have a child name the picture. If the name has /k/, have children make the letter *C* with their hand and hold it up in the air as they name the letter.

Objectives
- Identify the common sounds that letters represent.

Small Group Time

Pacing Small Group Instruction

20-30 mins.

5 Day Plan

DAY 1	• Phonemic Awareness/ Phonics • Decodable Story 10
DAY 2	• Phonics • Spelling • High-Frequency Words • Decodable Reader 10
DAY 3	• Independent Reader K.2.4 or Kindergarten Student Reader K.2.4
DAY 4	• Get Set, Roll! Reader 10 or Kindergarten Student Reader K.2.4
DAY 5	• Fluency and Comprehension • Independent Reader K.2.4

3 or 4 Day Plan

DAY 1	• Phonemic Awareness/ Phonics • Decodable Story 10
DAY 2	• Phonics • Spelling • High-Frequency Words • Decodable Reader 10
DAY 3	• Independent Reader K.2.4 or Kindergarten Student Reader K.2.4
DAY 4	• Get Set, Roll! Reader 10 or Kindergarten Student Reader K.2.4

3 Day Plan: Eliminate the shaded box.

More Practice

For additional practice with this week's phonics skills and to develop fluency, have children reread the Decodable Story (Day 1) and the Decodable Reader (Day 2).

A Advanced

DAY 1

Phonemic Awareness•Phonics

■ **Listen for /k/** Draw four boxes on the board. Have four children come to the board and stand by the boxes. The word is *cat*. If the word begins with /k/, write a letter *c* in your box. Check children's responses. Select a new set of children and continue with these words: *bird, camel, caterpillar, dog, cow, cardinal, duck, caribou.*

■ **Make Cotton Pictures** Give children construction paper, glue, and about ten cotton balls each. Tell children they will be making pictures of /k/*Cc* words using cotton balls. Give some ideas, such as making a caterpillar by connecting several cotton balls, a cat with cotton balls as fur, a car with cotton balls as wheels, or a cup with cotton balls as marshmallows. Have children share their cotton ball pictures with the class.

Objectives
• Identify the common sounds that letters represent.

A Advanced

DAY 2

Phonics•Spelling

■ **Connect /k/ to *Cc*** Display the *Cc* Alphabet Card. What are the names of these letters? What is the sound we learned for this letter?

■ **Spell Sounds** Write *Mac* on the board. *Mac* is a name so the letter *M* is capitalized. Have children blend the sound of each letter to read the word. /M/ /a/ /k/, *Mac.* This is the name *Mac. Mac* is a boy. Repeat the routine with the following words: *Cam, cap.*

■ **Review High-Frequency Words** Review the following high-frequency words with children: *we, my, am, to.*

Objectives
• Identify the common sounds that letters represent.
• Read at least 25 high-frequency words from a commonly used list.
• Use letter-sound correspondences to spell consonant-vowel-consonant (CVC) words.

A Advanced

DAY 3

For a complete lesson plan and additional practice, see the **Leveled Reader Teaching Guide**.

Independent Reader K.2.4

■ **Practice High-Frequency Words** Write *we* on the board. Have volunteers say the word and use it in a sentence. Continue with these words: *my, am, is, have, like, to, the.*

■ **Activate Prior Knowledge** Have children read the title and look at the picture. Have them tell what they think the story is about. Then have children take turns reading *Skip and Run* for their group.

Independent
Reader K.2.4

■ **Realism and Fantasy** Display the cover of the book *Skip and Run.* Ask children to describe the animals. As they tell about the animals, think about the information they give to decide whether the animals are real or make-believe.

■ **Reread for Fluency** After rereading with children, model reading fluently for them. I am going to read this selection aloud. I will read the words with no mistakes. I want you to read it aloud with me. Try to read the words just as I do.

Use echo reading of Independent Reader K.2.4 to model reading fluently. Use your oral reading to model for children where to pause, when to change pitch, and which words to stress. Then have children reread orally three to four times, or until they can read with few or no mistakes.

■ For more practice with phonics and high-frequency words and to develop fluency, have children read the Kindergarten Student Reader K.2.4. Use the instruction on pp. 354–355.

More Reading

Use Leveled Readers or other text at children's instructional level.

Objectives
• Identify the common sounds that letters represent.
• Read at least 25 high-frequency words from a commonly used list.
• Identify content as realism or fantasy.

Small Group Time

More Reading

Use Leveled Readers or other text at children's instructional level.

A Advanced · DAY 4

Kindergarten Student Reader K.2.4

- **Revisit Rebus Words** Write the word *cold* on the board. This is the word *cold.* Name the letters with me: *c, o, l, d, cold.* Repeat the routine for the words *door, snowballs, snowman,* and *snow.*

- **Reread** Use Kindergarten Student Reader K.2.4 to practice reading fluently.

- **Text to World** Ask children to think about being outside when it is very cold. Have them tell about a time when they were cold. Ask them to provide details.

- **Read** Have children read Get Set, Roll! Reader 10, *The Cap.* Use the instruction on p. 385.

Kindergarten Student Reader K.2.4

Objectives
- Read at least 25 high-frequency words from a commonly used list.

A Advanced · DAY 5

Fluency•Comprehension

- **Reread for Fluency** Use the Independent Reader K.2.4 to model reading fluently for children. I am going to read this story aloud. I will read the words with no mistakes. I want you to read it aloud with me. Try to read the words just as I do.

- **Comprehension** After children have finished reading the selection, have them retell what happened in the story. Then have children write or draw a picture of things to do to have fun in the winter. Allow time for children to show their pictures and tell about the winter fun.

Independent Reader K.2.4

Objectives
- Read at least 25 high-frequency words from a commonly used list.

Support for English Language Learners

 English Language Learners   **DAY 1**

Concept Development

■ **Read the Concept Literacy Reader** To build vocabulary, read *The Bear.* Have children describe what they see on the cover. Then have children look at the pictures in the book. Read the book aloud, pausing to discuss each page. Use your finger to show reading moves from left to right. Model sentence patterns and vocabulary that describe what the bear likes. The bear likes to play. The bear likes to climb. On a second reading, have children talk about what the bear is doing on each page.

■ **Develop Oral Language** Revisit *The Bear,* pointing out that the bear likes to do many things. Then have children sing this song to the tune of "The Farmer in the Dell":

> The bear likes to play.
> The bear likes to play.
> Hi-ho, the derry-o
> The bear likes to play.

Continue with other things the bear likes to do in the song.

Phonemic Awareness/Phonics

■ **Frontload Words with /k/** Have children look at the picture on pp. 72–73 of *My Skills Buddy.* This picture shows animals working in a garden and other animals playing outside. Have you played outside like these animals? Have you ever helped plant things? Listen to the word *carrot.* What sound does *carrot* begin with? *Carrot* begins with /k/; /k/, *carrot.* Then use the question and answer game below to introduce picture words beginning with /k/:

> Where is /k/?
> /k/ begins _____. (Pause for an answer: *carrot.*)

Repeat the question with other picture words that begin with /k/, including *cucumber, cart, cap, cards, cape, cane, coloring* or *colors,* and *cake.*

■ **Connect /k/ to Cc** Use letter tiles to show the word *cap* or write it on the board. This word is *cap:* /k/ /a/ /p/, *cap.* Say the word with me. Have children demonstrate knowledge of the relationships between sounds and letters of the English language by writing the word *cap* and circling the letter that stands for /k/. Continue with new words such as *can, cat,* and *cab.*

Objectives
• Learn new language structures heard during classroom instruction and interactions. • Use visual support to enhance and confirm understanding of increasingly complex and elaborated spoken language. • Learn relationships between sounds and letters of the English language.

Content Objective
• Develop content knowledge related to what bears do in the winter.

Language Objectives
• Understand and use grade-level content area vocabulary.
• Recognize the sounds of English.

Concept Literacy Reader K.2.4

Daily Planner	
DAY 1	• Concept Development • Phonemic Awareness/ Phonics • Listening Comprehension
DAY 2	• Reading Comprehension • Vocabulary
DAY 3	• Phonemic Awareness/ Phonics • Conventions
DAY 4	• Phonemic Awareness/ Phonics • Concepts and Oral Language
DAY 5	• Language Workshop • Writing

Support for English Language Learners

Content Objective

- Understand realism and fantasy.

Language Objective

- Learn and use academic vocabulary.

My Skills Buddy, pp. 74–75

Listening Comprehension: Realism and Fantasy

■ **Frontload Vocabulary** Discuss the illustrations on pp. 74–75 in *My Skills Buddy* to frontload vocabulary. What do you see in the illustrations on p. 74? (a fish) Point to the fish. What do you see in the illustrations on p. 75? (a fish) Think about the two fish. Can a real fish live in a fish bowl? Does a real fish teach school?

■ **Provide Scaffolding** Review the illustrations on pp. 74–75. Explain that one illustration shows something real and one shows something make-believe. Help children understand that things that are real can actually happen while things that are make-believe do not really happen. Have children tell why one illustration is real and the other is make-believe.

■ **Prepare for the Read Aloud** The modified Read Aloud below prepares children for listening to the oral reading "Bolie's First Winter" on p. 325.

Bolie's First Winter

Bolie is a baby bear. This is his first winter. He has never seen snow. Bolie catches a flake in his paws. He sniffs it.

Ma tells him it is snow. She hurries Bolie along. She knows about winter. Winter means cold weather and little food. It is time for the big sleep.

Bolie and Ma take a walk deep into the woods. Bolie asks a lot of questions. Then Bolie sees a cave. He peeks inside. The cave is dark but warm. Bolie is brave. "I'm not afraid," he says. Then he and Ma go in the cave. There they fall fast asleep.

■ **First Listening** Write the title of the Read Aloud on the board. This is about a bear named Bolie. When winter comes, the bear family goes to a cave to sleep for the winter. After reading, ask children to recall what happens in the story. Is this story real or make-believe? Help children conclude that real bears do hibernate, or sleep for the winter, so that part is real. Ask them to tell about the things in the story that are not real.

■ **Second Listening** Write the words *real* and *make-believe* on the board. As you listen, think about what is real and what is make-believe. After reading, point to each word on the board and ask children to tell things that fit each category.

Objectives

• Understand information in increasingly complex spoken language commensurate with grade-level learning expectations. • Demonstrate English comprehension by employing basic reading skills commensurate with content area needs.

 **DAY 2**

Comprehension

■ **Provide Scaffolding** Display *Bear Snores On.* Guide children as you look through the book with them. Tell children they will hear about what happens when a bear tries to hibernate or sleep for the winter. Use gestures and facial expressions to convey meaning.

  • **Set the Scene** Use the cover of the Big Book to help children understand that this story takes place in a cave in the woods. Describe what a cave is like. Winter is coming and Bear goes into his cave to sleep or hibernate. While Bear is sound asleep, some of his friends come to visit.

  • **Frontload Vocabulary** As you lead the picture walk, use the illustrations to introduce unfamiliar words in the text. Look at this picture on page 5. The bear is in his cave or den. The book uses the word *lair,* which is another word for den. Who can point to the bear in his den? Continue through the pages calling out the following words: *snores* (p. 7); *twigs* (p. 9); *coals* (p. 10); *scuttles* (p. 15); *twitters* (p. 21); *slumbering* (p. 23); *stokes* (p. 24); *snuck* (p. 30).

Vocabulary: Words for Seasons

■ **Frontload Vocabulary** Have children turn to p. 88 of *My Skills Buddy.* Talk about each picture, using the words for the seasons *spring, summer, fall,* and *winter*. For example: The first picture shows people walking outside. The sun is hiding behind the clouds and you can see the rain coming down. This shows the season of spring. Do you see people with umbrellas? What color is the grass? What do the trees have? Then invite children to talk about the pictures describing each season.

■ **Provide Scaffolding** Write the words *spring, summer, fall,* and *winter* on the board. Read the words aloud with children. These words tell us the names for the seasons. Point to the word *winter*. How does it look when it is winter? Repeat with the other seasons.

■ **Practice** Have children work in four groups. Assign one of the seasons to each group. Ask each group to draw a picture of its assigned season. Allow time for children to complete the picture. Then have each group show its picture. Have the group tell about the things that the members of the group drew and other things the group knows about the season.

Objectives
• Speak using learning strategies. • Comprehend English vocabulary used routinely in written classroom materials. • Use support from peers and teachers to develop vocabulary needed to comprehend increasingly challenging language.

Content Objective
• Develop background knowledge.

Language Objective
• Learn and use words for seasons.

Use Learning Strategies
Remind children that if they have trouble saying something, they can ask their partners for help.

Big Book

Support for English Language Learners

Content Objective
- Use learning strategies.

Language Objectives
- Connect /k/ and *Cc*.
- Use adjectives for sizes and numbers.

 **Transfer Skills**

Pronouncing /k/ Children's familiarity with /k/ in home language words will help them recognize /k/ in English. For example, these words for *cat* begin with /k/: *kat* (Afrikaans, Dutch), *kot* (Polish, Russian), *kedi* (Turkish).

Use Learning Strategies

Help children discover words that can describe the size and number of items. Give these examples: *a big bear, three bears.* The word *big* tells about the bear and the number word *three* tells how many bears.

Phonemic Awareness/Phonics

■ **Isolate initial and final /k/** Help children hear /k/ in the words *cat, can,* and *cap.* Say the words, emphasizing the initial sound in each word. Next, blend the phonemes /k/ /a/ /t/ to form the word *cat.* Repeat with *can* and *cap.* Help children hear that each word begins with the same /k/ sound. Then say the word *duck.* Segment the sounds: /d/ /u/ /k/, *duck.* Have children repeat the sounds with you. Where do you hear /k/ in *duck?* Yes, the last sound in the word is /k/. Continue with the words *pack, lick,* and *rock.*

■ **/k/ Spelled *Cc*** Write the word *picnic* on the board. As you read the word aloud, track the sounds and letters with your fingers. Help children recognize that the word ends with the letter *c* and the sound /k/.

Conventions: Adjectives for Sizes/Numbers

■ **Provide Scaffolding** Display pp. 14–15 of *Bear Snores On.* How many friends came to visit bear? (two) How many bears do you see? (one) The number words *two* and *one* tell how many. What size is bear? (big) What size is mouse? (little) The words *big* and *little* tell the size. Display pp. 18–19 of *Bear Snores On.* Now how many friends have come to visit bear? (three) Have children point and count each friend to check the number.

■ **Practice** Continue through the book asking children to tell how many friends they see. Also have them choose which animal is big and which is little in each picture. Help children conclude that the number and size words describe things. Remind children that words that describe are called adjectives.

Leveled LS Support

Beginning/Intermediate Point to a set of books in the classroom. Have children describe the size and number of books. Continue with other classroom items.

Advanced/Advanced-High Have the children identify the number of books and use the number word in a sentence, such as the following: *We have six books. I have six books.* Repeat using words to describe the size: *I have a big book. This is a little book.*

Objectives
- Give information ranging from using a very limited bank of high-frequency, high-need, concrete vocabulary, including key words and expressions needed for basic communication in academic and social contexts, to using abstract and content-based vocabulary during extended speaking assignments.

 **Grammar Jammer**

 **DAY 4**

Phonemic Awareness/Phonics

■ **Review /p/** To review /p/ in words, say the following sentences with words that begin with the sound: Pam is pals with Peter. Put the pig in the pen.

Have children repeat the sentences after you. Then have them pronounce just the words that begin with /p/. What sound do these words start with? Yes, they start with /p/.

■ **/p/ Spelled Pp** Compare words such as *cap* and *top*. Help children isolate the sounds in each word: /k/ /a/ /p/, *cap*. Repeat for /t/ /o/ /p/, *top*. How are the words alike? Yes, they both end with /p/.

Concepts and Oral Language

■ **Revisit Talk with Me Chart 10A** Display the chart. Point to the pictures on the chart. Have children describe the things in the pictures. Help them by pointing out the differences in the pictures. Where does the bear sleep? What do you know about a cave?

■ **Develop Oral Language** Introduce language patterns that help describe the things on Talk with Me Chart 10A. Write this sentence frame on the board: *The _____ is _____.* Let's use this sentence pattern to talk about the cave. *The cave is big. The cave is in a hill.* Have children use the same sentence pattern to talk about the bear. Then add this sentence frame: *The _____ has _____.* Now I will use a new pattern to talk about the bear. *The bear has fur. The bear has ears.* Point to one of the small pictures on the chart. Ask a volunteer to make up a sentence that describes the picture. Then have the volunteer point to another picture on the chart and choose someone to make up a sentence.

 Beginning Have children repeat the sentences that other children make up. Let them take a turn pointing to a picture on the chart.

Intermediate Ask questions to help children notice more details about the photographs, such as *What is a blustery winter day like?*

Advanced/Advanced-High Encourage children to use their prior knowledge about the pictures to think of other descriptive words, such as *cold, wintery, dark, snowy,* and *icy.*

Content Objectives
• Develop oral language.
• Use learning strategies.

Language Objectives
• Connect /k/ with *Cc.*
• Learn English language patterns.

Use Learning Strategies
Work with children to create a concept map titled *A Bear.* Include the categories *Size, Color,* and *What They Can Do.*

Talk with Me Chart 10A

Objectives
• Use prior knowledge to understand meanings in English. • Distinguish sounds of English with increasing ease. • Learn new language structures heard during classroom instruction and interactions. • Decode (sound out) words using a combination of skills.

Support for English Language Learners

Content Objective

- Take notes.

Language Objectives

- Distinguish realism and fantasy through speaking and writing.

- Write using grade-level vocabulary.

Monitor and Self-Correct

Remind children that if they don't know how to write the words, they can see if the notes on the class chart will help them.

Home Language Support

Invite children to share ideas in their home languages before creating their books.

Language Workshop: Realism and Fantasy

■ **Introduce and Model** Display the cover of the book *Bear Snores On.* Look at the animals on the cover. How many animals do you see? Let's make a list. Write a list on the animals (bear, mouse, raven, badger, gopher, rabbit, raven) on chart paper. What other animal was in the story? (a wren) Add the word to the list.

■ **Practice** Point to an animal name on the chart. Have a child point to the animal on the cover of the book. Review each animal name. Ask children to tell whether the book shows animals that are real or animals that are make-believe. Write the words *Real* and *Make-Believe* on the board. Have children tell how they know the animals in the story are make-believe.

Writing: Write About Make Believe

■ **Prepare for Writing** We have talked about the animals. Now let's write about the animals. Give each child a sheet of paper.

■ **Create Animal Books** Write these sentence sets on the board.

> **This is a _____. It is real.**
> **This is a _____. It is make-believe.**

Read the sentences together. Have children choose an animal and then choose a set of sentences to tell about their animal. Have children copy the sentences on their paper and draw a picture of their real or make-believe animal. When children have finished, collect the make-believe pages and make a book. Have children read their page to the class. Repeat with the pages for real animals.

Leveled Support

Beginning Help children complete the sentence frame on their papers. Show them where to find the animal name on the chart.

Intermediate Guide children in copying the sentences and writing words to complete the sentence.

Advanced/Advanced-High Encourage children to write their sentences on their own. You might also have children help less-proficient partners complete their sentences.

Objectives

- Express ideas ranging from communicating single words and short phrases to participating in extended discussions on a variety of social and grade-appropriate academic topics. • Write using content-based grade-level vocabulary.

This Week's ELL Overview

ELL Handbook

- Maximize Literacy and Cognitive Engagement
- Research Into Practice
- Full Weekly Support for Every Selection

  A Bed for the Winter
  - Routines to Support Instruction

- Transfer Activities
- Professional Development

Daily Leveled ELL Notes

ELL notes appear throughout this week's instruction and ELL Support is on the DI pages of your Teacher's Edition. The following is a sample of an ELL note from this week.

English Language Learners

Beginning Build Background English learners will benefit from additional visual support to understand words from the song. For example, point to the *den* and the *hive* in the art to scaffold meaning.

Intermediate Visual Support Scaffold the meaning of the word *he* by having all the boys in the class stand up. Point to each boy and say a sentence about the color shirt he is wearing using this sentence frame: *He is wearing a ____.*

Advanced High-Frequency Words After the Team Talk activity, have children continue to work in pairs to check understanding. Have one child read one of the sentences aloud while another child makes a simple drawing to illustrate the sentence.

Advanced High Support Writing Before writing, display each page in *A Bed for the Winter.* Have children describe each bed. Write the words they use in a list. Encourage children to use the list of words to help them write sentences. Allow them to write the word in their home language as well as in English.

ELL by Strand

The ELL lessons on this week's Support for English Language Learners pages are organized by strand. They offer additional scaffolding for the core curriculum. Leveled support notes on these pages address the different proficiency levels in your class. See pages DI•80–DI•85.

ELL Guy
Dr. Jim Cummins

The Three Pillars of ELL Instruction

ELL Strands	Activate Prior Knowledge	Access Content	Extend Language
Vocabulary p. DI•82	Frontload Vocabulary	Provide Scaffolding	Practice
Reading Comprehension p. DI•82	Provide Scaffolding	Set the Scene	Frontload Vocabulary
Phonics, Spelling, and Word Analysis pp. DI•80, DI•83–DI•84	Frontload Words with /i/	Isolate Medial /i/	Review /k/
Listening Comprehension p. DI•81	Prepare for the Read Aloud	First Listening	Second Listening
Conventions and Writing pp. DI•83, DI•85	Provide Scaffolding/ Introduce and Model	Practice	Leveled Practice Activities/ Leveled Writing Activities
Concept Development p. DI•80	Read the Concept Literacy Reader	Read the Concept Literacy Reader	Develop Oral Language

This Week's Practice Stations Overview

Six Weekly Practice Stations with Leveled Activities can be found at the beginning of each week of instruction. For this week's Practice Stations, see pp. 414–415.

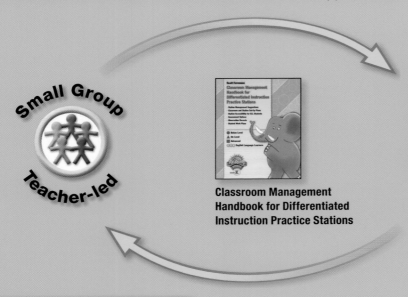

Practice Stations

Classroom Management Handbook for Differentiated Instruction Practice Stations

Daily Leveled Center Activities

⬤ Below   ▢ Advanced

△ On-Level   Ⓔ Ⓛ Ⓛ

Practice Stations Flip Charts

	Listen Up	Word Work	Words to Know	Let's Write	Read for Meaning	Let's Make Art
Objectives	• Identify and practice words with /k/.	• Identify and build words with /k/.	• Identify and use words for seasons.	• Write a poem about nature.	• Tell what is real and make-believe in a story.	• Draw a picture about a story.
Materials	• *Listen Up* Flip Chart Activity 11 • *black, cat, can, carrot, desk, duck, pig, top* Picture Cards	• *Word Work* Flip Chart Activity 11 • Alphabet Cards • *cap, caterpillar, crab, doll, van, wig* Picture Cards • Letter Tiles	• *Words to Know* Flip Chart Activity 11 • pictures that show landscapes of *spring, summer, fall, winter* • Teacher-made Word Cards: *spring, summer, fall, winter* • paper, pencils, crayons	• *Let's Write* Flip Chart Activity 11 • pictures that show examples of nature • crayons, paper, pencil	• *Read for Meaning* Flip Chart Activity 11 • Little Book *Bear Snores On* • Teacher-made Word Cards	• *Let's Make Art* Flip Chart Activity 11 • Little Book *Bear Snores On* • crayons, paper, pencil

This Week on Reading Street!

Week 5

Question of the Week

What kind of home does an animal need?

Daily Plan

Don't Wait Until Friday

Whole Group

- ◉ /i/ Spelled *Ii*
- ◉ Sequence
- • Vocabulary

MONITOR PROGRESS | **Success Predictor**

Day 1	Day 2	Day 3	Day 4	Day 5
Check Phonemic Awareness	Check Sound Spelling/ Retelling	Check Word Reading	Check Phonemic Awareness	Check Oral Vocabulary

Small Group

Teacher-Led

- • Reading Support
- • Skill Support
- • Fluency Practice

Practice Stations

Independent Activities

Customize Literacy More support for a Balanced Literacy approach, see pp. CL•1–CL•31.

Whole Group

- • Writing
- • Conventions: Adjectives for Opposites
- • Listening and Speaking

Assessment

- • Day 5 Assessment for Phonics
- • Day 5 Assessment for Comprehension

You Are Here! Unit 2 Week 5

Look at Us!

This Week's Reading Selections

A bed for the winter

Big Book
Genre: **Nonfiction**

Decodable Reader 11

Leveled Readers

Get Set Roll! Reader 11

Resources on Reading Street!

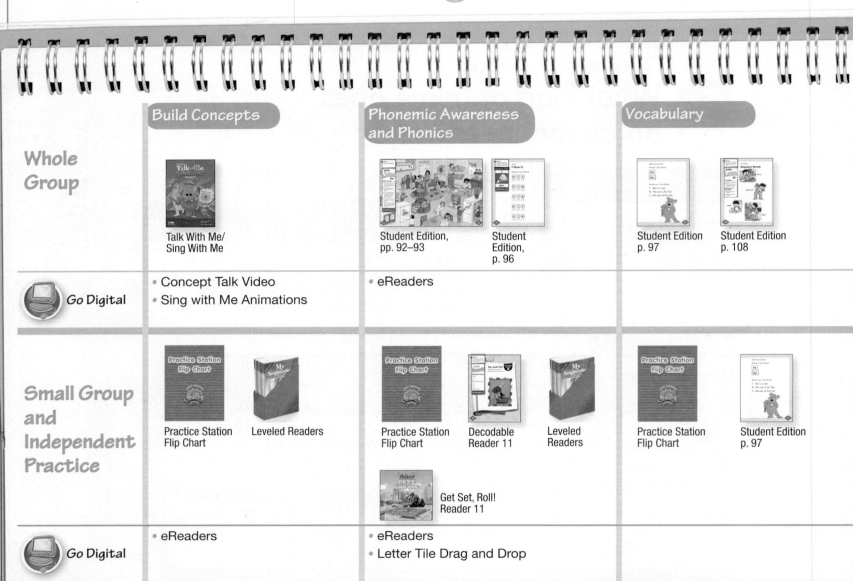

	Build Concepts	Phonemic Awareness and Phonics	Vocabulary
Whole Group	Talk With Me/ Sing With Me	Student Edition, pp. 92–93 Student Edition, p. 96	Student Edition p. 97 Student Edition p. 108
Go Digital	• Concept Talk Video • Sing with Me Animations	• eReaders	
Small Group and Independent Practice	Practice Station Flip Chart Leveled Readers	Practice Station Flip Chart Decodable Reader 11 Leveled Readers Get Set, Roll! Reader 11	Practice Station Flip Chart Student Edition p. 97
Go Digital	• eReaders	• eReaders • Letter Tile Drag and Drop	
Customize Literacy	• Leveled Readers	• Decodable Reader	• High-Frequency Word Cards
Go Digital	• Concept Talk Video • Big Question Video • eReaders	• eReaders	• Sing with Me Animations

What kind of home does an animal need?

Comprehension	Fluency	Conventions and Writing
 Student Edition pp. 94–95 Big Book	  Decodable Reader 11 Kdg. Student Reader K.2.5 Get Set, Roll! Reader 11	 Reader's and Writer's Notebook
• Envision It! Animations	• eReaders	• Grammar Jammer
Practice Station Flip Chart Leveled Readers Get Set, Roll! Reader 11	Practice Station Flip Chart Leveled Readers	Practice Station Flip Chart Reader's and Writer's Notebook
• Envision It! Animations • eReaders	• eReaders	• Grammar Jammer
• Leveled Readers	• Leveled Readers	• *Reader's and Writer's Notebook*
• Envision It! Aminations • eReaders	• eReaders	• Grammar Jammer

Week 5

You Are Here! Unit 2 Week 5

My 5-Day Planner for Reading Street!

Don't Wait Until Friday **MONITOR PROGRESS**

	Check Phonemic Awareness **Day 1** pages 416–431	**Check Sound-Spelling** **Check Retelling** **Day 2** pages 432–449
Get Ready to Read	**Concept Talk,** 416 **Oral Vocabulary,** 417 *nest, meadow, stump, tree trunk, hive, den* **Phonemic Awareness,** 418–419 ⊙ Initial /i/ **Phonics,** 420–421 ⊙ /i/ Spelled *Ii* **Handwriting,** 422 Letters *I* and *i* **High-Frequency Words,** 423 Introduce *he, for* **READ Decodable Story 11,** 424–425	**Concept Talk,** 432 **Oral Vocabulary,** 433 *nest, meadow* **Phonemic Awareness,** 434–435 ⊙ Initial and Medial /i/ **Phonics,** 436 ⊙ /i/ Spelled *Ii* **Handwriting,** 438 Words with *Ii* **High-Frequency Words,** 439 *he, for* **READ Decodable Reader 11,** 440–441
Read and Comprehend	**Listening Comprehension,** 426–427 ⊙ Sequence	**Listening Comprehension,** 442 ⊙ Sequence **READ Big Book—First Read,** 442 *A Bed for the Winter* **Retell,** 443 **Think, Talk, and Write,** 444
Language Arts	**Conventions,** 428 Adjectives for Opposites **Writing,** 429 Wonderful, Marvelous Me! **Daily Handwriting,** 429 Letters *I* and *i* **Listening and Speaking,** 430 Give a Description **Wrap Up Your Day,** 430 **Extend Your Day!,** 431	**Conventions,** 445 Adjectives for Opposites **Writing,** 446 Respond to Literature **Daily Handwriting,** 446 Letters *I* and *i* **Vocabulary,** 447 Sequence Words **Wrap Up Your Day,** 448 **Extend Your Day!,** 449

You Are Here! Unit 2 Week 5

Question of the Week
What kind of home does an animal need?

Check Word Reading	Check Phonemic Awareness	Check Oral Vocabulary
Day 3 pages 450–479	**Day 4** pages 480–491	**Day 5** pages 492–505
Concept Talk, 450 **Oral Vocabulary**, 451 *stump, tree trunk* **Phonemic Awareness**, 452–453 ◉ Medial /i/ **Phonics**, 454–455 ◉ /i/ Spelled *Ii* **READ Kindergarten Student Reader K.2.5**, 456–457	**Concept Talk**, 480 **Oral Vocabulary**, 481 *hive, den* Review **Phonemic Awareness**, 482 /k/ Review **Phonics**, 483 /k/ Spelled *Cc* **Spelling**, 484 ◉ /i/ Spelled *Ii* **READ Get Set, Roll! Reader 11**, 485	**Concept Wrap Up**, 492 **Oral Vocabulary**, 493 *nest, meadow, stump, tree trunk, hive, den* Review **Phonemic Awareness**, 494 ◉ /i/ Review **Phonics**, 495 ◉ /i/ Spelled *Ii* **Assessment**, 496–497 Monitor Progress
Comprehension, 458 ◉ Sequence **READ Big Book—Second Read**, 459–473 *A Bed for the Winter*	**Comprehension**, 486 ◉ Sequence Review Classify and Categorize **READ Big Book—Third Read**, 487 *A Bed for the Winter*	**Let's Practice It!**, 498–499 Poem **Assessment**, 500–501 Monitor Progress
Conventions, 474 Adjectives for Sizes and Numbers **Writing**, 475 Genre: Caption **Daily Handwriting**, 475 Letters *I* and *i* **Listening and Speaking**, 476–477 Give a Description **Wrap Up Your Day**, 478 **Extend Your Day!**, 479	**Conventions**, 488 Adjectives for Opposites **Writing**, 489 Extend the Concept **Daily Handwriting**, 489 Letters *I* and *i* **Vocabulary**, 490 Sequence Words **Wrap Up Your Day**, 490 **Extend Your Day!**, 491	Review **Conventions**, 502 Adjectives for Opposites **Writing**, 503 This Week We… **Daily Handwriting**, 503 Letters *I* and i **Wrap Up Your Week**, 504 What kind of home does an animal need? **Extend Your Day!**, 505

Week 5

Grouping Options for Differentiated Instruction
Turn the page for the small group time lesson plan.

Planning Small Group Time on Reading Street!

SMALL GROUP TIME RESOURCES

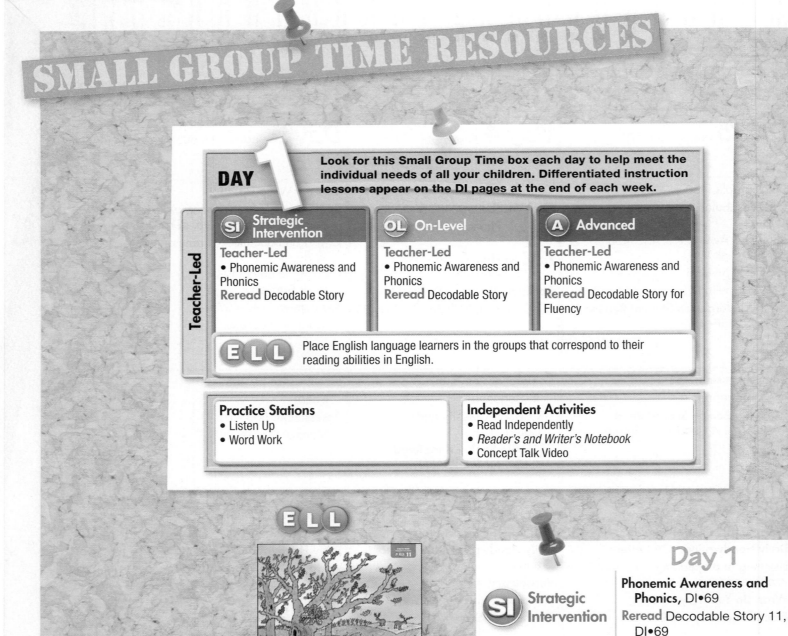

DAY 1

Look for this Small Group Time box each day to help meet the individual needs of all your children. Differentiated instruction lessons appear on the DI pages at the end of each week.

Teacher-Led

(SI) Strategic Intervention	**(OL) On-Level**	**(A) Advanced**
Teacher-Led	**Teacher-Led**	**Teacher-Led**
• Phonemic Awareness and Phonics	• Phonemic Awareness and Phonics	• Phonemic Awareness and Phonics
Reread Decodable Story	**Reread** Decodable Story	**Reread** Decodable Story for Fluency

(ELL) Place English language learners in the groups that correspond to their reading abilities in English.

Practice Stations
• Listen Up
• Word Work

Independent Activities
• Read Independently
• *Reader's and Writer's Notebook*
• Concept Talk Video

ELL

ELL Poster 11

		Day 1
	**Strategic Intervention**	**Phonemic Awareness and Phonics,** DI•69
		Reread Decodable Story 11, DI•69
	On-Level	**Phonemic Awareness and Phonics,** DI•74
		Reread Decodable Story 11, DI•74
	Advanced	**Phonemic Awareness and Phonics,** DI•77
		Reread Decodable Story 11 for Fluency, DI•77
	**English Language Learners**	DI•80–DI•81
		Frontload Concept
		Phonemic Awareness and Phonics
		Comprehension Skill

You Are Here! Unit 2 Week 5

Question of the Week
What kind of home does an animal need?

SI Strategic Intervention

Decodable
Reader

Concept Literacy Reader

Listen to Me Reader

Get Set, Roll! Reader

OL On-Level

Kindergarten
Student Reader

Decodable Reader

Get Set, Roll! Reader

A Advanced

Independent
Reader

Decodable Reader

Small Group Weekly Plan

Day 2	Day 3	Day 4	Day 5
Phonemic Awareness and Phonics, DI•70 **Reread** Decodable Reader 11, DI•70	**Phonemic Awareness and Phonics,** DI•71 **Read** Concept Literacy Reader K.2.5, DI•71	**Phonemic Awareness and Phonics,** DI•72 **Read** Get Set, Roll! Reader 11, DI•72	**Phonics Review,** DI•73 **Read** Listen to Me Reader K.2.5, DI•73
Phonemic Awareness and Phonics, DI•74 **Reread** Decodable Reader 11, DI•74	**Phonemic Awareness and Phonics,** DI•75 **Read** Kindergarten Student Reader K.2.5, DI•75	**Review Phonics and High-Frequency Words** **Read** Get Set, Roll! Reader 11, DI•76	**Phonics Review,** DI•76 **Reread** Leveled Books, DI•76
Phonics and Spelling, DI•77 **Reread** Decodable Reader 11 for Fluency, DI•77	**Read** Independent Reader K.2.5 or Kindergarten Student Reader K.2.5, DI•78	**Read** Get Set, Roll! Reader 11 or **Reread** Kindergarten Student Reader K.2.5, DI•79	**Fluency and Comprehension,** DI•79 **Reread** Independent Reader K.2.5, DI•79
DI•82 Comprehension Skill Frontload Vocabulary	DI•83 Review Phonemic Awareness and Phonics Scaffold Conventions	DI•84 Review Phonemic Awareness and Phonics Revisit Concepts and Oral Language	DI•85 Language Workshop Writing

Week 5

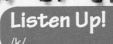
Practice Stations for Everyone on Reading Street!

Listen Up!
/k/

Objectives
• Identify and practice words with /k/.

Materials
• *Listen Up!* Flip Chart Activity 11
• *black, cat, can, carrot, desk, duck, pig, top* Picture Cards

Differentiated Activities

⬤ Find the *cat* Picture Card. Say the sound you hear at the beginning. Find another Picture Card with the same beginning sound.

🔺 Find the *cat* Picture Card. Say the sound you hear at the beginning. Point to a Picture Card with the same beginning sound. Find the *duck* Picture Card. Point to a Picture Card with the same end sound.

⬛ Find the *cat* Picture Card. Say the sound you hear at the beginning. Point to all Picture Cards with the same beginning sound. Find the *duck* Picture Card. Point to all Picture Cards with the same end sound.

Word Work
/k/ Spelled *Cc*

Objectives
• Identify and build words with /k/.

Materials
• *Word Work* Flip Chart Activity 11
• Alphabet Cards
• *cap, caterpillar, crab, doll, van, wig* Picture Cards
• Letter Tiles

Differentiated Activities

⬤ Find the *Cc* Alphabet Card. Look for Picture Cards that begin with /k/.

🔺 Find the *Cc* Alphabet Card. Find Picture Cards that begin with /k/. Look around the room. Find other objects that have /k/ at the beginning.

⬛ Find the *Cc* Alphabet Card. Find Picture Cards that begin with /k/. Use the Letter Tiles to spell other words that begin with /k/.

Technology
• Letter Tile Drag and Drop

Words To Know
Words for seasons

Objectives
• Identify and use words for seasons.

Materials
• *Words to Know* Flip Chart Activity 11
• Pictures that show landscapes of *spring, summer, fall, winter*
• Teacher-made Word Cards: *spring, summer, fall, winter*
• paper, pencils, crayons

Differentiated Activities

⬤ Look at the pictures that show *spring, summer, fall,* and *winter*. Say the name for each picture.

🔺 Match Word Cards and pictures that show *spring, summer, fall,* and *winter*.

⬛ Match the Word Cards and pictures that show *spring, summer, fall,* and *winter*. Draw pictures that show what you do in the *spring, summer, fall,* and *winter*. Label your pictures.

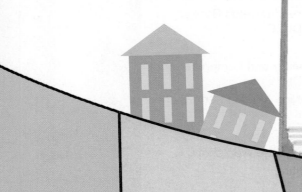

You Are Here! Unit 2 Week 5

Use this week's materials from the Reading Street Leveled Practice Stations Kit to organize this week's stations.

Key
● Below-Level Activities
▲ On-Level Activities
■ Advanced Activities

Practice Station Flip Chart

Let's Write!
Poem

Objectives
• Write a poem about nature.

Materials
• *Let's Write!* Flip Chart Activity 11
• pictures that show examples of nature
• crayons, paper, pencil

Differentiated Activities

● Look at the pictures of nature. Write a poem about your favorite part of nature. Use words that tell what you see and hear.

▲ Look at the pictures of nature. Write a poem about what you like to do outside. Draw a picture to go with your poem.

■ Look at the pictures of nature. Choose your favorite. Write a poem about what you see. Draw pictures for your poem.

Read For Meaning
Realism and fantasy

Objectives
• Tell what is real and make-believe in a story.

Materials
• *Read for Meaning* Flip Chart Activity 11
• Little Book *Bear Snores On*

Differentiated Activities

● Look at the Little Book. Point to something that is make-believe. Tell how you know it is make-believe.

▲ Look at the Little Book. Point to something that is realistic. Point to something that is make-believe. Tell how you know the difference.

■ Look at the Little Book. Find all pictures that show something realistic. Find all pictures that show something make-believe. Tell how you know the difference.

Let's Make Art!

Objectives
• Draw a picture about a story.

Materials
• *Let's Make Art!* Flip Chart Activity 11
• Little Book *Bear Snores On*
• crayons, paper, pencil

Differentiated Activities

● Look at the Little Book. Draw a picture of the bear sleeping in his cave.

▲ Look at the Little Book. Draw a picture of the Bear sleeping in his cave while the other animals have a party.

■ Look at the Little Book. Draw a picture of the bear sleeping in his cave while the other animals have a party. Write a sentence about your picture.

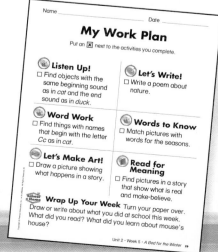

Name _____ Date _____

My Work Plan
Put an ☒ next to the activities you complete.

🎧 **Listen Up!**
☐ Find objects with the same beginning sound as in *cat* and the end sound as in *duck*.

✏️ **Let's Write!**
☐ Write a poem about nature.

📝 **Word Work**
☐ Find things with names that begin with the letter *Cc* as in *cat*.

📖 **Words to Know**
☐ Match pictures with words for the seasons.

🎨 **Let's Make Art!**
☐ Draw a picture showing what happens in a story.

📚 **Read for Meaning**
☐ Find pictures in a story that show what is real and make-believe.

Wrap Up Your Week Turn your paper over. Draw or write about what you did at school this week. What did you read? What did you learn about mouse's house?

Unit 2 · Week 5 · A Bed for the Winter

My Weekly Work Plan

Week 5

Objectives
- Share information and ideas about the concept.

Today at a Glance

Oral Vocabulary
nest, meadow, stump, tree trunk, hive, den

Phonemic Awareness
◉ Initial /i/

Phonics
◉ /i/ Spelled *Ii*

Handwriting
I and *i*

High-Frequency Words
he, for

Comprehension
◉ Sequence

Conventions
Adjectives for Opposites

Writing
Wonderful, Marvelous Me!

Listening and Speaking
Give a Description

TRUCKTOWN on Reading Street

Start your engines! Display p. 15 of *Truckery Rhymes*.

- Read aloud "Rock-a-Bye Mixer" and track the print.
  - Reread the rhyme and have children chime in.
    - Have children identify the rhyming words. (*fall, all*)

Truckery Rhymes

Concept Talk

Question of the Week

What kind of home does an animal need?

Introduce the concept

To build concepts and to focus their attention, tell children that this week they will talk, sing, read, and write about **animal homes.** Track each word as you read the question of the week.

Play the CD that asks the question, "What is the best home for you?" Animals live in many different places. Which animal lives in a nest? Can you hear some of the sounds of the different animals? What are they?

 Background Building Audio

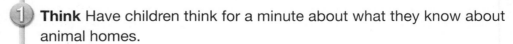

ROUTINE · Activate Prior Knowledge · Team Talk

(1) Think Have children think for a minute about what they know about animal homes.

(2) Pair Have pairs of children discuss the question of the week. Remind them to take turns speaking and to use complete sentences.

(3) Share Call on a few children to share their ideas with the group. Guide discussion and encourage elaboration with prompts such as: How are animal homes different from our homes?

Routines Flip Chart

Anchored Talk

Develop oral language

Display Talk with Me Chart 11A. This week we will be talking about the winter homes of many animals. The chart shows some of the animal homes. What do you see in this picture? What would live in a cave? What would live in these other places?

We are going to learn six new Amazing Words this week. Listen as I say the words. You may know some of them: *nest, meadow, stump, tree trunk, hive, den.* Have children say each word as you point to the picture.

Display Sing with Me Chart 11B. Today we are going to sing a song about a mouse looking for a safe, warm winter home. Listen for the Amazing Words *nest, meadow, stump, tree trunk, hive,* and *den.* Read the title. Have children describe the picture. Sing the song several times to the tune of "Twinkle, Twinkle, Little Star." Have children stand up and sing with you.

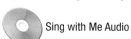 Sing with Me Audio

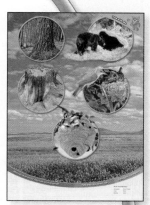

Talk with Me/Sing with Me Chart 11A

Little Mouse

Hurry, scurry, little mouse,
Where can you find a safe, warm house?
Not in the meadow, not in the bear's den,
Not in a bee hive where bees sleep in,
Hurry, scurry, little mouse,
Where can you find a safe, warm house?

Talk with Me/Sing with Me Chart 11B

ELL **Preteach Concepts** Use the Day 1 instruction on ELL Poster 11 to assess and build background knowledge, develop concepts, and build oral vocabulary.

 Poster 11

Amazing Words

nest	meadow
stump	tree trunk
hive	den

Differentiated Instruction

SI **Strategic Intervention**

Build Background To help children understand words in the song, such as *den* and *hive*, use the art. Make sure children know what a *bear* is and what *bees* are.

ELL

English Language Learners

Build Background English learners will benefit from additional visual support to understand words from the song. For example, point to the *den* and the *hive* in the art to scaffold meaning.

ELL Support Additional ELL support and modified instruction is provided in the *ELL Handbook* and in the ELL Support lessons on pp. DI•80–85.

Objectives

◎ Learn initial /i/.
- Identify words with initial /i/.
- Discriminate words with initial /i/.
- Review rhyming words.

Check Phonemic Awareness
SUCCESS PREDICTOR

My Skills Buddy, pp. 92–93

Phonemic Awareness
Initial /i/

Introduce

Today we are going to learn a new sound. Listen carefully: /i/ /i/ /i/. Say it with me: /i/ /i/ /i/. Display the *insect* Picture Card. *Insect* begins with /i/, *insect.* What sound does *insect* begin with? Continue the routine with the *inch, igloo,* and *iguana* Picture Cards.

Picture Card

Model

Have children look at the picture on pp. 92–93 of *My Skills Buddy.* Tell them that they will be listening for a new sound—/i/. Point to the poster that shows two men and an airplane. This poster shows men that are *inventors.* What sound do you hear at the beginning of *inventors?* I hear /i/ at the beginning of *inventors.* The first sound in *inventors* is /i/. What other things do you see that begin with that sound?

Guide practice

As children name example words from the picture, guide them in stating that /i/ is the beginning sound. Discuss with children some of the bulleted items on p. 92 of *My Skills Buddy.* Save the other bulleted items for discussion on Day 2.

Corrective feedback

If... children have difficulty naming words with /i/,
then... say *inventors* again, stretching the beginning sound, /i/ /i/ /i/, *inventors.*

Discriminate sounds

I am going to say two words. I want you to tell me which word begins with /i/. I will do the first one: *in, out.* Which word begins with /i/? *In* begins with /i/. Continue the routine with the following words: *inch, foot; igloo, apple; turtle, iguana; insect, dog.*

Have children stand in a circle. I am going to say a word. If it begins with /i/, clap your hands. If it does not begin with /i/, put your hands on your head. I will do the first ones with you. Listen: *iguana* (clap), *inch* (clap), *apple* (hands on head). Continue with these words: *insect, astronaut, infant, amuse, itch, ants, ask, Isabel, inside.*

Corrective feedback

If... children cannot discriminate initial /i/,
then... have them enunciate *infant.*

When you say /i/, does your mouth stay open and slightly up? Say /i/ with me: /i/.

Rhyming words

Remind children that rhyming words sound the same in the middle and end but not at the beginning. I am going to say three words. Two of the words rhyme; one does not. I want you to name the two rhyming words. Listen carefully: *pit, mitt, pan.* Which words rhyme? *Pit* and *mitt* rhyme, but *pan* does not. Continue the activity with the following words: *pan, man, cat; cat, map, hat; map, tip, tap; top, mop, bag; rag, big, pig.*

MONITOR PROGRESS — Check Phonemic Awareness — Words with Initial /i/

Say *inchworm* and *snake.* Have children identify the word that begins with /i/. Continue with *igloo, house; Isabel, Amy; iguana, alligator; ink, pencil;* and *itch, scratch.*

If... children cannot discriminate short *i* words,
then... use the small-group Strategic Intervention lesson, p. DI•69, to reteach /i/.

Day 1	Day 2	Day 3	Day 4	Day 5
Check Phonemic Awareness	Check Sound-Spelling/Retelling	Check Word Reading	Check Phonemic Awareness	Check Oral Vocabulary

Success Predictor

Objectives

• Recognize uppercase *I* and lowercase *i*.

◎ Associate the sound /i/ with the spelling *i*.

• Blend and read words with /i/.

Skills Trace

◎ **Short *i* Spelled *Ii***

Introduce U2W5D1; U2W6D1; U6W1D1

Practice U2W5D2; U2W5D3; U2W6D2; U2W6D3; U6W1D2; U6W1D3

Reteach/Review U2W5D5; U2W6D5; U3W1D4; U6W1D5; U6W2D4; U6W3D4

Assess/Test Benchmark Assessment U2; U6

KEY:
U=Unit   W=Week   D=Day

Phonics—Teach/Model
 /i/ Spelled *Ii*

Alphabet Card

Introduce

Display the *Ii* Alphabet Card. Point to the *igloo* on the Alphabet Card. *Igloo* begins with /i/. Say the word with me: *igloo*. Write the word *igloo* on the board and point to the *i*. *Igloo* begins with /i/ spelled *i*. Now point to the letters *Ii* on the card. One sound for this letter is /i/. The names of these letters are uppercase *I* and lowercase *i*. What is a sound for this letter? What are the names of these letters?

Model

Write on the board: *Izzy is an insect*. Point to the first *I*. When I see this letter, I think of the sound /i/. The first word is *Izzy*—/i/, *Izzy*. Point to *is*. This word begins with *i* too. I know that when I see an *i*, the sound may be /i/. This word is /i/, *is*. Repeat with the word *insect*. This sentence says *Izzy is an insect*.

Guide practice

Display Phonics Songs and Rhymes Chart 11. Teach children the song "In a Tin" sung to the tune of "Do You Know the Muffin Man?" Play the CD and sing the song several times. When children are familiar with the song, ask them to clap when they hear /i/ words. Have volunteers come up and point to words that begin with *i*. I will try the first one. Here is an *i*. *In* begins with /i/.

🔘 Phonics Songs and Rhymes Audio

In a Tin

In a tin on this big hill,
On this big hill, on this big hill,
In a tin on this big hill,
We hid from winter's chill.

It's winter still; the wind still whips,
The wind still whips, the wind still whips.
It's winter still; the wind still whips,
But we are warm in here!

Phonics Songs and Rhymes Chart 11

On their own

Have children use their "hand binoculars" to look around the room to find uppercase *I* and lowercase *i*. Each time they see a letter, have them point to it and say /i/.

Blend Words

Review

To review sound-spellings, use Alphabet Cards *Mm, Tt, Aa, Ss, Pp*, and *Cc* and the *map, top, apple, six, pig,* and *can* Picture Cards. Then use this routine for sound-by-sound blending to have children blend new words.

ROUTINE Sound-by-Sound Blending

1. **Connect** Write the letter *i*. What is the sound we learned for this letter? The sound is /i/. Say it with me: /i/ /i/ /i/. When you see this letter in a word, what sound will you say?

2. **Model** Write *tip* on the board.

   • Touch under the letter *t:* What is the sound for this letter? Say it with me: /t/ /t/ /t/. Repeat the routine touching under *i* and *p*.

   • Let's blend the sounds together. Listen as I blend the sounds: /t/ /i/ /p/. Say it with me: *tip*. Now say it without me.

   • Listen as I use *tip* in a sentence. *Please don't tip the cup over.* Say the sentence with me. Then have children use *tip* in their own sentences.

3. **Guide Practice** Continue the routine established in step 2 with the words below:

it	Tim	sit	pit	sip	pat	tap

   Children should successfully read these words before reading Decodable Story 11 on pp. 131–132 of *Reader's and Writer's Notebook*.

   Corrective Feedback If children have trouble reading a word, model blending the sounds to read the word. Then have children say it with you.

Routines Flip Chart

Differentiated Instruction

 Advanced

Connect Sound-Spelling Say the sounds /m/, /t/, /a/, /s/, /p/, /k/, or /i/ aloud one at a time. Have children write the correct letter for the sound in the air with their finger.

Handwriting

Introduce
Write *Ii* on the board. Words that begin with /i/ are written with either an uppercase *I* or a lowercase *i*. Which letter is uppercase *I*? Which letter is lowercase *i*?

Model uppercase *I*
Write the word *Isabel* on the board. This is the name *Isabel*. We use uppercase letters to begin sentences and for the first letter in a name. Watch as I trace the uppercase *I* with my finger. **Follow the stroke instructions pictured below.**

Guide practice
Have children write the uppercase *I* in the air. Use your finger to make an uppercase *I* in the air. Now write it on your hand.

Model lowercase *i*
Write the word *inch* on the board. This is the word *inch*. I use a lowercase *i* at the beginning of *inch*. Watch as I trace a lowercase *i* with my finger. Write another lowercase *i* on the board following the stroke instructions. Again, have children write *i* in the air and on their hands.

Guide practice
Have children use their Write-On Boards to write a row of uppercase *I* and a row of lowercase *i*.

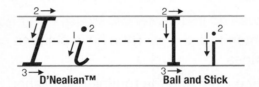

More practice
Use *Reader's and Writer's Notebook,* pp. 129, 130, for additional practice with initial *i*.

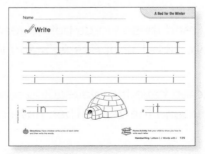
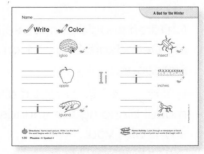

Reader's and Writer's Notebook, p. 129   Reader's and Writer's Notebook, p. 130

High-Frequency Words

Introduce Use the routine below to teach high-frequency words *he* and *for*.

ROUTINE **Nondecodable Words**

1. **Say and Spell** Some words we must learn by remembering the letters rather than saying the sounds. We will say and spell the words to help us learn them. Write *he* on the board. This is the word *he*. It has two letters. The letters in *he* are *h* and *e*. Have children say and spell the word, first with you and then without you.

2. **Demonstrate Meaning** I can use the word *he* in lots of sentences. Here is one sentence: *He likes the color blue.* Now you use the word in a sentence.

Repeat the routine with the word *for*.

Add the words *he* and *for* to the Word Wall.

Routines Flip Chart

Academic Vocabulary

Write the following words on the board:

adjective	informational text
description	sequence
caption	nursery rhyme

Point to the list. This week we are going to learn these important words. They are tools for learning. As we work this week you will hear them many times. Read the words. Preteach the Academic Vocabulary at point-of-use by providing a child-friendly description, explanation, or example that clarifies the meaning of each term. Then ask children to restate the meaning of the Academic Vocabulary in their own words.

Differentiated Instruction

 Advanced

High-Frequency Words Have children draw a picture to go along with the sentence they create. Have them copy the high-frequency word from the board onto their drawing.

English Language Learners

Visual Support Scaffold the meaning of the word *he* by having all the boys in the class stand up. Point to each boy and say a sentence about the color shirt he is wearing using this sentence frame: *He is wearing a _____.*

Decodable Story 11
/i/ Spelled *Ii* and High-Frequency Words

Review

Review the following high-frequency words. Have children read each word as you point to it on the Word Wall.

he	a	little	is	the

Teach rebus words

Write the word *pig* on the board. This is the word *pig*. Name the letters with me: *p, i, g, pig*. Look for the word *pig* in the story we read today. There will be a picture above the word to help you read it.

Read Decodable Story 11

Display Decodable Story 11. Today we will read a story about a pig named Tim. What is the title of the story? Point to the title of the story. The title of the story is *Tim the Pig*. We will read short *i* words in this story. Have children read Decodable Story 11 on pp. 131–132 in *Reader's and Writer's Notebook*.

Use the routine for reading decodable books to read Decodable Story 11.

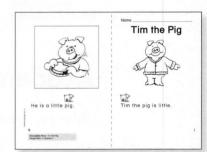

Reader's and Writer's Notebook, pp. 131–132

ROUTINE

Reading Decodable Books

1. **Read Silently** Have children whisper read the story page by page as you listen in.

2. **Model Fluent Reading** Have children finger point as you read a page. Then have children reread the page without you.

3. **Read Chorally** Have children finger point as they chorally read the page. Continue reading page by page, repeating steps 1 and 2.

4. **Read Individually** Have children take turns reading aloud a page.

5. **Reread and Monitor Progress** As you listen to individual children reread, monitor progress and provide support.

6. **Reread with a Partner** Have children reread the story page by page with a partner.

Routines Flip Chart

Differentiated Instruction

 Strategic Intervention
Practice High-Frequency Words Point to the word *he* on the Word Wall. Ask children to say the word and use it in a sentence. Continue with the words *a, little, is,* and *the.*

Small Group Time

DAY 1

Break into small groups after reading the Decodable Story and before the comprehension lesson.

Teacher-Led

SI Strategic Intervention	**OL On-Level**	**A Advanced**
Teacher-Led Page DI•69	Teacher-Led Page DI•74	Teacher-Led Page DI•77
• Phonemic Awareness and Phonics	• Phonemic Awareness and Phonics	• Phonemic Awareness and Phonics
• **Reread** Decodable Story 11	• **Reread** Decodable Story 11	• **Reread** Decodable Story 11 for Fluency

ELL Place English language learners in the groups that correspond to their reading abilities in English.

Practice Stations	**Independent Activities**
• Visit the Listen Up! Station	• Read independently
• Visit the Word Work Station	• Concept Talk Video
	• *Reader's and Writer's Notebook*

Objectives
◎ Identify and describe sequence.

Skills Trace
◎ **Sequence**
Introduce U1W3D1; U2W5D1;
U4W1D1; U4W3D1
Practice U1W3D2; U1W3D3;
U1W3D4; U2W5D2; U2W5D3;
U2W5D4; U4W1D2; U4W1D3;
U4W1D4; U4W3D2; U4W3D3;
U4W3D4
Reteach/Review U1W3D5;
U1W5D4; U2W2D4; U2W5D5;
U2W6D4; U4W1D5; U4W3D5;
U5W2D4
Assess/Test Benchmark
Assessment U4

KEY:
U=Unit   W=Week   D=Day

My Skills Buddy, pp. 94–95

Listening Comprehension
⊙ Sequence

Introduce

Envision It!

In most stories, many things happen. They happen in a certain order: something happens first, something happens next, and something happens last. The order in which things happen is the **sequence.** Good readers pay attention to the sequence because it helps them understand the story.

Have children turn to pp. 94–95 in *My Skills Buddy* and look at the three pictures. These pictures show a sequence, or order, of events.

• What happens in the first picture? (Mama Bird sits on her eggs.)

• What happens next? (Mama Bird feeds her babies.)

• What happens last? (The babies leave the nest.)

Model

Today I will read aloud a story about how a beaver builds its home. Read **"The Beaver's Lodge"** and model how to identify sequence.

Think Aloud

When I read, I pay attention to the sequence in which things happen. I look for clue words, such as *first, next,* and *last* to help me notice what happens. In "The Beaver's Lodge," the beaver uses trees to build his home. First, he uses his teeth to chop down the trees. Next, he chews off all of the branches. Last, the beaver rolls the tree to its new lodge.

Guide practice

Have children tell what happens in the story after the beaver chops down a tree. Next, the beaver chews off all of the branches. What happens last? (The beaver rolls the tree to its new lodge.)

More practice

Display Big Book *Bear Snores On*. Recall with children that several animals stop at Bear's den while he sleeps. Page through the story. Have children identify the order in which the animals appear. Who sneaks into the cave first? next? last?

Connect to everyday life

The days of the school week happen in the same sequence every week. First comes Monday. Next is Tuesday. What comes after that?

Differentiated Instruction

 Strategic Intervention

Access Content Have children tell the sequence of what happened when they got ready for school. Ask them what happened first, next, and last.

Academic Vocabulary

sequence the order of events in a selection

 E L L

English Language Learners
Oral Comprehension
To prepare English Learners for the Read Aloud, use the modified Read Aloud in the ELL Support lesson p. DI•81.

 Read Aloud

The Beaver's Lodge

The beaver is one of nature's best builders. This large brown rodent builds its home on the water. The beaver's home is called a lodge. From the outside, a lodge looks like a pile of tangled sticks and mud. But inside, there are many big rooms and tunnels.

A beaver uses trees to build its lodge. The first thing a beaver does is chop down a tree with its long, sharp teeth. Then it chews off all of the branches. Last, the beaver rolls the tree to its new lodge. The beaver's lodge is built strong and keeps the beaver safe from other animals.

Conventions
Adjectives for Opposites

Teach adjectives

Review adjectives with children. Adjectives are words that tell about, or describe, people, animals, places, and things. Today we are going to practice using adjectives to write about opposites, or things that are different from each other.

Model

Display the *black* Picture Card. Black is a very *dark* color. What is the opposite of *dark*? I know that *light* is the opposite of *dark*. Display the *box* Picture Card. This box is *open*. What is the opposite of *open? Closed* is the opposite of *open*. Continue modeling with *light/heavy* and *on/off*.

Guide practice

Tell children to look around the room. Have them find adjectives and then name their opposites. As children identify adjectives, ask them questions. What is the opposite of *high? small? wet? big? dark?*

As children name adjectives and their opposites, make a list of the words on the board. Let's read these adjectives together. Read the list with children, pointing to each adjective as you say it.

Write the following sentences on the board:

> **The door is closed.**
>
> **The door is _____.** (open)

Work with children to complete the sentence with an adjective for the opposite of *closed*. Repeat the procedure with other adjectives for opposites from the list children generated.

Team Talk Pair children and have them take turns using the adjectives from the list in complete sentences. Then have them use the opposite of that adjective in a complete sentence.

Daily Fix-It

Use the Daily Fix-It for more conventions practice.

Writing
Wonderful, Marvelous Me!
I Just Learned…

Introduce

Talk with children about learning. We learn new things all the time. We learn things at school and at home. How do we learn things? Sometimes people teach us new things. Sometimes we have to try something many times before we can do it. It's important not to give up. Have children share their ideas about why it is important to learn new things.

Model

Today we are going to tell about something wonderful and marvelous that we've learned. I'm going to close my eyes and think about the things I've learned lately. I really like sports, but I don't know how to play many of them. Last week my brother taught me how to shoot a basketball. The first time I tried to shoot a basket, I didn't make it. Draw a picture of a basketball and hoop. Write *basketball* and *hoop* below the drawing. The next time I tried, the ball was very close to going in. Demonstrate how you would follow through when shooting a basket. I tried one more time and I made a basket! I was so excited that I just learned how to shoot a basket. Demonstrate the entire movement of shooting a basket.

Guide practice

Have children stand up and pretend to shoot a basket. See how much fun learning new things can be?

Independent writing

Now you are going to write about something you learned. Close your eyes and think about something wonderful and marvelous that you have learned. Who helped you learn it? Have children write or dictate their ideas and then illustrate them.

Daily Handwriting

Write *Isaac* and *it* on the board. Review correct letter formations of uppercase *I* and lowercase *i*.

D'Nealian™   Ball and Stick

Have children write *Isaac* and *it* on their Write-On Boards. Remind them to use proper left-to-right and top-to-bottom progression and proper spacing between letters when writing *I* and *i*.

 Write Guy
Jeff Anderson

Writing to Learn

When a child writes a sentence, she is writing to learn. Let's provide her with at least one reader so that she learns how her language communicates. That reader may be a partner, a family member, the teacher, or a group of classmates. Writing comes alive and has a purpose when it has an audience. Young writers do as well.

Academic Vocabulary

adjective word that tells about a person, animal, place, or thing

Daily Fix-It

dormouse needs a house
Dormouse needs a house.

This week's practice sentences appear on Teacher Resources DVD-ROM.

Writing Routine

Day 1 Wonderful, Marvelous Me!

Day 2 Respond to Literature

Day 3 Genre Writing

Day 4 Extend the Concept

Day 5 This Week We…

Objectives
- Practice giving a description.
- Speak loudly and clearly.

Listening and Speaking
Give a Description

Teach If a story had no pictures, you could still imagine how things look by the words the author uses to describe the characters, setting, and events. When I give a description, I use words that tell more about my ideas.

Model Listen to the description in this short story: *On a hot summer day, the bright sun was shining. Alex ran down the sidewalk past the old houses. She was on her way to the beautiful park with the nice, cool sprinkler.*

What did I just describe? (a hot sunny day and a way to cool off)

Guide practice I am going to start a new story. Raise your hand when you want to add a sentence that will describe something else. *On a cold winter day, my father and I went outside to shovel the heavy, wet snow. I was wearing so many clothes I could hardly move.* Start a story and have children continue the story or describe an experience of their own. Refer children to the Rules for Listening and Speaking on pp. 1–2 of *Reader's and Writer's Notebook.* Remind them to speak loudly and clearly.

> Name _____
>
> 🔵 Listening Rules
>
> 1. Face the person who is speaking.
> 2. Be quiet while someone is speaking.
> 3. Pay attention to the speaker.
> 4. Ask questions if you don't understand.

Reader's and Writer's Notebook, p. 1

Wrap Up Your Day

✔ **Concept Talk** This week we are going to talk about animal homes. Today we read about a beaver's home. What kind of home does a beaver need?

✔ **Oral Language** Today we talked about homes for animals. Say the Amazing Words with me: *nest, meadow, stump, tree trunk, hive, den.*

✔ **Conventions** What is the opposite of *big? white? wet?*

✔ **Homework Idea** Send home the Family Times Newsletter on Let's Practice It! Teacher Resource DVD•21–22.

Preview

DAY 2

Tomorrow we will read about a little mouse who needs a home.

Science
Day-to-Day Weather Changes
Materials: indoor/outdoor thermometer, calendar, paper, markers

Track Day-to-Day Weather Changes
Divide each calendar day into three sections. Throughout the week, record the outside temperature on the calendar three times a day: first thing in the morning, before lunch, and just before going home. Discuss how the temperature usually rises from a morning low to an afternoon high and cools off again overnight. Point out the indoor temperature. Tell children that the school is heated so it never gets too cold inside. If the school has air conditioning, point out the indoor temperature on hot days too.

Write Sentences Have children write about the weather changes in a sequence and make illustrations for each sentence.

First, it rained.

Next, it snowed.

Finally, it got warm and dry.

Conventions
Adjectives for Opposites
Materials: labels—*tall, short, thin, wide, wet, dry, hot, cold, open, closed, dark, light, heavy, light, up, down;* paper; crayons or markers

Our Opposite Room Take an adjective walk around the classroom, attaching labels to objects and places the children identify. Have children draw a picture of two items described by adjectives for opposites and copy the labels onto their pictures.

Comprehension
Whose Tail Is It?
Materials: colored paper or large index cards, two copies of selected animals with distinctive tails from *Patterns* on the *Teacher Resources DVD-ROM;* cut tails off of one copy and mount bodies and tails on separate cards

Compare and Contrast Animal Tails Display pictures of animals. Ask volunteers to name each animal and describe its tail. Show a picture of an animal's tail to the children. Have them identify the animal with the tail.

Objectives
- Discuss the concepts to develop oral language.
- Build oral vocabulary.

Today at a Glance

Oral Vocabulary
nest, meadow

Phonemic Awareness
◉ Initial and Medial /i/

Phonics
◉ /i/ Spelled *Ii*

Handwriting
Words with *Ii*

Comprehension
◉ Sequence

Conventions
Adjectives for Opposites

Writing
Respond to Literature

Vocabulary
Sequence Words

TRUCKTOWN on Reading Street

Start your engines! Display p. 15 of *Truckery Rhymes.* Point to "Rock-a-Bye Mixer." What truck is this rhyme about? Yes, this rhyme is about Melvin. Let's read the rhyme together. Have a child point to the rhyming words as the class reads the rhyme again. What other words rhyme with *fall*?

Concept Talk

Question of the Week

 What kind of home does an animal need?

Build concepts

Write the question of the week on the board and track the print as you read it aloud. Have children answer the question in complete sentences. To reinforce the concept and to focus children's attention, display Sing with Me Chart 11B. Tell children that they are going to sing a song about a mouse looking for a safe, warm winter home.

Talk with Me/Sing with Me Chart 11B

🔘 Sing with Me Audio

Listen for Amazing Words

The Amazing Words *nest* and *meadow* are in this song. Read the title and have children describe the picture. Sing the song several times to the tune of "Twinkle, Twinkle, Little Star." Have children sing with you. Have them clap when they hear the Amazing Words *nest* and *meadow*.

ELL **Reinforce Vocabulary** Use the Day 2 instruction on ELL Poster 11 to reinforce the meanings of high-frequency words.

ELL Poster 11

Oral Vocabulary
Amazing Words

Teach Amazing Words

Amazing Words   Oral Vocabulary Routine

1. **Introduce the Word** Some animals live in a *nest*. A *nest* is a safe place made of grass, sticks, mud, or other things. What's our new Amazing Word for a safe place an animal makes of grass and other things? Say it with me: *nest.*

2. **Demonstrate** Provide examples to show meaning. *A bird builds a nest in a tree.* Where are some other places you may find a *nest*?

   Repeat steps 1 and 2.

   Introduce the Word A *meadow* is a large field filled with grass and other plants. Many animals live and find their food in a *meadow*. What's our new Amazing Word for a large grassy field? Say it with me: *meadow.*

   Demonstrate *Deer play and eat in the meadow.* What other animals live in the *meadow*?

3. **Apply** Tell children to use *nest* and *meadow* to describe places where animals live and make their homes.

Routines Flip Chart

Use Amazing Words

To reinforce the concept and the Amazing Words, have children supply the appropriate Amazing Word for each sentence.

The deer walked in the _____. (meadow)

The bird used twigs to build its _____. (nest)

Amazing Words

nest	meadow
stump	tree trunk
hive	den

Differentiated Instruction

SI Strategic Intervention

Sentence Production If children have difficulty completing the sentences below, model saying the completed sentence and then have them repeat it after you.

Teaching Tip

Building Nests Children may think that all nests look like a bird's twig home. If possible, show children pictures of a wasp's nest and show where it can be found. Show children other unusual nests.

 Get **Ready** to **Read**

DAY 2

Objectives

◎ Practice initial and medial /i/.

• Blend phonemes.

Phonemic Awareness
 Initial and Medial /i/

Isolate /i/

Display the *igloo* Picture Card. This is an *igloo. Igloo* begins with /i/. What is this? What sound does it begin with? Do *insect, iguana,* and *inch* begin the same?

Picture Card

Model medial /i/

Display the *pig* Picture Card. This is a *pig.* Listen as I say the sounds: /p/ /i/ /g/, *pig.* I hear /i/ in the middle of the word: /p/ /i/ /g/. Say it with me: /p/ /i/ /g/; /i/ is in the middle. Let's try some more. **Continue with the following words:** *tip, lick, pit, hit, big, dig, Jim, sit, pick, win, sip.*

Picture Card

Guide practice

Have children look at the picture on *My Skills Buddy* pp. 92–93. Remember that we saw inventors in the picture. *Inventors* begins with /i/. What things can you find that have /i/ in the middle? **Discuss with children those bulleted items on p. 92 not discussed on Day 1.**

My Skills Buddy, pp. 92–93

Listen to the sounds in *pit:* /p/ /i/ /t/. The middle sound is /i/. Raise your hand when I say a word that has the same middle sound as *pit: big, ram, dip, mat, sit, bib, crab, crib.*

Corrective feedback

If... children cannot discriminate medial /i/,

then... have them enunciate /i/ as they segment short i words.

Listen as I segment a word: /z/ /i/ /p/. Say it with me: /z/ /i/ /p/. What sound do you hear in the middle? I hear /i/ in the middle. What is the word? Say the word with me: *zip.* Continue with the following words: *fin, his, tin, will.*

On their own Display Phonics Songs and Rhymes Chart 11. Remind children of the song "In a Tin" sung to the tune of "Do You Know the Muffin Man?" Have them sing the song with you several times. This time I want you to clap your hands when you hear /i/ in the middle of a word. We can do it together the first time.

Review **Blending** Listen to the sounds in this word: /s/ /i/ /t/. Say the sounds with me: /s/ /i/ /t/. Now I'm going to blend the sounds together to say the word: /s/ /i/ /t/, *sit.* Now you try it with me: /s/ /i/ /t/, *sit.* Continue the blending routine with the following words: *tip, sip, pit, sat, tap, pat.*

In a Tin

In a tin on this big hill,
On this big hill, on this big hill,
In a tin on this big hill,
We hid from winter's chill.

It's winter still; the wind still whips,
The wind still whips, the wind still whips.
It's winter still; the wind still whips,
But we are warm in here!

Phonics Songs and
Rhymes Chart 11

Differentiated Instruction

 Strategic Intervention

Distinguish /i/ Words Say the title of the Phonics Song "In a Tin." Ask children to identify the word that begins with /i/ and the word that has /i/ in the middle.

E L L

English Language Learners
Support Phonemic Awareness English language learners from various language backgrounds may pronounce short *i* like the *ee* in *see.* Help children practice pronouncing word pairs such as *sit/seat; Tim/team; pit/Pete; mitt/meat.*

Phonics—Teach/Model
/i/ Spelled *Ii*

**Teach /i/ /Ii*

Display the *Ii* Alphabet Card. Point to the *igloo*. What is this? What sound does *igloo* begin with? *Igloo* begins with /i/. Write the word *igloo* on the board and point to the letter *i*. The letter for /i/ is *i*.

Model

Say the word *pit*. What are the sounds in *pit*? Say the sounds with me: /p/ /i/ /t/. Where do you hear /i/ in *pit*? I hear /i/ in the middle.

Write the word *pit* on the board. Point to each letter as you say the sounds: /p/ /i/ /t/, *pit*. Continue the routine with the following words: *sit, sip, tip*.

Guide practice

Envision It!

Have children open *My Skills Buddy* to p. 96. Demonstrate using the blending arrows on *My Skills Buddy* p. 96 as you model blending the first word. Put your finger on the red arrow below the *s*. Say the sound that *s* stands for: /s/. Continue with the letters *i* and *t*. Now I run my finger along the blue arrow as I blend the letters quickly to read *sit*. Have children work with a partner to blend the rest of the words on the page.

Alphabet Card

My Skills Buddy, p. 96

Blend Use the following routine to review blending *i* words.

ROUTINE Sound-by-Sound Blending

(1) Connect Write the letter *i*. What is the sound we learned for this letter? The sound is /i/. Say it with me: /i/ /i/ /i/. When you see this letter in a word, what sound will you say?

(2) Model Write the word *sit* on the board.

- Point to *s*. What is the sound we learned for this letter? Say it with me: /s/ /s/ /s/. Repeat the routine for *i* and *t*.

- Let's blend the sounds together. Listen as I blend the sounds: /s/ /i/ /t/, *sit*. Say it with me: /s/ /i/ /t/, *sit*. Now say it without me.

- Listen as I use *sit* in a sentence. *I will sit in the chair.* Say it with me. Have children use *sit* in a sentence.

(3) Guide Practice Continue the routine established in step 2 with these words:

Tip	it	pit	sip	Pat	cat	tap

Have children successfully read all the words before reading Decodable Reader 11 on pp. 98–105 of *My Skills Buddy*.

Corrective Feedback Model blending the sounds to read the word. Then have children say it with you.

Routines Flip Chart

MONITOR PROGRESS 🔊 **Check Sound-Spelling /i/ Spelled *Ii***

Give each child a blank card. Have children write the letters *Ii* on the card. I am going to read some words. When you hear a word with /i/, hold up your *Ii* card. Say: *Ingrid, like, fish, bus, dip, gift, fast, box, tag, win, inchworm.*

If... children cannot discriminate short *i* words,

then... use the small-group Strategic Intervention lesson, p. DI•70, to reteach /i/.

Continue to monitor children's progress using other instructional opportunities during the week so that children can be successful with the Day 5 Assessment.

Day 1	Day 2	Day 3	Day 4	Day 5
Check Phonemic Awareness	Check Sound-Spelling/ Retelling	Check Word Reading	Check Phonemic Awareness	Check Oral Vocabulary

Differentiated Instruction

SI Strategic Intervention

Connect Sound-Spelling
Display the *Ss, Ii, Tt, Mm,* and *Pp* Alphabet Cards. Have children review the correct sound-spelling for each letter.

Success Predictor

Sound-Spelling

Success Predictor

Handwriting
Write Words with *Ii*

Review

Write *Isabel* on the board. This is the word *Isabel*. I use an uppercase *I* for the first letter in *Isabel's* name. Watch me make an uppercase *I*. Write another uppercase *I* on the board using the strokes indicated in the model.

Write the word *it* on the board. What word is this? This is the word *it*. I use a lowercase *i* for the first letter in *it*. Watch me make a lowercase *i*. Write another lowercase *i* on the board using the proper strokes.

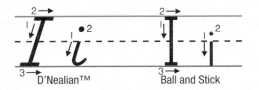

D'Nealian™   Ball and Stick

Guide practice

Have children use their Write-On Boards to make a row of uppercase *I* and a row of lowercase *i*. Circulate around the room, assisting children as necessary. Have children then write the following words: *sit, is, tip.*

High-Frequency Words

Model reading

Have children turn to p. 97 of *My Skills Buddy.* Read the high-frequency words *he* and *for* together. Then have children point to each word and read it themselves. Read the sentences on the *My Skills Buddy* page together to read the new high-frequency words in context.

Team Talk Pair children and have them take turns reading each of the sentences aloud.

High-Frequency Words

Words I Can Read

he

for

Sentences I Can Read

1. He is a cat.
2. The cat is for Tim.
3. He can sit for Tim.

97

My Skills Buddy, p. 97

On their own

Use *Reader's and Writer's Notebook,* p. 133, for additional practice with this week's high-frequency words.

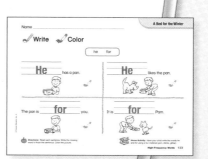

Reader's and Writer's Notebook, p. 133

Differentiated Instruction

A Advanced

High-Frequency Words Have children make up sentences using the high-frequency words.

English Language Learners

High-Frequency Words After the Team Talk activity, have children continue to work in pairs to check understanding. Have one child read one of the sentences aloud while another child makes a simple drawing to illustrate the sentence.

Objectives
• Read decodable text.
• Read high-frequency words.

Decodable Reader 11
🔄 /i/ Spelled *Ii* and High-Frequency Words

Review Review the previously taught high-frequency words. Have children read each word as you point to it on the Word Wall.

is	a	he	my	for

Have children turn to Decodable Reader 11, *Tip and Pat,* on p. 98 of *My Skills Buddy.* Today we will read a story about two cats named Tip and Pat. Point to the title of the story. The title of the story is *Tip and Pat.* What is the title of the story? Point to the author's name. The author of this story is Kate Brand. What does an author do? We will be able to read lots of short *i* words in this story.

Use the routine for reading decodable books to read Decodable Reader 11. Have children monitor their comprehension by asking them to think about whether they understand the story. To adjust comprehension, have them reread or read some part aloud.

My Skills Buddy, pp. 98–105

Differentiated Instruction

 Strategic Intervention

Recognize /i/ in Words Ask children which of the two names in the title has /i/, *Tip* or *Pat*. Have them pronounce words in the Decodable Reader that have /i/. (*Tip, it, sit*)

ROUTINE Reading Decodable Books

1 **Read Silently** Have children whisper read the book page by page as you listen in.

2 **Model Fluent Reading** Have children finger point as you read a page. Then have children reread the book without you.

3 **Read Chorally** Have children finger point as they chorally read the page. Continue reading page by page, repeating steps 1 and 2.

4 **Read Individually** Have children take turns reading aloud a page.

5 **Reread and Monitor Progress** As you listen to individual children reread, monitor progress and provide support.

6 **Reread with a Partner** Have children reread the book page by page with a partner.

Routines Flip Chart

Small Group Time

DAY 2

Break into small groups after reading the Decodable Reader and before the comprehension lesson.

Teacher-Led

 Strategic Intervention

Teacher-Led Page DI•70
- Phonemic Awareness and Phonics
- **Reread** Decodable Reader 11

OL On-Level

Teacher-Led Page DI•74
- Phonemic Awareness and Phonics
- **Reread** Decodable Reader 11

A Advanced

Teacher-Led Page DI•77
- Phonics and Spelling
- **Reread** Decodable Reader 11 for Fluency

 Place English language learners in the groups that correspond to their reading abilities in English.

Practice Stations
- Visit the Word Work Station
- Visit the Words to Know Station

Independent Activities
- Read independently
- Background Building Audio
- *Reader's and Writer's Notebook*

DAY 2 Read and Comprehend
20–25 mins.

Objectives
◉ Practice sequence.
• Preview and predict.
• Retell a selection.

Check Retelling
SUCCESS PREDICTOR

Listening Comprehension
 Sequence

Review

Have children turn to pp. 94–95 in *My Skills Buddy.* Remind children that stories happen in a certain order. Things happen first, next, and last. This is called the sequence. Good readers pay attention to sequence because it helps them understand the story.

Envision It!

My Skills Buddy, pp. 94–95

First Read—Big Book
A Bed for the Winter

Concepts of print

Display *A Bed for the Winter.* Explain that the printed words tell us the title of the story and who wrote the story.

Preview and predict

Think Aloud

Display *A Bed for the Winter.* On the cover I see a big bear, snowflakes, and trees. The title of this book is *A Bed for the Winter.* What do you think this book will be about?

Use photographs

Take children on a walk through the book. Have them describe the photographs.

Introduce genre

An informational text teaches us about things that happen in the world. In this selection we will learn about animal homes.

Set purpose

Tell children to listen to learn about animal homes as you read.

Model

Read *A Bed for the Winter* with expression for enjoyment.

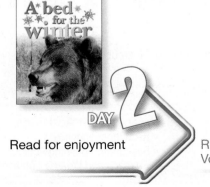

DAY 2
Read for enjoyment

DAY 3
Reread using Develop Vocabulary notes

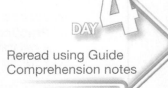
DAY 4
Reread using Guide Comprehension notes

Retell

Check retelling

Envision It!

Have children turn to p. 106 of *My Skills Buddy*. Walk through the retelling boxes as children retell the selection *A Bed for the Winter.* Let's retell what happens in the first box— the beginning of the selection. The dormouse stops in the meadow. She needs to find a bed for the winter. Let's retell what happens in the next box. Continue with the rest of the boxes. After children retell the selection as a group, have them draw pictures to retell a favorite part. Have them write or dictate a word or sentence to go with each picture.

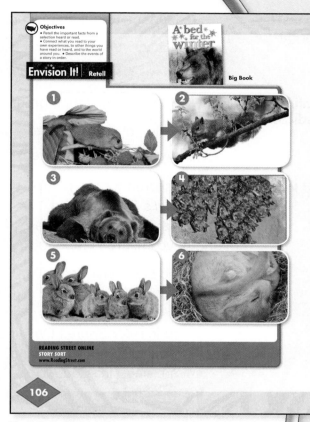

My Skills Buddy, p. 106

Top-Score Response A top-score response identifies the topic and details.

Differentiated Instruction

SI **Strategic Intervention**
Build Background To reinforce retelling, have children retell the day's activities.

Academic Vocabulary

informational text teaches readers about things that happen in the real word

Retelling Plan

☑ **Week 1** Assess Advanced students.

☑ **Week 2** Assess On-Level students.

☑ **Week 3** Assess Strategic Intervention students.

☑ **Week 4** Assess Advanced students.

☑ **This week assess On-Level students.**

☐ **Week 6** Assess Strategic Intervention students.

Don't Wait Until Friday

MONITOR PROGRESS **Check Retelling**

If... children have difficulty retelling the selection,

then... go through the selection one page at a time, and ask children to tell what they learn in their own words.

Day 1	Day 2	Day 3	Day 4	Day 5
Check Phonemic Awareness	Check Sound-Spelling/ Retelling	Check Word Reading	Check Phonemic Awareness	Check Oral Vocabulary

Success Predictor

Retelling

Success Predictor

Objectives

◎ Practice sequence.
• Confirm predictions.
• Practice adjectives for opposites.

Think, Talk, and Write

Discuss concept

We're learning about animal homes. Think about your home.

• What does your home look like?

• How does it feel to be in your own bed? Why is it best?

Confirm predictions

Have children recall their predictions before you read *A Bed for the Winter.*

• What did you think the story would be about?

• Was your prediction correct?

Text to text

Have children turn to p. 107 of *My Skills Buddy.* Read the questions and directives and have children respond.

1. Which bed reminded you of *Bear Snores On?* What kind of animal has a bed in *Bear Snores On?* Where does that same animal sleep in *A Bed for the Winter?*

◉ **Sequence**

2. Where does the dormouse go first in the story? **(the squirrel's nest)** Where does she go last? **(the tree trunk)**

Look back and write

3. Let's look back at our story and write about it. We remember that the dormouse is looking for a home for winter.

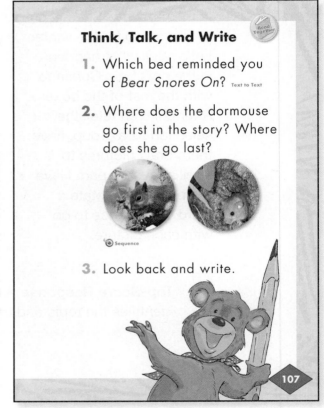

Think, Talk, and Write

1. Which bed reminded you of *Bear Snores On?* Text to Text

2. Where does the dormouse go first in the story? Where does she go last?

◎ Sequence

3. Look back and write.

107

My Skills Buddy, p. 107

Listen for why the dormouse does not want to sleep in the burrow with the rabbits. Read pp. 16–17 of *A Bed for the Winter.* Now let's write our ideas. Discuss with children why the rabbit's home is not a good home for the dormouse. Record children's responses on chart paper. (Possible responses: There are too many rabbits. There is no room for the dormouse.)

Conventions
Adjectives for Opposites

Review

Remind children of what they learned about adjectives. Adjectives are words that tell about people, animals, places, and things. This week we are learning about adjectives for opposites.

Guide practice

Guide children to identify places the dormouse visits in *A Bed for the Winter*. Have children say if the places are *high* or *low, cold* or *warm,* or *big* or very *small*. Read the text on p. 10 with children, emphasizing the adjective *wet*. Then read the text on p. 29 with children. Have them identify the adjective for the opposite of *wet*. (*dry*) Point out some opposites using positional words, such as *up in a tree* and *down on the ground*.

On their own

Use *Reader's and Writer's Notebook,* p. 134, for practice reading, writing, and saying adjectives for opposites.

Daily Fix-It

Use the Daily Fix-It for more conventions practice.

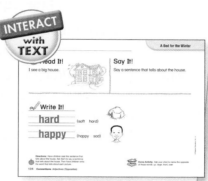

Reader's and Writer's Notebook, p. 134

Objectives

- Write about or dictate sentences about animal beds.
- Identify and use sequence words.
- Write *I* and *i*.

Writing
Respond to Literature

Discuss

Display *A Bed for the Winter*. Discuss with children the different beds the little dormouse visits.

Model

In the story, the dormouse visits different animal beds. We can use adjectives to describe the beds. I will write these two sentences:

> **The frog's bed is wet.**
>
> **The rabbit's bed is crowded.**

Guide practice

Have children help you write more sentences about the animal beds.

> **I like the high squirrel nest.**
>
> **I like the low frog bed.**

Independent writing

Have children write or dictate their own sentences about the different beds in *A Bed for the Winter*. Then have them illustrate their sentences.

Daily Handwriting

Write *Isis* and *is* on the board. Review correct letter formation of uppercase *I* and lowercase *i*.

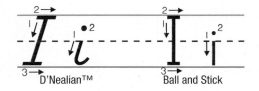

D'Nealian™   Ball and Stick

Have children write *Isis* and *is* on their Write-On Boards. Remind children to use proper left-to-right and top-to-bottom progression when writing *I* and *i*.

Vocabulary
Sequence Words

Model

Have children turn to p. 108 of *My Skills Buddy*. Read the first Vocabulary bullet on the page. These pictures tell a sequence, or order, of events. Direct them to look at the picture of the boy waking up in bed. This is what the boy does *first* in the morning. *First* is a sequence word. Direct them to look at the picture of the boy getting dressed. This is what the boy does *second*. *Second* is a sequence word. Direct them to the picture of the boy eating breakfast. *Next,* the boy eats breakfast. *Next* is a sequence word. Direct them to the picture of the boy getting on the school bus. The boy gets on the bus *last*. *Last* is a sequence word.

My Skills Buddy, p. 108

Guide practice

Write the words *first, second, next,* and *last* on the board. Point to each word as you read it.

first	second	next	last

Let's practice our new words. I'm going to tell you a sequence, or order, of actions. *First,* clap your hands. *Second,* put your hands on your head. *Next,* jump up and down. *Last,* sit down. What did I ask you to do *first? second? next? last?*

On their own

Have children take turns acting out a sequence, such as how to brush their teeth or tie their shoes. Have them tell what they are doing by using the sequence words *first, second, next,* and *last* in their explanation.

Differentiated Instruction

A **Advanced**

Access Content Have children work with a partner to tell how to make a bed using the words *first, second, next,* and *last*. Then have them discuss if it would be easier or harder to understand the order without the words *first, second, next,* and *last*.

English Language Learners

Support Writing Before writing, display each page in *A Bed for the Winter*. Have children describe each bed. Write the words they use in a list. Encourage children to use the list of words to help them write sentences. Allow them to write word their home language as well as in English.

Wrap Up Your Day

✔ **Concept Talk** Today we read about a dormouse looking for a bed. Why does she need a bed? What kind of place does she need?

✔ **Phonemic Awareness** I am going to read a poem. Clap when you hear /i/ words. *Iggy Inchworm inched along an igloo, inch by inch. If Iggy were a bit bigger, this trip would be a cinch!*

✔ **Vocabulary Skill** Today we learned sequence words. What is the *first* thing you did today? What are other sequence words besides *first*?

✔ **Homework Idea** Have children divide a sheet of paper into four sections. Have them draw the sequence of how to make a sandwich. Have them label the sections *first, second, next,* and *last*.

Preview

DAY 3

Tomorrow we will read about a home for a fish.

Science
Preparing for Winter Weather

Materials: On the Teacher Resources DVD-ROM, *Patterns* find—*boy, girl, winter clothing;* white construction paper; scissors; pencils; crayons; markers; glue

Get Protection from Winter Ask children what they would need if they were outside for a long time in the winter.

- What would you have to think about to prepare to be out in the cold weather for a long time?

- What would you need to protect yourself from the cold?

- Does it get dark earlier in the winter? What would you need to help you see in the dark?

Write a list of things children would need to protect themselves for the winter.

Give children a pattern of a boy or girl along with patterns for winter clothing. Ask them to cut out the child pattern and glue it to a sheet of paper. Then they can color, cut out, and glue patterns or draw other items needed for the winter. Have children label their pictures with an item needed for the winter.

Science
Real and Fantasy Animals

Materials: *Bear Snores On, A Bed for the Winter,* drawing paper, crayons or markers

Compare and Contrast Animals Show illustrations of the bear and the mouse in *Bear Snores On* and the photographs of the dormouse and the bear from *A Bed for the Winter.* Ask children how they know which animals are make-believe and which are real.

Have children draw two versions of the same animal, one lifelike and the other make-believe.

Phonemic Awareness
Sound Rhyme

Materials: small ball

Demonstrate Rhyme Knowledge Brainstorm words ending with -at, -it, -am, and -ip. Have children sit in a circle. Designate a target rime (-ip, -it, -am, or -at). Select a child to start the ball. Start by saying a word that ends with the target rime. Have each child name a rhyming word when the ball is passed to him or her. Change the word ending when necessary.

Objectives
- Share information and ideas about the concept.
- Build oral vocabulary.

Today at a Glance

Oral Vocabulary
stump, tree trunk

Phonemic Awareness
◉ Medial /i/

Phonics
◉ /i/ Spelled *Ii*

Comprehension
◉ Sequence

Conventions
Adjective for Numbers and Sizes

Writing
Caption

Listening and Speaking
Give a Description

TRUCKTOWN on Reading Street

Start your engines! Display p. 15 of *Truckery Rhymes.* Do you know the original "Rock-a-Bye Baby"? Recite it with children.

Rock-a-Bye baby, on the treetop.
When the wind blows, the cradle will rock.
When the bough breaks, the cradle will fall,
And down will come baby, cradle and all.

Truckery Rhymes

Concept Talk

Question of the Week

 What kind of home does an animal need?

Write the question of the week on the board. Read the question as you track the print. Talk with children about animal homes. Have them respond in complete sentences. Remind them to speak clearly and to take turns speaking.

Listen for Amazing Words

Let's Sing Display Sing with Me Chart 11B. Tell children that they are going to sing a song about a mouse looking for a safe, warm winter home. Tell them to listen for the Amazing Words *stump* and *tree trunk*. Read the title and ask children to describe the picture. Sing the song several times to the tune of "Twinkle, Twinkle, Little Star." Encourage children to sing with you. Have them clap when they hear the Amazing Word *stump* or *tree trunk*.

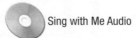 Sing with Me Audio

Talk with Me/Sing with Me Chart 11B

Oral Vocabulary
Amazing Words

Amazing Words

nest   meadow

stump   tree trunk

hive   den

Teach Amazing Words

Amazing Words — Oral Vocabulary Routine

1. **Introduce the Word** After a tree has been cut down, the bottom that is left is called a *stump*. What's our new Amazing Word for the bottom of a tree trunk that has been cut down? Say it with me: *stump*.

2. **Demonstrate** *If you see the stump of a tree, you might think of it as a chair and sit down on it.*

   Repeat steps 1 and 2.

   Introduce the Word A *tree trunk* is the thickest part of a tree that grows upward. What's our new Amazing Word for the thickest part of a tree that grows upward? Say it with me: *tree trunk*.

   Demonstrate *A tree trunk holds the tree up and carries water from its roots up to the branches and leaves.*

3. **Apply** Have children use the words *stump* and *tree trunk* to describe places where animals live and make their homes.

Routines Flip Chart

Use Amazing Words

To reinforce the concept and the Amazing Words, have children supply the appropriate Amazing Word for each sentence.

I sat down on the round, flat tree _____. (stump)

A dormouse lives in a _____. (tree trunk)

E L L Expand Vocabulary
Use the Day 3 instruction on ELL Poster 11 to help children expand vocabulary.

E L L Poster 11

Differentiated Instruction

SI Strategic Intervention
Sentence Production Use Talk with Me Chart 11A to help children complete the Amazing Word sentences below.

Phonemic Awareness
↻ Medial /i/

Review

Display the *pig* Picture Card. This is a *pig*. Listen to the sounds in *pig*: /p/ /i/ /g/. I hear /i/ in the middle of the word: /p/ /i/ /g/. Say it with me: /p/ /i/ /g/. Where do you hear /i/? Continue the routine with the following words: *dig, fit, hip, lip, ship, wig, zip.*

Identify syllables

Display p. 11 of *Trucktown ABCs*. Point to the picture of *Izzy*. Who is this? This is our Trucktown friend *Izzy*. Say his name with me: *Izzy*. Clap with me for each word part or syllable: *Iz-zy*. How many times did you clap? (2) There are two word parts or syllables in *Izzy*. Continue the routine with *alligator, elephant, gorilla, kangaroo, jellyfish, octopus, porcupine, raccoon,* and *walrus.*

On their own

Have children draw a picture of a word that has /i/ in the middle. Then have them show their pictures and say the name of what they drew.

Picture Card

Trucktown ABCs Big Book

Segment

Listen to the sounds in *zip*: /z/ /i/ /p/. Say the sounds with me: /z/ /i/ /p/. How many sounds do you hear? There are three sounds in *zip*. Continue the routine with the following words: *cat, fit, net, dot, lip, him, man, mop.*

Corrective feedback

If... children cannot segment the words into sounds, **then...** provide practice segmenting the words into chunks, such as *ca- /t/* or /k/ *-at.*

Substitute phonemes

Listen to the word I am going to say: *tip*. Say it with me: /t/ /i/ /p/, *tip*. I can make a new word by changing the last sound. Listen: /t/ /i/ /n/. Say it with me: /t/ /i/ /n/. What is the new word? The new word is *tin*. Continue practice with the following words: *pot, pop; cat, cap; sit, sip.*

Differentiated Instruction

SI Strategic Intervention

Distinguish /i/ Words Use Picture Cards to help children identify /i/ words. Show Picture Cards such as *cat, pig,* and *six.* Say the words and have children repeat them. Then have children help sort words with /i/ and words without /i/.

Objectives

◉ Practice /i/ spelled *Ii.*
- Substitute phonemes.
- Read /i/ words.
- Read high-frequency words.

Check Word Reading
⚲ **SUCCESS PREDICTOR**

Phonics—Teach/Model
/i/ Spelled *Ii*

Review | **/i/Ii** Display the *Ii* Alphabet Card and point to the *igloo*. What sound do you hear at the beginning of *igloo*? What letter spells that sound? Point to the letters *Ii*. What is the sound for this letter? What are the names of these letters?

Review | **Letter Names and Sounds** Use Alphabet Cards to review the following letter names and sounds: *Aa, Mm, Pp, Cc, Tt, Ss.*

Alphabet Card

Blend sounds | Write the word *sip* on the board. Point to each letter as you say the sound: /s/ /i/ /p/. When I blend these sounds together, I make the word *sip*. Say the sounds with me: /s/ /i/ /p/. Now blend the sounds together: /s/ /i/ /p/, *sip*. Change the *p* to *t*. Now we have a new word. Let's blend the sounds to read the word. Say them with me: /s/ /i/ /t/. What is the new word? The new word is *sit*. Repeat the blending routine with *pat, pit; cat, cap; tap, tip; map; tap.*

More practice | Use *Reader's and Writer's Notebook,* p. 135, for additional practice with /i/.

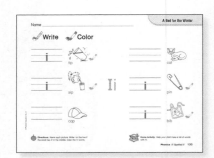

Reader's and Writer's Notebook, p. 135

Review **Sound-Spelling** Display the *Cc* Alphabet Card. What sound do you hear at the beginning of *cactus*? What letter can spell that sound? Yes, the letter *c* can spell /k/. Review the following sounds and letters with Alphabet Cards: *Pp, Ss, Aa, Tt, Mm*.

Review **High-Frequency Words** Write the word *he* on the board. This is the word *he*. What is this word? Continue the routine with *for, we, like, little, is, a, I, have,* and *my*.

Alphabet Card

Differentiated Instruction

A Advanced

Connect Sound-Spelling Say words that begin with /p/, /k/, /m/, /t/, /a/, /s/, or /i/. Have children write the correct letter for the sound in the air with their finger.

Don't Wait Until Friday

MONITOR PROGRESS ⟳ **Check Word Reading** **High-Frequency Words**

Write *I, little, a, have, is, my, like, he,* and *for* on the board. Have children take turns reading the words.

Practice reading these words from Kindergarten Student Reader K.2.5, *A House for Pip*.

it	Sam	Pip

If... children cannot read the high-frequency words,

then... write the words on cards for them to practice at home.

If... children cannot blend sounds to read the words,

then... provide practice blending the words in chunks, /p/ *-ip*.

If... children can successfully blend sounds to read the words,

then... have them read Kindergarten Student Reader K.2.5, *A House for Pip*.

Day 1	Day 2	Day 3	Day 4	Day 5
Check Phonemic Awareness	Check Sound-Spelling/ Retelling	Check Word Reading	Check Phonemic Awareness	Check Oral Vocabulary

Success Predictor

Kindergarten Student Reader K.2.5
/i/ Spelled *Ii* and High-Frequency Words

Review Review the previously taught high-frequency words. Have children read each word as you point to it on the Word Wall.

for	have	a	little	like	I	he	my

Teach rebus words Write the word *fish* on the board. This is the word *fish*. Name the letters with me: *f, i, s, h, fish*. Look for the word *fish* in the book we read today. Write the word *house* on the board. This is the word *house*. Name the letters with me: *h, o, u, s, e, house*. Look for this word in the book we read today. Write the word *ship* on the board. This is the word *ship*. Name the letters with me: *s, h, i, p, ship*. Look for this word in the book we read today. There will be pictures above these words to help you read them.

Read Kindergarten Student Reader K.2.5 Display Kindergarten Student Reader K.2.5. Today we are going to read a new book. Point to the title of the book. The title of the book is *A House for Pip*. The author's name is Christina Rivas. David Sheldon illustrated the book.

Use the reading decodable books routine to read the Kindergarten Student Reader.

ROUTINE — Reading Decodable Books — *Small Group*

1. **Read Silently** Have children whisper read the book page by page as you listen in.
2. **Model Fluent Reading** Have children finger point as you read a page. Then have children reread the page without you.
3. **Read Chorally** Have children finger point as they chorally read the page. Continue reading page by page, repeating steps 1 and 2.
4. **Read Individually** Have children take turns reading aloud a page.
5. **Reread and Monitor Progress** As you listen to individual children reread, monitor progress and provide support.
6. **Reread with a Partner** Have children reread the book page by page with a partner.

Routines Flip Chart

Pip is my fish.

He is little.

Sam, I have a house for Pip.

Kindergarten Student Reader K.2.5

It is little, like Pip.

Sam, I have a ship for Pip.

It is little, like Pip.

I like Pip.

Differentiated Instruction

SI Strategic Intervention

Access Content Have children draw a picture of a *house,* a *fish,* and a *ship* to better understand the rebus words.

Small Group Time

DAY 3 Break into small groups to read the Kindergarten Student Reader before the comprehension lesson.

Teacher-Led

SI Strategic Intervention	**OL** On-Level	**A** Advanced
Teacher-Led Page DI•71	Teacher-Led Page DI•75	Teacher-Led Page DI•78
• Phonemic Awareness and Phonics	• Phonemic Awareness and Phonics	• **Read** Independent Reader K.2.5 or Kindergarten Student Reader K.2.5
• **Read** Concept Literacy Reader K.2.5 or Kindergarten Student Reader K.2.5	• **Read** Kindergarten Student Reader K.2.5	

ELL Place English Language learners in the groups that correspond to their reading abilities in English.

Practice Stations
• Visit the Words to Know Station
• Visit the Let's Write! Station

Independent Activities
• Read independently
• Audio Text of Big Book
• *Reader's and Writer's Notebook*

ELL

English Language Learners

Access Content Have children identify the nouns in the story (*fish, house, ship*) and the adjective for size (*little*).

Objectives
- Recall and retell the selection.
- ◎ Practice sequence.
- Develop and use vocabulary.
- Develop and use comprehension skills.

Comprehension

Retell the story

Have children turn to p. 106 of *My Skills Buddy* and use the retelling boxes to retell the selection *A Bed for the Winter*.

 **Envision It!**

 Think Aloud — Direct children to the first retell box. This is when the dormouse looks for a bed for the winter. Tell me about the beds she tries.

Continue reviewing the retelling boxes and having children retell the selection.

 **Review**

Sequence Remind children that the animals in *A Bed for the Winter* sense changes in the weather, and then they react by trying to find a winter home.

- What happens first to make animals begin to look for a bed for winter? (cold rain, colder weather)
- Next, what season is it when animals begin to look for shelter before the winter? (fall, autumn)
- When an animal finds a bed for the winter, what does it usually do last? (It falls asleep.)

More practice

Use *Reader's and Writer's Notebook,* p. 136, to practice sequence.

My Skills Buddy, p. 106

Reader's and Writer's Notebook, p. 136

 **Triple Day Read!**

Second Read—Big Book
A Bed for the Winter

Reread *A Bed for the Winter.* Follow the Day 3 arrow beginning on p. 459, and use the Develop Vocabulary notes to prompt conversations about the story.

Have children use the Amazing Words *nest, meadow, stump, tree trunk, hive,* and *den* to talk about the story.

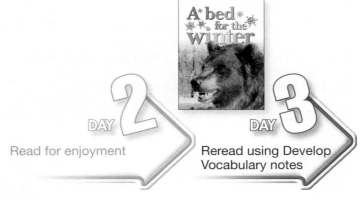

DAY 2 — Read for enjoyment

DAY 3 — Reread using Develop Vocabulary notes

DAY 4 — Reread using Guide Comprehension notes

Develop Vocabulary

Wh- question
Where does the dormouse stop? (the meadow)

- The dormouse stops in the meadow. What is the dormouse looking for?

Develop Vocabulary bed

Expand Vocabulary dormouse

A fluffy-tailed dormouse stops by a meadow.

Cold rain is falling.
Soon snow will be coming.

The dormouse is looking for somewhere to sleep. She needs a bed for the winter.

meadow

4

5

Big Book, pp. 4–5

Guide Comprehension

Monitor and Fix Up
Why does the dormouse need a bed? If you don't understand why the dormouse needs a bed, what could you do? (If I don't understand what is read, I need to raise my hand and ask if we could reread the page.)

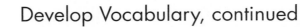
Develop Vocabulary, continued

DAY 3

Recall
Who does the dormouse meet?
(a squirrel)

- The squirrel's nest is in the treetops. Why can't the dormouse stay here?

Develop Vocabulary winter

A squirrel gathers leaves
high in a tree.
He makes his nest warm
for the cold winter weather.

But a nest in the treetops
is too high for a dormouse.
The dormouse looks up,
then scurries by.

nest

6

7

Big Book, pp. 6–7

Guide Comprehension, continued

DAY 4

Wh- **question**
Why does the squirrel gather leaves? (The squirrel gathers leaves because he is making a warm nest for the winter.)

Wh- question

Who does the dormouse meet next? (a queen wasp)

- The queen wasp stays in a crack under a tree stump. What other insect could fit in a crack in a tree stump?

stump

A queen wasp sleeps
under an oak stump.
She has squeezed through
a crack in the rotten wood.

But a crack in an oak stump
is too small for a dormouse.
The dormouse looks in,
then scurries by.

8   9

Big Book, pp. 8–9

Open-ended

How do you know this place is too small for the dormouse? (The dormouse is little, but she is still too big to squeeze through the small crack in the stump.)

Develop Vocabulary, continued

DAY 3

Distancing

The dormouse meets a toad. Why doesn't she stop here? (**It's too wet.**)

• The toad needs to keep his skin wet. What other animals must stay wet?

A golden-eyed toad sleeps under a stone.
It is muddy and wet and the toad's skin is cold.

But it's too wet for a dormouse under a stone.
The dormouse looks in, then scurries by.

10   11

Big Book, pp. 10–11

Guide Comprehension, continued

DAY 4

Sequence • *Wh-* question

Which animal does the dormouse meet first? Who does she meet after that? (The dormouse meets the squirrel first. Then she meets the wasp. Now she meets the toad.) If children have trouble answering the question, then walk through the pages together to review the order.

Wh- question

What kind of animal is this? **(a bear)**

- The dormouse meets a sleeping bear.
  Where does the bear sleep?

A mother brown bear
sleeps in a den.
She is furry and warm.
She stretches and yawns.

den

The dormouse looks in.
The bear's teeth are huge!
The dormouse trembles ...
then scurries by.

12

13

Big Book, pp. 12–13

Open-ended • Inferential

What do you think the bear would do if it
woke up when the dormouse was in the den?
(I think the bear might growl at the dormouse.)

Develop Vocabulary, continued

Open-ended

Where do bats live? (in a cave)

- Bats live in a cave during the day and come out at night. What would you do if you were awake all night?

Develop Vocabulary cave

cave

Bats hang in a cave
and cling to the rock.
They huddle together
and sleep through the winter.

The cave is damp and dark.
It's too cold for a dormouse.
The dormouse looks in,
then scurries by.

14   15

Big Book, pp. 14–15

Guide Comprehension, continued

Inferential

Why do you think the bats huddle together? (I think the bats huddle together to keep warm.)

Distancing

Where do the rabbits live? (in an underground burrow)

- The rabbits live in an underground burrow to stay warm. What do you do to stay warm?

Develop Vocabulary burrow

A family of rabbits
hop into their burrow.
They live underground
when the weather is cold.
But there are too many rabbits
to make room for a dormouse.

burrow

The dormouse
looks in,
then scurries by.

16   17

Big Book, pp. 16–17

Open-ended

How are the dormouse and the rabbits alike? How are they different? (The dormouse and the rabbits are alike because they are both furry and little. They are different because rabbits have big ears and they hop. The dormouse has little ears and she scurries.)

Develop Vocabulary, continued

Recall
Why does the dormouse hide?
(The owl is hunting.)

DAY 3

- The owl is hunting because he is hungry. What is he hunting for?

An owl
with sharp claws
flies over the meadow.
He is hungry
and watchful.
He is hunting
for mice.

The owl swoops!
The dormouse
hides in a bush.

Where can she find
a safe bed
for the winter?

18   19

Big Book, pp. 18–19

Guide Comprehension, continued

DAY 4

Sequence • *Wh-* question
Who does the dormouse meet
before the owl? (The dormouse
meets the rabbits before the owl.)

Open-ended

What does the dormouse see now? (a deer)

- The dormouse sees a deer in the meadow. The deer's coat gets thicker to keep her warm. What happens to her coat in the summer?

Expand Vocabulary coat

A deer comes to the meadow.
She nibbles the grass.
Her coat has grown thick
for the cold winter weather.

The dormouse shivers in the wind,
then scurries by.

20   21

Big Book, pp. 20–21

Open-ended

Why do you think the deer's coat grows thick in the winter? (The deer's coat grows thick to keep her warm in the winter.) What do you think happens to her coat in the summer?

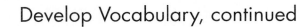
Develop Vocabulary, continued

DAY 3

Wh- question

What two kinds of animals do you see here? **(bees and ants)**

- Bees live in hives, and ants live in nests. What are the names of their homes?

A storm is coming.
The sky has turned black.

Bees fly home
to their hive.

hive

Ants run to their nest.

The dormouse waits
under a branch
for the storm to pass by.
Where can she find
a safe bed for the winter?

22

23

Big Book, pp. 22–23

Guide Comprehension, continued

DAY 4

Sequence • *Wh-* question

Why do the bees and the ants go to their homes? (The sky has turned black. A storm is coming.)

Distancing

What does the dormouse see here? **(a snake)**

- The dormouse is afraid of the snake. Tell me what the snake looks like.

A snake slides through the grass.
He has hungry black eyes.
He stares at the dormouse.
His tongue flicks in and out.

The dormouse
is trapped.
She's too scared
to move.

24

25

Big Book, pp. 24–25

Open-ended

Look at the picture of the snake. Why do you think the dormouse is afraid of the snake? (I think the dormouse is afraid of the snake because he looks really hungry and mean.) If you were the dormouse, what would you do?

Develop Vocabulary, continued

DAY 3

Open-ended

What is about to happen in this picture? (a storm)

- How does the snake act before the storm begins? What does the snake do after the thunder rumbles and the lightning flashes?

The snake slithers closer. His forked tongue comes nearer.

The snake stops for a second, then shoots into the grass.

BOOM!
Thunder rumbles.
CRACK!
Lightning flashes.

26

27

Big Book, pp. 26–27

Guide Comprehension, continued

DAY 4

Recall

What sound does the thunder make? What sound does the lightning make? (The thunder goes BOOM! The lightning goes CRACK!)

Wh- question

Where is the dormouse? (in a hole in a tree trunk)

- The dormouse crawls in a hole in a tree trunk. Why is she safe and dry?

The dormouse runs
through the meadow.
Her heart pounds like a drum.
She climbs up a tree trunk.

tree trunk

She crawls into a hole.
She finds a place
that is safe and dry!

28

29

Big Book, pp. 28–29

Wh- question

Why is the dormouse's heart pounding?
(The dormouse's heart is pounding because she is really scared.)

Develop Vocabulary, continued

DAY 3

Wh- question

The little dormouse finds a safe, warm place. Where is it? (in the tree hole)

- The dormouse finds a bed in the tree hole. What will she do now?

Snow falls on the meadow.
The ground is
frozen and hard.
Snug in the tree hole,
the dormouse is sleeping.
Her long, fluffy tail
is wrapped tightly
around her.

Her search is over.
The dormouse is safe.
At last she has found
her bed for the winter!

30

31

Big Book, pp. 30–31

Guide Comprehension, continued

DAY 4

Distancing

Why do you think the dormouse rolls up in a ball? (I think the dormouse is rolled up because she wants to stay warm.)

Open-ended

This page shows us all the places the dormouse goes. Where is she at the beginning of the story? **(the meadow)**

- The dormouse starts in the meadow. Name the places the dormouse visits.

Continue with DAY **3**
Conventions p. 47

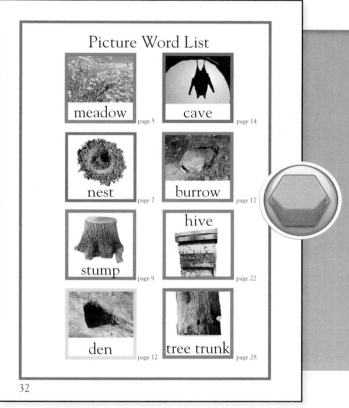

Big Book, p. 32

Sequence • Recall

Where does the dormouse begin? Where does she end up? **(She begins in the meadow and ends up in a hole in a tree trunk.)**

Skip to DAY **4**
Conventions p. 48

Objectives
- Review adjectives for sizes and numbers.
- Dictate or write a caption.

Conventions
Adjectives for Numbers and Sizes

Review

Remind children of what they learned about adjectives for numbers and sizes. Words for numbers and sizes are describing words, or adjectives. They tell more about a person, animal, place, or thing.

Display a calendar. How many days are in a week? There are seven days in a week. *Seven* describes how many days. Size words such as *small, tall, little,* and *big* are adjectives too. What two adjectives are in the phrase *three little pigs? Three* is an adjective for a number and *little* is an adjective for a size.

Guide practice

Write the following phrases on the board.

> **nine tiny puppies**
> **two small houses**
> **eight tall flowers**
> **one big dog**

Read the first phrase and point to the word *nine.* How many puppies are there? There are *nine.* What size are the puppies? They are *tiny.* The word *nine* is an adjective for a number, and the word *tiny* is an adjective for a size. Read the other phrases.

Write the phrases on the board again, this time leaving a blank for one of the adjectives. Point to the phrase _____ *tiny puppies.* Let's think of an adjective for a number we can write on this line. Repeat the routine with the other phrases, replacing either the adjective for number or for size.

Team Talk Pair children and have them take turns saying phrases that have adjectives for numbers and sizes.

On their own

Use *Reader's and Writer's Notebook,* p. 137, for practice reading, writing, and saying adjectives for sizes and numbers.

Daily Fix-It

Use the Daily Fix-It for more conventions practice.

Reader's and Writer's Notebook, p. 137

Writing
Caption

Teach Display simple pictures you have drawn of an igloo, an apartment building, and a teepee. Let's look at the pictures I drew of different places people live. Pictures can show us the size or shape of something. This picture shows a teepee. It is shaped like a triangle. This picture shows an apartment building. It is tall. Pictures can show us what things look like that we may not have seen before. This picture shows an igloo. The top of the igloo is round.

Model Draw or display a picture of a tree house. This is another kind of house. What makes this house different? It's in a tree. This is a tree house. This picture shows where this type of house is located. I am going to write a caption for this picture. A *caption* is a word next to a picture that tells about the picture. Write *tree house* under the picture. Read the caption. This caption tells me that this is a picture of a tree house.

Guide practice Have children provide captions for the other pictures you drew. Write their captions under the pictures.

Independent writing Have children turn to p. 138 of *Reader's and Writer's Notebook.* Have them draw a picture of an animal home. Then have them write or dictate a caption for their picture on the lines below it.

Reader's and Writer's Notebook, p. 138

Daily Handwriting

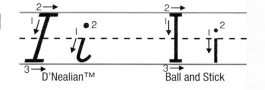

D'Nealian™   Ball and Stick

Write *Isis* and *sip* on the board. Review correct letter formation of uppercase *I* and lowercase *i*.

Have children write *Isis* and *sip* on their Write-On Boards. Remind children to use proper left-to-right and top-to-bottom progression and proper spacing between letters when writing *I* and *i*.

Differentiated Instruction

 A Advanced

Adjectives for Numbers and Sizes Use objects to show adjectives for numbers and sizes. Bring in five different sized pencils, some short and some long. Have children sort the pencils into a *short* or *long* category. Then count the number of pencils for each category. Have children give phrases to tell about the pencils: *two short pencils.*

Academic Vocabulary

caption word or words next to a picture that tells about the picture

Daily Fix-It

a Dormouse lives in a tree hole.
A dormouse lives in a tree hole.

This week's practice sentences appear on Teacher Resources DVD-ROM.

Listening and Speaking
Give a Description

Review

Remind children that when they give a description, they use words that tell about a person, place, animal, or thing. Tell children that when they share their ideas, they need to speak clearly and loudly so everyone can hear and understand them.

Model

AlphaBuddy is going to give a description. **Have AlphaBuddy say:** There is a bird outside the window. Do you know which window? Do you know which bird? **Now have AlphaBuddy say:** There is a pretty red bird outside the small, round window. Now we know where to look.

Guide practice

Have children turn to p. 109 of *My Skills Buddy.* I see a picture of a dog. Do you know which dog I am talking about? What can I say to help you understand which dog I am talking about? Discuss with children how they can describe the dogs in order to distinguish the pictures from each other. Then have them discuss how they can describe the two clocks. Use the Listening and Speaking bullets on p. 108 of *My Skills Buddy* in your discussion.

My Skills Buddy, p. 109

Independent practice

Have children think about the animals in *A Bed for the Winter* and decide which animal is their favorite. Have each child come to the front of the class to share one or two descriptive details about his or her favorite animal without saying the animal's name. Ask the other children to figure out the mystery animals from the descriptions. Have each child share different details when it is his or her turn to speak. Refer children to their Rules for Listening and Speaking from pp. 1–2 of *Reader's and Writer's Notebook.* Tell children to speak clearly and loudly and to use complete sentences in their descriptions.

Name _____

🔊 Speaking Rules

1. Speak clearly.
2. Tell only important ideas.
3. Choose your words carefully.
4. Take turns speaking.
5. Speak one at a time.

2 Listening and Speaking Rules

Reader's and Writer's Notebook, p. 2

Get Ready For Grade 1

Be a Good Speaker

1. Speak clearly and loudly.
2. Tell only important ideas.
3. Choose your words carefully.
4. Take turns speaking.
5. Speak one at a time.

Differentiated Instruction

 Strategic Intervention

Access Content If children have difficulty understanding how to describe an animal, prompt them with questions such as these: Is it big or little? Is it smooth or furry? Help children use their answers in their descriptions.

Academic Vocabulary

description words that tell more about a person, place, animal, or thing

Objectives
- Review skills learned and practiced today.

Wrap Up Your Day

✔ **Concept Talk** Today we read about a dormouse trying to find a winter bed. What kinds of beds does the dormouse find? Does the dormouse like the beds she finds?

✔ **Respond to Literature** Today we also read about getting a house for a fish named Pip. What kind of house does Pip get?

✔ **Conventions** Have children look at the front and back of their hands. Let's think of some adjectives to describe our hands. Ask children for number and size descriptions. How many fingers do you have? Are your hands big or little?

✔ **Homework Idea** Have children draw a picture of something they find at home with /i/ in its name.

Preview DAY 4

Tomorrow we will read about one of our Trucktown friends.

Extend Your Day!

Science
What Do We Do in the Four Seasons?
Materials: *Patterns* on *Teacher Resources DVD-ROM,* seasonal props and clothing; drawing paper divided into four sections labeled *Spring, Summer, Fall,* and *Winter;* scissors; glue; crayons

Name Characteristics and Activities for Different Seasons The story we've been reading, *A Bed for the Winter,* is about which of the four seasons? Who remembers the other three seasons? Review characteristics of each season, asking children to name some differences between opposite seasons and some activities appropriate to each season.

Display a paper divided into four sections. I'm going to show you a picture, and I want you to tell me what it is, what season it belongs in, and how you know that.

Pass out patterns and have children color and cut them out. Guide them to glue the pictures in appropriate boxes.

Comprehension
The Dormouse's Trip
Materials: *A Bed for the Winter,* mural paper, crayons

Make a Sequence Take a picture walk through *A Bed for the Winter* with children. On the board, record each home the dormouse sees before finding a place for herself. Divide a long roll of paper into nine sections. Divide children into nine groups. Instruct the groups to draw one animal and its home. When finished, display the mural and review the sequence.

Phonics
Letter People

 **s i p**

Build Words Write the following letters on large cards: *a, c, i, m, p, s, t.* Have seven children come to the front of the group. Give each child a letter card. Tell the other children you are going to use the "letter people" to build words. Listen to this word: *sip.* What letters do we need to build the word *sip?* The first sound is /s/. What is the letter for /s/? Yes, *s* is the letter for /s/. Have the "*s* person" move to the front of the group. Continue with the other letters. Let's blend the sounds of the letters together to read the word: /s/ /i/ /p/, *sip.* Continue building the following words: *mat, tap, sat, tip, sit, pit, cat, pat.*

Objectives

- Discuss the concept to develop oral language.
- Build oral vocabulary.

Today at a Glance

Oral Vocabulary
hive, den

Phonemic Awareness
Initial /k/

Phonics
/k/ Spelled *Cc*

Comprehension
◉ Sequence

Conventions
Adjectives for Opposites

Writing
Extend the Concept

Vocabulary
Sequence Words

TRUCKTOWN on Reading Street

Start your engines!

- Display "Rock-a-Bye Mixer" and say the rhyme together.
- Have children sway in rhythm with the rhyme as they recite it.
- When children master the rhythm, have them march around the room as they say the rhyme.

Truckery Rhymes

Concept Talk

Question of the Week

 What kind of home does an animal need?

Build concepts

Write the question of the week on the board. Read the question as you track the print. Tell children to respond in complete sentences. Display Sing with Me Chart 11B.

Listen for Amazing Words

We are going to sing "Little Mouse" again. Listen for the Amazing Words *hive* and *den.* Sing the song several times to the tune of "Twinkle, Twinkle, Little Star." Tell children to sing with you. Have them clap when they hear the Amazing Word *hive* or *den.*

💿 Sing with Me Audio

Little Mouse

Hurry, scurry, little mouse,
Where can you find a safe, warm house?
Not in the meadow, not in the bear's den,
Not in a bee hive where bees sleep in,
Hurry, scurry, little mouse,
Where can you find a safe, warm house?

Talk with Me/Sing with Me Chart 11B

ELL **Produce Oral Language** Use the Day 4 instruction on ELL Poster 11 to extend and enrich language.

ELL Poster 11

Oral Vocabulary
Amazing Words

Amazing Words

nest   meadow
stump   tree trunk
hive   den

Teach Amazing Words

> **Amazing Words** — **Oral Vocabulary Routine**
>
> **1** **Introduce the Word** When a storm comes, bees fly back to their *hive*. A *hive* is a shelter where bees live. What's our new Amazing Word for a home for bees? Say it with me: *hive*.
>
> **2** **Demonstrate** *Many bees live together in a hive. Sometimes they make their hive in a tree.*
>
> Repeat steps 1 and 2.
>
> **Introduce the Word** All winter the bear sleeps in its *den*. A *den* is a shelter where a bear makes its home. What's our new Amazing Word for a bear's home? Say it with me: *den*
>
> **Demonstrate** *A den can be found dug into a hillside or under the roots of a tree.*
>
> **3** **Apply** Tell children to use *hive* and *den* in complete sentences. Have them illustrate the words.

Routines Flip Chart

Use Amazing Words

To reinforce the concept and the Amazing Words, have children supply the appropriate Amazing Word for each sentence.

From the flower the bee flew to its _____. (hive)

The bear was sound asleep in its _____. (den)

Differentiated Instruction

SI **Strategic Intervention**
Sentence Production If children's oral sentences lack subject-verb agreement, say each sentence correctly and have children repeat it.

Objectives
• Review /k/ spelled *Cc*.

Check Phonemic Awareness

SUCCESS PREDICTOR

Phonemic Awareness
Review /k/

Picture Card

Review

Display the *carrot* Picture Card. This is a *carrot*. *Carrot* begins with /k/. What sound does *carrot* begin with? Continue the routine with the following Picture Cards: *can, cap, cat, caterpillar.* Then display the *rock* Picture Card. This is a *rock*. Where do you hear /k/ in the word *rock? Rock* ends with /k/. What sound does *rock* end with?

I am going to say three words. Tell me which words begin with /k/: *cat, canoe, pig. Cat* and *canoe* begin with /k/. *Pig* begins with /p/. Continue the activity with the following sets of words: *camel, moose, caterpillar; cup, cow, milk; chameleon, iguana, cactus; peas, carrots, corn; cab, car, taxi.*

Picture Card

Corrective feedback

If... children cannot discriminate /k/,
then... have them say /k/ several times.

When you say /k/, the back of your tongue is humped and touching the top of your mouth. Have children practice saying /k/, and then repeat the discrimination activity.

Phonics
/k/ Spelled Cc

Review

Display the *Cc* Alphabet Card. This is a *cactus.* *Cactus* begins with /k/. What letter spells the sound /k/? Yes, the letter *c.*

Write the word *cat* on the board. Help me blend this word. Listen as I say each sound: /k/ /a/ /t/. Say it with me: /k/ /a/ /t/. Now let's blend the sounds together to read the word: /k/ /a/ /t/, *cat.* What is the word? (*cat*) Let's try one more. Write *cap* on the board and repeat the routine.

Alphabet Card

Don't Wait Until Friday

MONITOR PROGRESS — Check Phonemic Awareness

Phoneme Segmentation Practice segmenting the sounds in these words after I say each word.

cap	cat	tap	sat	Sam	pat

If... children cannot segment the sounds,

then... use the small-group Strategic Intervention lesson, p. DI•72, to reteach segmentation skills.

Continue to monitor children's progress using other instructional opportunities during the week so that children can be successful with the Day 5 Assessment. See the Skills Trace on p. 420.

Day 1	Day 2	Day 3	Day 4	Day 5
Check Phonemic Awareness	Check Sound-Spelling/ Retelling	Check Word Reading	Check Phonemic Awareness	Check Oral Vocabulary

Success Predictor

Differentiated Instruction

 Advanced

Support Phonemic Awareness Have children look around the classroom and find things that begin with /k/.

Phonemic Awareness

Success Predictor

Objectives
- Spell words.
- Blend and segment words.
- Read decodable text.
- Read high-frequency words.

Spelling
↻ /i/ Spelled *Ii*

ROUTINE Spell Words

Spell words

1. **Review Sound-Spellings** Display the *Ii* Alphabet Card. This is an *igloo. Igloo* begins with /i/. What is the letter we learned for /i/? (*i*) Continue the routine with the following letters: *Aa, Mm, Ss, Tt, Pp, Cc.*

2. **Model** Today we are going to spell some words. Listen to the three sounds in *tip:* /t/ /i/ /p/.

- What is the first sound in *tip?* (/t/) What is the letter for /t/? (*t*) Write *t* on the board.

- What is the middle sound you hear? (/i/) What is the letter for /i/? (*i*) Write *i* on the board.

- What is the last sound you hear? (/p/) What is the letter for /p/? (*p*) Write *p* on the board.

- Point to *tip.* Help me blend the sound of each letter together to read this word: /t/ /i/ /p/. The word is *tip.* Repeat the modeling with the word *sit.*

3. **Guide Practice** Now let's spell some words together. Listen to this word: /s/ /i/ /p/. What is the first sound in *sip?* (/s/) What is the letter for /s/? (*s*) Write *s* on the board. Now you write *s* on your paper. What is the middle sound in *sip?* (/i/) What is the letter for /i/? (*i*) Write *i* on the board. Now you write *i* on your paper. What is the last sound in *sip?* (/p/) What is the letter for /p/? (*p*) Write *p* on the board. Now you write *p* on your paper. Now we can blend the sounds of the letters together to read the word: /s/ /i/ /p/. What is the word? (*sip*) Continue spell and blend practice with the following words: *Tim, bit.*

4. **On Your Own** This time I am going to say a word. I want you to write it on your paper. Remember, first, say the word slowly in your head and then write the letter for each sound. Listen carefully. Write the word *pit.* Give children time to write the word. How do you spell the word *pit?* Listen to the sounds: /p/ /i/ /t/. The first sound is /p/. What is the letter for /p/? Did you write *p* on your paper? What is the letter for /i/? Did you write *i* on your paper? What is the letter for /t/? Did you write *t* on your paper? Name the letters in *pit. Pit* is spelled *p, i, t.* Continue the activity with the following words: *Sis, tap, mat, it.*

Routines Flip Chart

Get Set, Roll! Reader 11
Practice /k/ Spelled Cc

Review Review the high-frequency words *he, for, is,* and *a.* Have children find each word on the Word Wall.

Teach rebus words Write the word *Pete* on the board. This is the word *Pete.* Name the letters with me: *P, e, t, e, Pete.* Continue with the words *dig* and *building.* Look for the words *Pete, dig,* and *building* in the story we read today. A picture above the word will help you read it.

Read Get Set, Roll! Reader 11 Today we will read a story about our friend Payloader Pete. Point to the title of the story. What is the title of the story? (*Pete Can Dig*) We will read words with /i/ in this story.

Use the routine for reading decodable books found in the Routines Flip Chart to read Get Set, Roll! Reader 11.

Get Set, Roll! Reader 11

Differentiated Instruction

SI Strategic Intervention
Activate Prior Knowledge To reinforce the meaning of the rebus words, have children act out how to *dig.* Then have them draw a picture of a *building.*

Small Group Time

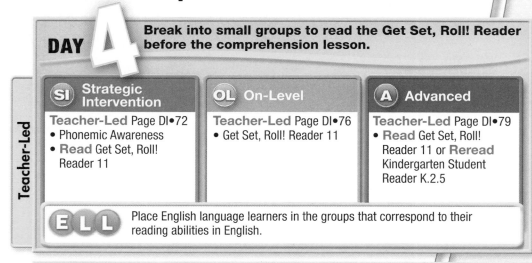

DAY 4 Break into small groups to read the Get Set, Roll! Reader before the comprehension lesson.

Teacher-Led

SI Strategic Intervention	**OL** On-Level	**A** Advanced
Teacher-Led Page DI•72 • Phonemic Awareness • **Read** Get Set, Roll! Reader 11	Teacher-Led Page DI•76 • Get Set, Roll! Reader 11	Teacher-Led Page DI•79 • **Read** Get Set, Roll! Reader 11 or **Reread** Kindergarten Student Reader K.2.5

ELL Place English language learners in the groups that correspond to their reading abilities in English.

Practice Stations
• Visit the Let's Write! Station
• Visit the Read for Meaning Station

Independent Activities
• Read independently
• Audio Text of the Big Book
• *Reader's and Writer's Notebook*

English Language Learners
Frontload Reader Do a picture walk with children to preview the reader before starting the routine.

Comprehension
↻ Sequence

Practice sequence

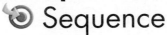

Have children turn to pp. 94–95 of *My Skills Buddy*. As you look at the pictures, remind children that in most stories things happen in a certain order: first, next, last. This is called the sequence.

Team Talk Pair children and have them take turns telling the sequence of what they have done today. Remind them to use the sequence words *first, next,* and *last.*

My Skills Buddy, pp. 94–95

Classify and Categorize

Review

Review Classify and Categorize with children.

Remember, we can say that things in a group belong together if they are alike in some way. Good readers look for ways that things are alike when they are reading to help them understand the selection.

More practice

For more practice with classify and categorize, use *Reader's and Writer's Notebook,* p. 139.

Reader's and Writer's Notebook, p. 139

Third Read—Big Book
A Bed for the Winter

Guide comprehension

Display *A Bed for the Winter.* The animals in this selection are alike in many ways. We can group the animals by things that are the same about them.

- How are the dormouse and the snake alike? (They are both looking for a bed for the winter.)

- How are the squirrel and the dormouse alike? (They both live in the trees.)

Reread *A Bed for the Winter*. Return to p. 459. Follow the Day 4 arrow and use the Guide Comprehension notes to give children the opportunity to gain a more complete understanding of the selection.

DAY **2**
Read for enjoyment

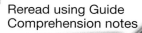
DAY **3**
Reread using Develop Vocabulary notes

DAY **4**
Reread using Guide Comprehension notes

Differentiated Instruction

 Strategic Intervention

Access Content Give pairs of children 3 markers and 3 crayons. Have them sort the items into 2 groups (crayons and markers). Then have them tell why they put the items into those groups.

Objectives

- Identify adjectives for opposites.
- Practice adjectives for opposites.
- Write about or dictate experiences that connect to ideas to *A Bed for the Winter*.

Conventions
Adjectives for Opposites

Review

Remind children of what they learned about adjectives. We have been talking about adjectives, or describing words. Adjectives are words that tell more about people, places, animals, and things. Some adjectives have opposites.

I know the opposite of *dark* is *light*. The opposite of *small* is *big*. These words are adjectives that tell opposites.

Guide practice

Have children identify opposite pairs. What other pairs of words can you think of that are opposites? Write children's responses in a two-column chart. Have children echo read the list with you.

On their own

Use *Reader's and Writer's Notebook,* p. 140, for more practice with adjectives for opposites.

Daily Fix-It

Use the Daily Fix-It exercise for more conventions practice.

Reader's and Writer's Notebook, p. 140

Writing
Extend the Concept: Text to Self

Discuss homes

We just read a story about animal homes. The animals in the story have a home and a bed that fit them. All the animal homes or beds are different. Like these animals, we have homes and beds that fit us.

Ask children to think about their homes and beds and how they are a good fit for them. Talk about what makes their homes and beds good ones for them.

Guide practice

Use children's contributions to the discussion to write sentences.

> **My home . . .**   **is small and cozy.**
>   **has all of my toys.**
>
> **My bed . . .**   **has four pillows.**
>   **is in my own room.**

Encourage children to help you write more sentences. Have them read the sentences with you.

Independent writing

Have children write or dictate their own sentences about their home, or copy one of the sentences from the board. Encourage them to read their sentences to the class. Have them draw a picture to go along with the sentence.

Daily Handwriting

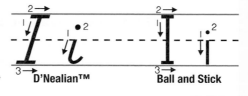

Write uppercase *I* and lowercase *i* on the board. Review correct letter formation with children.

Have children write a row of uppercase *I* and a row of lowercase *i* on their Write-On Boards. Remind them to use proper left-to-right and top-to-bottom progression when writing *I* and *i*.

Vocabulary
Sequence Words

| first | second | next | last |

Teach

Write the words *first, second, next,* and *last* on the board. Point to each word as you read it. These are words that tell the sequence, or order, of things. Have children turn to p. 108 of *My Skills Buddy.* Look at these pictures. What does the boy do *first?* What does he do *second?* What happens *next?* What happens *last?* Then discuss the second Vocabulary bullet on the page. Have children use the words *first, second, next,* and *last* in their responses.

My Skills Buddy, p. 108

Team Talk Pair children and have them make up a story about an animal together. Have them alternate sentences using the words *first, second, next,* and *last.*

Wrap Up Your Day

✔ **Oral Language** Sing "Little Mouse" with me. Clap when you hear an Amazing Word—*nest, meadow, stump, tree trunk, hive, den.*

✔ **Phonemic Awareness** I am going to read two sentences. Clap when you hear words that begin with /k/: *Carl the chameleon eats carrots and corn on the court. Carolyn Cow counts cars.*

✔ **Homework Idea** Have children draw a picture of two things that are opposites.

Preview DAY 5

Tell children that tomorrow they will review some of the books and stories they have read this week.

Extend Your Day!

Social Studies
Last Week, This Week, Next Week

Materials: chart paper, calendar, drawing paper, crayons or markers

Describe Activities Draw a three-column chart with the headings *Last Week, This Week,* and *Next Week.* Using the calendar, demonstrate how to find last week by looking at the row of squares above the current week, and next week by looking at the row of squares below the current week. Have children tell what they have done, are doing, and are looking forward to doing. Write their responses on the chart. Have them choose one sentence to copy or illustrate.

Illustrate the Year Flip the calendar back to the first month of school. Ask children what the class did that month. Make a list on the board. Have children copy a sentence and illustrate it, writing the name of the month at the top of the page. Do the same with the next month. Save children's pages and combine them at the end of the year for individual memory books.

Last week it rained.

Science
Cycle of Seasons

Discuss Animals in Winter Page through *A Bed for the Winter* and discuss how the different animals in the book spend the winter.

When is it time for the animals to wake up? What season comes after spring? What season comes after summer? What season comes after fall? And then what happens?

Let's pretend we are animals waking up in the spring. What type of animal would you like to be? We've been asleep for a long time. What might we do first?

Science
Shoe Sort

Classify and Categorize Sit in a circle and ask children to take off one of their shoes. Put the shoes in the center of the circle. Discuss the different attributes of the shoes (type of closure, color, material). Decide on an attribute and sort shoes into appropriate piles.

When all the shoes have been sorted, return them to the middle of the circle.

Objectives
- Review the concepts.
- Build oral vocabulary.

Today at a Glance

Oral Vocabulary
nest, meadow, stump, tree trunk, hive, den

Phonemic Awareness
◉ Initial and Medial /i/

Phonics
◉ /i/ Spelled *Ii*

Comprehension
◉ Sequence

Conventions
Adjectives for Opposites

Writing
This Week We…

Check Oral Vocabulary
SUCCESS PREDICTOR

TRUCKTOWN
on Reading Street

Start your engines!

- Display "Rock-a-Bye Mixer" and lead children in saying the rhyme several times with you.
  - Have half the group recite the rhyme while the other half acts like Melvin.
  - Then have the groups change roles.

Truckery Rhymes

Concept Wrap Up

 Question of the Week
What kind of home does an animal need?

Listen for Amazing Words

Write the question of the week on the board. Track the print as you read it. Have children use the Amazing Words in their responses (*nest, meadow, stump, tree trunk, hive, den*). Display Sing with Me Chart 11B. Let's sing "Little Mouse." I want you to listen for the Amazing Words we learned this week. Say them with me: *nest, meadow, stump, tree trunk, hive, den.* Sing the song several times to the tune of "Twinkle, Twinkle, Little Star." Discuss the different kinds of animal homes and why animals need special homes. Follow the agreed-upon rules for discussion, including speaking one at a time.

Little Mouse

Hurry, scurry, little mouse,
Where can you find a safe, warm house?
Not in the meadow, not in the bear's den,
Not in a bee hive where bees sleep in,
Hurry, scurry, little mouse,
Where can you find a safe, warm house?

Sing with Me Chart 11B

 Sing with Me Audio

E L L **Check Concepts and Language** Use the Day 5 instruction on ELL Poster 11 to monitor children's understanding of the lesson concept.

E L L Poster 11

Oral Vocabulary
Amazing Words

Amazing Words

nest	meadow
stump	tree trunk
hive	den

Review

Let's Talk Display Talk with Me Chart 11A. We learned six new Amazing Words this week. Let's say the Amazing Words as I point to the pictures on the chart. Point to each photo and give children a chance to say the appropriate Amazing Word before offering it.

Have children supply the appropriate Amazing Word to complete each sentence.

> **The bees flew out of the _____.** (hive)
>
> **The _____ was filled with bright flowers.** (meadow)
>
> **I couldn't wrap my arms around the _____.** (tree trunk)
>
> **The bear went in its _____ to hibernate.** (den)
>
> **We could hear birds chirping in the _____.** (nest)
>
> **After my dad cut the tree down, the _____ was left.** (stump)

Talk with Me/Sing with Me Chart 11A

It's Friday

MONITOR PROGRESS | **Check Oral Vocabulary**

Demonstrate Word Knowledge Monitor the Amazing Words by asking the following questions. Have children use the Amazing Word in their answer.

- **What do birds build in the spring?** (nest)
- **Where might you finding deer eating grass?** (meadow)
- **What are the bees flying in and out of?** (hive)
- **What do squirrels run up and down?** (tree trunk)
- **What do bears sleep in?** (den)
- **What part of the tree is left after you cut the tree down?** (stump)

If... children have difficulty using the Amazing Words,

then... reteach unknown words using the Oral Vocabulary Routine on the Routines Flip Chart.

Day 1	Day 2	Day 3	Day 4	**Day 5**
Check Phonemic Awareness	Check Sound-Spelling/ Retelling	Check Word Reading	Check Phonemic Awareness	**Check Oral Vocabulary**

Success Predictor

Differentiated Instruction

 Strategic Intervention

Match for Meaning Display Talk with Me Chart 11A and draw a simple bird, bee, and bear on the board. Work with children to match the animal with its home. Where does a bird live? Point from the bird drawing to the nest on the chart. A bird lives in a nest. Continue with the other images.

Oral Vocabulary

Success Predictor

Phonemic Awareness Review

↺ /i/

Isolate initial and medial /i/

Display the *iguana* Picture Card. What is the first sound in *iguana*? Say the word with me: *iguana*, /i/ /i/ /i/, *iguana*. Review initial /i/ with the following words: *igloo, inch, insect.*

Display the *six* Picture Card. What is the middle sound in *six*? Say the sounds: /s/ /i/ /ks/. The middle sound is /i/. Continue isolating medial /i/ with the words *tip* and *pit.*

Discriminate medial sounds

I am going to read some words. When you hear /i/ in the word, I want you to point to the tip of your nose. When you hear /a/ in the word, I want you to tap your knee. Let's try the first one together. Listen carefully: *dip.* Do you hear /i/ or /a/ in *dip*? I hear /i/ in *dip* so I am going to point to the tip of my nose. **Continue with the following words:** *jam, bit, cap, bat, dim, yam, hip, wit, cat, him.*

Picture Card

Picture Card

Phonics Review
/i/ Spelled *Ii*

Teach /i/ Ii

Display the *Ii* Alphabet Card. This is an *igloo*. What sound do you hear at the beginning of *igloo*? What letter spells that sound?

High-frequency words

Write the word *he* on the board. This is the word *he*. What is this word? Repeat the routine with *for*.

Apply phonics in familiar text

Let's Reread Have children reread one of the books specific to the target letter sound. You may wish to review the decodable words and high-frequency words that appear in each book prior to rereading.

Alphabet Card

Decodable Reader 11
My Skills Buddy, p. 98

Kindergarten
Student Reader K.2.5

Get Set, Roll!
Reader 11

Differentiated Instruction

SI Strategic Intervention

Connect Sound-Spelling Say words that have either initial /i/ or medial /i/. Have children say where they hear the /i/ sound in the word. Use words such as *mix, wish, igloo,* and *ignore.*

Small Group Time

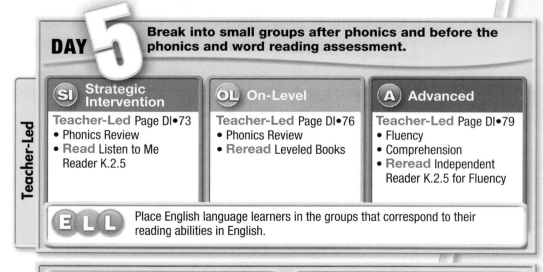

DAY 5

Break into small groups after phonics and before the phonics and word reading assessment.

Teacher-Led

SI Strategic Intervention

Teacher-Led Page DI•73
• Phonics Review
• **Read** Listen to Me Reader K.2.5

OL On-Level

Teacher-Led Page DI•76
• Phonics Review
• **Reread** Leveled Books

A Advanced

Teacher-Led Page DI•79
• Fluency
• Comprehension
• **Reread** Independent Reader K.2.5 for Fluency

ELL Place English language learners in the groups that correspond to their reading abilities in English.

Practice Stations
• Visit the Read for Meaning Station
• Visit the Let's Make Art Station

Independent Activities
• Read independently
• Story Sort
• Concept Talk Video

Objectives
◎ Read words with /i/.
• Read high-frequency words.
• Read sentences.

Assessment
Monitor Progress

/i/ Spelled *Ii*   **Whole Class** Divide a paper into four equal sections for each child. Tell children to draw a picture of something that begins with /i/ or something that has a medial /i/ in each section. Instruct them to label their pictures with the word or the letter *i.*

MONITOR PROGRESS   **Check Word and Sentence Reading**

If... children cannot complete the whole-class assessment,
then... use the Reteach lesson in *First Stop.*

If... you are unsure of a child's grasp of this week's skills,
then... use the assessment below to obtain a clearer evaluation of the child's progress.

/i/ Spelled *Ii* and high-frequency words   **One-on-One** To facilitate individual progress monitoring, assess some children on Day 4 and the rest on Day 5. While individual children are being assessed, the rest of the class can reread this week's books and look for words with /i/.

Word reading   Use the word lists on reproducible p. 497 to assess a child's ability to read words with short *i* and high-frequency words. We are going to read some words. I'll read the first word, and you read the rest. The first word is *sip,* /s/ /i/ /p/. For each child, record any decoding problems.

Sentence reading   Use the sentences on reproducible p. 497 to assess a child's ability to read these words in sentences. Have the child read two sentences aloud. Have each child read different sentences. Start over with sentence one if necessary.

Record scores   Monitor children's accuracy by recording their scores using the Word and Sentence Reading Chart for this unit in *First Stop.*

Read the Words

sip	☐	tip	☐	
he	☐	for	☐	
Tim	☐	sit	☐	
Sis	☐	pit	☐	

Read the Sentences

1. I have a map for Sis.

2. He likes to sit.

3. He likes Tim.

4. I have a cat for Tip.

Note to Teacher: Children read each word. Children read two sentences.

Scoring for Read the Words: Score 1 point for each correct word.

Short i (*sip, Tim, Sis, tip, sit, pit*) _____ /___6___

High-Frequency Words (*he, for*) _____ /___2___

MONITOR PROGRESS
• /i/ Spelled *Ii*
• High-frequency words

Objectives

- Recognize a poem.
- Identify rhythm.
- Make inferences based on illustrations.

My Skills Buddy, pp. 110–111

Let's Practice It!
Nursery Rhyme

Teach

Tell children that today they will listen to a nursery rhyme. A nursery rhyme is a song or poem written especially for children. Review the features of a nursery rhyme with children.

- A nursery rhyme tells a story.
- A nursery rhyme has words that rhyme.
- A nursery rhyme has rhythm. **Rhythm** is a strong beat found in songs and poems.

Have children turn to pp. 110–111 of *My Skills Buddy.* I am going to read you a nursery rhyme called "The House That Jack Built." Look at the pictures as I read. Read the text of "The House That Jack Built." As you read, direct children to look at the appropriate picture.

Guide practice

Discuss the features of a nursery rhyme with children and discuss the bulleted text on *My Skills Buddy* p. 110.

- A nursery rhyme tells a story. This nursery rhyme tells a story about Jack's house. **Direct children to the first picture of Jack by his house.** How does Jack feel about his house? How can you tell? (He looks proud as he stands next to the house he built.)

- A nursery rhyme has words that rhyme. What are the rhyming words in "The House That Jack Built?" (*cat, rat*)

- What are some other words that rhyme with *cat* and *rat*? (*mat, bat, sat, pat*)

- Tell about a time when you made or did something you were proud of, just like Jack is proud of the house he built. (I was very proud of a family picture I drew.)

- A poem has rhythm. Listen to the rhythm of "The House That Jack Built" as I read and clap my hands to the beat. **Reread the poem, clapping your hands to the rhythm. Then reread the nursery rhyme and have children clap to the rhythm with you.**

The House That Jack Built

This is the house that Jack built.

This is the corn
That lay in the house that Jack built.

This is the rat
That smelled the corn
That lay in the house that Jack built.

This is the cat
That spotted the rat
That smelled the corn
That lay in the house that Jack built.

This is the dog
That barked at the cat
That spotted the rat
That smelled the corn
That lay in the house that Jack built.

This is the rain
That fell on the dog
That barked at the cat
That spotted the rat
That smelled the corn
That lay in the house that Jack built.

Comprehension Assessment
Monitor Progress

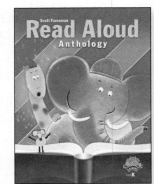

Read Aloud Anthology

Review

Sequence In most stories things happen in a certain order: *first, next, last.* The order in which things happen is called sequence. What do we call the order in which things happen? (sequence)

Good readers listen for the sequence of a story to help them understand the story.

Read "Willy's Winter Rest"

Tell children that you are going to read them a story about a family of dormice getting ready for winter. Ask them to listen for what happens first, next, and last in the selection. Listen carefully while I read you a story. When I'm done, I will ask you to tell me the sequence, or what happens *first, next,* and last. Read "Willy's Winter Rest" on p. 22 of the *Read Aloud Anthology.*

Check sequence

After you read the story, have children tell what happens first, next, and last.

* When autumn comes, what does Papa Dormouse do first to prepare the family for winter? (He finds a place for the family to spend the winter.)

* What does the family do next to prepare for winter? (They bring bark and grass for a nest. They bring berries, grains, and nuts for food.)

* What is the last thing the family does at the end of the story before they go to sleep? (They eat extra food.)

Corrective feedback

If... children cannot identify sequence in text,
then... reteach sequence using the Reteach lesson in *First Stop.*

Assess sequence

Use the blackline master on p. 501. Make one copy for each child. Have children cut out the three scenes and glue them on another sheet of paper in the correct order.

Name _____

Sequence

Put these events from "Willy's Winter Rest" in order.

Note to Teacher: Have children cut out the three scenes and glue them to another sheet of paper in the correct order.

MONITOR
PROGRESS

• Sequence

Objectives
- Review adjectives for opposites.
- Write a poem.

Conventions
Adjectives for Opposites

Review   Remind children of what they learned about adjectives. Adjectives are describing words. They are words that tell more about people, animals, places, and things. Some adjectives are opposites.

Model   Display a Picture Card and describe it with an adjective that has an opposite. For example, show the *alligator* Picture Card. This is a picture of a *small* alligator. The opposite of *small* is *big*. Then show the *elephant* Picture Card. This is a picture of a *young* elephant. The opposite of *young* is *old*.

Guide practice   Continue this exercise using several other Picture Cards, asking children to determine opposite adjectives for images on the cards. Then choose a card and see if a child can use an adjective to describe it and tell its opposite.

On their own   Have children locate an object in the classroom. Then have them draw that object two ways, using adjectives for opposites. For example, children can draw a *long* pencil and a *short* pencil. Have children write or dictate a label for their pictures. Then have children show their drawings to the class.

Daily Fix-It   Use the Daily Fix-It exercise for more conventions practice.

Writing
This Week We...

Review

Display *A Bed for the Winter,* Sing with Me Chart 11B, Phonics Songs and Rhymes Chart 11, Decodable Reader 11 from *My Skills Buddy,* Kindergarten Student Reader K.2.5, and Get Set, Roll! Reader 11. This week we learned about animal homes. We read new books, and we sang some new songs. Which book or song was your favorite? Let's share our ideas with each other.

Team Talk Pair children and have them take turns telling which book or song was their favorite and why.

Model writing a poem

Today we will write a poem about the animals and winter homes in our songs and stories. Write the poem below on the board. Let's think about the animals and the winter homes from our story *A Bed for the Winter.* Model how to complete the poem by filling in the blanks with information about animals and their homes.

> The _____ lives in a _____.
> The _____ lives in a tree.
> But at home with my family,
> This is the best home for me.

Guide practice

Work with children to make a list of animals and their homes. Have them use the words on the list to complete the poem. Have children echo read the poem each time it is completed.

On their own

Have children illustrate an animal home and label it with a word or sentence. Collect their illustrations to create a class book.

Daily Handwriting

Write uppercase *I* and lowercase *i* on the board. Review correct letter formation with children.

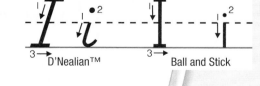

D'Nealian™   Ball and Stick

Have children write a row of uppercase *I* and a row of lowercase *i* on their Write-On Boards. Remind them to use proper left-to-right and top-to-bottom progression.

Differentiated Instruction

SI Strategic Intervention

Support Writing Display parts of *A Bed for the Winter* to assist children with generating ideas for the poem.

Daily Fix-It

he has a sad face
He has a sad face.

This week's practice sentences appear on Teacher Resources DVD-ROM.

ELL

English Language Learners

Poster Preview Prepare children for next week by using Week 6 ELL Poster number 12. Read the Poster Talk-Through to introduce the concept and vocabulary. Ask children to identify and describe objects and actions in the art.

Wrap Up Your Week!

Question of the Week
What kind of home does an animal need?

Amazing Words

You've learned
| 0 | 0 | 6 |
words this week!

You've learned
| 0 | 6 | 6 |
words this year!

Illustrate sequence

This week we talked about animal homes.

- Make a two-column chart like the one pictured or use Graphic Organizer 4 and fill it with children's responses.
- Have children choose an animal from the chart and draw a picture of the animal in its home.
- Have children write or dictate a sentence about their picture.
- Then have children arrange the pictures to show the order of animal homes the dormouse visited in *A Bed for the Winter*.

Animal	Good Home
Dormouse	
Squirrel	
Bee	
Toad	
Bear	

Next Week's Question
How are real and make-believe plants alike and different?

Discuss next week's question. Talk with children about how plants can be an animal's home.

Preview NEXT WEEK

Tell children that next week they will read about real and make-believe plants.

Extend Your Day!

Science
Animal Characteristics

Materials: Big Book *A Bed for the Winter*, chart paper, markers or crayons

Compare and Contrast Animals Display pp. 12–13 of *A Bed for the Winter*. Have children describe, one at a time, how the dormouse and the bear are the same. Then have children describe how they are different. List children's responses in a T-chart or Graphic Organizer 4. You may wish to compare and contrast several animals in the selection.

Write About Animal Characteristics Have children choose one comparison the class discussed, such as the sizes of the dormouse and the bear. Ask them to illustrate the similarity or the difference on paper. Then ask children to write or dictate labels or simple sentences that tell about their pictures.

The bear is big.

The dormouse is small.

Math
Graph Colorful Mice

Materials: *Patterns* on the Teacher Resources DVD-ROM,—mouse, paper, scissors, crayons

Make a Bar Graph Give each child a mouse pattern. Ask each child to color the mouse in his or her favorite color. Then have children cut out their mice. When everyone has finished, sort the mice by color. Then create a bar graph on the board or wall by attaching the mice in columns or rows by color. When the graph is finished, have children count the number of mice in each color row or column.

Science
Animals in Each Season

Materials: *Patterns* p. 57—bare tree, crayons or markers

Review Seasons Discuss seasons with children—how the appearance of trees will change and what animals will do in each season. Have children choose a season, label the picture, and complete the tree drawing for that season. Then have them choose an animal and draw it in the picture, showing something that animal would do in that season.

fall

Weekly Assessment

Use the whole-class assessment on pages 496–497 and 500–501 in this Teacher's Edition to check:

✔ 🔊 **Short *i* Spelled *Ii***

✔ 🔊 **Comprehension Skill** *Sequence*

✔ **High-Frequency Words** *he for*

Teacher's Edition, Day 5

Managing Assessment

Use the Assessment Handbook for:

✔ **Observation Checklists**

✔ **Record-Keeping Forms**

✔ **Portfolio Assessment**

Assessment Handbook

Teacher Notes

Small Group Time

Pacing Small Group Instruction

20–30 mins.

5 Day Plan

DAY 1	• Phonemic Awareness/ Phonics • Decodable Story 11
DAY 2	• Phonemic Awareness/ Phonics • Decodable Reader 11
DAY 3	• Phonemic Awareness/ Phonics • Concept Literacy Reader K.2.5 or Kindergarten Student Reader K.2.5
DAY 4	• Phonemic Awareness/ Phonics • Get Set, Roll! Reader 11
DAY 5	• Phonics Review • Listen to Me Reader K.2.5

3 or 4 Day Plan

DAY 1	• Phonemic Awareness/ Phonics • Decodable Story 11
DAY 2	• Phonemic Awareness/ Phonics • Decodable Reader 11
DAY 3	• Phonemic Awareness/ Phonics • Concept Literacy Reader K.2.5 or Kindergarten Student Reader K.2.5
DAY 4	• Phonemic Awareness/ Phonics • Get Set, Roll! Reader 11

3 Day Plan: Eliminate the shaded box.

SI Strategic Intervention — DAY 1

Phonemic Awareness•Phonics

■ **Discriminate /i/** I am going to say three words. I want you to tell me which word begins with /i/. Listen carefully: *apple, insect, banana.* Say the words with me: *apple, insect, banana.* Which word begins with /i/? *Insect* begins with /i/. *Apple* and *banana* do not begin with /i/. Continue discriminating /i/ with the following sets of words: *outside, inside, under; igloo, lizard, lemon; mitten, egg, ink; otter, inch, elbow.*

■ **Connect /i/ to *Ii*** I am going to say three words. I want you to tell me which word begins with /i/. Listen carefully: *on, an, in.* Which word begins with /i/? *In* begins with /i/. *On* and *an* do not begin with /i/. Write the letters *Ii* on the board. The letter *i* stands for /i/ in words. Continue discriminating /i/ in the middle of words using the following sets of words: *bag, big, beg; bid, bed, bad; hat, hit, hot; Tim, Tom, Tam.*

Decodable Story 11

■ **Review High-Frequency Words** Review the following high-frequency words. Have children read each word as you point to it on the Word Wall.

he	a	little	is	the	for

> **If...** children have difficulty reading the words,
> **then...** say a word and have children point to the word. Repeat several times, giving assistance as needed.

Have children read the story Tim the Pig orally. Then have them reread the story several times individually.

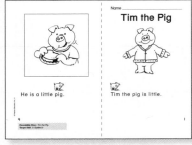

Reader's and Writer's Notebook, pp. 131–132

Objectives
• Identify the common sounds that letters represent.
• Read at least 25 high-frequency words from a commonly used list.

SI *Strategic Intervention*

DAY 2

Phonemic Awareness•Phonics

■ **Discriminate /i/** Display Phonics Songs and Rhymes Chart 11. Sing "In a Tin" to the tune of "Do You Know the Muffin Man?" several times with children. Have children clap when they hear an /i/ word.

■ **Recognize Ii** Ask children to name words that begin with /i/. List the words as they say them. Have children echo read the list of words. Then ask children to take turns circling the *i*'s on the list.

Decodable Reader 11

■ **Review High-Frequency Words** Review the previously taught high-frequency words. Have children read each word as you point to it on the Word Wall.

My Skills Buddy

is	a	he	my	for	we

If... children have difficulty reading the words,
then... say a word and have children point to the word. Repeat several times, giving assistance as needed.

Display the story *Tip and Pat* on p. 98 of *My Skills Buddy.*
The title of this story is *Tip and Pat.* The author is Kate Brand. The illustrator is Carl Johnson. Look at the picture on the cover. What do you think the story will be about? Let's read the story together.

More Reading
Use Leveled Readers or other text at children's instructional level.

Objectives
• Identify the common sounds that letters represent.
• Read at least 25 high-frequency words from a commonly used list.

SI *Strategic Intervention* **DAY 3**

Phonemic Awareness•Phonics

■ **Isolate /i/** Display the *iguana* Picture Card. This is an *iguana. Iguana* begins with /i/. Say it with me: /i/ /i/ /i/, *iguana.* Repeat with *inch* and *igloo.*

■ **Discriminate /i/** Display the *insect* Picture Card. This is an *insect. Insect* begins with /i/. Say it with me: /i/ /i/ /i/, *insect.* Write the letters *Ii* on the board. The letter *i* stands for /i/. Say it with me: /i/ /i/ /i/, *insect.* Give children two chenille sticks. Have them bend them at the tip to form antennas. When you hear a word that has initial or medial /i/, hold up your antennas and place them behind your head. Use the following words: *inch, ladybug, it, Tim, moose, Tip, inside, sip.*

■ **Blend Sounds** Write *Pip* on the board. *Pip* is a name so the first letter *P* is capitalized. Have children blend the sound of each letter to read the word: /p/ /i/ /p/, *Pip. Pip* is the name of a fish.

■ **Review High-Frequency Words** Write *for* on the board. Have volunteers say the word and use it in a sentence. Continue with the words *my, he, I, have, a, like, is,* and *we.*

■ To practice phonics and high-frequency words, have children read Kindergarten Student Reader K.2.5. Use the instruction on p. 456.

For a complete lesson plan and additional practice, see the **Leveled Reader Teaching Guide**.

Concept Literacy Reader K.2.5

■ **Preview and Predict** Display the cover of the Concept Literacy Reader K.2.5. Point to the cover of the book. The title of the book is *Animal Homes.* What do you think the book is about? Have children tell about the picture and what they think the story might be about.

■ **Set a Purpose** We talked about the title of the book. Let's read the book to find out about animal homes. Have children read the Concept Literacy Reader.

■ **Read** Provide corrective feedback as children read the book orally. During reading, ask them if they were able to confirm any of the predictions they made prior to reading.

If... children have difficulty reading the book individually,

then... read a sentence aloud as children point to each word. Then have the group reread the sentences as they continue pointing to the words.

■ **Retell** Have children retell what kind of home each animal has. Help them identify the information in the pictures to provide details about each animal and its home.

Concept Literacy Reader K.2.5

Objectives
• Identify the common sounds that letters represent.   • Predict what might happen next based on the cover.
• Predict what might happen next based on the title.   • Retell important facts in a text, heard or read.

DI•71   Look at Us! • Unit 2 • Week 5

Phonemic Awareness•Phonics

■ **Isolate /i/** Say the word *ink*. Ask children to say the word with you and listen to the beginning sound. *Ink* begins with /i/. Say it with me: /i/ /i/ /i/, *ink*. Repeat with *igloo, insects,* and *iguana.*

■ **Segmenting** Listen to the sounds in *dip:* /d/ /i/ /p/. Say the sounds with me: /d/ /i/ /p/. There are three sounds in *dip.* Continue with *sit, mat, tip,* and *tap.*

■ **Connect /i/ to Ii** Display the *inch* Picture Card. This is an *inch. Inch* begins with /i/. Say it with me: /i/ /i/ /i/, *inch.* Write the letters *Ii* on the board. The word *inch* begins with the letter *i.* Listen for other words that begin with the letter *i.* Say the following words and have children write the letter *i* in the air for each word that begins with /i/: *inside, otter, index, ink, uncle, into.*

Get Set, Roll! Reader 11

■ **Review** Review the high-frequency words *he, for, is,* and *a.* Have children find each word on the Word Wall.

■ **Review Rebus Words** Write the word *dig* on the board. This is the word *dig.* Name the letters with me: *d, i, g, dig.* Continue with the words *Pete* and *building.* Look for the words *dig, Pete,* and *building* in the story we read today. A picture above the word will help you read it.

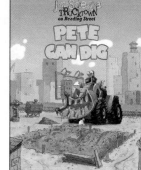
Get Set, Roll! Reader 11

■ **Read** Display the Get Set, Roll! Reader 11, *Pete Can Dig.* Today we will read a story about our friend Payloader Pete. Point to the title of the story. What is the title of the story? (*Pete Can Dig*) We will read words with /i/ in this story. Point to the picture on the cover. What do you think the story will be about?

> **If...** children have difficulty reading the story individually,
> **then...** read a sentence aloud as children point to each word. Then have the group reread the sentences as they continue pointing to the words.

■ **Reread** Use echo reading of Get Set, Roll! Reader 11 to model fluent reading. Use your oral reading to model for children where to pause, when to change pitch, and which words to stress. Then have children reread orally three to four times, or until they can read with few or no mistakes.

Objectives
• Identify the common sounds that letters represent.
• Read at least 25 high-frequency words from a commonly used list.
• Predict what might happen next based on the cover.

Small Group Time

More Reading

Use Leveled Readers or other text at children's instructional level.

SI *Strategic Intervention*

DAY 5

Phonics Review

■ **Recognize /i/** Gather the following Picture Cards: *inch, insect, igloo, iguana, six, wig, pig.* Mix the cards and display them one at a time. Have a child name the picture and tell whether /i/ is at the beginning or in the middle of the word.

■ **Discriminate /i/** Draw pictures of igloos on the board. Gather about ten Picture Cards, including the following /i/*Ii* cards: *igloo, iguana, inch, insect.* Mix the cards and display them one at a time. Have a child name the picture. If the name has /i/, have the child write a lowercase *i* in one of the igloos.

Listen to Me Reader K.2.5

■ **Preview and Predict** Display the book. The title of this story is *The Iguana.* The author is Carmie Ruiz. The illustrator is Sheila Bailey. Look at the cover of the book. What do you think the story will be about?

■ **Set a Purpose** Review children's ideas. Point out that they will know more about the iguana when they read the story. Tell children that you will read the story with them. Follow along with your finger as I read. Then we will take turns reading this page. Repeat this routine through all of the pages. Guide children to decode words. Provide support with decoding as necessary.

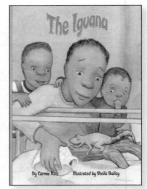

Listen to Me Reader K.2.5

■ **Reread for Fluency** Use echo reading of Listen to Me Reader K.2.5 to model reading fluently. Use your oral reading to model for children where to pause, when to change pitch, and which words to stress. Then have children reread orally three to four times, or until they can read with few or no mistakes.

Objectives
• Identify the common sounds that letters represent.
• Predict what might happen next based on the cover.
• Predict what might happen next based on the title.

 **eReaders**

 **On-Level** **DAY 1**

Phonemic Awareness•Phonics

■ **Look for /i/** Tell children that you will say two words. Have them listen to the words to tell which word has /i/. Listen to these words: *pat, pit*. Say the words with me—*pat, pit*. Which word has /i/? When the word *pit* has been identified, write the word on the board. Have a volunteer circle the letter that stands for /i/. Continue with these word sets: *bit, bat; dig, dog; lid, led; wig, wag; kit, cat; big, bag; fin, fan.*

■ **Picture an Igloo** Give children copies of a drawing of an igloo. Where can you find igloos? What would you see around igloos? Have children draw pictures of other words that have the /i/ sound like *igloo*, such as *fish, tin, six, sit* and *fin*. Have children share their pictures with the class.

Objectives
• Identify the common sounds that letters represent.

Pacing Small Group Instruction 20–30 mins.

5 Day Plan

DAY 1	• Phonemic Awareness/ Phonics • Decodable Story 11
DAY 2	• Phonemic Awareness/ Phonics • High-Frequency Words • Decodable Reader 11
DAY 3	• Phonemic Awareness/ Phonics • Kindergarten Student Reader K.2.5
DAY 4	• Get Set, Roll! Reader 11
DAY 5	• Phonics Review • Reread Leveled Books

 **On-Level** **DAY 2**

Phonemic Awareness•Phonics

■ **Clap for /i/** Tell children you will tell them a story and they should listen for /i/. When you say a word that begins with /i/, the children should clap and repeat the word. Tell a simple story, emphasizing the /i/ words and pausing to give children a chance to clap and repeat the word. *In* the jungle, you can find *insects*. *If* you go deeper, *iguanas* may show up. *In* an *igloo,* you cannot find *insects* or *iguanas* because *it is* too cold. Repeat the activity. Have children write *Ii* on their paper every time they hear a word with /i/.

■ **High-Frequency Words** Write *he* on the board. This is the word *he*. What word is this? Continue with the following words: *little, for, a, is, we, my, like.*

Objectives
• Identify the common sounds that letters represent.
• Read at least 25 high-frequency words from a commonly used list.

3 or 4 Day Plan

DAY 1	• Phonemic Awareness/ Phonics • Decodable Story 11
DAY 2	• Phonemic Awareness/ Phonics • High-Frequency Words • Decodable Reader 11
DAY 3	• Phonemic Awareness/ Phonics • Kindergarten Student Reader K.2.5
DAY 4	• Get Set, Roll! Reader 11

3 Day Plan: Eliminate the shaded box.

More Practice

For additional practice with this week's phonics skills, have children reread the Decodable Story (Day 1) and the Decodable Reader (Day 2).

Phonemic Awareness•Phonics

■ **Listen for Sounds** Read children the following sets of words. Have them hold up one finger if they hear /i/ in one word. Have them hold up two fingers if they hear /i/ in both words. Use the following set of words: *sit, kit; bit, bat; fox, fix; hill, heel; lid, lead; ten, tin; mice, miss; pit, lip.*

■ **Pass the Lid** Have children stand in a circle. Give a box lid (or paper) to one child. Have the child say a word with /i/ and pass the lid to the next child in the circle. That child must say a word with /i/. Continue around the circle having children name words with /i/. Provide clues for words as needed to help children.

■ **Connect /i/ to Ii** Write this sentence on the board: *The tin is in the bin.* Have children copy the sentence and circle the letters that stand for /i/.

Kindergarten Student Reader K.2.5

Kindergarten Student
Reader K.2.5

■ **Preview and Predict** Display Kindergarten Student Reader K.2.5. Point to the title of the book. The title of the book is *A House for Pip.* The author's name is Christina Rivas. David Sheldon illustrated the book. Read the title of the book with me. What do you think the story is about?

■ **Set a Purpose** Review the list of things that children think might happen in the story. Remind children that they want to find out about a house for Pip.

■ **Read** Have children follow along as they read the story with you. After reading p. 2, ask children to tell who Pip is. Have them point to the fish and tell what it looks like. Continue with each page and ask the following questions:

  • What size is Pip?
  • What did the girl have? Why did she think it was a good house?
  • What else did she have for Pip?

■ **Summarize** Have children retell the story to a partner and tell why all the things were good for Pip.

■ **Text to Self** Help children make personal connections to the story as they tell why the girl finds things to put in the fish bowl with Pip. Ask them to tell how they would feel if they got some new things.

Objectives
• Identify the common sounds that letters represent.
• Read at least 25 high-frequency words from a commonly used list.

 OL On-Level

DAY **4**

Get Set, Roll! Reader 11

■ **Review** Review the high-frequency words *he, for, is,* and *a.* Have children find each word on the Word Wall.

■ **Review Rebus Words** Write the word *building* on the board. This is the word building. Name the letters with me: *b, u, i, l, d, i, n, g, building.* Continue with the words *Pete* and *dig.* Look for the words *Pete, dig,* and *building* in the story we read today. A picture above the word will help you read it.

■ **Read** Today we will read a story about our friend Payloader Pete. Point to the title of the story. What is the title of the story? (*Pete Can Dig*) We will read words with /i/ in this story.

Objectives
• Read at least 25 high-frequency words from a commonly used list.

More Reading
Use Leveled Readers or other text at children's instructional level.

OL On-Level

DAY **5**

Phonics Review

■ **In and Out Boxes** Assign words to children and have them draw pictures of the words. Include the following initial and medial /i/ words, such as *igloo, insect, iguana, ink, pig, wig,* and *hill.* Also assign words that do not begin with or have /i/, such as *jet, cat, frog, hat, octopus,* and *mug.* Label boxes with the words "in box" and "out box." Collect children's drawings and mix them up. Give each child a different drawing and have him or her name the picture and put it in the "in box" if the word has initial or medial /i/. If not, have them put it in the "out box."

■ **Connect /i/ to *Ii*** Show these picture cards and say the name of each animal: alligator, bat, hippopotamus, iguana, insect, tiger, pig. If children hear /i/ in the word, they write *i* on their paper.

Objectives
• Identify the common sounds that letters represent.

Small Group Time

Pacing Small Group Instruction

⏱ 20–30 mins.

5 Day Plan

DAY 1	• Phonemic Awareness/ Phonics • Decodable Story 11
DAY 2	• Phonics • Spelling • High-Frequency Words • Decodable Reader 11
DAY 3	• Independent Reader K.2.5 or Kindergarten Student Reader K.2.5
DAY 4	• Get Set, Roll! Reader 11 or Kindergarten Student Reader K.2.5
DAY 5	• Fluency/ Comprehension • Independent Reader K.2.5

3 or 4 Day Plan

DAY 1	• Phonemic Awareness/ Phonics • Decodable Story
DAY 2	• Phonics • Spelling • High-Frequency Words • Decodable Reader 11
DAY 3	• Independent Reader K.2.5 or Kindergarten Student Reader K.2.5
DAY 4	• Get Set, Roll! Reader 11 or Kindergarten Student Reader K.2.5

3 Day Plan: Eliminate the shaded box.

More Practice

For additional practice with this week's phonics skills and to develop fluency, have children reread the Decodable Story (Day 1) and the Decodable Reader (Day 2).

A  Advanced — **DAY 1**

Phonemic Awareness•Phonics

■ **Insect Legs** Draw a picture on the board of an insect with six legs. Give each child a sheet of paper. Have children draw a similar picture on their paper. Display the following *Ii* Picture Cards on the ledge of the board: *igloo, pig, six, iguana, inch,* and *wig.* Also include six Picture Cards that are not /i/ words. Say the names of the pictures together. Have children draw a picture on each leg that has /i/. After children have finished, review the pictures to see that all the words with /i/ were used.

■ **Build Words** Write *t__p* on the board. Have a volunteer add the missing letter to make the word *tap.* Then have a child change the letter to make the word *tip.* Continue with these words using /a/ and /i/: *s__t, b__t, b__g, l__d, p__n, f__n.*

Objectives
• Identify the common sounds that letters represent.
• Recognize that new words are created when letters are changed.

A  Advanced — **DAY 2**

Phonics•Spelling

■ **Connect /i/ to Ii** Display the *Ii* Alphabet Card. What are the names of these letters? What is the sound we learned for this letter?

■ **Spell Sounds** Write *Tip* on the board. *Tip* is a name so the letter *T* is capitalized. Have children blend the sound of each letter to read the word: /t/ /i/ /p/, *Tip.* This is the name *Tip. Tip* is a cat. Repeat the routine with the following words: *cat, Pat, it, sit.*

■ **Review High-Frequency Words** Review the following high-frequency words with children: *he, is, my, a, for.*

Objectives
• Identify the common sounds that letters represent.
• Read at least 25 high-frequency words from a commonly used list.
• Use letter-sound correspondences to spell consonant-vowel-consonant (CVC) words.

DAY 3

For a complete lesson plan and additional practice, see the **Leveled Reader Teaching Guide**.

Independent Reader K.2.5

Independent Reader
K.2.5

■ **Practice High-Frequency Words** Write *little* on the board. Have volunteers say the word and use it in a sentence. Continue with the words *I, am, a, the, have,* and *is.*

■ **Activate Prior Knowledge** Have children read the title and look at the picture. Have them tell what they think the story is about and add any information they may have about the topic. Then have children take turns reading *A Winter Home* for their group.

■ **Sequence** Ask children to retell the chipmunk's search for a bed. Think about the story. What is the first place the chipmunk looks? (in a den) What is the next place he looks? (at a pond) What is the last place he looks? (in a tree) Review the sequence of events with children and have them use the words *first, next,* and *last.*

■ **Reread for Fluency** After rereading with children, model reading fluently for them. I am going to read this selection aloud. I will read the words with no mistakes. I want you to read it aloud with me. Try to read the words just as I do.

Use echo reading of Independent Leveled Reader K.2.5 to model reading fluently. Use your oral reading to model for children where to pause, when to change pitch, and which words to stress. Then have children reread orally three to four times, or until they can read with few or no mistakes.

■ For more practice with phonics and high-frequency words and to develop fluency, have children read the Kindergarten Student Reader K.2.5. Use the instruction on pp. 456.

More Reading
Use Leveled Readers or other text at children's instructional level.

More Reading

Use Leveled Readers or other text at children's instructional level.

A Advanced — DAY 4

Kindergarten Student Reader K.2.5

■ **Revisit Rebus Words** Write the word *fish* on the board. This is the word *fish.* Name the letters with me: *f, i, s, h, fish.* Repeat the routine with the words *house* and *ship.* There will be pictures above these words to help you read them.

■ **Reread** Use Kindergarten Student Reader K.2.5 to practice reading fluently.

■ **Text to World** Ask children to describe where Pip lives. Have them tell about other places fish live. Make a list of places. Have them tell about places they have visited.

■ **Read** Have children read Get Set, Roll! Reader 11, *Pete Can Dig.* Use the instruction on p. 485.

Kindergarten Student Reader K.2.5

Objectives
• Read at least 25 high-frequency words from a commonly used list.
• Use words that name locations.

A Advanced — DAY 5

Fluency•Comprehension

■ **Reread for Fluency** Use the Independent Reader K.2.5 to model reading fluently for children. I am going to read this story aloud. I will read the words with no mistakes. I want you to read it aloud with me. Try to read the words just as I do.

■ **Comprehension** After children have finished reading the selection, have them retell what happened in the story. Ask children to tell what happens first (The chipmunk tries to sleep in a den.), next (The chipmunk thinks about sleeping in a pond.), next (He thinks about sleeping in a nest.), and last (Chipmunk finds an old tree to sleep in.). Have children draw pictures to show the events.

Independent Reader K.2.5

Objectives
• Read at least 25 high-frequency words from a commonly used list.
• Use words that name sequences.

Support for English Language Learners

 **DAY 1**

Concept Development

- **Read the Concept Literacy Reader** Read *Animal Homes* with children. Have children describe what they see on the cover. Then have children look at the pictures in the book. What animal lives in this home? Read the book aloud, pausing to discuss each page. Model sentence patterns and vocabulary that identify the animal home. The squirrel is rolled up in a ball. The squirrel is in the leaves. On a second reading, invite children to talk about the animal shown on each page.

- **Develop Oral Language** Revisit *Animal Homes,* pointing out the different animal homes. Then have children sing the following song with you to the tune of "Frère Jacques."

> Where is my home? Where is my home?
> It is here. It is here.
> I live here today. I live here today.
> I'm a ____. I'm a ____.

Phonemic Awareness/Phonics

- **Frontload Words with /i/** Have children look at the illustration on pp. 92–93 of *My Skills Buddy.* This drawing shows children in the library. Look at all the things in the library. What do you see? Listen to the word *igloo.* What sound does *igloo* begin with? *Igloo* begins with /i/; /i/, *igloo.* Then use this chant to introduce picture words beginning with /i/:

> Izzy and Inga go to the library.
> They see an insect.
> They see the ink.
> They see an iguana.
> They read about things that begin with /i/.

Repeat the chant with other words that begin with /i/, including *inch, itch, in.*

- **Connect /i/ to Ii** Use letter tiles to display the word *it* or write it on the board. This word is *it:* /i/ /t/, *it.* Say the word with me. Have children write the word *it* and circle the letter that makes /i/. Write and read aloud the following sentence: *Izzy and Isabel use ink to make an igloo.* Point to *i* in *Izzy* and ask: What letter is this? Yes, this is *i.* Continue with *Isabel, ink,* and *igloo.*

Objectives
- Distinguish sounds of English with increasing ease. • Use visual support to enhance and confirm understanding of increasingly complex and elaborated spoken language. • Learn relationships between sounds and letters of the English language.

Content Objective
- Develop content knowledge about homes for animals.

Language Objectives
- Understand and use grade-level content area vocabulary.
- Recognize the sounds of English.

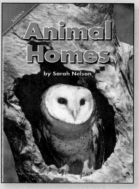

Concept Literacy Reader K.2.5

Daily Planner

DAY 1	• Concept Development • Phonemic Awareness/Phonics • Listening Comprehension
DAY 2	• Comprehension • Vocabulary
DAY 3	• Phonemic Awareness/Phonics • Conventions
DAY 4	• Phonemic Awareness/Phonics • Concepts and Oral Language
DAY 5	• Language Workshop • Writing

A Bed for the Winter **DI•80**

Support for English Language Learners

Content Objective
• Understand sequence.

Language Objective
• Learn and use academic vocabulary.

My Skills Buddy, pp. 94–95

English Opportunity

Help children understand that when they answer a question with a complete sentence, they are using formal language. When they answer with just a few words, they are using informal language. Informal language can be used when talking to friends.

Listening Comprehension: Sequence

■ **Frontload Vocabulary** Discuss the illustrations on pp. 94–95 in *My Skills Buddy* to frontload vocabulary. Show p. 94. Point to the bird. What do you see? (a bird) Where is the bird? (on a nest) Point to the nest. What do you see in the nest? (some eggs) What is the bird doing? (sitting on the eggs in the nest) Look at the next picture. What happens next? (the eggs hatch) Look at the next picture. What happens next? (the birds grow up and leave home) Tell the story for me. What happens first? Have children respond and point to the things in the illustration. Use the word *first* as you help children tell the first part of the story. What happens second? What happens last?

■ **Provide Scaffolding** Point to the illustrations on pp. 94–95. Explain that things happen in order. Write the words *first, second,* and *last* on the board. Look at the pictures of the bird story. Point to the word *first* on the board. What happens first? Continue with *second* and *last*. Help children conclude that things happen in a special order, and when they tell about it they can use the words *first, second,* and *last*.

■ **Prepare for the Read Aloud** The modified Read Aloud below prepares children for listening to the oral reading "The Beaver's Lodge" on p. 427.

The Beaver's Lodge

The beaver is a large brown animal. It is also a very good builder. It builds its home on the water. The beaver's home is called a lodge. Outside, a lodge looks like a pile of sticks and mud. But inside, there are many big rooms and tunnels.

A beaver uses trees to build its lodge. First, a beaver uses its sharp teeth to chop down a tree. Then it chews off all of the branches. Last, the beaver rolls the tree to its new lodge. The beaver's lodge is strong. It keeps the beaver safe from other animals.

■ **First Listening** Write the title of the Read Aloud on the board. This is about a beaver. It tells how a beaver builds its home or lodge. Listen as I read for the words *first, then,* and *last.* After reading, ask children to retell what happens *first, next,* and *last.*

■ **Second Listening** Write the words *first, next,* and *last* on the board. As you listen, think about the order things happen. After reading, point to *first* on the board and ask children to tell what the beaver does first. Repeat for *next* and *last.*

Objectives
• Understand the main points of spoken language ranging from situations in which topics are familiar to unfamiliar. • Read linguistically accommodated content area material with a decreasing need for linguistic accommodations as more English is learned.

DAY 2

Comprehension

- **Provide Scaffolding** Display *A Bed for the Winter.* Lead a detailed picture walk through the selection, naming what you see in the photographs and describing what is happening. Use gestures and facial expressions to convey meaning.

  - **Set the Scene** Use the cover of the Big Book to help children understand that this selection is about animals and how the animals get ready for winter. Describe what happens when winter begins. Winter is a season. As winter begins, it starts to get cold. Animals look for places to stay during the winter. They look for places to keep their food.

  - **Frontload Vocabulary** As you lead the picture walk, use the pictures to introduce the dormouse. Show pp. 4–5. Continue by using the vocabulary boxes on various pages to introduce unfamiliar words as you go through the book. If children do not know the English word for an animal shown in the book, have them identify the animal with a word they know, such as the Spanish word *oso* for bear. Supply the English word, and have children repeat it.

Vocabulary: Sequence Words

- **Frontload Vocabulary** Have children turn to p. 108 of *My Skills Buddy.* Talk about each illustration, using the sequence words *first, second, next,* and *last.* The boy is getting ready for school. The first thing he does in the morning is wake up. Then invite children to tell about the illustrations using the sequence words.

- **Provide Scaffolding** Write the words *first, second, next,* and *last* on the board. These words help us figure out the order in which things happen. What did you do *first* this morning? Repeat with the other sequence words.

- **Practice** Write the words *first, second, next,* and *last* on the board. Tell children that you want to show someone how to make a sandwich. Talk about the steps: Get bread, peanut butter, and jelly. Put the peanut butter on the bread. Put the jelly on the bread. Put the slices of bread together. Have children draw four pictures to show the steps and write the words *first, second, next,* and *last* by each picture. Then have them share their drawings by narrating the steps using the sequence words.

Objectives

• Use prior experiences to understand meanings in English. • Demonstrate listening comprehension of increasingly complex spoken English by following directions commensurate with content and grade-level needs. • Narrate with increasing specificity and detail as more English is acquired.

Content Objective

- Develop background knowledge.

Language Objective

- Learn and use sequence words.

Use Learning Strategies

Remind children that if they have trouble remembering the order of things, they can use the words on the board or they can ask their classmates for help.

Big Book

Support for English Language Learners

Content Objective
- Use learning strategies.

Language Objectives
- Connect /i/ with *Ii*.
- Use adjectives for opposites.

Use Learning Strategies
Help children understand that when we talk about opposites we are talking about words that have very different meanings. For example, *dark, light; hot, cold;* and *big, little.*

Phonemic Awareness/Phonics

- **Isolate Medial /i/** Say *pin*, and then model segmenting sounds by saying /p/ /i/ /n/. Emphasize the medial sound in the word. Help children identify the medial sound.

- **/i/ Spelled *Ii*** Say the following word pair: *pat, pit.* Have children say the words and listen for the middle sound. Have them tell which word has /i/. Write the word *pit* and segment the sounds: /p/ /i/ /t/. Repeat several times with children to be sure they distinguish /i/ in the middle of the word. Continue with these pairs: *sit, sat; mat, mitt; sap, sip; Tam, Tim.*

Conventions: Adjectives for Opposites

- **Provide Scaffolding** Point to the large photograph on pp. 4–5 of *A Bed for the Winter.* Look at the picture. Point to and read the first sentence on p. 5. What word tells about the rain? The word *cold* tells about the rain. What is the opposite of *cold?* If something is not *cold,* it can be *hot. Hot* and *cold* are opposites. Display pp. 6–7 and read the first sentence. Where does the squirrel gather leaves? What is the opposite of *high?* If something is not *high,* it can be *low. High* and *low* are opposites.

- **Practice** What are some other words that we can find opposites? Page through the Big Book and have children name an opposite for each word you point to. Include the following words: *warm* (p. 6), *small* (p. 9), *wet* (p. 10), *dark* (p. 15), *long* (p. 30).

  Leveled Support

  Beginning/Intermediate For each word, have a child think of a word that is the opposite. Help them remember that opposites are words that have meanings that are very different from each other. Use these examples: *tall tree (short tree), big branch (little branch), high limb (low limb), small bush (large bush).*

  Advanced/Advanced-High Have children use the opposites in sentences. Use these examples: *It is a hot summer day. It is a cold winter day. This is a tall tree. This is a short tree.*

Objectives
- Use prior knowledge to understand meanings in English. • Develop repertoire of learning strategies commensurate with grade-level learning expectations. • Decode (sound out) words using a combination of skills. • Comprehend English language structures used routinely in written classroom materials.

 ELL English Language Learners

DAY 4

Phonemic Awareness/Phonics

■ **Review /k/** To review /k/, use these sentences that contain initial and final /k/:

Can a cat put a cap on a duck?
Can the duck pack the picnic sack?

Then remind children that some words have /k/ at the beginning, and others have /k/ at the end. Repeat the sentences one word at a time, and have children repeat the word after you. Does the word have /k/? Say the word *can* with me: *can*, /k/ /a/ /n/. Where do you hear /k/? Yes, the word begins with /k/. Say each /k/ word and have children tell whether /k/ is at the beginning or the end of the word.

■ **/k/ Spelled Cc** Tell children they will read words with /k/. Write the words *cat* and *cot* on the board. As you read them aloud, track the sounds and letters with your fingers. Help children recognize that *cat* and *cot* begin with the same sound. Have children write the words and underline the letter *c*. Continue with the words *can, cap, cab,* and *cut.*

Concepts and Oral Language

■ **Revisit Talk with Me Chart 11A** Display the chart. The chart shows some places that animals live. Point to the picture of the tree stump. What do you see in this picture? What animals live in a tree stump? Continue with the other pictures.

■ **Develop Oral Language** Introduce language patterns that help describe the winter homes on Talk with Me Chart 11A. Write this sentence frame on the board: *A _____ is a home for a _____.* Let's use this sentence pattern to talk about the picture: *A nest is a home for a bird.* What picture am I talking about? Have a child point to the picture of the bird and its nest. Ask children to suggest sentences for other pictures using the frame. Then play a game with children in which you ask a question about the pictures, such as: Where is the nest? Have children point to the correct picture and then answer your question with a sentence, such as *The nest is in the tree.* Help children understand that answering with a complete sentence instead of with just a few words is using formal language. Formal language should be used when speaking to an adult.

Objectives

• Use strategic learning techniques to acquire basic vocabulary. • Speak using a variety of grammatical structures with increasing accuracy and ease as more English is acquired. • Speak using grade-level content area vocabulary in context to internalize new English words.

Content Objectives

• Develop oral language.

• Use learning strategies.

Language Objectives

• Connect /k/ with *Cc*.

• Learn English language patterns.

 Transfer Skills

Pronouncing /k/ Children's familiarity with /k/ in names such as *California* or home language words will help them recognize /k/ in English. For example, most Spanish speakers know the words *casa* (house) and *cómo* (how).

Use Learning Strategies

Create a two-column chart titled *Homes for the Winter.* Label column 1 *Animal* and column 2 *Home.* Have children name an animal in the selection and write the name in column 1. Then have them name the animal's home and write the word in column 2. Children can also draw pictures for the chart.

Talk with Me Chart 11A

Support for English Language Learners

Content Objectives

- Understand *A Bed for the Winter*.
- Practice Sequence.

Language Objectives

- Retell a selection through speaking and writing.
- Write using grade-level vocabulary.

Monitor and Self-Correct

Remind children that if they don't know how to say a word, they can ask their partners for help.

Home Language Support

Invite children to share ideas in their home languages before creating their sentences.

Language Workshop: Retell

■ **Introduce and Model** Display Big Book *A Bed for the Winter.* Guide children as you look through the book with them. Point out that each pair of pages shows an animal getting ready for winter. Have children tell how animals get ready for winter.

■ **Practice** Help children recognize and name these animals.

dormouse	squirrel	wasp	toad	snake
bats	rabbits	bear	deer	owl

Page through the book as children describe each animal and its home. On chart paper, write simple sentences such as the following to tell about each animal:

A **squirrel** lives in a nest.
A **wasp** lives in a stump.
A **toad** lives under a stone.
A **bear** lives in a den.
A **bat** lives in a cave.

Writing: Write About *A Bed for the Winter*

■ **Prepare for Writing** Together review the list of animals and their homes for the winter. Have children choose an animal to write about.

■ **Create Sentences** Review the animals and add these sentences to the chart. Then have children write the sentence about their animal or create a new sentence.

A **rabbit** lives in a burrow.
A **toad** lives under a stone.
A **snake** lives in the grass.
A **deer** lives in the woods.
A **dormouse** lives in a hole.

Leveled Support

Beginning /Intermediate Guide children in finding the animal they choose and copying the sentence.

Advanced/Advanced-High Have children write their sentences on their own. Have children help less-proficient partners complete their sentences.

Objectives
• Monitor oral language production and employ self-corrective techniques or other resources. • Demonstrate listening comprehension of increasingly complex spoken English by responding to questions and requests commensurate with content and grade-level needs. • Write using newly acquired basic vocabulary.

This Week's ELL Overview

ELL Handbook

- Maximize Literacy and Cognitive Engagement
- Research Into Practice
- Full Weekly Support for Every Selection

   ### *Jack and the Beanstalk*
   - Routines to Support Instruction

- Transfer Activities
- Professional Development

Daily Leveled ELL Notes

ELL notes appear throughout this week's instruction and ELL Support is on the DI pages of your Teacher's Edition. The following is a sample of an ELL note from this week.

English Language Learners

Beginning Support Phonics English language learners from various backgrounds may pronounce short *i* like the long *e* in *see.* Model correct pronunciation by saying a short phrase or sentence with both the short *i* and long *e* sounds: *You can eat it.* Have children repeat the sentence. Call attention to the differences in pronouncing *eat* and *it.*

Intermediate High-Frequency Words All languages do not use gender-specific pronouns. Point out to English learners that *he* stands for males, such as *Ian* or *Mr. Jones,* or animals with male names, such as *Rob the Robin.*

Advanced High-Frequency Words After the Team Talk activity, have children continue to work in pairs to check understanding. Have one child read one of the sentences aloud while the other child makes a simple drawing to illustrate the sentence.

Advanced High Amazing Words Explain to children that *lad* means *boy* and is more commonly used in British English than American English. Use this opportunity to point out that the same language may be spoken differently in different regions of the world. Talk with children about other places in the world that speak their home languages.

ELL by Strand

The ELL lessons on this week's Support for English Language Learners pages are organized by strand. They offer additional scaffolding for the core curriculum. Leveled support notes on these pages address the different proficiency levels in your class. See pages DI•97–DI•102.

ELL Guy
Dr. Jim Cummins

The Three Pillars of ELL Instruction

ELL Strands	Activate Prior Knowledge	Access Content	Extend Language
Vocabulary p. DI•99	Frontload Vocabulary	Provide Scaffolding	Practice
Reading Comprehension p. DI•99	Provide Scaffolding	Set the Scene	Frontload Vocabulary
Phonics, Spelling, and Word Analysis pp. DI•97, DI•100–DI•101	Frontload Words with /i/, /a/, /s/, /p/, /k/	Isolate Initial and Medial /i/	Review /k/
Listening Comprehension p. DI•98	Prepare for the Read Aloud	First Listening	Second Listening
Conventions and Writing pp. DI•100, DI•102	Provide Scaffolding/ Introduce and Model	Practice	Leveled Practice Activities/ Leveled Writing Activities
Concept Development p. DI•97	Read the Concept Literacy Reader	Read the Concept Literacy Reader	Develop Oral Language

This Week's Practice Stations Overview

Six Weekly Practice Stations with Leveled Activities can be found at the beginning of each week of instruction. For this week's Practice Stations, see pp. 514–515.

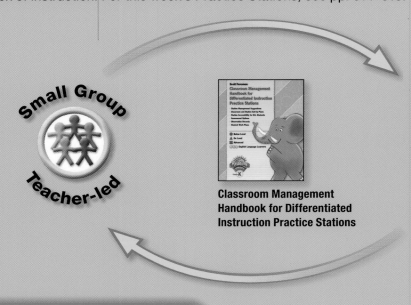

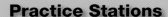
Practice Stations

Small Group Teacher-led

Classroom Management Handbook for Differentiated Instruction Practice Stations

Daily Leveled Center Activities

⬤ Below   ▢ Advanced

△ On-Level   Ⓔ Ⓛ Ⓛ

Practice Stations Flip Charts

	Listen Up	Word Work	Words to Know	Let's Write	Read for Meaning	Let's Make Art
Objectives	• Identify and practice words with /i/.	• Identify and build words with /i/.	• Identify and use sequence words.	• Write a caption for a picture.	• Identify events in a story. • Sequence the events using time-order words	• Use paper shapes to make an animal home.
Materials	• *Listen Up* Flip Chart Activity 12 • *brick, inch, igloo, kitten, iguana, mitten* Picture Cards	• *Word Work* Flip Chart Activity 12 • *Ii, Tt, Uu, Bb* Alphabet Cards • *insect, pig, six* Picture Cards • Letter Tiles	• *Words to Know* Flip Chart Activity 12 • four pictures that show a sequence of events • Teacher-made Word Cards: *first, second, next, last* • paper, pencils, crayons	• *Let's Write* Flip Chart Activity 12 • Picture Cards that show examples of nature • calendar pictures that show examples of nature • crayons, paper, pencil	• *Read for Meaning* Flip Chart Activity 12 • Little Book *A Bed for the Winter* • pencil, crayons, paper	• *Let's Make Art* Flip Chart Activity 12 • Little Book *A Bed for the Winter* • art paper, crayons, safety scissors

This Week on Reading Street!

Question of the Week

How are real and make-believe plants alike and different?

Look at Us!

Daily Plan

Don't Wait Until Friday

Whole Group

- /i/ Spelled *Ii*
- Realism and Fantasy
- Vocabulary

MONITOR PROGRESS — Success Predictor

Day 1	Day 2	Day 3	Day 4	Day 5
Check Phonemic Awareness	Check Sound Spelling/ Retelling	Check Word Reading	Check Phonemic Awareness	Check Oral Vocabulary

Small Group

Teacher-Led

- Reading Support
- Skill Support
- Fluency Practice

Practice Stations

Independent Activities

Customize Literacy More support for a Balanced Literacy approach, see pp. CL•1–CL•31.

Whole Group

- Writing
- Conventions: Adjectives
- Listening and Speaking

Assessment

- Day 5 Assessment for Phonics
- Day 5 Assessment for Comprehension

You Are Here!
Unit 2
Week 6

This Week's Reading Selections

Big Book
Genre: **Fairy Tale**

Decodable Reader 12

Leveled Readers

Get Set Roll!
Reader 12

Resources on Reading Street!

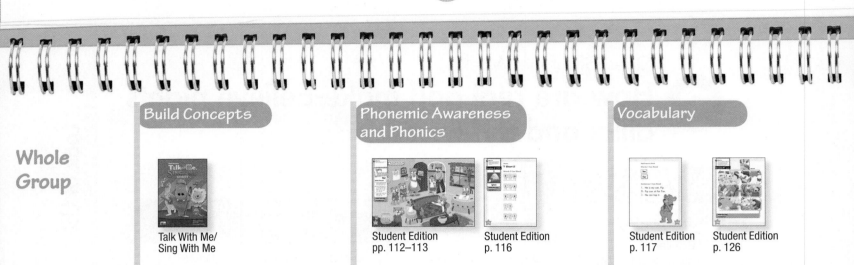

	Build Concepts	Phonemic Awareness and Phonics	Vocabulary
Whole Group	Talk With Me/ Sing With Me	Student Edition pp. 112–113 Student Edition p. 116	Student Edition p. 117 Student Edition p. 126
Go Digital	• Concept Talk Video • Sing with Me Animations	• eReaders	
Small Group and Independent Practice	Practice Station Flip Chart Leveled Readers	Practice Station Flip Chart Decodable Reader 12 Leveled Readers  Get Set, Roll! Reader 12	Practice Station Flip Chart Student Edition p. 117
Go Digital	• eReaders	• eReaders • Letter Tile Drag and Drop	
Customize Literacy	• Leveled Readers	• Decodable Reader	• High-Frequency Word Cards
 *Go Digital*	• Concept Talk Video • Big Question Video • eReaders	• eReaders	• Sing with Me Animations

Question of the Week

How are real and make-believe plants alike and different?

Week 6

Comprehension

Student Edition
pp. 114–115

Big Book

- Envision It! Animations

Fluency

Decodable
Reader 12

Kdg. Student
Reader K.2.6

Get Set, Roll!
Reader 12

- eReaders

Conventions and Writing

Reader's and
Writer's Notebook

- Grammar Jammer

Practice Station
Flip Chart

Leveled
Readers

Get Set, Roll!
Reader 12

Practice Station
Flip Chart

Leveled Readers

Practice Station
Flip Chart

Reader's and
Writer's Notebook

- Envision It! Animations
- eReaders

- eReaders

- Grammar Jammer

- Leveled Readers

- Leveled Readers

- *Reader's and Writer's Notebook*

- Envision It! Aminations
- eReaders

- eReaders

- Grammar Jammer

You Are Here!
Unit 2
Week 6

My 5-Day Planner for Reading Street!

	Check Phonemic Awareness **Day 1** pages 516–531	**Check Sound-Spelling** **Check Retelling** **Day 2** pages 532–549
Get Ready to Read	**Concept Talk,** 516 **Oral Vocabulary,** 517 *beanstalk, lad, ogre, magic, naughty, lend* **Phonemic Awareness,** 518–519 ◉ Initial Sounds **Phonics,** 520–521 ◉ /i/ Spelled *Ii* **Handwriting,** 522 Letters *I* and *i* **High-Frequency Words,** 523 *he, for* **READ Decodable Story 12,** 524–525	**Concept Talk,** 532 **Oral Vocabulary,** 533 *beanstalk, lad* **Phonemic Awareness,** 534–535 ◉ Medial, and Final Sounds **Phonics,** 536 ◉ /i/ Spelled *Ii* **Handwriting,** 538 Words with *Ii* **High-Frequency Words,** 539 *he, for* **READ Decodable Reader 12,** 540–541
Read and Comprehend	**Listening Comprehension,** 526–527 ◉ Realism and Fantasy	**Listening Comprehension,** 542 ◉ Realism and Fantasy **READ Big Book—First Read,** 542 *Jack and the Beanstalk* **Retell,** 543 **Think, Talk, and Write,** 544
Language Arts	**Conventions,** 528 Adjectives **Writing,** 529 Writing Process: Plan a Story **Listening and Speaking,** 530 Listen for Plot **Wrap Up Your Day,** 530 **Extend Your Day!,** 531	**Conventions,** 545 Adjectives **Writing,** 546 Writing Process: Draft a Story **Vocabulary,** 547 Direction Words **Wrap Up Your Day,** 548 **Extend Your Day!,** 549

You Are Here! Unit 2 Week 6

Question of the Week
How are real and make-believe plants alike and different?

Check Word Reading	Check Phonemic Awareness	Check Oral Vocabulary
Day 3 pages 550–577	**Day 4** pages 578–589	**Day 5** pages 590–603

Concept Talk, 550 **Oral Vocabulary,** 551 *ogre, magic* **Phonemic Awareness,** 552–553 ◉ Initial and Medial /i/ **Phonics,** 554–555 ◉ /i/ Spelled *Ii* **READ Kindergarten Student Reader K.2.6,** 556–557	**Concept Talk,** 578 **Oral Vocabulary,** 579 *naughty, lend* Review **Phonemic Awareness,** 580 /k/ Review **Phonics,** 581 /k/ Spelled *Cc* **Spelling,** 582 ◉ /i/ Spelled *Ii* **READ Get Set, Roll! Reader 12,** 583	**Concept Wrap Up,** 590 **Oral Vocabulary,** 591 *beanstalk, lad, ogre, magic, naughty, lend* Review **Phonemic Awareness,** 592 ◉ /i/ Review **Phonics,** 593 ◉ /i/ Spelled *Ii* **Assessment,** 594–595 Monitor Progress
Comprehension, 558–559 ◉ Realism and Fantasy **READ Big Book—Second Read,** 560–571 *Jack and the Beanstalk*	**Comprehension,** 584 ◉ Realism and Fantasy Review Sequence **READ Big Book—Third Read,** 585 *Jack and the Beanstalk*	**Let's Practice It!,** 596–597 Expository Text **Assessment,** 598–599 Monitor Progress
Conventions, 572 Adjectives for Opposites **Writing,** 573 Writing Process: Revise a Story **Listening and Speaking,** 574–575 Listen for Plot **Wrap Up Your Day,** 576 **Extend Your Day!,** 577	**Conventions,** 586 Adjectives **Writing,** 587 Writing Process: Edit a Story **Vocabulary,** 588 Direction Words **Wrap Up Your Day,** 588 **Extend Your Day!,** 589	Review **Conventions,** 600 Adjectives **Writing,** 601 Writing Process: Share a Story **Wrap Up Your Week,** 602 How are real and make-believe plants alike and different? **Extend Your Day!,** 603

Week 6

Grouping Options for Differentiated Instruction
Turn the page for the small group time lesson plan.

Planning Small Group Time on Reading Street!

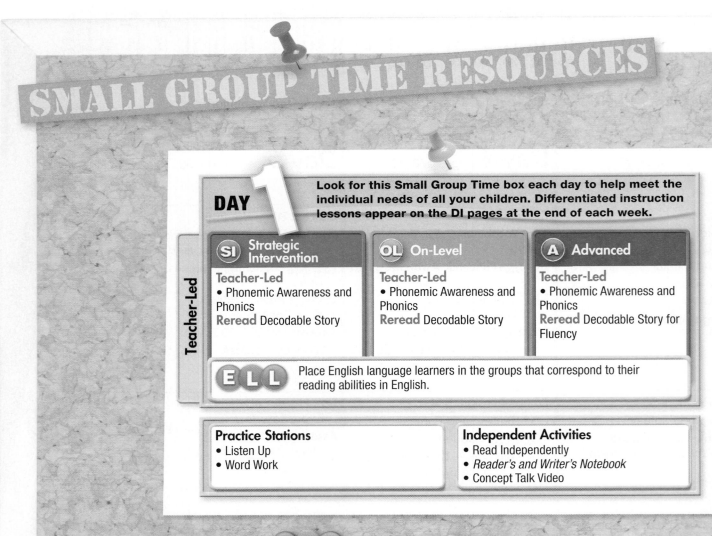

SMALL GROUP TIME RESOURCES

DAY 1

Look for this Small Group Time box each day to help meet the individual needs of all your children. Differentiated instruction lessons appear on the DI pages at the end of each week.

Teacher-Led

SI Strategic Intervention

Teacher-Led
- Phonemic Awareness and Phonics

Reread Decodable Story

OL On-Level

Teacher-Led
- Phonemic Awareness and Phonics

Reread Decodable Story

A Advanced

Teacher-Led
- Phonemic Awareness and Phonics

Reread Decodable Story for Fluency

ELL Place English language learners in the groups that correspond to their reading abilities in English.

Practice Stations
- Listen Up
- Word Work

Independent Activities
- Read Independently
- *Reader's and Writer's Notebook*
- Concept Talk Video

ELL

ELL Poster 12

Day 1

SI Strategic Intervention	**Phonemic Awareness and Phonics,** DI•86 **Reread** Decodable Story 12, DI•86	
OL On-Level	**Phonemic Awareness and Phonics,** DI•91 **Reread** Decodable Story 12, DI•91	
A Advanced	**Phonemic Awareness and Phonics,** DI•94 **Reread** Decodable Story 12 for Fluency, DI•94	
ELL English Language Learners	DI•97–DI•98 Frontload Concept Phonemic Awareness and Phonics Comprehension Skill	

You Are Here!
Unit 2
Week 6

Reading Street Response to Intervention Kit

Practice Station Flip Chart
Reading

Reading Street Leveled Practice Stations Kit

Question of the Week
How are real and make-believe plants alike and different?

SI Strategic Intervention

I Can Read!
Tim and Sam
Written by Joel Shawitz
Illustrated by Lawrence Paul

Decodable Reader

All About Me!
By Claire Alvorado
Listen to Me Reader

In the Garden
by Dennis Benjamin
Concept Literacy Reader

TIRES
Get Set, Roll! Reader

OL On-Level

Tim's Garden
Kindergarten Student Reader

I Can Read!
Tim and Sam
Written by Joel Shawitz
Illustrated by Lawrence Paul
Decodable Reader

TIRES
Get Set, Roll! Reader

A Advanced

A Yard
By D.M. Longo
Illustrated by Jackie Snider
Independent Reader

I Can Read!
Tim and Sam
Written by Joel Shawitz
Illustrated by Lawrence Paul
Decodable Reader

Decodable Reader

Small Group Weekly Plan

Day 2	Day 3	Day 4	Day 5
Phonemic Awareness and Phonics, DI•87 **Reread** Decodable Reader 12, DI•87	**Phonemic Awareness and Phonics,** DI•88 **Read** Concept Literacy Reader K.2.6, DI•88	**Phonemic Awareness and Phonics,** DI•89 **Read** Get Set, Roll! Reader 12, DI•89	**Phonics Review,** DI•90 **Read** Listen to Me Reader K.2.6, DI•90
Phonemic Awareness and Phonics, DI•91 **Reread** Decodable Reader 12, DI•91	**Phonemic Awareness and Phonics,** DI•92 **Read** Kindergarten Student Reader K.2.6, DI•92	Review Phonics and High-Frequency Words **Read** Get Set, Roll! Reader 12, DI•93	**Phonics Review,** DI•93 **Reread** Leveled Books, DI•93
Phonics and Spelling, DI•94 **Reread** Decodable Reader 12 for Fluency, DI•94	**Read** Independent Reader K.2.6 or Kindergarten Student Reader K.2.6, DI•95	**Read** Get Set, Roll! Reader 12 or **Reread** Kindergarten Student Reader K.2.6, DI•96	**Fluency and Comprehension,** DI•96 **Reread** Independent Reader for Fluency, DI•96
DI•99 Comprehension Skill Frontload Vocabulary	DI•100 Review Phonemic Awareness and Phonics Scaffold Conventions	DI•101 Review Phonemic Awareness and Phonics Revisit Concept and Oral Language	DI•102 Language Workshop Writing

Practice Stations for Everyone on Reading Street!

Listen Up!
/i/

Objectives
• Identify and practice words with /i/.

Materials
• *Listen Up!* Flip Chart Activity 12
• *brick, inch, igloo, kitten, iguana, mitten* Picture Cards

Differentiated Activities

● Find the Picture Card for *inch*. Say the sound you hear at the beginning. Find another Picture Card with /i/ at the beginning.

▲ Find the Picture Card for *inch*. Say the sound you hear at the beginning. Point to another Picture Card with /i/ at the beginning. Find the Picture Card for *kitten*. Point to another Picture Card with /i/ in the middle.

■ Find the Picture Card for *inch*. Say the sound you hear at the beginning. Point to all the Picture Cards with /i/ at the beginning. Find the Picture Card for *kitten*. Point to all the Picture Cards with /i/ in the middle.

Word Work
/i/ Spelled *Ii*

Objectives
• Identify and build words with /i/.

Materials
• *Word Work* Flip Chart Activity 12
• *Ii, Tt, Uu, Bb* Alphabet Cards
• *insect, pig, six* Picture Cards
• Letter Tiles

Differentiated Activities

● Find the Alphabet Card for the letter *Ii*. Look for the Picture Card with beginning /i/.

▲ Find the Alphabet Card for the letter *Ii*. Find a Picture Card with beginning /i/. Find Picture Cards with the sound of /i/ in the middle. Look around the room. Find objects in the room that have /i/ at the beginning or in the middle.

■ Find the Alphabet Card for the letter *Ii*. Find the Picture Card with beginning /i/. Find Picture Cards with /i/ in the middle. Use the Letter Tiles to spell other words that begin with /i/ or have /i/ in the middle.

Technology
• Letter Tile Drag and Drop

Words To Know
Sequence words

Objectives
• Identify and use sequence words.

Materials
• *Words to Know* Flip Chart Activity 12
• four pictures that show a sequence of events
• Teacher-made Word Cards: *first, second, next, last*
• paper, pencils, crayons

Differentiated Activities

● Look at the pictures. Put them in order to show what happens *first, second, next,* and *last*.

▲ Put the pictures in order to show what happens *first, second, next,* and *last*. Tell what happens in each picture. Use the words *first, second, next,* and *last*.

■ Put the pictures in order to show what happens *first, second, next,* and *last*. Then draw four pictures that show how to make a sandwich. Tell about the pictures. Use the words *first, second, next,* and *last*.

You Are Here! Unit 2 Week 6

Key
● Below-Level Activities
▲ On-Level Activities
■ Advanced Activities

Practice Station
Flip Chart

Use this week's materials from the Reading Street Leveled Practice Stations Kit to organize this week's stations.

Let's Write!
Caption

Objectives
• Write a caption for a picture.

Materials
• *Let's Write!* Flip Chart Activity 12
• Picture Cards that show examples of nature
• calendar pictures that show examples of nature
• crayons, paper, pencil

Differentiated Activities

● Choose a nature picture. Tell what you see in the picture. Write a caption about what you see.

▲ Draw a picture of your favorite animal in nature. Write a caption that tells about your picture.

■ Choose three nature pictures. Write a caption for each picture. Make sure the caption tells about the picture.

Read For Meaning
Sequence

Objectives
• Identify events in a story.
• Sequence the events using time-order words.

Materials
• *Read for Meaning* Flip Chart Activity 12
• Little Book *A Bed for the Winter*
• pencil, crayons, paper

Differentiated Activities

● Read the Little Book. What happened? Point to pictures in the story that show what happened *first*, what happened *next*, and what happened *last*.

▲ Read the Little Book. Think about what happened. Draw pictures to show what happened *first*, what happened *next*, and what happened *last*.

■ Read the Little Book. Draw pictures to show what happened *first*, what happened *next*, and what happened *last*. Use your pictures to retell what happened using the words *first, next,* and *last*.

Let's Make Art!

Objectives
• Use paper shapes to make an animal home.

Materials
• *Let's Make Art!* Flip Chart Activity 12
• Little Book *A Bed for the Winter*
• art paper, crayons, safety scissors

Differentiated Activities

● Choose an animal from the Little Book. What is its home? Draw the shape of its home on your paper. Cut it out and add details with your crayons.

▲ Choose an animal from the Little Book. What is its home? Draw the shape of its home on your paper. Cut out the home and draw a picture of the animal in it.

■ Choose an animal from the Little Book. Draw the shape of its home on your paper and cut it out. Draw a picture of your animal in its home. Label your picture.

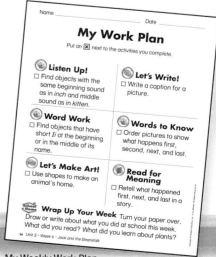

Name _____ Date _____
My Work Plan
Put an ☒ next to the activities you complete.

Listen Up!
☐ Find objects with the same beginning sound as in *inch* and middle sound as in *kitten*.

Let's Write!
☐ Write a caption for a picture.

Word Work
☐ Find objects that have short *Ii* at the beginning or in the middle of its name.

Words to Know
☐ Order pictures to show what happens first, second, next, and last.

Let's Make Art!
☐ Use shapes to make an animal's home.

Read for Meaning
☐ Retell what happened first, next, and last in a story.

Wrap Up Your Week Turn your paper over. Draw or write about what you did at school this week. What did you read? What did you learn about plants?
Unit 2 • Week 6 • *Jack and the Beanstalk*

My Weekly Work Plan

Week 6

Objectives
• Share information and ideas about the concept.

Today at a Glance

Oral Vocabulary
beanstalk, lad, ogre, magic, naughty, lend

Phonemic Awareness
◉ Initial Sounds

Phonics
◉ /i/ Spelled *Ii*

Handwriting
I and *i*

High-Frequency Words
he, for

Comprehension
◉ Realism and Fantasy

Conventions
Adjectives

Writing
Plan a Story

Listening and Speaking
Listen for Plot

TRUCKTOWN
on Reading Street

Start your engines! Display p. 16 of *Truckery Rhymes*.

• Read aloud "Wrecker Rosie Sat on a Wall" and track the print.

• Reread the rhyme and have children chime in as they wish.

• Ask children to identify the rhyming words. (*wall, fall*)

Truckery Rhymes

Concept Talk

Question of the Week

 How are real and make-believe plants alike and different?

Introduce the concept

To build concepts and to focus their attention, tell children that this week they will talk, sing, read, and write about **real and make-believe plants.** Track each word as you read the question of the week.

Play the CD that features a rhyming song about how plants grow.
Plants need things to help them grow. What does a plant need to grow?

🔘 Background Building Audio

ROUTINE **Activate Prior Knowledge** **Team Talk**

① **Think** Have children think for a minute about plants.

② **Pair** Have pairs of children discuss the question of the week. Remind them to take turns speaking. Have children use complete sentences in their discussions about plants.

③ **Share** Call on a few children to share their ideas with the group. Guide discussion and encourage elaboration with prompts such as: Where do you see plants in real life? How are they like make-believe plants?

Routines Flip Chart

Anchored Talk

Develop oral language

Display Talk with Me Chart 12A. What do you see in the pictures? Point to the first picture. What are the girls doing in this picture? They are coloring on the walls. Are they being good or naughty? Point to the boy below them. Another name for boy is *lad.* What else could we call this boy?

We are going to learn six new Amazing Words this week. Listen as I say each word: *beanstalk, lad, ogre, magic, naughty, lend.* Have children say each word as you point to the picture.

Display Sing with Me Chart 12B. Tell children that they are going to sing a song about a boy climbing up a very tall plant. Read the title. Have children describe the picture. Sing the song several times to the tune of "I've Been Working on the Railroad." Listen for the Amazing Words: *beanstalk, lad, ogre, magic, naughty, lend.* Have children stand up and sing with you.

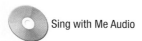 Sing with Me Audio

Talk with Me/Sing with Me Chart 12A

Talk with Me/Sing with Me Chart 12B

ELL **Preteach Concepts** Use the Day 1 instruction on ELL Poster 12 to assess and build background knowledge, develop concepts, and build oral vocabulary.

 Poster 12

Amazing Words

beanstalk	lad
ogre	magic
naughty	lend

Differentiated Instruction

A **Advanced**

Build Background Display the *garden* Picture Card. Discuss with children plants that grow in real gardens. Then have children make up things that might grow in make-believe gardens, such as gloves, trucks, or traffic signs. Have children draw a picture of their make-believe gardens.

ELL

English Language Learners
Build Background Use the pictures on Talk with Me Chart 12A to help children understand words such as *ogre* and *naughty.*

ELL Support Additional ELL support and modified instruction is provided in the *ELL Handbook* and in the ELL Support lessons on pp. DI•97–102.

Objectives

◎ Review initial /i/, /a/, /s/, /p/, and /k/.

• Identify words with initial /i/, /a/, /s/, /p/, and /k/.

• Discriminate words with initial /i/, /a/, /s/, /p/, and /k/.

• Distinguish words with initial /i/ and /a/.

Check Phonemic Awareness
SUCCESS PREDICTOR

My Skills Buddy, pp. 112–113

Phonemic Awareness
Initial Sounds

Picture Card

Reteach

Today we will practice a sound. Listen carefully: /i/ /i/ /i/. Say it with me: /i/ /i/ /i/. Display the *iguana* Picture Card. *Iguana* begins with /i/; /i/, *iguana*. What sound does *iguana* begin with? Continue the routine with the sounds /i/, /a/, /s/, /p/, and /k/ with the following Picture Cards: *insect, ant, astronaut, seal, six, pail, pen, cap, carrot.*

Model

Have children look at the picture on pp. 112–113 of *My Skills Buddy.* Let's listen for words that begin like *iguana, ant, seal, pail,* and *cap.* I see two cats coming in the door. I hear /i/ at the beginning of *in.* The first sound of *in* is /i/. What other things do you see that begin with /i/? Repeat for the sounds /a/, /s/, /p/, and /k/.

Guide practice

As children name example words from the picture, guide them in stating the beginning sound. Discuss some of the bulleted items on p. 112 of *My Skills Buddy.* Save the other bulleted items for Day 2.

Corrective feedback

If... children have difficulty naming words that begin with /i/, /a/, /s/, /p/, or /k/,

then... say *in* (an example word) again, stretching the beginning sound— /i/ /i/ /i/, *in.*

Discriminate sounds

I am going to say two words; one word will begin with /i/. I want you to tell me which one begins with /i/. Listen carefully as I do the first one: *infant, baby.* Which one begins with /i/? *Infant* begins with /i/. Now try it with me. Continue the routine with these sounds and pairs of words: /i/ *itch, scratch;* /a/ *apple, orange;* /a/ *bug, ant;* /s/ *ten, six;* /s/ *well, sick;* /p/ *peach, berry;* /p/ *pickle, sandwich;* /k/ *hot, cold;* /k/ *cabin, house.*

I am going to say a word. If it begins with /i/, clap your hands. If it does not begin with /i/, keep your hands at your side. I will do the first few with you. Listen carefully: *iguana* (clap), *tiger* (hands at side), *it* (clap). Repeat the routine with these sounds and words: /a/ *alligator, anteater, crocodile;* /s/ *otter, seal, whale;* /p/ *pear, banana, peach;* /k/ *pen, carry, color.*

Corrective feedback

If... children cannot discriminate initial sounds,
then... have them enunciate the initial sound in each word: /i/ /i/ /i/, *is.*

When you say /i/, your mouth is open and the front part of your tongue is high in your mouth. Repeat by having children pay attention to their mouth positions as they say /a/, /s/, /p/, and /k/.

Distinguish /i/ and /a/

Remind children that the first sound in *igloo* is /i/ and the first sound in *apple* is /a/. Tell children that you are going to read some words. When you hear /i/ at the beginning of the word, wriggle your fingers. When you hear /a/ at the beginning of the word, clap your hands. Use the following words: *and, in, itch, ant, it, ask, insect, Alex, Isabel, ill, alligator, iguana.*

MONITOR PROGRESS ⟳ **Check Phonemic Awareness   Initial Sounds**

Say *inside* and *outside.* Have children identify the word that begins with /i/. Continue using the following word pairs: /a/ *animal, insect;* /s/ *sand, beach;* /p/ *take, pick;* /k/ *cap, hat.*

If... children cannot discriminate initial sounds,
then... use the small-group Strategic Intervention lesson, p. DI•86, to reteach /i/, /a/, /s/, /p/, and /k/.

Day 1	**Day 2**	**Day 3**	**Day 4**	**Day 5**
Check Phonemic Awareness	Check Sound-Spelling/ Retelling	Check Word Reading	Check Phonemic Awareness	Check Oral Vocabulary

Differentiated Instruction

 Advanced

Support Phonemic Awareness
After studying the picture on pp. 112–113 of *My Skills Buddy,* have children draw their own picture. Ask them to include objects that begin with /i/, /a/, /s/, /p/, and /k/.

Teacher Tip

Be patient and consistent in teaching /i/. Make sure children can distinguish it from /e/ and /a/.

E L L

English Language Learners
Support Phonemic Awareness
Make up a nonsense phrase, such as *The kitty cat likes to tip tap,* to help children hear the difference between /i/ and /a/.

Phonics—Teach/Model
 /i/ Spelled *Ii*

Introduce

Display the *Ii* Alphabet Card. Point to the *igloo* on the Alphabet Card. *Igloo* begins with /i/. Say the word with me: *igloo.* Write the word *igloo* on the board and point to the *i. Igloo* begins with /i/ spelled *i.* Now point to the *Ii* on the card. A sound we learned for this letter is /i/. The names of these letters are uppercase *I* and lower-case *i.* What is a sound for this letter? What are the names of these letters?

Alphabet Card

Model

Write *Six Little Silly Fish* on the board. Point to the *i* in *Six.* The letter *i* can also come in the middle of words. When I see this letter, I think of the sound /i/. The first word is *Six.* Where do you hear /i/ in *Six?* Yes, /i/ is in the middle of *Six.* Point to *Little.* The next word has /i/ too. I know that when I see an *i,* the sound may be /i/. The second word is *Little.* Where do you hear /i/ in *Little?* Repeat for the words *Silly* and *Fish.*

Guide practice

Display Phonics Songs and Rhymes Chart 12. Teach children the song "Six Little Silly Fish" sung to the tune of "The Farmer in the Dell." Play the CD and sing the song several times. When children are familiar with the song, ask them to wriggle their fingers when they hear /i/ words. As you sing the song, point to words with *i.*

Phonics Songs and Rhymes Chart 12

🔘 Phonics Songs and Rhymes Audio

On their own

Pair children and give each pair a familiar book. Have them find words with uppercase *I* and lower-case *i.* Tell them to say /i/ each time they see the letter *I* or *i.*

Blend Words

To review sound-spellings, use Alphabet Cards *Aa, Mm, Pp, Ss,* and *Tt* and the *apple, moon, pillow, sock,* and *tiger* Picture Cards to practice previously taught letters. Then use this routine for sound-by-sound blending to have children blend new words.

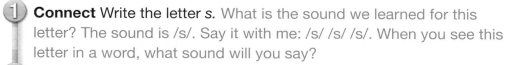 **Sound-by-Sound Blending**

① **Connect** Write the letter *s.* What is the sound we learned for this letter? The sound is /s/. Say it with me: /s/ /s/ /s/. When you see this letter in a word, what sound will you say?

② **Model** Write *Sam* on the board.

- Touch under the letter *S:* What is the sound for this letter? Say it with me: /s/ /s/ /s/. Repeat the routine for *a* and *m*.

- Let's blend the sounds together. Listen as I blend the sounds: /s/ /a/ /m/. Say it with me: /s/ /a/ /m/, *Sam*. Now say it without me.

- Listen as I use *Sam* in a sentence: *Sam is my dog.* Say it with me. Then have children use *Sam* in their own sentences.

③ **Guide Practice** Continue the routine established in step 2 with the words below:

> sit   pat   sip

Children should successfully read these words before reading Decodable Story 12 on pp. 143–144 of *Reader's and Writer's Notebook.*

Corrective feedback If children have trouble reading a word, model blending the sounds to read the word. Then have children say it with you.

Routines Flip Chart

Objectives
- Write *I* and *i*.
- Learn high-frequency words.

Handwriting

Introduce

Write *Ii* on the board. Words that begin with /i/ are written with an uppercase *I* or a lowercase *i*. Which letter is uppercase *I*? Which letter is lowercase *i*?

Model uppercase *I*

Write the name *Ingrid* on the board. Point to the uppercase *I*. This is the uppercase *I*. We use uppercase letters to begin sentences and for the first letter in a person's name. Watch as I trace the uppercase *I* with my finger. Follow the stroke instructions pictured below.

Guide practice

Have children write the uppercase *I* in the air. Use your finger to make an uppercase *I* in the air. Now write it on your hand.

Model lowercase *i*

Point to the lowercase *i* in *Ingrid*. This is a lowercase *i*. Watch as I trace a lowercase *i* with my finger. Write another lowercase *i* on the board following the stroke instructions. Again, have children write *i* in the air and on their hands.

Guide practice

Have children use their Write-On Boards to write a row each of uppercase *I* and lowercase *i*.

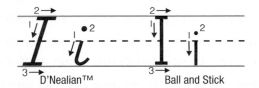

More practice

Use *Reader's and Writer's Notebook,* pp. 141, 142, for additional practice with *i*.

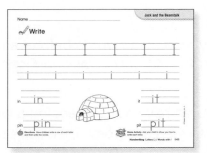

Reader's and Writer's Notebook, p. 141

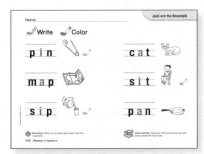

Reader's and Writer's Notebook, p. 142

High-Frequency Words

Introduce Use the routine below to teach high-frequency words *he* and *for.*

 ROUTINE **Nondecodable Words**

1. **Say and Spell** Some words we must learn by remembering the letters rather than saying the sounds. We will say and spell the words to help learn them. **Write *he* on the board.** This is the word *he.* It has two letters. The letters in *he* are *h* and *e.* **Have children say and spell the word, first with you and then without you.**

2. **Demonstrate Meaning** I can use the word *he* in lots of sentences. Here is one sentence: *He is a good police officer.* Now you use the word in a sentence.

Repeat the routine with the word *for.*

Routines Flip Chart

Academic Vocabulary

Write the following on the board:

realism	**fantasy**
draft	**revise**
plot	**sequence**
edit	**expository text**

Point to the list. This week we are going to learn these important words. They are tools for learning. As we work this week, you will hear them many times. **Read the words.** Preteach the Academic Vocabulary at point-of-use by providing a child-friendly description, explanation, or example that clarifies the meaning of each term. Then ask children to restate the meaning of the Academic Vocabulary in their own words.

Differentiated Instruction

SI Strategic Intervention

High-Frequency Words Write this week's high-frequency words on cards for children to tape to the tops of their desks. As they read this week's stories, remind them to look at the high-frequency words and practice saying them.

English Language Learners
High-Frequency Words
All languages do not use gender-specific pronouns. Point out to English learners that *he* stands for males, such as *Ian* or *Mr. Jones,* or animals with male names, such as *Rob the Robin.*

Decodable Story 12
/i/ Spelled Ii and High-Frequency Words

Review

Review the previously taught high-frequency words by having children read each word as you point to it on the Word Wall.

he	for	we	my	like	have	is

Read Decodable Story 12

Display Decodable Story 12. Today we will read a story about a dog named Sam. What is the title of the story? Point to the title of the story. The title of the story is *Sam, Sit!* What sound do you hear in the middle of *sit?* We will read lots of words that have /i/ in this story. Have children read Decodable Story 12 on pp. 143–144 in *Reader's and Writer's Notebook.*

Reader's and Writer's Notebook, pp. 143–144

Use the routine for reading decodable books to read Decodable Story 12.

ROUTINE Reading Decodable Books

1 Read Silently Have children whisper read the story page by page as you listen in.

2 Model Fluent Reading Have children finger point as you read a page. Then have children reread the page without you.

3 Read Chorally Have children finger point as they chorally read the page. Continue reading page by page, repeating steps 1 and 2.

4 Read Individually Have children take turns reading aloud a page.

5 Reread and Monitor Progress As you listen to individual children reread, monitor progress and provide support.

6 Reread with a Partner Have children reread the story page by page with a partner.

Routines Flip Chart

Small Group Time

DAY 1

Break into small groups after reading the Decodable Story and before the comprehension lesson.

Teacher-Led

SI Strategic Intervention	**OL On-Level**	**A Advanced**
Teacher-Led Page DI•86	Teacher-Led Page DI•91	Teacher-Led Page DI•94
• Phonemic Awareness and Phonics	• Phonemic Awareness and Phonics	• Phonemic Awareness and Phonics
• **Reread** Decodable Story 12	• **Reread** Decodable Story 12	• **Reread** Decodable Story 12 for Fluency

ELL Place English language learners in the groups that correspond to their reading abilities in English.

Practice Stations
• Visit the Listen Up! Station
• Visit the Word Work Station

Independent Activities
• Read independently
• Concept Talk Video
• *Reader's and Writer's Notebook*

Differentiated Instruction

SI Strategic Intervention

Build Background Before reading *Sam, Sit!* talk with children about things pets and other animals do. Encourage children to act out their suggestions.

English Language Learners

Frontload Decodable Story Before children read *Sam, Sit!* review /i/ and /a/ words with the *can, cat, pig, wig, six, inch, jam,* and *bag* Picture Cards.

Objectives
◎ Identify and describe realism and fantasy.

Skills Trace

◉ **Realism and Fantasy**
Introduce U2W4D1; U2W6D1; U5W1D1
Practice U2W4D2; U2W4D3; U2W4D4; U2W6D2; U2W6D3; U2W6D4; U5W1D2; U5W1D3; U5W1D4
Reteach/Review U2W4D5; U2W6D5; U3W2D4; U4W6D4; U5W1D5; U6W5D4

KEY:
U=Unit W=Week D=Day

My Skills Buddy, pp. 114–115

Listening Comprehension
Realism and Fantasy

Introduce
Envision It!

Some stories show realism; some show fantasy. If a story shows realism, then everything in it could really happen. If it shows fantasy, then it has things that could not really happen. Good readers pay attention to **realism and fantasy** because it helps them understand the story.

Have children turn to pp. 114–115 in *My Skills Buddy.* One of these pictures shows realism; the other shows fantasy.

• Point to the first picture. What tells you that this picture could really happen? (The fish looks like ones in real life.)

• How can you tell that the second picture is fantasy? (Fish do not sit at desks or hold crayons.)

Model

Read **"Jack and the Beanstalk"** and model how to identify and describe realism and fantasy.

Think Aloud

This story is about a boy who climbs up a very tall plant that grows from magic seeds. That doesn't sound like something that could really happen, so I know that this story shows fantasy.

Guide practice

After reading, ask children questions about realism and fantasy.

- Why does Jack's mother send him to the market? (to sell the family cow) Could this really happen? (yes)
- What does Jack trade for the cow? (five magic beans) Could this really happen? (no)
- What do the beans grow into? (a giant beanstalk) Could this really happen? (no)
- If even one thing in a story could not really happen, then it is a fantasy. Is this story realistic, or is it a fantasy? (fantasy)

More practice

Display Big Book *A Bed for the Winter.* Recall with children that a dormouse looks for a winter home. Page through the story. Have children look at each picture. Is this story realistic or fantasy?

Connect to everyday life

Living animals you can see and hear are real. Can real animals talk to you with words? (no) That's right. Real animals can make noises, but only fantasy animals can talk with words.

Academic Vocabulary

realism the showing of things that could happen in real life

fantasy the showing of make-believe things that could not really happen

English Language Learners
Oral Comprehension To prepare English learners for the Read Aloud, use the teaching routine in the *ELL Handbook* p. DI•98.

Jack and the Beanstalk

Once upon a time, Jack and his mother lived in a little house. They were very poor. His mother told Jack to take their cow to the market and sell it. On his way there, Jack met a man who told him he would give Jack five magic beans for the cow. Jack agreed to the trade. When his mother found out what he had done, she was so angry that she threw the beans out the window into the yard.

By the next day, a giant beanstalk had grown up into the clouds. Jack climbed the beanstalk and followed a path to a castle. A mean giant and his wife lived in the castle. The giant's wife was nice to Jack and helped him hide when the giant came home. After the giant fell asleep, Jack took a bag of gold coins, ran back to the beanstalk, and climbed down. His mother was glad to see him— and the gold coins.

Jack made more trips up the beanstalk. One time he took a hen that laid golden eggs, and another time he took a golden harp that sang. The giant saw Jack take the harp and ran after him. Jack and his mother cut down the beanstalk so the giant couldn't climb down.

Jack and his mother shared the hen's golden eggs and the harp's beautiful music with their neighbors, and they all lived happily ever after.

Objectives
- Identify and use adjectives.
- Generate ideas for a class story.
- Choose an idea for a class story.

Conventions
Adjectives

Teach adjectives

Remind children that adjectives are words that describe people, animals, places, or things. Adjectives can be words that tell about color, shape, size, opposites, or other describing words.

Model

Display the *alligator* Picture Card. *The green alligator walks.* What word describes the alligator? (*green*) *The big alligator has long claws.* What word describes the alligator? (*big*) Repeat the sentence. What word describes the claws? (*long*) What words would you use to describe an alligator?

Guide practice

Display the *apple, bus, fan, playground, queen, rug, starfish, sun, taxi, volcano, wagon, yarn,* and *zebra* Picture Cards. Have children use describing words to tell about the picture on each card. Point out that many different adjectives can be used to describe an object. For example, *red, one, large,* and *delicious* could all describe the same apple.

Team Talk Pair children and have them take turns describing themselves using an adjective. Then have their partner identify the adjective in the sentence.

Daily Fix-It

Use the Daily Fix-It exercise for more conventions practice.

Writing
Writing Process: Plan a Story

**Teach:
Generate
ideas**

Talk with children about narrative writing. We just read a story called *Jack and the Beanstalk.* Display Big Book *Jack and the Beanstalk.* This is the story we are going to read this week. It is another writer's way of telling the same story about Jack and his giant beanstalk.

A story tells about people, places, things, and events. In this story, Jack is a make-believe person, and the beanstalk is a make-believe plant. This week we are going to write a story about a child who has an adventure with a make-believe plant.

**Model:
Generate
ideas**

When we write a story, the first thing we need to do is decide what our story will be about. Who is the child? What is the plant? What can it do that a real plant cannot do? Write *Child, Plant,* and *What Plant Can Do* on the board. I am thinking about a girl named Sue, who grows a sunflower that can talk. Write *Sue* under *Child, sunflower* under *Plant,* and *talk* under *What Plant Can Do.*

**Guide
practice:
Generate
ideas**

Encourage children to use their imaginations to generate other story ideas for the list. Think about plants you know. Think about things you would like these plants to do that real plants cannot do. Think about a child for our story.

Have children turn to p. 145 in *Reader's and Writer's Notebook* and draw pictures of children with plants that can do things real plants cannot. When children are finished, add their ideas to the lists on the board. As a class, choose one set of ideas (for example, a girl named Dina who sees a daisy that can dance). Write the story idea *Dina sees a daisy that can dance* on the board.

**Independent
writing**

Have children draw a picture for the chosen story idea on p. 146 in *Reader's and Writer's Notebook.* Encourage them to make their picture as detailed as possible.

Reader's and Writer's
Notebook, p. 146

i ride in a red wagon
I ride in a red wagon.

This week's practice sentences appear on Teacher Resources DVD-ROM.

ELL

English Language Learners
Professional Development

Access Content Make sure you include the input of English learners as you plan your class story. According to Dr. Jim Cummins of the University of Toronto: "We should constantly search for ways to link academic content with what students already know or what is familiar to them from their family or cultural experiences. This not only validates children's sense of identity, but it also makes the learning more meaningful."

Listening and Speaking
Listen for Plot

Teach

In a story, many different things happen. The things that happen in a story are called the plot.

Model

I will tell you a story. I want you to listen for the things that happen in the story. *Emma wants to give Ana a special present, but she does not have enough money. Dad says they can buy the gift together. Dad and Emma go to the store. They buy a pretty flower and hurry home to give it to Ana.*

Everything that happens in the story makes up the plot. What does Emma want to do? (give Ana a present) What happens in the story? (Emma does not have enough money, so she and Dad buy the present together.)

Guide practice

Reread *A Bed for the Winter* and guide children to tell the plot of the selection. Refer children to the Rules for Listening and Speaking on pp. 1–2 of the *Reader's and Writer's Notebook.* Remind them to face the speaker when listening and to ask questions if they don't understand something. What does the dormouse need? What happens in the selection?

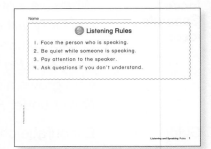

Reader's and Writer's Notebook, p. 1

Wrap Up Your Day

✔ **Oral Language** Today we talked about how make-believe plants are different from real plants. Let's say the Amazing Words again: *beanstalk, lad, ogre, magic, naughty, lend.*

✔ **Homework Idea** Send home the Family Times Newsletter Let's Practice It! TR DVD•23–26.

Tomorrow we will read about a girl and her cat.

Science
The Food Pyramid

Materials: complete food pyramid, copies of food pyramid outline, crayons or markers

Where Does Food Come From? Explain to children that a lot of the food we eat comes from plants. In one of the stories we are reading this week, Jack climbs up a beanstalk. A beanstalk is a plant that gives us beans. Discuss with children different types of beans they have eaten, such as green beans, lima beans, or soybeans.

Color a Food Pyramid Display the food pyramid and discuss its purpose with children. Then point to and describe each section of the pyramid and name several foods that belong in each group. Give each child a copy of a black-and-white food pyramid. Have children color and write or dictate labels for each food group. Then explain that some beans are in the vegetable food group and others are in the meat food group. Have children draw a bean in each of these sections on their food pyramids.

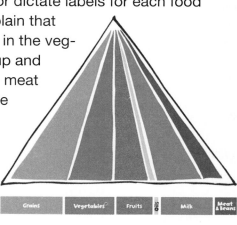

Phonics
Sort Names

Materials: magazine pictures of animals, construction paper, glue

Sort /a/ and /i/ Words Glue the animal pictures onto the construction paper. Label each animal with a name that begins with /a/ or /i/, such as *Izzie, Isabel, Iggy, Annie, Adam,* or *Abby.* Read each name to children and have them identify uppercase *I* or *A* at the beginning of the name. Then have them sort the animals into those with names that begin with /a/ and those with names that begin with /i/. Ask children to choose an animal and write or dictate a sentence using its name. Have them illustrate their sentences.

Math
How Many Animals?

Materials: chalk, chart paper, markers

Count Animals Have children name animals that fly. List the animals on the board. Have children count the animals with you. Record this number on a bar graph. Repeat the routine for animals that run and animals that slither. Have children tell which group has the most and least animals.

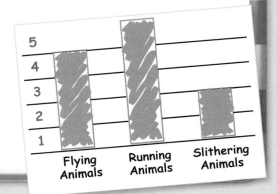

Objectives

- Discuss the concepts to develop oral language.
- Build oral vocabulary.

Today at a Glance

Oral Vocabulary
beanstalk, lad

Phonemic Awareness
◉ Medial and Final Sounds

Phonics
◉ /i/ Spelled *Ii*

Handwriting
Words with *Ii*

Comprehension
◉ Realism and Fantasy

Conventions
Adjectives

Writing
Draft a Story

Vocabulary
Direction Words

TRUCKTOWN on Reading Street

Start your engines! Display p. 16 of *Truckery Rhymes.* Point to "Wrecker Rosie Sat on a Wall." Who remembers the truck in this rhyme? Yes, Wrecker Rosie. Let's read the rhyme together. Now have a child point to the rhyming words as the class reads the rhyme again. Give additional children the opportunity to say the rhyme aloud and track the print.

Truckery Rhymes

Concept Talk

 Question of the Week

How are real and make-believe plants alike and different?

Build concepts

Write the question of the week on the board and track the print as you read it aloud. Have children answer the question in complete sentences. To reinforce the concept and focus children's attention, display Talk with Me/Sing with Me Chart 12B. Tell children that they are going to sing about Jack climbing the beanstalk.

 Sing with Me Audio

Listen for Amazing Words

The Amazing Words *beanstalk* and *lad* are in the song "I've Been Climbing Up a Beanstalk." Have children describe the characters in the picture. Sing the song several times to the tune of "I've Been Working on the Railroad." Ask children to sing along with you. Have them clap when they hear *beanstalk* and *lad.*

ELL Reinforce Vocabulary Use the Day 2 instruction on ELL Poster 12 to reinforce the meanings of high-frequency words.

Talk with Me/Sing with Me Chart 12B

ELL Poster 12

Oral Vocabulary
Amazing Words

Amazing Words **Oral Vocabulary Routine**

Teach Amazing Words

① **Introduce the Word** A *beanstalk* is the tall stem of a plant that grows beans. What's our new Amazing Word for the tall stem of a bean plant? Say it with me: *beanstalk*.

② **Demonstrate** Provide examples to show meaning. *I like to eat beans fresh off the beanstalk.*

Repeat steps 1 and 2.

Introduce the Word A *lad* is a boy. The story we will read this week is about a *lad* named Jack. What's our new Amazing Word for a boy? Say it with me: *lad.*

Demonstrate *I have twelve lads in my class.*

③ **Apply** Tell children to use *beanstalk* and *lad* in complete sentences. Have them draw a picture of a lad and a beanstalk.

Routines Flip Chart

Use Amazing Words

To reinforce the concept and the Amazing Words, have children supply the appropriate Amazing Word for each sentence.

> **The _____ grew up to be a man.** (lad)
>
> **He planted a _____ in his garden.** (beanstalk)

Amazing Words

beanstalk	lad
ogre	magic
naughty	lend

Differentiated Instruction

SI **Strategic Intervention**

Sentence Production If children have difficulty completing the sentences, say a sentence using each Amazing Word and ask children to choose the one that makes sense. Say the sentence together.

English Language Learners

Amazing Words Explain to children that *lad* means *boy* and is more commonly used in British English than American English. Use this opportunity to point out that the same language may be spoken differently in different regions of the world. Talk with children about other places in the world that speak their home languages.

Objectives

◎ Review medial /i/ and /a/ and final /s/, /p/, and /k/.

• Identify words with medial /i/ and /a/ and final /s/, /p/, and /k/.

• Discriminate words with medial /i/ and /a/ and final /s/, /p/, and /k/.

Phonemic Awareness
Medial and Final Sounds

Picture Card

Isolate medial and final sounds

Display the *wig* Picture Card. This is a *wig. Wig* has /i/ in the middle. What is this? What sound does it have in the middle? Continue the routine for medial /i/ and /a/ with the *pig, cat,* and *pan* Picture Cards.

Display the *bus* Picture Card. This is a *bus. Bus* has /s/ at the end. What is this? What sound does it have at the end? Continue the routine for final /s/, /p/, and /k/ with the *dress, cap, mop, brick,* and *rock* Picture Cards.

Picture Card

Model

Display a picture of a fish and point to its fin. This is a *fin.* Listen as I say the sounds: /f/ /i/ /n/. I hear /i/ in the middle of the word *fin:* /f/ /i/ /n/. Say it with me: /f/ /i/ /n/, *fin;* /i/ is in the middle. Let's try some more. Continue the routine with medial /i/ and /a/ and final /s/, /p/, and /k/ with the following words: *dig, bag, tan, toss, grass, hop, tip, pick, tuck.*

Guide practice

Have children look at the picture on *My Skills Buddy* pp. 112–113. Remember, we saw people coming *in* the door. *In* begins with /i/. Now let's look for things in the picture that have /i/ in the middle. Repeat for medial /a/ and final /s/, /p/, and /k/. Discuss with children those bulleted items on p. 112 not discussed on Day 1.

My Skills Buddy, pp. 112–113

Corrective feedback

If... children cannot discriminate medial and final sounds, **then...** have them segment the words.

Listen as I segment a word: /s/ /i/ /k/, *sick.* Say it with me: /s/ /i/ /k/, *sick.* What sound do you hear at the end of *sick?* I hear /k/ at the end of *sick.* Continue with medial sounds in *kiss* and *cat* and final sounds in *purse* and *cup.*

On their own Display Phonics Songs and Rhymes Chart 12. Remind children of the song "Six Little Silly Fish" sung to the tune of "The Farmer in the Dell." Have them sing the song with you several times. This time I want you to raise your hand each time you hear a word that has /i/ in the middle. I will do it with you the first time. After children have identified /i/ words, point out that *splash* has /a/ in the middle; *this* ends with /s/; and *flip, skip,* and *dip* end with /p/.

Six Little Silly Fish

Six little silly fish,
Six little silly fish,
They flip and skip; in water they dip.
Six little silly fish.

The fishies splash and splish,
The fishies splash and splish,
They splash and splish in water like this.
The fishies splash and splish.

Phonics Songs and
Rhymes Chart 12

Review **Blend Sounds** Listen to the sounds in the name *Tim*: /t/ /i/ /m/. Say them with me: /t/ /i/ /m/. Now I'm going to blend the sounds together to say the word: /t/ /i/ /m/, *Tim.* Now you try it with me: /t/ /i/ /m/, *Tim.* Continue the blending routine with the following words: *Sam, pass, tip, sack.*

Differentiated Instruction

SI Strategic Intervention

Support Phonemic Awareness Say /a/ and have children find something in the classroom that has that sound in the middle. If they can't find anything, have them say a word they know that has that sound. Repeat for medial /i/ and final /s/, /p/, and /k/.

ELL

English Language Learners

Phonemic Awareness Point to details in the picture on pp. 112–113 of *My Skills Buddy* as you say the corresponding words. To clarify understanding, have children point to the details as you say the words. Then have children say the words.

Objectives

◎ Practice /i/ spelled *Ii*.

• Blend /i/ words.

⎯ **Check Sound-Spelling**

SUCCESS PREDICTOR

Phonics—Teach/Model
🎯 /i/ Spelled *Ii*

Review

/i/Ii Point to the *igloo* on the *Ii* Alphabet Card. What is this? What sound does *igloo* begin with? *Igloo* begins with /i/. Write *igloo* on the board and point to the letter *i*. The letter we learned for /i/ is *i*.

Model

Write *sit* on the board. This is the word *sit*. Say the sounds in *sit* with me: /s/ /i/ /t/, *sit*. Where do you hear /i/ in *sit*? I hear /i/ in the middle. Point to each letter as you say the sounds: /s/ /i/ /t/, *sit*. Continue the routine with the following words: *tip, Tim, sip*.

Alphabet Card

Guide practice

Envision It!

Have children open *My Skills Buddy* to p. 116. Demonstrate using the blending arrows on *My Skills Buddy* p. 116 as you model blending the first word. Put your finger on the red arrow below the *T*. Say the sound that *T* stands for: /t/. Continue with the letters *i* and *m*. Now I run my finger along the blue arrow as I blend the letters quickly to read *Tim*. Repeat with the word *tip*. Explain that when the letter *m* in *Tim* is changed to the letter *p*, a new word is created. Have children work with a partner to blend the rest of the words on the page.

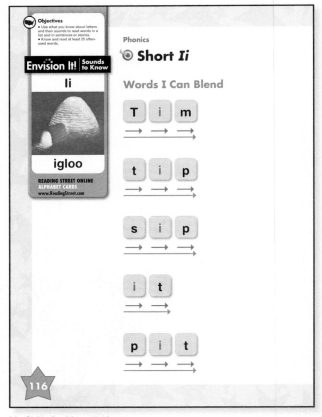

My Skills Buddy, p. 116

Blend

Use the following routine to review blending *i* words.

ROUTINE   Sound-by-Sound Blending

(1) Connect Write the letter *i*. What is the sound we learned for this letter? The sound is /i/. Say it with me: /i/ /i/ /i/. When you see this letter in a word, what sound will you say?

(2) Model Write the word *sit* on the board.

- Point to *s*. What is the sound for this letter? Say it with me: /s/ /s/ /s/. Repeat the routine for *i* and *t*.

- Let's blend the sounds together. Listen as I blend the sounds: /s/ /i/ /t/. Say it with me: /s/ /i/ /t/. Now say it without me.

- Listen as I use *sit* in a sentence: *I sit in my chair.* Say it with me. Have children use *sit* in a sentence.

(3) Guide Practice Continue the routine established in step 2 with these words:

| Sam | Tim | sat | cat | pat | tip | it | mat |

Have children successfully read all of the words before reading Decodable Reader 12 on pp. 118–125 of *My Skills Buddy*.

Corrective Feedback Model blending the sounds to read the word. Then have children say it with you.

Routines Flip Chart

MONITOR PROGRESS ↻ Check Sound-Spelling /i/ Spelled *Ii*

Have children write the letters *Ii* on a blank card. I'm going to read some words. When you hear a word with /i/, hold up your *Ii* card. Say: *fish, igloo, apple, tap, inch, it, man, insect, sink, cup, gift, pin, fun, map, iguana, thin, wish.*

If... children cannot discriminate /i/ words,

then... use the small-group Strategic Intervention lesson, p. DI•87, to reteach /i/.

Continue to monitor children's progress using other instructional opportunities during the week so that children can be successful with the Day 5 Assessment.

Day 1	Day 2	Day 3	Day 4	Day 5
Check Phonemic Awareness	**Check Sound-Spelling/ Retelling**	Check Word Reading	Check Phonemic Awareness	Check Oral Vocabulary

Differentiated Instruction

 Advanced

Support Phonics Write the words *top, sap, pot, sat,* and *Tom* on the board. Have children change the middle letter in each word to *i* and identify the new words that are formed.

537

Success Predictor

DAY 2 Get Ready to Read

Objectives
- Write *I* and *i*.
- Read high-frequency words.

Handwriting
Write Words with *Ii*

Review

Tell children the rule for writing words that begin with /i/. Words that begin with /i/ are written with either an uppercase *I* or a lowercase *i*. We use uppercase *I* at the beginning of sentences or for the first letter of a person's name.

Write *tip* on the board. This is the word *tip.* I use a lowercase *i* in the middle of *tip.* See how I make a lowercase *i.* Write another *i* on the board following the stroke instructions below.

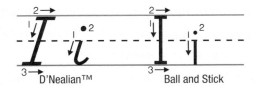

D'Nealian™   Ball and Stick

Guide practice

Have children use their Write-On Boards to make a row of uppercase *I* and a row of lowercase *i.* Circulate around the room, assisting children as necessary. Have children then write the following words: *sip, mat, pit, sit, Tim, Sam, cat.*

High-Frequency Words

Model reading

Have children turn to p. 117 of *My Skills Buddy.* Read the high-frequency words *he* and *for* together. Then have children point to each word and read it themselves. Read the sentences on the *My Skills Buddy* page together to read the new high-frequency words in context.

Team Talk Pair children and have them take turns reading each of the sentences aloud.

High-Frequency Words

Words I Can Read

he

for

Sentences I Can Read

1. He is my cat, Pip.
2. Pip can sit for Tim.
3. He can tap it.

117

My Skills Buddy, p. 117

On their own

Use *Reader's and Writer's Notebook,* p. 147, for additional practice with this week's high-frequency words.

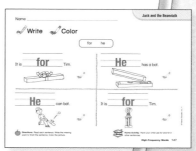

Reader's and Writer's Notebook, p. 147

Differentiated Instruction

 Advanced

Handwriting Have children practice writing the letters *Aa, Cc, Ii, Mm, Pp, Ss,* and *Tt* on their Write-On Boards. Then have them put three of the letters together to write a word, such as *tip* or *sat.*

English Language Learners

High-Frequency Words After the Team Talk activity, have children continue to work in pairs to check understanding. Have one child read one of the sentences aloud while the other child makes a simple drawing to illustrate the sentence.

Objectives
- Read decodable text.
- Read high-frequency words.

Decodable Reader 12
/i/ Spelled *Ii* and High-Frequency Words

Review Review the previously taught high-frequency words. Have children read each word as you point to it on the Word Wall.

I	am	have	he	is	my	we	a	for

Have children turn to Decodable Reader 12, *Tim and Sam,* on p. 118 of *My Skills Buddy*. Today we will read a story about a girl named Sam and her cat, Tim. **Point to the title.** The title of this story is *Tim and Sam.* What is the title? **Point to the name of the author.** The author's name is Joei Shavitz. What does the author do? The illustrator's name is Lawrence Paul. What does the illustrator do?

Use the routine for reading decodable books to read Decodable Reader 12. Have children monitor their comprehension by asking them to think about whether they understand the story. To adjust comprehension, have them reread or read some part aloud.

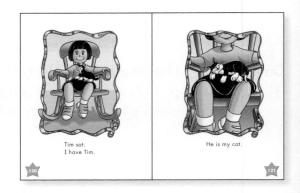

My Skills Buddy, pp. 118–125

 Reading Decodable Books

1. **Read Silently** Have children whisper read the book page by page as you listen in.

2. **Model Fluent Reading** Have children finger point as you read a page. Then have children reread the book without you.

3. **Read Chorally** Have children finger point as they chorally read the page. Continue reading page by page, repeating steps 1 and 2.

4. **Read Individually** Have children take turns reading aloud a page.

5. **Reread and Monitor Progress** As you listen to individual children reread, monitor progress and provide support.

6. **Reread with a Partner** Have children reread the book page by page with a partner.

Routines Flip Chart

Small Group Time

DAY 2

Break into small groups after reading the Decodable Reader and before the comprehension lesson.

Teacher-Led

SI Strategic Intervention	**OL** On-Level	**A** Advanced
Teacher-Led Page DI•87	Teacher-Led Page DI•91	Teacher-Led Page DI•94
• Phonemic Awareness and Phonics	• Phonemic Awareness and Phonics	• Phonics and Spelling
• **Reread** Decodable Reader 12	• **Reread** Decodable Reader 12	• **Reread** Decodable Reader 12 for Fluency

ELL Place English language learners in the groups that correspond to their reading abilities in English.

Practice Stations
• Visit the Word Work Station
• Visit the Words to Know Station

Independent Activities
• Read independently
• Background Building Audio
• *Reader's and Writer's Notebook*

SI **Strategic Intervention**
Support Reading Ask children which name in the book's title has /i/ and which name has /a/. Then ask what letter spells each of these sounds.

English Language Learners
Frontload Decodable Reader
Before children read *Tim and Sam,* have volunteers model the actions sit, pat, and tip.

Listening Comprehension
 Realism and Fantasy

Review

Envision It!

Have children turn to pp. 114–115 of *My Skills Buddy.* Remind them that stories can show realism or fantasy. If a story is realistic, all of the events could really happen. If it is a fantasy, at least one of the events could not really happen.

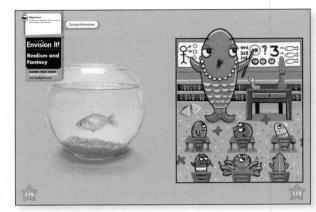

My Skills Buddy, pp. 114–115

First Read—Big Book
Jack and the Beanstalk

Concepts of print

Display the cover of *Jack and the Beanstalk*. Explain that the printed words tell us the title of the story and who wrote and illustrated it.

Preview and predict

Think Aloud

The title of this book is *Jack and the Beanstalk*. What you see on the cover? What do you think this book will be about?

Use illustrations

Take children on a picture walk through the book. Have children tell about what they see in each picture.

Introduce genre

A modern fairy tale is a story with magical characters and events. A fairy tale has been passed down for many years, but a *modern* fairy tale has been updated to sound like it is happening right now.

Set purpose

Say the question of the week: *How are real and make-believe plants alike and different?* Listen as I read to see how the plant in the story and real plants are alike and different.

Model

Read *Jack and the Beanstalk* with expression for enjoyment.

DAY 2
Read for enjoyment

DAY 3
Reread using Develop Vocabulary notes

DAY 4
Reread using Guide Comprehension notes

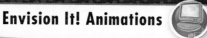
Retell

Check retelling

Envision It!

Have children turn to p. 126 of *My Skills Buddy*. Walk through the retelling boxes as children retell *Jack and the Beanstalk.* Let's retell what happens in the first box—the beginning of the story. Jack trades the family cow for five magic beans. Let's retell what happens in the next box. Continue with the rest of the boxes. After children retell the story as a group, have them draw a picture to retell a favorite part of the story. Have them write or dictate a word or sentence to go with their picture.

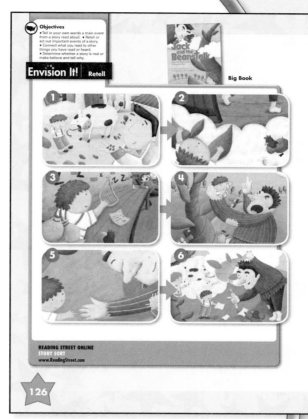

My Skills Buddy, p. 126

Top-Score Response A top-score response describes events in sequence with details.

 Don't Wait Until Friday

MONITOR PROGRESS | **Check Retelling**

 Grade K Retelling Cards

If... children have difficulty retelling the story,

then... go through the story one page at a time, and ask children to tell what happens in their own words.

Day 1	**Day 2**	**Day 3**	**Day 4**	**Day 5**
Check Phonemic Awareness	Check Sound-Spelling/ Retelling	Check Word Reading	Check Phonemic Awareness	Check Oral Vocabulary

 Success Predictor

Differentiated Instruction

A **Advanced**

Retell Have two children volunteer to be Jack and the ogre. Have the rest of the children work together to retell the story. As the children retell parts of the story, have the volunteers act out what is being told. Have the children retelling the story "direct" the children playing Jack and the ogre.

Retelling Plan

☑ **Week 1** Assess Advanced students.

☑ **Week 2** Assess On-Level students.

☑ **Week 3** Assess Strategic Intervention students.

☑ **Week 4** Assess Advanced students.

☑ **Week 5** Assess On-Level students.

☑ **This week assess Strategic Intervention students.**

E L L

English Language Learners

Support Comprehension Other languages have words for realism and fantasy too. In Spanish, the word for realism is *realismo* and the word for fantasy is *fantasía.*

Objectives

◎ Practice realism and fantasy.
• Confirm predictions.
• Practice adjectives.

Think, Talk, and Write

Discuss concept

We're learning about how real and make-believe plants are alike and different.

• What are some plants that you like to look at?

• What are some plants that give us food?

• What are the tallest plants you can think of?

Confirm predictions

Have children recall their predictions before you read *Jack and the Beanstalk*.

• What did you think the story would be about?

• Was your prediction correct?

Have children turn to p. 127 of *My Skills Buddy*. Read the questions and directives and have children respond.

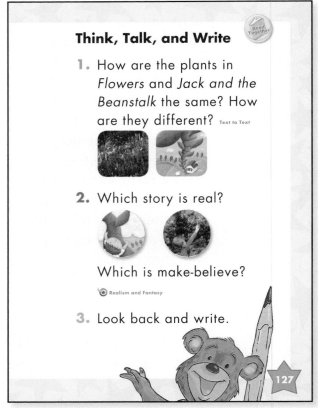

My Skills Buddy, p. 127

Text to text

1. Do you remember the real plants we read about in the selection *Flowers*? How are the plants in *Flowers* and *Jack and the Beanstalk* the same? How are they different? Do you think you could see a beanstalk like the one Jack climbs in real life?

◉ Realism and fantasy

2. Which story is real, *Flowers* or *Jack and the Beanstalk*? (*Flowers*) Which is make-believe? (*Jack and the Beanstalk*)

Look back and write

3. Let's look back at our story and write about it. We remember that Jack took things from the ogre's house. Listen for all the things he took. Read pp. 7–11 of *Jack and the Beanstalk.* Now let's write our ideas. Discuss with children each item that Jack took from the ogre's house. Record their responses on chart paper. (Possible responses: magic hen that lays gold eggs, bags of gold, golden harp.)

Conventions
Adjectives

Remind children of what they learned about adjectives.
We call words that describe people, animals, places, and
things *adjectives*. Adjectives can describe size, color, number,
or shape. Adjectives can also describe opposites.

Guide practice I am going to use an adjective in a sentence. Tell me which word
describes the size, color, number, shape, or opposite of something
in the sentence. Write these sentences on the board and draw a
plant above the word *beanstalk* wherever it occurs:

> **I see a big beanstalk.** (big)
>
> **Do you see a green beanstalk?** (green)
>
> **I see three beanstalks.** (three)

Read the sentences aloud with children. Have them identify the
adjective in each sentence. Have children copy one of the adjectives onto their Write-On Boards.

On their own Use *Reader's and Writer's Notebook*,
p. 148, for more practice with
adjectives.

Daily Fix-It Use the Daily Fix-It exercise for more
conventions practice.

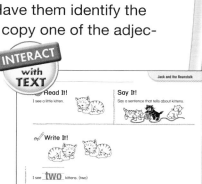

Reader's and Writer's
Notebook, p. 148

Differentiated Instruction

 Strategic Intervention
Look Back and Write Tell
children how you would feel if
Jack came into your house and
took things that belonged to
you. Explain why you would be
angry with him, as the ogre was.

Daily Fix-It

jim sits on a big hill
Jim sits on a big hill.

This week's practice sentences
appear on Teacher Resources
DVD-ROM.

ELL

English Language Learners
Think, Talk, and Write To help
children see the difference
between real and make-believe
plants, take a picture walk
through *Flowers* and *Jack and
the Beanstalk* before the Think,
Talk, and Write activity. Help
children use the photographs
and illustrations to see the
differences between the two
kinds of plants.

Objectives
- Develop and write a first draft of a class story.
- Identify and use direction words.

Writing
Writing Process: Draft a Story

Teach

Today we're going to decide what will happen in our story about Dina and the dancing daisy. Then we're going to write a draft of our story. A draft is a first try at writing. We'll come back to our draft later and make it better. Right now we want to figure out how to get our words down on paper in the right order.

Model

Explain that a story has a beginning, a middle, and an end. In a story, things that happen first are at the beginning, things that happen next are in the middle, and things that happen last are at the end. Display *Jack and the Beanstalk*. At the beginning, Jack and the ogre talk about the past. In the middle, Jack asks the ogre to share with him. At the end, Jack and the ogre write down their story.

In a row on the board, write three short sentences or draw three simple illustrations that tell about these story events. Label them *Beginning, Middle,* and *End.*

Guide practice

Write *Beginning, Middle,* and *End* in a row on the board. What happens at the beginning of our story? What happens first? Where is Dina? (Possible event: *Dina is in the garden.*) Write or illustrate children's suggestions under *Beginning.* What happens in the middle of our story? What happens next? What does Dina see? (Possible event: *She sees a daisy.*) Write or illustrate children's suggestions under *Middle.* What happens at the end of our story? What happens last? What is the daisy doing? (Possible event: *It is dancing a jig.*) Write or illustrate children's suggestions under *End.*

Reread and discuss the events you wrote on the board. As a class, choose a beginning event, a middle event, and an ending event for the story.

Independent writing

On p. 149 in *Reader's and Writer's Notebook,* have children draw pictures of the events at the beginning, in the middle, and at the end of the class story. Then have them write or dictate words or sentences about the events or copy your sentences from the board on p. 150 in *Reader's and Writer's Notebook.*

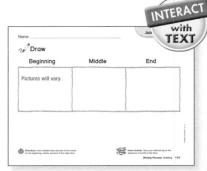

Reader's and Writer's Notebook, p. 149

Vocabulary
Direction Words

Model

Have children turn to p. 128 of *My Skills Buddy.* Use the first Vocabulary bullet on the page to guide the discussion. Direct children to the girl's left hand. This is the girl's *left* hand. This is her *left* leg and her *left* ear. Everything on this side of her body is *left*. Direct children to the girl's right hand. This is the girl's *right* hand. This is her *right* leg and her *right* ear. Everything on this side of her body is *right*. Turn around so your back is facing children. Hold up your left hand. This is my *left* hand. Hold up your right hand. This is my *right* hand.

My Skills Buddy, p. 128

Guide practice

Write the words *left* and *right* on the board. Point to each word as you read it.

> **left**　　**right**

Let's practice our new words. Remember, it doesn't matter which way you are facing. Hold up your left hand. This is always your *left* hand. Hold up your right hand. This is always your *right* hand. Sing the "Hokey Pokey" and teach children the movements. Remind them to pay special attention to the words *left* and *right* in the song.

On their own

Hold up AlphaBuddy and name a body part with the word *left* or *right*, such as *left foot*. Have a child point to that part on AlphaBuddy. Repeat until each child correctly identifies a body part using the word *left* or *right*.

Wrap Up Your Day

✔ **Concept Talk** Today we read a story about a boy who climbs a beanstalk. What does the boy do when he gets to the top of the beanstalk? Who does he meet there?

✔ **Conventions** I am going to say a sentence. Tell me which word is the adjective, or describing word, in the sentence: *Juan drew a colorful picture.* Which word describes Juan's picture?

✔ **Vocabulary Skill** Today we talked about words for directions: *left, right.* Stand with your back to children. Hold up your left hand. Is this my left hand or my right hand? Stick out your right foot. Is this my left foot or my right foot?

✔ **Homework Idea** Ask children to make up a complete sentence about themselves that uses an adjective.

Preview DAY 3

Tomorrow we will reread the story about Jack and the beanstalk.

Science
Six, Four, Two, None

Materials: pictures of animals clipped from magazines, poster board, markers, glue

Sort Animals Pair children and give each pair assorted animal pictures. Be sure each pair has animals with six, four, two, and no legs. Have pairs count how many legs each animal has and sort them into groups.

Talk with children about their observations of the animals in each group. Some shared characteristics might include:

- 6-legged: insects, most have wings, body cover is hard

- 4-legged: many have fur; some have scales; may be good climbers, runners, or jumpers

- 2-legged: birds, bats, people; not as good at jumping and climbing

- legless: worms, snakes, fish; use muscles to move

Make and Label Posters Make four posters titled *Animals with Six Legs, Animals with Four Legs,* and so on. Have each pair of children glue one appropriate picture on each poster.

Comprehension
Real or Make-Believe

Materials: Big Book *Jack and the Beanstalk,* encyclopedia or nature magazine

Analyze Illustrations Ask children if they think the drawings in *Jack and the Beanstalk* look real or make-believe. Compare a drawing of the beanstalk in the story with a photograph of a real beanstalk. Guide children to conclude that the cartoon-style illustrations show some aspects of the plant that are real and some that are make-believe. Have children help you list things that are *Real* about the illustrations in the book and things that are *Make-Believe*.

Phonics
Alphabet Partners

Materials: letter cards for *A, a, C, c, I, i, M, m, P, p, S, s, T, t*

Match Organize 14 children into 2 groups. Have them stand on opposite sides at the front of the room. The other children stay seated. Give one group of children cards with uppercase letters and the other group cards with lowercase letters. Have children find their uppercase/lowercase match. Say one of the letter sounds while standing behind each pair of alphabet partners. When you stand behind the correct letters for one of the sounds, seated children should say, "Yes!".

Objectives
- Share information and ideas about the concept.
- Build oral vocabulary.

Today at a Glance

Oral Vocabulary
ogre, magic

Phonemic Awareness
◉ Initial and Medial /i/

Phonics
◉ /i/ Spelled *Ii*

Comprehension
◉ Realism and Fantasy

Conventions
Adjectives for Opposites

Writing
Revise a Story

Listening and Speaking
Listen for Plot

TRUCKTOWN on Reading Street

Start your engines! Display p. 16 of *Truckery Rhymes.* Do you know the original "Humpty Dumpty"? Recite it first, and then have children repeat it with you:

Humpty Dumpty sat on a wall,
Humpty Dumpty had a great fall.
All the King's horses,
and all the King's men
Couldn't put Humpty
together again!

Truckery Rhymes

Concept Talk

 Question of the Week
How are real and make-believe plants alike and different?

Write the question of the week on the board. Read the question as you track the print. Talk with children about feelings. Remind children to speak clearly and to take turns speaking.

Listen for Amazing Words

Let's Sing Display Sing with Me Chart 12B. Remind children that yesterday they sang "I've Been Climbing Up a Beanstalk" and listened for the words *beanstalk* and *lad.* Today we are going to listen for the Amazing Words *ogre* and *magic.* Sing the song several times to the tune of "I've Been Working on the Railroad." Have children sing along with you, clapping their hands when they say the Amazing Word *ogre* or *magic.*

I've Been Climbing Up a Beanstalk

I've been climbing up a beanstalk,
A clever lad am I!
A magic, tall, wide beanstalk
To find an ogre in the sky.
I hope he doesn't think I'm naughty,
For climbing up so high.
Lend me all of your riches,
Then I'll say goodbye!

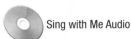 Sing with Me Audio

Talk with Me/Sing with Me
Chart 12B

Oral Vocabulary
Amazing Words

Amazing Words

beanstalk   lad
ogre   magic
naughty   lend

Teach Amazing Words

Amazing Words   Oral Vocabulary Routine

1. Introduce the Word One of the characters in the story *Jack and the Beanstalk* is an *ogre*. An *ogre* is a giant or monster in a fairy tale. What's our new Amazing Word for a giant or monster in a fairy tale? Say it with me: *ogre*.

2. Demonstrate Provide examples to show meaning. *The ogre got mad at Jack.*

Repeat steps 1 and 2.

Introduce the Word *Magic* is the skill of performing tricks that seem to be impossible. What's our new Amazing Word for performing tricks that seem to be impossible? Say it with me: *magic*.

Demonstrate *The magic beans grew into a tall beanstalk.*

3. Apply Have children use *ogre* and *magic* in a sentence to talk about *Jack and the Beanstalk.* Have them illustrate their sentences.

Routines Flip Chart

Differentiated Instruction

A Advanced

Build Vocabulary Have children draw a picture of an *ogre*. Remind children that ogres are make-believe characters that do not really exist. Encourage them to use their imaginations as they draw their ogres.

Use Amazing Words

To reinforce the concept and the Amazing Words, have children supply the appropriate Amazing Word for each sentence.

The _____ jumped out from behind a bush. (ogre)

The little girl performed a _____ trick. (magic)

ELL Expand Vocabulary
Use the Day 3 instruction on ELL Poster 12 to help children expand vocabulary.

 Poster 12

ELL

English Language Learners
Visual Support Use the pictures on the Talk with Me Chart to help children complete the Amazing Word sentences.

Objectives

◎ Isolate initial and medial /i/.

• Discriminate initial and medial /i/.

• Substitute sounds.

Phonemic Awareness
↻ Initial and Medial /i/

Review	**Initial /i/** Display the *inch* Picture Card. This is an *inch. Inch* begins with /i/, *inch.* What sound do you hear at the beginning of *inch*? Continue with the *igloo, iguana,* and *insect* Picture Cards.
Practice medial /i/	Display the *pig* Picture Card. This is a *pig.* Listen to the sounds in *pig:* /p/ /i/ /g/. Where do you hear /i/ in *pig*? (in the middle) The /i/ in *pig* is in the middle. Continue the routine with the words *pin, sit, tip,* and *wig.*
Discriminate sounds	Listen to the middle sound in *pit. Pit* has /i/ in the middle. Now listen to these two words: *cap, tip.* Which word has the same middle sound as *pit*? Does *cap* have /i/ in the middle? (no) Does *tip* have /i/ in the middle? (yes) *Pit* and *tip* have /i/ in the middle. Continue the routine with these pairs of words: *jog, big; dot, pin; sit, pod; Tim, Sam.*
On their own	Display the *kitten, doll, pig,* and *quilt* Picture Cards. Have children choose one of the words with /i/ in the middle and illustrate it.

Picture Card

Picture Card

Identify and count syllables

We have been reading and talking about Jack and his beanstalk. Listen as I say the word slowly: *bean-stalk*. Clap your hands for each word part, or syllable, in the word: *bean-stalk*. How many times did you clap? (two) How many word parts, or syllables, are in the word *bean-stalk*? What are those words parts? (*bean* and *stalk*) Continue the activity by having children identify and count syllables in these spoken words: *Jack, ogre, cow, morning, magic*.

Corrective feedback

If... children cannot identify the syllables in the words, **then...** provide practice saying each syllable separately before saying the word again.

Substitute phonemes

Listen to the word I am going to say: *tip*. Say it with me: /t/ /i/ /p/, *tip*. I can make a new word by changing the middle sound. Listen: /t/ /a/ /p/. Sat it with me: /t/ /a/ p/, *tap*. What is the new word? The new word is *tap*. We can change the first, middle, and last sounds to make new words. **Continue practice with the following string of words:** *pit, pat, cat, cap, map, mat, sat, sit.*

Differentiated Instruction

 Advanced

Isolate Medial Sounds Say the words *hit* and *hot.* What sound is different—the beginning, the middle, or the end? Repeat the routine with *pit, pat* and *tip, top.*

Phonics—Teach/Model

 ## /i/ Spelled *Ii*

Review   **/i/Ii** Display the *Ii* Alphabet Card and point to the *igloo*. What sound do you hear at the beginning of *igloo*? What letter spells that sound? Point to the letters *Ii*. What is the sound we learned for this letter? What are the names of these letters?

Review   **Letter Names and Sounds** Use Alphabet Cards to review the following letter names and sounds: *Aa, Cc, Mm, Pp, Ss, Tt.*

Blend sounds   Write the word *sip* on the board. Point to each letter as you say the sound: /s/ /i/ /p/. When I blend these sounds together, I make the word *sip*. Say the sounds with me: /s/ /i/ /p/. Now blend the sounds together: /s/ /i/ /p/, *sip*. Repeat the blending routine with *Tim, pit,* and *sit.*

s	i	p

More practice   Use *Reader's and Writer's Notebook,* p. 151, for additional practice with /i/.

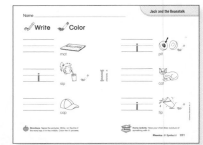

Reader's and Writer's Notebook, p. 151

Review **Sound-Spelling** Display the *Cc* Alphabet Card. What sound do you hear at the beginning of *cactus?* What letter spells that sound? Yes, the letter *c* spells /k/. Review the following sounds and letters with Alphabet Cards: *Aa, Ii, Mm, Pp, Ss, Tt.*

Review **High-Frequency Words** Write *for* on the board. This is the word *for.* What is this word? Continue the routine with *he, the, is,* and *like.*

MONITOR PROGRESS   Check Word Reading   High-Frequency Words

Write *for, he, the, is,* and *like* on the board. Have children take turns reading the words.

Practice reading these words from Kindergarten Student Reader K.2.6, *Tim's Garden.*

Tim	sits	at	it

If... children cannot read the high-frequency words, **then...** write the words on cards for them to practice at home.

If... children cannot blend sounds to read the words, **then...** provide practice blending the words in chunks, /t/ -im.

If... children can successfully blend sounds to read the words, **then...** have them read Kindergarten Student Reader K.2.6, *Tim's Garden.*

Day 1	Day 2	Day 3	Day 4	Day 5
Check Phonemic Awareness	Check Sound-Spelling/ Retelling	Check Word Reading	Check Phonemic Awareness	Check Oral Vocabulary

Success Predictor

Differentiated Instruction

 Strategic Intervention

High-Frequency Words Have children work in pairs to review high-frequency words. Write the words on flash cards. Have the first child display the flash card for his or her partner who then says the word aloud.

Word Reading

Success Predictor

Objectives
- Read /i/ words.
- Read high-frequency words.

Kindergarten Student Reader K.2.6
🔄 /i/ Spelled *Ii* and
High-Frequency Words

Review

Review the previously taught high-frequency words. Have children read each word as you point to it on the Word Wall.

the	is	for	he	likes

Teach rebus words

Write the word *garden* on the board. This is the word *garden*. Name the letters with me: *g, a, r, d, e, n*. Look for the word *garden* in the story we read today. There will be a picture above the word to help you read it. Continue with the words *bunny, worm, bird,* and *happy*.

Read Kindergarten Student Reader K.2.6

Display Kindergarten Student Reader K.2.6. Today we are going to read a new book. Point to the title of the book. The title of this book is *Tim's Garden*. The author's name is Benton Walston. The author writes the words in the story.

Use the reading decodable books routine to read the Kindergarten Student Reader.

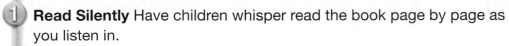

ROUTINE   **Reading Decodable Books**   *Small Group*

1. **Read Silently** Have children whisper read the book page by page as you listen in.

2. **Model Fluent Reading** Have children finger point as you read a page. Then have children reread the page without you.

3. **Read Chorally** Have children finger point as they chorally read the page. Continue reading page by page, repeating steps 1 and 2.

4. **Read Individually** Have children take turns reading aloud a page.

5. **Reread and Monitor Progress** As you listen to individual children reread, monitor progress and provide support.

6. **Reread with a Partner** Have children reread the book page by page with a partner.

Routines Flip Chart

Kindergarten Student Reader K.2.6

Differentiated Instruction

 Advanced

Expand Rebus Word The word *worm* is in this book. Have you ever touched a worm? What does a worm feel like? Write children's suggestions on the board. Have children tell how they feel about worms and other animals found in gardens.

Small Group Time

DAY 3 Break into small groups to read the Kindergarten Student Reader before the comprehension lesson.

Teacher-Led

SI Strategic Intervention
Teacher-Led Page DI•88
• Phonemic Awareness and Phonics
• **Read** Concept Literacy Reader K.2.6 or Kindergarten Student Reader K.2.6

OL On-Level
Teacher-Led Page DI•92
• Phonemic Awareness and Phonics
• **Read** Kindergarten Student Reader K.2.6

A Advanced
Teacher-Led Page DI•95
• **Read** Independent Reader K.2.6 or Kindergarten Student Reader K.2.6

ELL Place English language learners in the groups that correspond to their reading abilities in English.

Practice Stations
• Visit the Words to Know Station
• Visit the Let's Write! Station

Independent Activities
• Read independently
• Audio Text of Big Book
• *Reader's and Writer's Notebook*

Objectives
- Recall and retell a story.
- Practice realism and fantasy.
- Develop and use vocabulary.
- Develop and use comprehension skills.

Comprehension

Retell the selection

Have children turn to p. 126 of *My Skills Buddy* and use the retelling boxes to retell the story *Jack and the Beanstalk*.

Envision It!

My Skills Buddy, p .126

> **Think Aloud** Direct children to the first retell box. This is when Jack trades the family cow for five magic beans. Tell me what happens next.

Continue reviewing the retelling boxes and having children retell the story.

Review

Realism and Fantasy Display illustrations in *Jack and the Beanstalk*. Let's think about whether or not this story could really happen.

- What does Jack get when he trades the family cow? (five magic beans) Could this really happen? (no)

- What do the beans grow into? (a beanstalk that is so tall you can't see the top) Could this really happen? (no)

- How does Jack get to the ogre's house? (He climbs to the top of the beanstalk.) Could this really happen? (no)

- Could this story happen in real life? (no)

More practice

Use *Reader's and Writer's Notebook,* p. 152, for additional practice with realism and fantasy.

Reader's and Writer's Notebook, p. 152

Second Read—Big Book
Jack and the Beanstalk

Reread *Jack and the Beanstalk*. Follow the Day 3 arrow beginning on p. 560 and use the Develop Vocabulary notes to prompt conversations about the story.

Have children use the Amazing Words *beanstalk, lad, ogre, magic, naughty,* and *lend* to talk about the story.

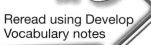

DAY **2**
Read for enjoyment

DAY **3**
Reread using Develop Vocabulary notes

DAY **4**
Reread using Guide Comprehension notes

Differentiated Instruction

A **Advanced**

Build Vocabulary Remind children that a modern fairy tale is a new version of an old story. Have them choose a different plant that Jack could climb and use it to make up a new version of *Jack and the Beanstalk*.

English Language Learners

Access Content Review the terms *realism* (things that can really happen) and *fantasy* (things that are make-believe).

Develop Vocabulary

DAY 3

Wh- question

Who are the characters in this fairy tale? (Jack and the ogre)

- The characters are Jack and the ogre. Tell me about the ogre. Does he look like an ogre to you?

Big Book, pp. 2–3

Guide Comprehension

DAY 4

Wh- question

What do you notice about the text on this page? (It rhymes. It has a rhythm.)

- The text rhymes and has rhythm. What types of texts usually have rhythm and rhyme?

Inferential

How does Jack get the magic beans? (He trades a cow for them.)

- Jack trades the family cow for the magic beans. What do you think would be a fair trade for the cow?

Develop Vocabulary trade

I lost our milk cow
In a trade.

You got five beans.
That's all you made.

Big Book, pp. 4–5

Monitor and Fix Up

Who says, "You got five beans. That's all you made"? (the ogre)

- There are little pictures next to all of the words that show who is talking. If you don't know which character is talking, how can you use the little pictures to help you understand the story?

Develop Vocabulary, continued

Wh- question

DAY 3

What does Jack do when he gets to the top of the beanstalk? (steals the magic hen)

- Jack stole the ogre's magic hen. How do you think that made the ogre feel?

Develop Vocabulary stole

Big Book, pp. 6–7

Guide Comprehension, continued

DAY 4

Realism and Fantasy

What about this beanstalk is like a real plant? (It is green. It has leaves.)

- The plant is green and has leaves like a real plant. What about this plant is make-believe?

Distancing

What is the ogre doing in this picture?
(sleeping)

- The ogre is sleeping in a chair at the table.
  Where do you like to sleep?

Expand Vocabulary confess, harp

Big Book, pp. 8–9

Recall

What has happened in the story so far? (First,
Jack trades the cow for beans that grow
into a giant beanstalk. Then he climbs the
beanstalk and goes into the ogre's house.
Finally, Jack takes the ogre's magic hen,
bags of gold, and golden harp.)

Develop Vocabulary, continued

DAY 3

Open-ended

What are the rhyming words on these pages? (*true* and *do*)

- What other words rhyme with *true* and *do*?

Big Book, pp. 10–11

Guide Comprehension, continued

DAY 4

Inferential

What does the ogre say about what Jack does? (He says it is naughty.)

- Do you think what Jack does is naughty? Why or why not?

Open-ended

Why does Jack say he took the ogre's things? (because he and his mother are poor and hungry)

- He says he took the hen, bags of gold, and harp because he and his mother are poor and hungry. Do you think the ogre is poor? Why or why not?

Develop Vocabulary poor

Now Mister Ogre,
Don't be mad.
I do admit
That I was bad,
But we were poor
And hungry, too.

You give them back
Or I'll eat you!

Big Book, pp. 12–13

Distancing

What is the ogre doing in this picture? (yelling at Jack; shaking his finger at Jack)

- The ogre is yelling and shaking his finger at Jack because he is mad. What do you do when you are mad?

Develop Vocabulary, continued

DAY 3

Wh- question

Where is this part of the story happening? (outside near the beanstalk)

- The setting of the story here is outside by the beanstalk. When is the story taking place?

Big Book, pp. 14–15

Guide Comprehension, continued

DAY 4

Distancing

What does Jack want from the ogre? (He wants the ogre to lend him his hen.)

- Jack wants the ogre to let him borrow his hen once in a while.

How is borrowing different from just taking?

Distancing

Now what does Jack want to borrow from the ogre? (his harp)

- Jack says it would be a special treat to borrow the ogre's harp. Have you ever heard the music of a harp? How does it sound?

Develop Vocabulary treat

Expand Vocabulary tone

Not all the time.
Just now and then.
And also for
A special treat,
Please lend your harp.
It sounds so sweet.

Why, yes, it has
A lovely tone.
But don't forget,
It's just a loan!

Big Book, pp. 16–17

Recall

How often does Jack say he wants to borrow the ogre's hen? (now and then)

- Jack wants to borrow the hen "now and then." What does "now and then" mean?

Develop Vocabulary, continued

DAY 3

Distancing

What does Jack ask the ogre for now? (a bag of gold)

- Now Jack asks the ogre for a bag of gold, or a bag of money. What would you do with a bag full of money?

Expand Vocabulary spare

> A bag of gold
> Perhaps you'd share?

> A half-bag's all
> That I can spare.

18 19

Big Book, pp. 18–19

Guide Comprehension, continued

DAY 4

Open-ended

What is the hen doing in this picture? (laughing)

- The hen seems to be laughing. Why do you think the hen is laughing?

Realism and Fantasy

Who is shaking hands in this picture? (Jack, the ogre, and the hen)

- Jack, the ogre, and the hen are all shaking hands in this picture. Can a hen shake hands in real life?

Now that's all settled
And we're friends
And that's the way
Our story ends.

Let's write it down.   Let's write it now.

20   21

Big Book, pp. 20–21

Inferential

What do Jack and the ogre decide to do? (write their story down)

- They decide to write their story down. Who do you think will read their story?

Develop Vocabulary, continued

Wh- question

Why is there a white cloud above Jack's head? (It shows his thoughts.)

* The cloud shows what Jack is thinking. What is Jack thinking about in this picture?

DAY 3

Big Book, pp. 22–23

Guide Comprehension, continued

DAY 4

Recall

How did the ogre feel earlier in the story? (He was mad.)

* How do you think the ogre feels now?

Distancing

How do you think Jack and the ogre feel about each other now? **(They are friends.)**

- Jack makes a new friend when he climbs up the beanstalk. Have you ever made a new friend in a strange way?

Continue with DAY **3**

Conventions p. 572

And when our story
Is all through,
You'll read to me!
I'll read to you!

Big Book, p. 24

Distancing

What do Jack and the ogre want to do once their story is written? **(read it to each other)**

- They want to read their story to each other. Who do you like to read with?

Skip to DAY **4**

Conventions p. 586

Objectives
- Review adjectives for opposites.
- Revise a class story by adding details and sentences.

Conventions
Adjectives for Opposites

Review Write these adjectives on the board in two columns:

tall	good
dark	sad
happy	short
bad	light

Remind children of what they learned about adjectives for opposites. Some adjectives tell how things are opposites. Read each word on the board to children. Have them echo read the words with you. Then have volunteers come to the board and draw lines to connect the adjectives that describe opposites. (*tall, short; dark, light; happy, sad; bad, good*)

Guide practice Hold up AlphaBuddy. Let's think of adjectives for opposites. Is AlphaBuddy a big bear or a small bear? (a small bear) The words *big* and *small* are opposites, and they are words that describe things, or adjectives.

What is the opposite of *short*? (*tall*) Continue by asking for the opposites of other words, such as *loud* (*soft*), *wide* (*narrow*), *heavy* (*light*), and *sweet* (*sour*).

Team Talk Pair children and have them find two things in the room that they can describe with adjectives for opposites. Have one partner stand next to each object. When you call on them, have children tell a descriptive sentence, such as *This cabinet is tall, but this bookcase is short.* Help children write one of the adjectives they used on their Write-On Boards.

On their own Use *Reader's and Writer's Notebook,* p. 153, for more practice with adjectives for opposites.

Daily Fix-It Use the Daily Fix-It exercise for more conventions practice.

Reader's and Writer's Notebook, p. 153

Writing
Writing Process: Revise a Story

Teach

Yesterday we wrote a draft of our story about Dina and the dancing daisy. We wrote sentences for the beginning, middle, and end. Today we're going to revise our story. When we revise our writing, we make it better. One way to make our story better is to add more details and sentences. A detail is more information about something. If I tell you I have a dog, then you know I have a dog. But if I tell you I have a big dog, then you know more about it. *Big* is a detail about my dog. How can adding more details make our story better? **Encourage children to share their thoughts. (Adding more details can make the story more interesting and fun for readers.)**

Model

Let's look at the writing we did yesterday. We wrote three sentences about Dina and the dancing daisy. **Review the story with children.** We wrote that Dina is in the garden, but we didn't say what she is doing there. I think we should add that detail. Let's change the verb *is* in our first sentence to an action verb. What is Dina doing *in the garden? Dina walks in the garden*. Let's change the sentence at the beginning of our story.

Guide practice

We wrote that the daisy is dancing a jig, but we didn't say what Dina does after she sees the daisy dancing. That would make a better ending for our story because it tells readers more details. What does Dina do after she sees the daisy dancing a jig? **Let children suggest a concluding sentence.** *Dina dances with the daisy*. Good! That ending will surprise readers. They won't expect it. Let's add that sentence to the end of our story. **Review the revised story together.** (*Dina walks in the garden. She sees a daisy. It is dancing a jig. Dina dances with the daisy.*)

Independent writing

On p. 154 in *Reader's and Writer's Notebook,* have children draw more pictures and/or write or dictate more words or sentences that can be added to the story.

Reader's and Writer's Notebook, p. 154

Differentiated Instruction

SI Strategic Intervention

Practice Revising Write this sentence on the board: *AlphaBuddy* is a *bear*. Read it to children as you point to each word. How can I make this sentence better? I can explain more. How can we describe AlphaBuddy? We can say he is brown. Write this sentence below the first sentence: *AlphaBuddy is a brown bear*. We made the sentence better by adding more information.

Academic Vocabulary

revise to look over and improve

Daily Fix-It

many plants live in gardens
Many plants live in gardens.

This week's practice sentences appear on Teacher Resources DVD-ROM.

ELL

English Language Learners

Support Writing If children struggle to find the correct words to add to the story, allow them to pantomime the details they wish to add. Then supply English words to help them put their thoughts in writing.

Listening and Speaking
Listen for Plot

Review Remind children that when they listen, they should focus their attention on the speaker and ask questions if they don't understand something.

Model Have children turn to p. 129 of *My Skills Buddy.* Listen carefully as I retell what happens in *Jack and the Beanstalk*. After I retell the story, we'll talk about what happens. Incorporate the Listening and Speaking bullet on p. 128 of *My Skills Buddy* into the discussion.

Jack trades his cow for magic beans that grow into a very tall beanstalk. Jack climbs to the top of the beanstalk and takes the ogre's magic hen, bags of gold, and golden harp. The ogre tells him to give them back. Jack does, but asks the ogre to share them sometimes. The ogre agrees, and he and Jack become friends. They write their story down and read it to each other.

What happens in this story? I'll tell one of the first things that happens: Jack climbs to the top of a beanstalk where he takes things from an ogre. What happens next? (The ogre gets mad and asks for the items back. Jack and the ogre agree to share the items, and they become friends.)

The important things that happen in a story are called the plot. If I know the plot, I know I understand the story. For example, in the story *Jack and the Beanstalk,* Jack and the ogre become friends because they find a way to share what makes them both happy.

My Skills Buddy, p. 129

Independent practice

Pair children and give each pair a Big Book, Trade Book, Decodable Reader, or Kindergarten Student Reader they have already read. Have pairs take a picture walk through the story. Have one partner retell the main events in the story. Then have the other partner tell the plot. Refer children to their Rules for Listening and Speaking from pp. 1–2 of the *Reader's and Writer's Notebook*. Remind children to face their partner when listening and to ask questions if they don't understand something.

Name _____

⊙ Listening Rules

1. Face the person who is speaking.
2. Be quiet while someone is speaking.
3. Pay attention to the speaker.
4. Ask questions if you don't understand.

Listening and Speaking Rules 1

Reader's and Writer's Notebook, p.1

Be a Good Listener

1. Face the speaker.
2. Be quiet while someone is speaking.
3. Pay attention to the speaker.
4. Ask questions if you don't understand

Differentiated Instruction

 Strategic Intervention

Support Retelling If children cannot recall the story after looking at the pictures, then page through the story with them. Point out important words and remind them of key events in the story.

Academic Vocabulary

plot a series of related events at the beginning, middle, and end of a story; the action of a story

ⒺⓁⓁ

English Language Learners
Support Listening and Speaking Pair struggling students with more able students so that they can learn from each other's strengths.

Wrap Up Your Day

✔ **Concept Talk** Today we reread the story of Jack and the ogre. How do these two become friends?

✔ **Respond to Literature** Today we read about a boy who likes gardens. Draw a picture of your favorite part of a garden.

✔ **Conventions** Let's think of adjectives that are opposites. What is the opposite of a *high* fence? (a *low* fence) a *fast* car? (a *slow* car) a *big* fish? (a *little* fish)

✔ **Homework Idea** Have children draw a picture of something big or something little and write a caption that names the object and includes the word *big* or *little.*

Preview

DAY 4

Tomorrow we will read a story about two of our Trucktown friends, Jack and Ted.

Science
Growing Plants

Materials: lima bean seeds (or any fast-growing plant seeds), soil, water, plastic cups, paper, pencils, crayons

What All Plants Need Have each child plant a seed in a plastic cup filled two-thirds with soil. Make sure each child has his or her name on the cup. Discuss what they think the seed needs to grow.

Place the seeds near a source of sunlight. Have children water their seeds as needed. Also plant some other seeds in cups and place them in a place where there is no sunlight and do not water these seeds. Have children periodically tell how all of the plants are doing and what the plants needed to grow.

Write Sentences Have children fold a sheet of drawing paper in half. On the left side, ask them to draw and color a picture of their plant. On the right side, tell them to draw and color a picture of one of the cups containing a seed that did not receive water or sunlight. Have children write or dictate a sentence on each side to tell about the plant.

Phonemic Awareness
Guess the Plant

Materials: paper bag, plant pictures on index cards

Blend Word Segments Place the cards with pictures of plants in a paper bag. Choose one picture without showing it to children. Tell children what you see by orally segmenting the plant's name into onset and rime. *I see a /t/ -ulip. What plant do I see? Blend together the word parts to name the plant.* After children guess the plant's name, show them the picture for confirmation. Continue to choose cards, segment the plant's names, and have the class guess them. As an alternative, use other categories of objects, such as colors, clothing, or school supplies.

Comprehension
Goofy Grower

Materials: nature magazines, construction paper, scissors, glue, markers or crayons

Real/Make-Believe Give each child a sheet of paper with a line drawn down the middle. Tell children to look through old magazines to find a picture of a plant. Have them cut out the photo and glue it to the left side of their paper. Have children write or dictate a title for this picture, such as *Real Aloe.* Ask children to draw a make-believe picture of their plant on the opposite side and give it a title such as *Make-Believe Aloe.*

Objectives

- Discuss the concept to develop oral language.

Today at a Glance

Oral Vocabulary
naughty, lend

Phonemic Awareness
Initial and Final /k/

Phonics
/k/ Spelled *Cc*

Comprehension
◉ Realism and Fantasy

Conventions
Adjectives

Writing
Edit a Story

Vocabulary
Direction Words

TRUCKTOWN on Reading Street

Start your engines!

- Display "Wrecker Rosie Sat on a Wall" and lead the group in saying the rhyme a few times.

- Have the group clap the rhythm as they recite the rhyme.

- When children master the rhythm, have them march around the room as they say the rhyme.

Truckery Rhymes

Concept Talk

Question of the Week

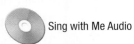

How are real and make-believe plants alike and different?

Build concepts

Write the question of the week on the board. Read the question as you track the print. Tell children to respond in complete sentences. Display Sing with Me Chart 12B.

Listen for Amazing Words

We are going to sing this song again. Listen for the Amazing Words *naughty* and *lend.* Sing the song several times with children to the tune of "I've Been Working on the Railroad." Have them stand up when they hear the Amazing Word *naughty* or *lend.*

🔘 Sing with Me Audio

I've Been Climbing Up a Beanstalk

I've been climbing up a beanstalk,
A clever lad am I!
A magic, tall, wide beanstalk
To find an ogre in the sky.
I hope he doesn't think I'm naughty,
For climbing up so high.
Lend me all of your riches,
Then I'll say goodbye!

Talk with Me/Sing with Me Chart 12B

ELL **Produce Oral Language** Use the Day 4 instruction on ELL Poster 12 to extend and enrich language.

ELL Poster 12

Oral Vocabulary
Amazing Words

Teach Amazing Words

> **Amazing Words** **Oral Vocabulary Routine**
>
> ① **Introduce the Word** Someone that does something *naughty* is bad or does not behave well. What's our new Amazing Word for bad or not well-behaved? Say it with me: *naughty*.
>
> ② **Demonstrate** *It was naughty for the girl to hit her sister.*
>
> Repeat steps 1 and 2.
>
> **Introduce the Word** To *lend* is to let someone have or use something for a short time. What's our new Amazing Word for letting someone have or use something for a short time? Say it with me: *lend*.
>
> **Demonstrate** *I will lend you my bicycle for an hour.*
>
> ③ **Apply** Have children use *naughty* and *lend* to tell about Jack and the ogre.

Routines Flip Chart

Use Amazing Words

To reinforce the concept and the Amazing Words, have children supply the appropriate Amazing Word for each sentence.

Will you _____ me your book? (lend)

It was _____ of Drew to draw on his shirt. (naughty)

Differentiated Instruction

Ⓐ **Advanced**

Physical Response Have pairs of children act out how they would *lend* an item in the classroom to each other. Remind them to use polite words like *please* and *thank you*.

English Language Learners

Build Vocabulary If children need help completing the sentences, say a sentence using each Amazing Word and ask children to choose the sentence that makes sense.

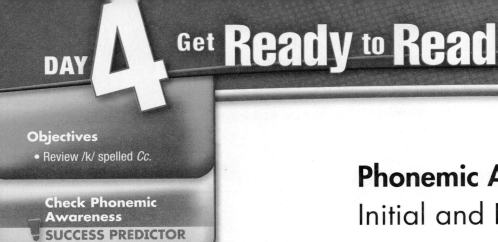

Phonemic Awareness
Initial and Final /k/

Review | Display the *cap* Picture Card. This is a *cap*. *Cap* begins with /k/. What sound does *cap* begin with? Continue with the *can, cat,* and *caterpillar* Picture Cards. Then display the *brick* Picture Card. This is a *brick*. Where do you hear /k/ in the word *brick*? *Brick* ends with /k/. What sound does *brick* end with? Continue the routine with the *duck, rock,* and *sock* Picture Cards.

Give each child a paper cap to wear. I will say some words. Touch your cap when you hear a word that begins with /k/: *lad, hen, cow.* I touched my cap for *cow; cow* begins with /k/. Let's try some more. Listen carefully. Continue with the following words: *cub, fish, puppy, camel, cat, bear, caterpillar.*

Picture Card

Corrective feedback | **If...** children cannot discriminate /k/,
then... have them say /k/ several times, /k/ /k/ /k/.

When you say /k/, the back of your tongue is humped and touching the top of your mouth. Have children practice saying /k/ before repeating the discrimination activity.

Picture Card

Phonics
/k/ Spelled Cc

Review

Display the *Cc* Alphabet Card. This is a *cactus. Cactus* begins with /k/. What letter spells the sound /k/? Yes, the letter *c.*

Write the word *cap* on the board. Help me blend this word. Listen as I say each sound. /k/ /a/ /p/. Now let's blend the sounds together to read the word: /k/ /a/ /p/, *cap.* What is the word? (*cap*) Let's try more. Repeat the routine with the words *Cam* and *cat.*

Don't Wait Until Friday

MONITOR PROGRESS **Check Phonemic Awareness**

Phoneme Segmentation I am going to say a word. Tell me each sound in the word.

tip	cat	Sam	it	sat	pat	Tam

If... children cannot segment the sounds,

then... use the small-group Strategic Intervention lesson, p. DI•89, to reteach segmentation skills.

Continue to monitor children's progress using other instructional opportunities during the week so that they can be successful with the Day 5 Assessment. See the Skills Trace on p. 520.

Day 1	Day 2	Day 3	**Day 4**	Day 5
Check Phonemic Awareness	Check Sound-Spelling/ Retelling	Check Word Reading	Check Phonemic Awareness	Check Oral Vocabulary

Success Predictor

Differentiated Instruction

SI Strategic Intervention

Connect Sound-Spelling Have each child write the letter *c* on a card. Then segment and blend the following words. Have children hold up the *c* card when they hear /k/. Have children then say each word, segmenting the sounds: *Cam, cap, cat, pack, pick, sack, sick, tack, tick.* Ask them to tell whether they hear /k/ at the beginning or end of each word.

Phonemic Awareness

Success Predictor

Objectives
- Spell words.
- Blend and segment words.
- Read decodable text.
- Read high-frequency words.

Spelling
↻ /i/ Spelled *Ii*

ROUTINE **Spell Words**

Spell words

1 **Review Sound-Spellings** Display the *Cc* Alphabet Card. This is a *cactus. Cactus* begins with /k/. What is the letter we learned for /k/? (*c*) Continue the routine with the following Alphabet Cards: *Aa, Ii, Mm, Pp, Ss, Tt.*

2 **Model** Today we are going to spell some words. Listen to the three sounds in *tip:* /t/ /i/ /p/.

- What is the first sound in *tip*? (/t/) What is the letter for /t/? (*t*) Write *t* on the board.
- What is the middle sound you hear? (/i/) What is the letter for /i/? (*i*) Write *i* on the board.
- What is the last sound you hear? (/p/) What is the letter for /p/? (*p*) Write *p* on the board.
- Point to *tip.* Help me blend the sound of each letter together to read this word: /t/ /i/ /p/. The word is *tip.* Repeat with the word *mat.*

3 **Guide Practice** Now let's spell some words together. Listen to this word: /s/ /a/ /t/. What is the first sound in *sat*? (/s/) What is the letter for /s/? (*s*) Write *s* on the board. Now you write *s* on your paper. What is the middle sound in *sat*? (/a/) What is the letter for /a/? (*a*) Write *a* on the board. Now you write *a* on your paper. What is the last sound in *sat*? (/t/) What is the letter for /t/? (*t*) Write *t* on the board. Now you write *t* on your paper. Now we can blend the sound of each letter together to read the word: /s/ /a/ /t/. What is the word? (*sat*) Continue spell and blend practice with the following words: *pit, tap, Tim, Sam.*

4 **On Your Own** I am going to say a word. I want you to write it on your paper. Remember, first, say the word slowly in your head and then write the letter for each sound. Listen carefully. Write the word *sip.* Give children time to write the word. How do you spell *sip*? The first sound is /s/. What is the letter for /s/? Did you write *s* on your paper? What is the letter for /i/? Did you write *i* on your paper? What is the letter for /p/? Did you write *p* on your paper? Name the letters in *sip: s, i, p.* Continue with the words *cat, am, it, pit, pat,* and *sit.*

Routines Flip Chart

Get Set, Roll! Reader 12
↻ Practice /i/ Spelled *Ii*

Review
Review the high-frequency words *for, the,* and *he.* Have children find each word on the Word Wall.

Teach rebus words
Write the word *tires* on the board. This is the word *tires.* Name the letters with me: *t, i, r, e, s, tires.* Repeat the procedure with *Ted, Jack, see, rock, zigs,* and *zags.* Look for these words in the story today. A picture above the word will help you read it.

Read Get Set, Roll! Reader 12
Today we will read a story about our friends Jack and Ted. Point to the title of the book. What is the title of the book? (*Tires*) We will read some words with /i/ in this book.

Use the routine for reading decodable books found in the Routines Flip Chart to read Get Set, Roll! Reader 12.

Get Set, Roll! Reader 12

Small Group Time

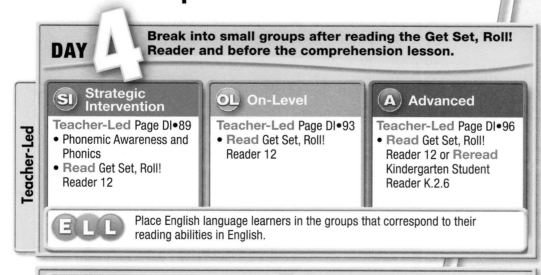

DAY 4 Break into small groups after reading the Get Set, Roll! Reader and before the comprehension lesson.

Teacher-Led

SI Strategic Intervention	**OL On-Level**	**A Advanced**
Teacher-Led Page DI•89 • Phonemic Awareness and Phonics • Read Get Set, Roll! Reader 12	Teacher-Led Page DI•93 • Read Get Set, Roll! Reader 12	Teacher-Led Page DI•96 • Read Get Set, Roll! Reader 12 or Reread Kindergarten Student Reader K.2.6

ELL Place English language learners in the groups that correspond to their reading abilities in English.

Practice Stations
• Visit the Let's Write! Station
• Visit the Read for Meaning Station

Independent Activities
• Read independently
• Audio Text of the Big Book
• *Reader's and Writer's Notebook*

 **ELL**

English Language Learners
Frontload Reader Do a picture walk with children to preview the reader before starting the routine.

Objectives
◎ Practice realism and fantasy.
• Review and practice sequence.

Comprehension
🎯 Realism and Fantasy

Practice realism and fantasy

Envision It!

Have children turn to the Realism and Fantasy picture on pp. 114–115 of *My Skills Buddy.* As you look at the pictures, remind children that stories that show realism have events that could really happen. Stories that show fantasy have events that are make-believe, or could not really happen.

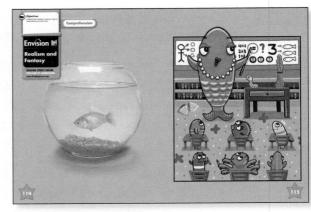

My Skills Buddy, pp. 114–115

Team Talk Pair children.

Have one child tell something a plant could or could not do, such as *The plant grows in the garden*. Next, have the second child tell if the sentence shows realism or fantasy. Then have children switch roles and repeat the activity.

Sequence

Review

Direct children to the Sequence picture on pp. 94–95 of *My Skills Buddy.*

In most stories, something happens first, something happens next, and something happens last. The order in which things happen in a story is called sequence. Good readers pay attention to the sequence to follow the events in the story.

• What happens first? (The mama bird sits on eggs in a nest.)

• What happens next? (The mama bird feeds the baby birds.)

• What happens last? (The baby birds grow up and fly away.)

More practice

For more practice with sequence, use *Reader's and Writer's Notebook,* p. 155.

Reader's and Writer's Notebook, p. 155

Third Read—Big Book
Jack and the Beanstalk

Guide comprehension

Display *Jack and the Beanstalk.* In this story, something happens first, something happens next, and something happens last.

Display the pictures on pp. 4–5.

• What happens first? (Jack trades the cow for magic beans that grow into a tall beanstalk.)

Display the pictures on pp. 7–9.

• What happens next? (Jack takes the ogre's hen, bags of gold, and harp.)

Display the pictures on pp. 20–21.

• What happens last? (Jack and the ogre become friends and write their story together.)

Reread *Jack and the Beanstalk.* Return to p. 560. Follow the Day 4 arrow and use the Guide Comprehension notes to give children the opportunity to gain a more complete understanding of the story.

DAY **2**
Read for enjoyment

DAY **3**
Reread using Develop Vocabulary notes

DAY **4**
Reread using Guide Comprehension notes

Differentiated Instruction

 SI **Strategic Intervention**

Practice Sequence Have children tell three things they have done so far today. Then have them tell how their day would be different if they changed the order of these events.

Academic Vocabulary

sequence the order of events in a selection or story

Objectives
- Identify and use adjectives.
- Edit a class story by checking letter and word spacing.
- Use a picture dictionary.

Conventions
Adjectives

Review

Remind children of what they learned about adjectives. Adjectives are describing words. They can describe a person, animal, place, or thing. They can tell about its shape, color, size, number, or opposite.

Have AlphaBuddy hold up two yellow pencils.

How can I describe the pencils AlphaBuddy has? He has two pencils. *Two* is an adjective. The pencils are yellow. *Yellow* is an adjective.

Let's use some more adjectives to describe the pencils. Are the pencils new or old? Are they long or short? List children's responses on the board. Have children echo read the list of adjectives with you.

Guide practice

Display a colorful blanket or quilt. There are lots of colors in this blanket. Let's use adjectives to describe the colors in the blanket. Have children turn to p. 133 of *My Skills Buddy.* This is a picture dictionary. It can help you find out what a word means or how to spell it. Ask children to find pictures on p. 133 that best match the colors in the blanket. We can use the picture dictionary to help us write color words. Have children suggest a sentence using color words to describe the blanket, such as *The blanket is red and orange.* Write the sentence on the board and read it with children. Then have them copy the sentence and illustrate it.

On their own

Use *Reader's and Writer's Notebook,* p. 156, for more practice with adjectives.

Daily Fix-It

Use the Daily Fix-It for more conventions practice.

Reader's and Writer's Notebook, p. 156

Writing
Writing Process: Edit a Story

Teach

Remind children of the work they have done on their story so far. What steps in the writing process have we done so far in writing our story? (We chose an idea when we planned our story; we wrote sentences for the beginning, middle, and end when we drafted our story; we added more details and sentences when we revised our story.) Today we will edit our story. When we edit our writing, we check to make sure we've written everything correctly. Did we use correct spacing between letters and words? Remind children that we leave small spaces between the letters in a word and bigger spaces between the words in a sentence. Correct letter and word spaces help make our words and sentences clear and easy for others to read.

Model

Reread the story you wrote. Point out the correct spacing between letters and words. Have children point out anything they think needs to be fixed. Show them how you would mark these corrections.

Guide practice

Help children complete the editing activity on p. 157 in *Reader's and Writer's Notebook*. Ask them what needs to be fixed in each sentence. After children circle the errors, you may wish to have them write the words or sentences correctly on the lines.

Reader's and Writer's Notebook, p. 157

Independent writing

Children can practice proper letter and word spacing by copying on p. 158 in *Reader's and Writer's Notebook* some or all of the sentences from the class story. Remind them to use small spaces between the letters in a word and bigger spaces between the words in a sentence. Point out that children can use your sentences on the board as models.

Differentiated Instruction

Ⓐ Advanced

Support Conventions Have children use the picture dictionary to find other describing words, such as words for shapes. Have them use one of the words they find in a sentence to describe something in the classroom.

Daily Fix-It

julis is a big pig
Julius is a big pig.

This week's practice sentences appear on Teacher Resources DVD-ROM.

Academic Vocabulary

edit to correct errors

ELL

English Language Learners
Editing Have children edit the story they wrote for standard grammar and usage, such as subject-verb agreement. Provide support for children by modelling short simple sentences with incorrect and correct subject and verb agreement. Use the following examples:
The boy are short. The boy is short.
The dog were barking. The dog was barking.

Objectives
- Practice using words for directions.

Vocabulary
Direction Words

Teach

Write the words *left* and *right* on the board. Point to each word as you read it. These words tell about directions, or where something is. Have children turn to p. 128 of *My Skills Buddy.* Point to the girl's left hand. This is her *left* hand. Point to the girl's right hand. This is her *right* hand. Use the last two Vocabulary bullets on the page to help children act out the words *left* and *right.*

Team Talk Pair children and have them take turns giving each other commands with the words *left* and *right.* As an example, start children off with the command *Touch your nose with your right hand.*

My Skills Buddy, p. 128

Wrap Up Your Day

✔ **Oral Language** Sing "I've Been Climbing Up a Beanstalk" with me. Pretend to climb when you hear an Amazing Word—*beanstalk, lad, ogre, magic, naughty, lend.*

✔ **Phonemic Awareness** I am going to say a sentence. Clap when you hear a word that has /i/ in it. Say: *Izzie will sing about lizards. Nick will sing about kittens. Jill will dance a jig.*

✔ **Homework Idea** Ask children to use an adjective to tell about something they have at home.

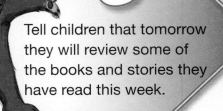

Preview **DAY 5**

Tell children that tomorrow they will review some of the books and stories they have read this week.

Extend Your Day!

Science
Plant Life
Materials: chart paper, copies of a main idea web (one per child), crayons or markers

What Do Plants Need? Draw a main idea web on chart paper or use Graphic Organizer 18. Write the word *Plants* and draw a plant in the center circle. All living things need certain things to help them grow. We need food, water, and rest. What do plants need to help them grow? Use the following questions to prompt, if necessary.

• What do plants need that comes from a hose or from rain?

• What do plants need that shines in the sky?

• What do plants need that we breathe?

• What do plants need that is where the roots grow?

As children identify items, draw and label an item in each circle. Distribute copies of the web to children. Have them complete it with pictures and labels.

Math
Patterns
Materials: four red flower shapes, four green leaf shapes, and four yellow sun shapes for each child; construction paper; glue

Make a Nature Pattern Ask children to place the following shapes in a line on their desks: one red flower, one green leaf, one yellow sun, one red flower, and one green leaf. Ask what shape comes next. Continue with various patterns. Choose volunteers to create patterns. Finally, allow children to make their own patterns and glue them to a sheet of construction paper.

Phonemic Awareness
Sing a Song
Materials: Phonics Songs and Rhymes Chart 12

Six Little Silly Fish

Six little silly fish,
Six little silly fish,
They flip and skip; in water they dip.
Six little silly fish.

The fishies splash and splish,
The fishies splash and splish,
They splash and splish in water like this.
The fishies splash and splish.

Listen and Act Out
Display Phonics Songs and Rhymes Chart 12. Tell children you are going to play the song again. Ask them to clap when they hear /i/ words. This time let's sing the song and make up some actions to go with the words. Sing the song again with actions. Have some children act as song leaders to model the actions.

Phonics Songs and Rhymes Chart 12

Objectives
• Review the concepts.
• Build oral vocabulary.

Today at a Glance

Oral Vocabulary
beanstalk, lad, ogre, magic, naughty, lend

Phonemic Awareness
◉ Initial and Medial /i/

Phonics
◉ /i/ Spelled *Ii*

Comprehension
◉ Realism and Fantasy

Conventions
Adjectives

Writing
Share a Story

Check Oral Vocabulary
SUCCESS PREDICTOR

TRUCKTOWN on Reading Street

Start your engines!

• Display "Wrecker Rosie Sat on a Wall" and lead the group in saying the rhyme a few times.

• Have half the group recite the rhyme while the other half acts it out.

• Then have the groups change roles.

Truckery Rhymes

Concept Wrap Up

Question of the Week

How are real and make-believe plants alike and different?

Listen for Amazing Words

Write the question of the week on the board. Track the print as you read it to children. Have them use the Amazing Words in their responses (*beanstalk, lad, ogre, magic, naughty, lend*) and answer in complete sentences. Display Sing with Me Chart 12B. Let's sing "I've Been Climbing Up a Beanstalk." I want you to listen for the Amazing Words we learned this week. Remind children that the words *beanstalk, lad, ogre, magic, naughty,* and *lend* are in the song. Sing the song several times to the tune of "I've Been Working on the Railroad." Have children pretend to wave a magic wand each time they hear an Amazing Word. Then discuss how the beanstalk in the song is like a real plant. Remind children to speak one at a time.

I've Been Climbing Up a Beanstalk

I've been climbing up a beanstalk,
A clever lad am I!
A magic, tall, wide beanstalk
To find an ogre in the sky.
I hope he doesn't think I'm naughty,
For climbing up so high.
Lend me all of your riches,
Then I'll say goodbye!

Sing with Me Chart 12B

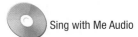 Sing with Me Audio

ELL Check Concepts and Language Use the Day 5 instruction on ELL Poster 12 to monitor children's understanding of the lesson concept.

ELL Poster 12

Oral Vocabulary
Amazing Words

beanstalk	lad
ogre	magic
naughty	lend

Review

Let's Talk Display Talk with Me Chart 12A. We learned six new Amazing Words this week. Let's say the Amazing Words as I point to the pictures on the chart. Point to each picture and give children the chance to say the appropriate Amazing Word before offering it.

Have children supply the appropriate Amazing Word.

> My _____ puppy ate my homework. (naughty)
>
> She was scared of the _____ in the fairy tale. (ogre)
>
> I am growing a _____ in my garden. (beanstalk)
>
> The _____ was tall for his age. (lad)
>
> He performed a _____ trick with a coin. (magic)
>
> My sister and I _____ each other clothes. (lend)

Talk with Me/Sing with Me
Chart 12A

Differentiated Instruction

 Strategic Intervention
Sentence Production Have children choose one Amazing Word. Ask them to say a complete sentence using that word.

 It's Friday

MONITOR PROGRESS **Check Oral Vocabulary**

Demonstrate Word Knowledge Monitor the Amazing Words by asking the following questions. Have children use the Amazing Word in their answer.

- **What is another name for a boy?** (lad)
- **What is a monster or giant in a fairy tale called?** (ogre)
- **What is another word for bad or not well-behaved?** (naughty)
- **What is it called when you let someone have something for a short time?** (lend)
- **What is the tall stem of a plant that grows beans?** (beanstalk)
- **What is the skill of performing tricks that seem to be impossible?** (magic)

If... children have difficulty using the Amazing Words,

then... reteach the words using the Oral Vocabulary Routine on the Routines Flip Chart.

Day 1	Day 2	Day 3	Day 4	Day 5
Check Phonemic Awareness	Check Sound-Spelling/ Retelling	Check Word Reading	Check Phonemic Awareness	**Check Oral Vocabulary**

Success Predictor

Oral Vocabulary

Success Predictor

Objectives
◎ Review initial and medial /i/.
◎ Review /i/ spelled *Ii*.

Phonemic Awareness Review

↺ /i/

Isolate initial and medial /i/

Display the *insect* Picture Card. What is the beginning sound in *insect*? Say the word with me: /i/ /i/ /i/, *insect*. Continue to review initial /i/ with the *igloo, iguana,* and *inch* Picture Cards.

Display the *six* Picture Card. What is the middle sound in *six*? Say it again: *six*. The middle sound in *six* is /i/. Continue to review medial /i/ with the *wig, pig,* and *zipper* Picture Cards.

Discriminate medial sounds

I am going to read some words. If you hear /i/ in the word, I want you to hold up a fist. If you hear /a/ in the word, I want you to clap. Let's try the first one together. Listen carefully: *tap.* Do you hear /i/ or /a/ in *tap*? I hear /a/ in *tap,* so I am going to clap. Continue with the following words: *fat, bin, tack, sit, sat, mat, pit, sand, cap, will, map, Tim, Sam, Sal, Pip.*

Picture Card

Picture Card

Phonics Review
 /i/ Spelled *Ii*

Teach /i/ *Ii*

Display the *Ii* Alphabet Card. This is an *igloo*. What sound do you hear at the beginning of *igloo*? What letter spells that sound?

High-frequency words

Write the word *he* on the board. This is the word *he*. What is this word? Repeat the routine with *for*.

Apply phonics in familiar text

Have children reread one of the books specific to the target letter sounds. You may wish to review the decodable words and high-frequency words that appear in each book prior to rereading.

Alphabet Card

Decodable Reader 12
My Skills Buddy, p. 118

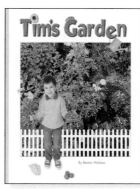

Kindergarten
Student Reader K.2.6

Get Set, Roll!
Reader 12

Small Group Time

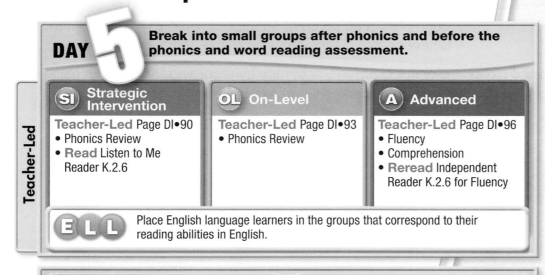

DAY 5 Break into small groups after phonics and before the phonics and word reading assessment.

Teacher-Led

SI Strategic Intervention
Teacher-Led Page DI•90
• Phonics Review
• **Read** Listen to Me Reader K.2.6

OL On-Level
Teacher-Led Page DI•93
• Phonics Review

A Advanced
Teacher-Led Page DI•96
• Fluency
• Comprehension
• **Reread** Independent Reader K.2.6 for Fluency

ELL Place English language learners in the groups that correspond to their reading abilities in English.

Practice Stations
• Visit the Read for Meaning Station
• Visit the Let's Make Art Station

Independent Activities
• Read independently
• Story Sort
• Concept Talk Video

Assess

◎ Read words with /i/.
• Read high-frequency words.
• Read sentences.

Assessment
Monitor Progress

/i/ Spelled Ii

Whole Class Divide a paper in half for each child. Ask children to draw something that begins with /i/ in the first box and label the picture with the word. Then have children draw something that has /i/ in the middle in the second box and label that picture with the word.

> **MONITOR PROGRESS** **Check Word and Sentence Reading**
>
> **If...** children cannot complete the whole-class assessment,
> **then...** use the Reteach lesson in *First Stop*.
>
> **If...** you are unsure of a child's grasp of this week's skills,
> **then...** use the assessment below to obtain a clearer evaluation of the child's progress.

/i/ Spelled Ii and high-frequency words

To facilitate individual progress monitoring, assess some children on Day 4 and the rest on Day 5. While individual children are being assessed, the rest of the class can reread this week's books and look for words with /i/.

Word reading

Use the word lists on reproducible p. 595 to assess each child's ability to read words with /i/ and high-frequency words. We're going to read some words. I'll read the first word, and you read the rest. The first word is *sip:* /s/ /i/ /p/. For each child, record any decoding problems.

Sentence reading

Use the sentences on reproducible p. 595 to assess each child's ability to read words in sentences. Have each child read two sentences aloud. Have each child read different sentences. Start over with sentence one if necessary.

Record scores

Monitor children's accuracy by recording their scores using the Word and Sentence Reading Chart for this unit in *First Stop*.

Read the Words

sip ☐   Tim ☐
for ☐   he ☐
pit ☐   tip ☐
sit ☐   Sis ☐

Read the Sentences

1. I have a cap for Tim.

2. He tips the cap.

3. He likes little Tim.

4. Pip is a cat for Pam.

Note to Teacher: Children read each word. Children read two sentences.

Scoring for Read the Words: Score 1 point for each correct word.

Short *i* (*sip, pit, sit, Tim, tip, Sis*) ———— / __6__
High-Frequency Words (*for, he*) ———— / __2__

MONITOR PROGRESS
• Short *i*
• High-frequency words

Objectives
- Recognize an expository text.
- Identify the topic of an expository text.

My Skills Buddy, pp. 130–131

Let's Practice It!
Expository Text

Teach

Today you will listen to an expository text. Expository text tells information about a topic. Review the features of an expository text with children.

- Readers use expository text to learn about a topic.
- Expository text tells facts about one topic.
- Expository text uses details to give more information about the topic.

Have children turn to p. 130 of *My Skills Buddy*. I am going to read an expository text called "Parts of a Plant." Look at the pictures. What do you think this expository text will be about? Continue to look at the pictures as I read. Read the text of "Parts of a Plant." As you read, direct children to look at the appropriate picture.

Guide practice

Discuss the features of an expository text with children and the bulleted text on p. 130 of *My Skills Buddy.*

- Readers use expository text to learn about a topic. What is one thing you learned from this expository text? (Possible answer: leaves make food for the plant.)

- Expository text tells facts about one topic. What is the topic of this expository text? (plant parts) How do you know? (The photographs are of plants and their parts. The text is called "Parts of a Plant.")

- Expository text uses details to give more information about the topic. This text gives us details about the parts of a plant. What are the four parts of a plant? (roots, stem, leaves, flowers)

Parts of a Plant

All plants have four main parts: roots, stems, leaves, flowers. Roots hold a plant in the soil, like an anchor. They also take in water from the soil.

The stem makes the plant stand up. The stem also connects all the parts of the plant. Water travels from the roots through the stem to the leaves. Food travels from the leaves through the stem to the rest of the plant.

Leaves make food for the plant. The leaves take in light from the sun. They use the sunlight, air, and water to make food.

Flowers make seeds for the plant. Seeds from the flowers fall to the ground. Then new plants grow from the seeds.

Comprehension Assessment
Monitor Progress

Review

🎯 **Realism and Fantasy** Stories can show realism or fantasy. A story that shows realism tells about things that could really happen. A story that shows fantasy tells about things that are make-believe, or could not really happen. Good readers look for realism and fantasy to help them understand and remember the story.

Read "The Ants and the Grasshopper"

Tell children that you are going to read them a story about a grasshopper that learns an important lesson. Ask children to think about whether the story shows realism or fantasy as they listen. Listen carefully as I read the story. When I am done, I am going to ask you to tell me if it shows realism or fantasy. Read "The Ants and the Grasshopper" on p. 26 of *Read Aloud Anthology*.

Read Aloud Anthology

Check realism and fantasy

After you read the story, have children tell you whether parts of the story show realism or fantasy.

- What does the grasshopper like to do? (**make music**) Is this something that grasshoppers really do? (**no**)

- What do the ants do while the grasshopper makes music? (**work in the garden**) Is this something that ants really do? (**no**)

- What makes the ants go inside their anthill? (**winter comes**) Is this something that really happens? (**yes**)

- Is this story realistic or a fantasy? (**fantasy**)

Corrective feedback

If... a child cannot identify realism and fantasy,
then... reteach realism and fantasy using the Reteach lesson in *First Stop*.

Assess realism and fantasy

Use the blackline master on p. 599. Make one copy for each child. Have children color the pictures that show fantasy and circle the picture that shows realism.

Realism and Fantasy

Color the make-believe pictures.
Circle the real picture.

Note to Teacher: Have children color the pictures that are make-believe and circle the picture that is real.

Objectives
- Review adjectives.
- Prepare a final copy of a class story.
- Share a class story with others.

Conventions
Adjectives

Review   Remind children of what they learned about adjectives. Adjectives are words that describe people, animals, places, or things.

Model   Display an object such as a cup and describe it using an adjective. This is a red cup. *Red* is an adjective that tells about the cup.

Guide practice   What is another adjective we could use to describe the cup? It is also a *shiny* cup. Have children suggest more adjectives, such as *plastic* and *little.* Line up several objects and ask children to describe each one. Write children's adjectives on the board and read them with children.

On their own   Ask children to choose another object in the room to describe. Have them think of two adjectives that describe the object and then draw a picture that illustrates those qualities. Ask children to write or dictate the adjectives to label their pictures.

Daily Fix-It   Use the Daily Fix-It exercise for more conventions practice.

Writing
Writing Process: Share a Story

Teach

Display the story you have written together. Now it's time to share our work with other people. But before we share our work, we need to write a clean copy of our story. We will fix any mistakes we found while we were editing our story. We will use our best handwriting. We can add pictures if we choose, and we will make a cover. Then our story will be ready to share with others.

Model

Now I will rewrite our story using my best handwriting. Quickly check spacing between letters and words.

Guide practice

Work with children to write their stories on a separate sheet of paper. Encourage them to personalize their stories by drawing pictures to accompany the text.

Children can use p. 159 in *Reader's and Writer's Notebook* to make a cover for their story. Explain that the cover has a picture that goes with the story, a title that tells what the story is about, and the name of the author. With children, think of a title for the class story. After they have drawn a picture, help children write the title and their name on the lines. Place each child's story between the cover and a blank sheet of paper and staple the pages together to make a booklet.

Reader's and Writer's Notebook, p. 159

After they have shared their story with others, have children complete p. 160 in *Reader's and Writer's Notebook.* As a group, discuss reviewers' reactions to the stories. Have children save their stories to add to the classroom library.

Daily Fix-It

a tree grows in the garden
A tree grows in the garden.

This week's practice sentences appear on Teacher Resources DVD-ROM.

ELL

English Language Learners
Poster Preview Prepare children for next week by using Week 1 ELL Poster number 13. Read the Poster Talk-Through to introduce the concept and vocabulary. Ask children to identify and describe objects and actions in the art.

Objectives
- Review weekly concept.
- Review realism and fantasy.

Wrap Up Your Week!

 Question of the Week

How are real and make-believe plants alike and different?

This week we talked about real and make-believe plants and how they are alike and different.

- Make a three-column chart like the one shown or use Graphic Organizer 11. Fill it with children's responses about real and make-believe actions for the given characters.
- Have children draw pictures to illustrate one row of the chart.
- Have children write or dictate a complete sentence about their pictures.

Real Action	Character	Make-Believe Action
	plant	
	pig	
	teacher	
	boy	

Amazing Words

You've learned
0 0 6
words this week!

You've learned
0 7 2
words this year!

Illustrate realism and fantasy

 Next Week's Question

How does a panda change in its first year of life?

Discuss next week's question. Talk with children about what they know about pandas.

Preview NEXT WEEK

Tell children that next week they will read about a baby panda bear.

Extend Your Day!

Social Studies
Respect for Living Things
Materials: several garbage bags

Naming Native Living Things Discuss what kinds of plants and animals make their homes in the neighborhood around your school. If children struggle to name plants, remind them that trees, shrubs, and grass are all kinds of plants.

Texas Plants	Texas Animals
oak trees	deer
buffalo grass	lizards
daisies	armadillos
saguaro cacti	squirrels

Cleaning Up the Playground Talk with children about what might happen to a plant or animal when people litter. Then take a walk around your schoolyard and playground. Help children pick up paper and other garbage. When you return to the classroom, review the chart you made with children. Talk about how a cleaner neighborhood could help each plant and animal on the chart.

Phonics
Letter People
Materials: letter cards: *a, c, i, m, p, s, t*

Build Words Have 6 children come to the front of the room. Give each child a letter card. Tell the other children you are going to use the "letter people" to build words. What letters do we need to build the word *sip?* The first sound is /s/. What is the letter for /s/? (s) Have the "*s* person" move to the front of the group. Continue with *i* and *p.* Let's blend the sound of each letter together: /s/ /i/ /p/, *sip.* Continue with: *mat, tap, sat, tip, sit, pit, cat, pat.*

Math
Plant Pattern
Materials: line drawings: cactus, tree, flower; crayons; scissors; poster board; glue

Follow a Pattern Place children into 3 groups. Give each child in the first group a cactus, the second group a tree, and the third group a flower. Have children color their plants and cut them out. Then have one child from each group glue their pictures onto a poster board in a row. Ask children what plant should come next to repeat the pattern. Have children come forward and glue their shapes in the same pattern until all plants are used.

Unit Wrap-Up

 The Big Question

How are animals and plants unique?

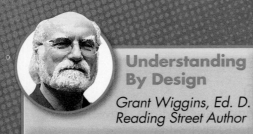

Understanding By Design

Grant Wiggins, Ed. D.
Reading Street Author

"A big idea is not necessarily vast in the sense of a vague phrase covering lots of content. Nor is a big idea a 'basic' idea. Rather, big ideas are at the 'core' of the subject; they need to be uncovered; we have to dig deep until we get to the core."

WEEK 1

Flowers
by Vijaya Khisty Bodach
Gail Saunders-Smith, PhD, Consulting Editor

 Question of the Week

How are flowers unique?

Concept Knowledge

Children understand that flowers:

- have parts that do different jobs
- make fruit and seeds

WEEK 2

NATURE SPY
written by SHELLEY ROTNER and KEN KREISLER
photographs by SHELLEY ROTNER

Question of the Week

What can we learn about nature when we look closely?

Concept Knowledge

Children understand that looking closely at nature:

- helps them see new and different things
- helps them appreciate nature

Discuss the Big Question

Help children relate the theme question for this unit to the selections and their own experiences. Write the big question and prompt discussion with questions such as the following:

How do the stories we read describe how plants and animals are unique? Possible Responses:

- *Flowers* describes how plants grow flowers and seeds and what they are used for.
- *Nature Spy* shows how ordinary plants and animals can look very different when we look closely.
- We read about the many different baby animals that live in the grasslands with their mothers.

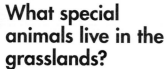

animal babies
in grasslands

Question of the Week

 **What special animals live in the grasslands?**

Concept Knowledge

Children learn that the baby animals of the grasslands:

- look very different
- do many things with their mothers

Bear Snores On

Question of the Week

What unique thing does a bear do in the winter?

Concept Knowledge

Children learn that in the winter a bear:

- sleeps in a cave or den
- keeps warm and quiet

A bed for the winter

KAREN WALLACE

Question of the Week

What kind of home does an animal need?

Concept Knowledge

Children understand that some animals:

- look for a winter home
- find a warm place to stay

Jack and the Beanstalk

from You Read to Me, I'll Read to You

by Mary Ann Hoberman
illustrated by Natalia Vasquez

Question of the Week

How are real and make-believe plants alike and different?

Concept Knowledge

Children understand that, no matter where or how they grow, all plants:

- need the same things
- are amazing in their own way

- In *Bear Snores On,* Bear hibernates, and the other animals visit him.
- We read about a mouse that searches and finds that there are many different animal homes in the meadow. But he finds just the right one for himself.

Can you describe some animals that you read about and how they live?

(Answers will vary.)

Can you think of ways that you and your friends are unique? Possible responses:

- Children live with their own families in different homes.
- Children look distinctly like themselves.
- Children are talented in different ways.

Weekly Assessment

Use the whole-class assessment on pages 594–595 and 598–599 in this Teacher's Edition to check:

✔ 🔊 **Short *i* Spelled *Ii***

✔ 🔊 **Comprehension Skill** *Realism and Fantasy*

✔ **High-Frequency Words**   *he*   *for*

Teacher's Edition, Day 5

Managing Assessment

Use the Assessment Handbook for:

✔ **Observation Checklists**

✔ **Record-Keeping Forms**

✔ **Portfolio Assessment**

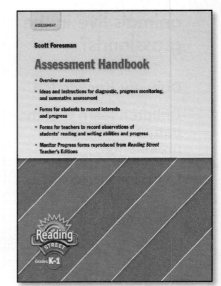

Assessment Handbook

Unit Assessment

Use the Unit 2 Assessment to check progress in:

✔ **Phonological Awareness**

✔ **Phonics**

✔ **High-Frequency Words**

✔ **Comprehension Skill** *Setting; Realism and Fantasy*

✔ **Conventions in Writing**

Unit Assessment

Teacher Notes

Small Group Time

Pacing Small Group Instruction

⏱ 20–30 mins.

5 Day Plan

DAY 1	• Phonemic Awareness/ Phonics • Decodable Story 12
DAY 2	• Phonemic Awareness/ Phonics • Decodable Reader 12
DAY 3	• Phonemic Awareness/ Phonics • Concept Literacy Reader K.2.6 or Kindergarten Student Reader K.2.6
DAY 4	• Phonemic Awareness/ Phonics • Get Set, Roll! Reader 12
DAY 5	• Phonics Review • Listen to Me Reader K.2.6

3 or 4 Day Plan

DAY 1	• Phonemic Awareness/ Phonics • Decodable Story 12
DAY 2	• Phonemic Awareness/ Phonics • Decodable Reader 12
DAY 3	• Phonemic Awareness/ Phonics • Concept Literacy Reader K.2.6 or Kindergarten Student Reader K.2.6
DAY 4	• Phonemic Awareness/ Phonics • Get Set, Roll! Reader 12

3 Day Plan: Eliminate the shaded box.

SI Strategic Intervention   **DAY 1**

Phonemic Awareness•Phonics

■ **Initial Sounds** Say the words *inch* and *insect* with me. Listen to the beginning sound as we say each word: /i/ /i/ /i/, *inch*; /i/ /i/ /i/, *insect*. Do these words begin with the same sound? Yes, the words begin with /i/. Now let's say the word *ant*. Does this word begin like *inch* and *insect*? No, the word does not begin like *inch* and *insect*. Repeat with words for initial /a/, /s/, /p/ and /k/.

■ **Connect /i/ to *Ii*** I am going to say three words. I want you to tell me which word begins with /i/. Listen carefully: *inch, foot, yard.* Say the words with me: *inch, foot, yard.* Which word begins with /i/? *Inch* begins with /i/. *Foot* and *yard* do not begin with /i/. Write the letters *Ii* on the board. The letter *i* stands for /i/ in words. Continue discriminating /i/ with the following sets of words: *in, out, under; juice, itch, lamp; mask, gate, ink; gum, it, yarn.*

■ **Discriminate Initial Sounds** To practice discriminating initial /a/, use *apple, it, an;* for /s/ use *cat, sat, silly;* for /p/ use *big, pig, pat;* for /k/ use *corn, dig, can.*

Decodable Story 12

■ **Review High-Frequency Words** Review the previously taught high-frequency words by writing each of these words and having children say the words with you.

he	for	we	my	like	have	is

If... children have difficulty reading the words,
then... say a word and have children point to the word. Repeat several times, giving assistance as needed.

Have children read the story *Sam, Sit!* orally. Then have them reread the story several times individually.

Reader's and Writer's Notebook, pp. 143–144

Objectives
• Identify the common sounds that letters represent.
• Read at least 25 high-frequency words from a commonly used list.

 **DAY 2**

Phonemic Awareness•Phonics

■ **Discriminate /i/** Display Phonics Songs and Rhymes Chart 12. Sing "Six Little Silly Fish" to the tune of "The Farmer in the Dell" several times with children. Have children clap when they hear an /i/ word.

■ **Connect /i/ to *Ii*** Ask children to name words that have /i/. List the words as they say them. Have children echo read the list of words. Then ask children to take turns circling the *i*'s on the list.

Decodable Reader 12

■ **Review High-Frequency Words** Review the previously taught high-frequency words. Have children read each word as you point to it on the Word Wall.

I	am	have	he	is	my	we	a	for

My Skills Buddy

If... children have difficulty reading the words,
then... say a word and have children point to the word. Repeat several times, giving assistance as needed.

Display the story *Tim and Sam* on p. 118 of *My Skills Buddy*. The title of this story is *Tim and Sam*. The author is Joei Shavitz. The illustrator is Lawrence Paul. What do you think the story will be about? Let's read the story together.

More Reading

Use Leveled Readers or other text at children's instructional level.

Objectives
• Identify the common sounds that letters represent.
• Read at least 25 high-frequency words from a commonly used list.

Phonemic Awareness•Phonics

■ **Isolate /i/** Display the *igloo, iguana, inch,* and *insect* Picture Cards. Say the picture names with me: *igloo, iguana, inch, insect.* The words begin with /i/. Say the word *igloo* with me: /i/ /i/ /i/, *igloo.* Repeat with *iguana, inch,* and *insect.*

■ **Discriminate /i/** Display the *inch* Picture Card. This is an *inch. Inch* begins with /i/. Say it with me: /i/ /i/ /i/, *inch.* Write the letters *Ii* on the board. The letter *i* stands for /i/. Show children how long an inch is using your thumb and index fingers. When you hear a word that has initial or medial /i/, show how long an inch is. Use the following words: *sip, tip, frog, it, gum, flip, little, mat, itch.*

■ **Blend Sounds** Write *Tim* on the board. Have children blend the sound of each letter to read the word: /t/ /i/ /m/, *Tim. Tim* is a name. Repeat the routine with the following words: *sit, it.*

■ **Review High-Frequency Words** Write *the* on the board. Have volunteers say the word and use it in a sentence. Continue with the words *is, for, he,* and *like.*

■ To practice phonics and high-frequency words, have children read Kindergarten Student Reader K.2.6. Use the instruction on pp. 555–556.

For a complete lesson plan and additional practice, see the **Leveled Reader Teaching Guide**.

Concept Literacy Reader K.2.6

■ **Preview and Predict** Display the cover of the Concept Literacy Reader K.2.6. Point to the title of the book. The title of the book is *In the Garden.* What do you think the book is about? Have children tell about the picture and what they think the book might be about.

■ **Set a Purpose** We talked about the title of the story. Let's read the story to find out what is in the garden. Have children read the Concept Literacy Reader.

■ **Read** Provide corrective feedback as children read the book orally. During reading, ask them if they were able to confirm any of the predictions they made prior to reading.

If... children have difficulty reading the book individually,
then... read a sentence aloud as children point to each word. Then have the group reread the sentences as they continue pointing to the words.

■ **Retell** Have children retell the information as you page through the book. Help them identify each animal and how it moves.

Concept Literacy Reader K.2.6

Objectives
• Identify the common sounds that letters represent.   • Predict what might happen next based on the cover.
• Predict what might happen next based on the title.   • Retell important facts in a text, heard or read.

 **SI** *Strategic Intervention* **DAY 4**

Phonemic Awareness•Phonics

■ **Isolate /i/** Display the *inch* and *igloo* Picture Cards. Listen to the words *inch* and *igloo.* Do these words begin with the same sound? Yes, *inch* and *igloo* begin with /i/. Say the words with me: /i/ /i/ /i/, *inch;* /i/ /i/ /i/, *igloo.* Repeat with *insect* and *iguana.*

■ **Connect /i/ to *Ii*** Display the *igloo* Picture Card. This is an *igloo. Igloo* begins with /i/. Write the letters *Ii* on the board. Listen to the beginning sound. *Igloo* begins with /i/. The letter *i* stands for /i/. Say it with me: /i/ /i/ /i/, *igloo.* Does *kangaroo* begin with the same letter as *igloo?* No, *kangaroo* does not begin with /i/.

■ **Segmenting** Say *cat.* It has three sounds, /k/ /a/ /t/. Say them with me. Now say *tap.* How many sounds are in *tap?* (three) What are they? (/t/ /a/ /p/) Continue with *dig, Tim, bat, cab,* and *Pam.*

Get Set, Roll! Reader 12

■ **Review** Review the high-frequency words *for, the,* and *he.* Have children find each word on the Word Wall.

■ **Review Rebus Words** Write the word *rock* on the board. This is the word rock. Name the letters with me: *r, o, c, k, rock.* Repeat the procedure with *Ted, Jack, see, tires, zigs,* and *zags.* Look for these words in the story today. A picture above the word will help you read it.

Get Set, Roll! Reader 12

■ **Read** Display the Get Set, Roll! Reader 12, *Tires.* Today we will read a story about our friends Jack and Ted. Point to the title of the book. What is the title of the book? (*Tires*) We will read some words with /i/ in this book.

> **If...** children have difficulty reading the story individually,
> **then...** read a sentence aloud as children point to each word. Then have the group reread the sentences as they continue pointing to the words.

■ **Reread** Use echo reading of Get Set, Roll! Reader 12 to model fluent reading. Use your oral reading to model for children where to pause, when to change pitch, and which words to stress. Then have children reread orally three to four times, or until they can read with few or no mistakes.

Objectives
• Identify the common sounds that letters represent.
• Read at least 25 high-frequency words from a commonly used list.

Small Group Time

More Reading
Use Leveled Readers or other text at children's instructional level.

SI *Strategic Intervention*

DAY 5

Phonics Review

■ **Recognize** *Ii* Write the uppercase *I* on the board. Name the letter as you write it several times. Then give each child a sheet of construction paper and have him or her cut out the shape of a capital *I*. Then write a lowercase *i* on the board. Name the letter and ask a volunteer to write the letter on the board.

■ **Discriminate** /i/ Draw an insect with six legs on the board. Gather about ten Picture Cards, including the following *Ii*/i/ cards: *igloo, insect, iguana, inch.* Mix the cards and display them one at a time. Have a child name the picture. If the name has /i/, have the child write a lowercase *i* in one of the insect's legs.

Listen to Me Reader K.2.6

■ **Preview and Predict** Display the book. The title of this story is *All About Me!* The author is Claire Albrecht. The illustrator is Yoshiko Z. Jaeggi. Point to the title on the cover and read it again. Ask children to tell what they think the book is about.

Listen to Me Reader K.2.6

■ **Set a Purpose** Review children's ideas. Point out that they will know more about the book when they read the story. Tell children that you will read the story with them. Follow along with your finger as I read. Then we will take turns reading this page. Reread the book several times giving children several opportunities to read the text. Provide support with decoding as necessary.

■ **Reread for Fluency** Use echo reading of Listen to Me Reader K.2.6 to model reading fluently. Use your oral reading to model for children where to pause, when to change pitch, and which words to stress. Then have children reread orally three to four times, or until they can read with few or no mistakes.

Objectives
• Identify the common sounds that letters represent.
• Predict what might happen next based on the cover.
• Predict what might happen next based on the title.

OL On-Level **DAY 1**

Phonemic Awareness•Phonics

■ **Identify /i/** Tell children you will tell them a story and they should listen for words with /i/. When you say a word that has /i/, the children should clap their hands and repeat the word. Tell the following story, emphasizing the /i/ words and pausing to give children a chance to clap and repeat the word. *Tim likes to fish. Izzy likes to fish. Tim dips his fishing line in water. The fish splash and splish in water. Tim caught six fish! Izzy did the same. Izzy caught six fish. Tim and Izzy like to fish.*

■ **Match /i/ to /i** Retell the story and have children take turns writing *i* or *I* on the board when they hear a word that has /i/.

Objectives
• Identify the common sounds that letters represent.

Pacing Small Group Instruction

 20–30 mins.

5 Day Plan	
DAY 1	• Phonemic Awareness/ Phonics • Decodable Story 12
DAY 2	• Phonemic Awareness/ Phonics • High-Frequency Words • Decodable Reader 12
DAY 3	• Phonemic Awareness/ Phonics • Kindergarten Student Reader K.2.6
DAY 4	• Get Set, Roll! Reader 12
DAY 5	• Phonics Review • Reread Leveled Books

OL On-Level **DAY 2**

Phonemic Awareness•Phonics

■ **Discriminate /i/** Draw a large bib on a sheet of chart paper. Ask children to decorate the bib by drawing a picture of something that has /i/ in the middle of the picture name. Give children paper for their pictures. When children are done, have each child show his or her picture and tell the picture name. Have the class decide if the picture name has /i/. If it does, have the child paste the picture on the bib and write an *i* below it.

■ **High-Frequency Words** Display the following word cards: *I, a, the, for, he, is, have, little, to.* Say the word *have* and select a child to point to the word. Have children say the word and use it in a sentence. Continue with the other words.

Objectives
• Identify the common sounds that letters represent.
• Read at least 25 high-frequency words from a commonly used list.

3 or 4 Day Plan	
DAY 1	• Phonemic Awareness/ Phonics • Decodable Story 12
DAY 2	• Phonemic Awareness/ Phonics • High-Frequency Words • Decodable Reader 12
DAY 3	• Phonemic Awareness/ Phonics • Kindergarten Student Reader K.2.6
DAY 4	• Get Set, Roll! Reader 12

3 Day Plan: Eliminate the shaded box.

More Practice

For additional practice with this week's phonics skills, have children reread the Decodable Story (Day 1) and the Decodable Reader (Day 2).

Small Group Time

Phonemic Awareness•Phonics

■ **Listen for Sounds** Have children listen to three words and identify the ones that have the same middle sound. Use the following words: *pit, tip, tan; big, bag, hit; kit, can, lid; dog, dig, pig; sit, sat, sip.*

■ **Recognize /i/** Display the *inch* and *otter* Picture Cards. This is *inch.* This is *otter:* /i/ /i/, *inch,* /o/ /o/, *otter.* Which word begins with /i/? What other words can you name that begin with /i/? List the words children name. Then display the *pig* and *pen* Picture Cards. This is a *pig* and this is a *pen.* Which word has /i/ in the middle, *pig* or *pen?* What other words can you name that have /i/ in the middle? List the words children name. Circle the *i* in each word. The letter *i* stands for the sound /i/ in these words.

Kindergarten Student Reader K.2.6

■ **Preview and Predict** Display Kindergarten Student Reader K.2.6.Today we are going to read a new book. Point to the title of the book. The title of this book is *Tim's Garden.* The author's name is Benton Walston. The author writes the words in the story. Who do you think is the boy on the cover? Yes, his name is Tim. Where is Tim?

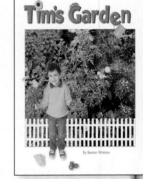

Kindergarten Student
Reader K.2.6

■ **Set a Purpose** Review the list of places where children think Tim is. Remind children that they want to find out about Tim as they read the story.

■ **Read** Have children follow along as they read the story with you. After reading p. 2, ask children to tell where Tim is. Help them identify the things they see in the picture. Continue through the book. Then ask the following questions:

• Which animals are in the garden?

• What things does Tim like?

■ **Summarize** Have children retell the story to a partner and tell how Tim feels at the end of the story.

■ **Text to Self** Help children make personal connections to the story as they tell about a garden they have or would like to have. Ask them to tell what things are in their garden and why they like those things.

Objectives
• Identify the common sounds that letters represent.
• Read at least 25 high-frequency words from a commonly used list.
• Retell important facts in a text, heard or read.

 **OL** On-Level

DAY **4**

More Reading
Use Leveled Readers or other text at children's instructional level.

Get Set, Roll! Reader 12

■ **Review** Review the high-frequency words *for, the,* and *he.* Have children find each word on the Word Wall.

■ **Review Rebus Words** Write the word *tires* on the board. This is the word *tires.* Name the letters with me: *t, i, r, e, s, tires.* Repeat the procedure with *Ted, Jack, see, rock, zigs,* and *zags.* Look for these words in the story today. A picture above the word will help you read it.

■ **Read** Today we will read a story about our friends Jack and Ted. Point to the title of the book. What is the title of the book? (*Tires*) We will read some words with /i/ in this book. Point to the picture on the cover. What do you think this story is about?

Objectives
• Read at least 25 high-frequency words from a commonly used list.
• Predict what might happen next based on the cover.

OL On-Level

DAY  **5**

Phonics Review

■ **Recognize /i/** Display the *can, brick, kitten, pig, pillow, dog, quilt, six, fan, wig, hat,* and *zipper* Picture Cards. Have a child take a card and say the picture name. If the word has /i/, have the child write *i* on the board. Continue with the other cards.

Objectives
• Identify the common sounds that letters represent.

Small Group Time

Pacing Small Group Instruction

20-30 mins.

5 Day Plan

DAY 1	• Phonemic Awareness/ Phonics • Decodable Story 12
DAY 2	• Phonics • Spelling • High-Frequency Words • Decodable Reader 12
DAY 3	• Independent Reader K.2.6 or Kindergarten Student Reader K.2.6
DAY 4	• Get Set, Roll/Reader 12 or Kindergarten Student Reader K.2.6
DAY 5	• Fluency/ Comprehension • Independent Reader K.2.6

3 or 4 Day Plan

DAY 1	• Phonemic Awareness/ Phonics
DAY 2	• Phonics • Spelling • High-Frequency Words
DAY 3	• Independent Reader K.2.6 or Kindergarten Student Reader K.2.6
DAY 4	• Get Set, Roll/Reader 12 or Kindergarten Student Reader K.2.6

3 Day Plan: Eliminate the shaded box.

More Practice

For additional practice with this week's phonics skills and to develop fluency, have children reread the Decodable Story (Day 1) and the Decodable Reader (Day 2).

A Advanced **DAY 1**

Phonemic Awareness•Phonics

■ **Discriminate /i/** Have children clap if they hear /i/ in the beginning or middle of these words. Say *plant, pick, inch, tulip, dig, grow, grip, insect.*

■ **Connect /i/ to Ii** Write the following words on the board: *sat, pat, tap.* Have a volunteer read the first word. Say the word *sit* and ask children what letter stands for the middle sound. Have a volunteer write the word *sit* below the word *sat.* Continue with the words *pat* and *tap* to form the words *pit* and *tip.* Repeat the procedure with these words: *bag, hat, lap.*

Objectives
• Identify the common sounds that letters represent.
• Recognize that new words are created when letters are changed.

A Advanced **DAY 2**

Phonics•Spelling

■ **Connect /i/ to Ii** Display the *Ii* Alphabet Card. What are the names of these letters? What is the sound we learned for this letter?

■ **Spell Sounds** Write *tip* on the board. Have children blend the sound of each letter to read the word: /t/ /i/ /p/, *tip.* This is the word *tip.* Repeat the routine with the following words: *sit, Tim, pit, Pip, it.*

■ **Review High-Frequency Words** Review the following high-frequency words with children: *I, am, have, he, is, my, we, like, a, for.*

Objectives
• Identify upper-case letters. • Identify lower-case letters.
• Identify the common sounds that letters represent.
• Use letter-sound correspondences to spell consonant-vowel-consonant (CVC) words.

A Advanced

DAY 3

For a complete lesson plan and additional practice, see the **Leveled Reader Teaching Guide**.

Independent Reader K.2.6

Independent Reader K.2.6

- **Practice High-Frequency Words** Write *little* on the board. Have volunteers say the word and use it in a sentence. Continue with the words *I, am, a, the, have,* and *is.*

- **Activate Prior Knowledge** Have children read the title and look at the picture. Have them tell what they think the story is about and add any information they may have about the topic. Then have children take turns reading *A Yard for All* for their group.

- **Realism and Fantasy** Remind children that a realistic story tells about something that could happen in real life. A fantasy is a story about something make-believe. Do you think this story could really happen or is it make-believe? Why?

- **Reread for Fluency** After rereading with children, model reading fluently for them. I am going to read this selection aloud. I will read the words with no mistakes. I want you to read it aloud with me. Try to read the words just as I do.

  Use echo reading of Independent Reader K.2.6 to model reading fluently. Use your oral reading to model for children where to pause, when to change pitch, and which words to stress. Then have children reread orally three to four times, or until they can read with few or no mistakes.

- For more practice with phonics and high-frequency words and to develop fluency, have children read Kindergarten Student Reader K.2.6. Use the instruction on pp. 555–556.

More Reading
Use Leveled Readers or other text at children's instructional level.

Objectives
- Identify the common sounds that letters represent.
- Read at least 25 high-frequency words from a commonly used list.

Small **Group Time**

More Reading
Use Leveled Readers or other text at children's instructional level.

A Advanced | DAY 4

Kindergarten Student Reader K.2.6

■ **Revisit Rebus Words** Write the word *bunny* on the board. *This is* bunny. *Name the letters with me:* b, u, n, n, y. *Look for the word* bunny. *There will be a picture above the word to help you.* Continue with: *garden, worm, bird,* and *happy.*

■ **Reread** Use Kindergarten Student Reader K.2.6 to practice reading fluently.

■ **Text to World** Ask children to describe the garden in the book. Have them tell about gardens they have seen and what plants and animals are found there.

■ **Read** Have children read Get Set, Roll! Reader 12, *Tires.* Use the instruction on p. 583.

Kindergarten Student Reader K.2.6

Objectives
• Read at least 25 high-frequency words from a commonly used list.

A Advanced | DAY 5

Fluency•Comprehension

■ **Reread for Fluency** Use the Independent Reader K.2.6 to model reading fluently for children. *I am going to read this story aloud. I will read the words with no mistakes. I want you to read it aloud with me. Try to read the words just as I do.*

■ **Comprehension** After children have finished reading the selection, have them retell the events in the story. Divide the class into two groups. Have one group draw a picture of a real garden and the other group draw pictures of a make-believe garden. Have the groups share their pictures

Independent Leveled Reader K.2.6

Objectives
• Read at least 25 high-frequency words from a commonly used list.
• Identify content as realism or fantasy.

 **English Language Learners**

DAY 1

Concept Development

- **Read the Concept Literacy Reader** To build background and vocabulary, read *In the Garden* with children. Begin by reading the title and author's name. Have children describe what they see on the cover. Then have children look at the pictures in the book. *What different things do you see in the garden?* Read the book aloud, pausing to discuss each page. Model sentence patterns and vocabulary that describe things in the garden. *The bird is green and white. It flies around the garden.* On a second reading, invite children to talk about the pictures on each page.

- **Develop Oral Language** Revisit *In the Garden,* pointing out that many different plants and animals live in the garden. Then have children sing the following song with you to the tune of "If You're Happy and You Know It":

  If you live inside the garden clap your hands,
  If you live inside the garden clap your hands.
  If you're a bird it's really neat,
  A tasty flower is a treat.
  If you live inside the garden clap your hands.

Repeat the song with other animals that live in the garden.

Phonemic Awareness/Phonics

- **Frontload Words with /i/, /a/, /s/, /p/, /k/** Have children look at the picture on pp. 112–113 of *My Skills Buddy.* This picture shows a crowded house. How many animals are in the house? (8) How many people do you live with? In the picture, the cat on the couch is ill. *Ill* is another way to say someone is sick. What sound does *ill* begin with? *Ill* begins with /i/; /i/, *ill.* Repeat with other words in the picture that begin with /p/ or /k/, including *pair, pears, pen, picture, pants, cry, cat, crayon, color, cup, covers,* and *cap.*

- **Connect Sound to Letters** Use letter tiles to display the word *in.* This word is *in:* /i/ /n/, *in.* Say the word with me. Have children write the word *in* and circle the letter that makes /i/. Write and read aloud the following sentence: *Andy is into reading about igloos.* Point to *i* in *is* and ask: What letter is this? Yes, this is *i.* Continue with *into* and *igloos.*

Content Objective

- Develop content knowledge about what is real and make-believe.

Language Objectives

- Understand and use grade-level content area vocabulary.

- Recognize the sounds of English.

Concept Literacy Reader K.2.6

Daily Planner

DAY 1	• Concept Development • Phonemic Awareness/ Phonics • Listening Comprehension
DAY 2	• Comprehension • Vocabulary
DAY 3	• Phonemic Awareness/ Phonics • Conventions
DAY 4	• Phonemic Awareness/ Phonics • Concepts and Oral Language
DAY 5	• Language Workshop • Writing

Objectives
- Distinguish sounds of English with increasing ease. • Use visual support to enhance and confirm understanding of increasingly complex and elaborated spoken language. • Learn relationships between sounds and letters of the English language.

Support for English Language Learners

Content Objective
• Understand realism and fantasy.

Language Objective
• Learn and use academic vocabulary.

My Skills Buddy, pp. 114–115

Listening Comprehension: Realism and Fantasy

■ **Frontload Vocabulary** Discuss the illustrations on pp. 114–115 in *My Skills Buddy* to frontload vocabulary. Look at page 114. What animal do you see? (a fish) What color is the fish? (gold) Where does the fish live? (a fishbowl) What else is in the fishbowl? (pebbles) How does the fish get around? (It swims.) Can the fish talk? (no) Now look at page 115. Where is everyone? (a classroom) Who is teaching the class? (a big fish)

■ **Provide Scaffolding** Point to the illustrations on p. 114. Explain that this illustration shows realism, or something that could really happen. A fish can really live in a fishbowl. A fish can really swim. Point to the illustration on p. 115. Explain that this illustration shows fantasy. Fantasy is another word for make-believe. A fish cannot really teach a class. Sea creatures would not really sit in desks. Compare the real fish on p. 114 to the fantasy fish on p. 115. How are the two fish different?

■ **Prepare for the Read Aloud** Prepare children for listening to "Jack and the Beanstalk" on p. 527.

Jack and the Beanstalk

Jack and his mother are poor. Jack's mom tells him to sell their cow. Jack meets a man. The man says he will give Jack five magic beans for the cow. Jack agrees. His mother finds out, and throws the beans out the window.

The next day, there is a giant beanstalk. Jack climbs it. A mean giant and his wife live there. The giant's wife is nice to Jack. When the giant falls asleep, Jack sneaks out and takes a bag of gold coins.

Jack makes more trips up the beanstalk. One time the giant sees Jack and runs after him. Jack gets away. Then he and his mother cut down the beanstalk.

■ **First Listening** Write the title of the Read Aloud on the board. This is about a boy named Jack. He climbs a magic beanstalk. Listen to find out about what he finds at the top of the beanstalk. After reading, ask children to recall the events. What does Jack find at the top? What does he take back home?

■ **Second Listening** Explain to children that many fairy tales mix realism with fantasy. Make a chart on the board. Title one side *Realism* and the other side *Fantasy*. As you listen to the story, think about the realism and fantasy. What in the story could be real? (A boy lives with his mother. They are poor. He is sent to sell the cow.) What is made up? (magic beans, the beanstalk, the giant,) Write the children's answers in the chart.

Objectives
• Understand the main points of spoken language ranging from situations in which contexts are familiar to unfamiliar. • Use visual and contextual support to enhance and confirm understanding needed to comprehend increasingly challenging language.

Comprehension

■ **Provide Scaffolding** Display *Jack and the Beanstalk.* Lead a detailed picture walk through the story, naming what you see in the illustrations and describing what is happening. Use gestures and facial expressions to convey meaning.

• **Set the Scene** Use the cover of the Big Book to help children understand that this story takes place in a fantasy world, a place that is not like the real world. Explain that stories that take place in fantasy worlds are often called fairy tales. Look at the pictures in the story. What things happen in the story that do not happen in the real world? (A boy rides a cow, there is an ogre, there is a magic beanstalk.)

• **Frontload Vocabulary** As you lead the picture walk, use the illustrations to introduce unfamiliar words in the text, including some of the adjectives. Look at the picture on page 7. There is a magic laying hen. What does magic mean? (It means the hen is able to do something special.) Look at the picture. What do you think the hen can do that is magic? (lay golden eggs) Include some of the following words: *golden* (p. 9); *hungry* (p. 12); *special, sweet* (p. 16); *lovely* (p. 17).

Vocabulary: Direction Words

■ **Frontload Vocabulary** Have children turn to p. 128 of *My Skills Buddy.* Talk about the picture, using the direction words *left* and *right*. Tell children to stand like the girl in the picture. This is my *left*. (Shake your left arm. Tell children to shake their left arm also.) This is my *right*. (Shake your right arm. Tell children to shake their right arm also.) Then practice by asking children to raise their left or right hands.

■ **Provide Scaffolding** Write the words *left* and *right* on the board. Read the words aloud with children. These words tell us about direction. Stand so you're facing the same direction as the children. Point out classroom objects based on the direction words *left* and *right*.

■ **Practice** Ask for volunteers. Explain that you are going to use direction words to walk a child through the classroom. Start a child at one end of the class. Direct the child to take a number of steps to the left or right. Then have him or her stop. Continue to have the child follow your direction cues until he or she get to where you want. Repeat with other children.

Content Objective
• Develop background knowledge.

Language Objective
• Learn and use direction words.

Use Learning Strategies
Remind children that if they have trouble remembering their left from their right, they can ask other children for help.

Big Book

Content Objective

- Use learning strategies.

Language Objectives

- Connect /i/ and *Ii*.
- Use adjectives.

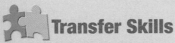

Transfer Skills

Pronouncing /i/ English language learners from various language backgrounds may pronounce short *i* like the *ee* in *see*. Model correct pronunciation by saying a short phrase or sentence with both the short *i* and long *e* sounds, such as *You can eat it.* Have children repeat the sentence, and call their attention to the differences in pronouncing *eat* and *it*.

Use Learning Strategies

In *Jack and the Beanstalk*, at one point Jack says "Just now and then." Explain to children that this is an expression that mean "sometimes." Have children look through the story or other books to find more expressions. Help children analyze the expressions to understand meaning.

Phonemic Awareness/Phonics

- **Isolate Initial and Medial /i/** Say *if,* and then model segmenting sounds by saying /i/ /f/. Emphasize the initial sound in the word. Repeat for initial /i/ with *it* and *ill*. Help children identify the initial sound in each word. Then say *hid*. Model segmenting sounds by saying /h/ /i/ /d/. Emphasize the medial sound in the word. Repeat for medial /i/ with *pin* and *hit*. Help children identify the medial sound in each word.

- **/i/ Spelled *Ii*** Say the following word pairs: *sat/sit.* Have children say the words and listen for the middle sound. Have them tell which word has /i/. Segment the sounds in the word: /s/ /i/ /t/. Have children tell you which letter to write for each sound in the word *sit*. Repeat several times with children to be sure they distinguish /i/ in the middle of the word. Continue with these pairs: *bit/bat, pit/pot, mitt/mat, pick/pack.*

Conventions: Adjectives

- **Provide Scaffolding** Point to the first image on p. 6 of *Jack and the Beanstalk.* Look at the picture. You can see the beanstalk. How would you describe the beanstalk? Explain that adjectives are words used to describe something. In the book, it says the beanstalk is *tall*. *Tall* is an adjective. It describes the beanstalk.

- **Practice** What are some other adjectives in this story? Page through the Big Book and name more adjectives from the story. Include the adjectives mentioned on Day 2: *golden* (p. 9); *hungry* (p. 12); *special, sweet* (p. 16); *lovely* (p. 17). Then ask children to name as many other adjectives as they can think of. Have children answer with the sentence frame: _____ is an adjective. Encourage them to look at classroom objects for ideas. Write the adjectives on the board.

- **Leveled LS Support** **Beginning/Intermediate** Give a sentence frame for some of the nouns in the story. See if children can name an adjective that describes the noun. Write the adjectives on the board. The boy is ____. The ogre is ____. The hen is ____. The house is ____. The eggs are ____.

  Advanced/Advanced-High Read a series of adjectives: *tall, happy, strong, small, blue.* Ask children to use each adjective in a sentence.

Objectives

- Internalize new academic language by using and reusing it in meaningful ways in speaking activities that build concept and language attainment. • Develop repertoire of learning strategies commensurate with grade-level learning expectations. • Decode (sound out) words using a combination of skills.

Phonemic Awareness/Phonics

■ **Review /k/** To review /k/ in words, say the sentence with words that begin or end with the sound:

> Can we color cards in the back of the car?

Have children repeat the sentence after you. Have them pronounce just the words that begin with /k/. What sound do these words begin with? Yes, they start with /k/. Then have them pronounce the word that ends with /k/. What sound does this word end with? Yes, it ends with /k/.

■ **/k/ Spelled *Cc*** Use letter tiles to form the following words: *can, cat, cap.* Model reading the words, isolating /k/ and pointing out *c*. Show all the sound-letter correspondences (for example, /k/ /a/ /n/ = *can*).

Concepts and Oral Language

■ **Revisit Talk with Me Chart 12A** Display the chart. Have children describe the things and ideas in the photos. Then say a sentence for each picture. After that, ask a question about each Amazing Word. Is an *ogre* real or make-believe?

■ **Develop Oral Language** Introduce language patterns that help describe the pictures on Talk with Me Chart 12A. Describe the things or ideas in each by using adjectives. The beanstalk is *tall. Tall* describes the beanstalk. Have children repeat your sentences. Then repeat with the rest of the Amazing Words.

Beginning Have children point to each picture on the chart and use the Amazing Word to identify the picture.

Intermediate With your assistance, have children use the Amazing Words in a sentence unrelated to the picture on the Talk With Me Chart.

Advanced/Advanced-High Encourage children to use their prior knowledge about the Amazing Words to think of examples for each word.

Content Objectives

• Develop oral language.

• Use learning strategies.

Language Objectives

• Connect /k/ with *Cc*.

• Learn English language patterns.

Use Learning Strategies

Work with children to create a two-column chart titled *Nouns and Adjectives.* Label one side of the chart *Nouns* and the other side *Adjectives*. Then write a sentence on the board and read it aloud. Ask children which word is a noun. Write the word on the *Noun* side of the chart. Ask children what word is an adjective. Write that on the *Adjective* side of the chart. Repeat with other examples.

Talk with Me Chart 12A

Objectives

• Use strategic learning techniques to acquire basic vocabulary. • Recognize elements of the English sound system in newly acquired vocabulary. • Share information in cooperative learning interactions. • Decode (sound out) words using a combination of skills.

Support for English Language Learners

Content Objectives

- Understand *Jack and the Beanstalk.*
- Practice compare and contrast.

Language Objectives

- Retell a selection through speaking and writing.
- Write using grade-level vocabulary.

Monitor and Self-Correct

Remind children that if they don't know how to say a word, they can ask their partners for help.

Home Language Support

Invite children to share ideas in their home languages before creating their sentences.

Language Workshop: Retell *Jack and the Beanstalk*

- **Introduce and Model** Display Big Book *Jack and the Beanstalk.* Point out that the words in the story are written like a poem with rhyming words.

- **Practice** Read pp. 21–24 and have children identify the rhyming words: friends, ends; now, cow; grew, through, you. Remind children that rhyming words have the same middle and ending sounds. As children identify the rhyming words, help them say other rhyming words.

Writing: Write About Jack and the Beanstalk

- **Prepare for Writing** Review other sets of rhyming words by writing simple word patterns on the board. Use these word patterns for children to spell words that rhyme: __at, __an, __in, __op. Let's write a poem about Jack and the things in the story. We can use the rhyming words to write a poem. Think of something we read about. We can write real things or make-believe things.

- **Create Sentences** Read the sentence frames for rhyming words:

  My cow can _____. (hop)   I see my ____. (friends)
  It will not _____. (stop)   My story ____. (ends)

Have children work together to create a poem. Have them copy the poem and draw a picture about it. Children can also work with a partner to create their own poem.

Leveled LS Support

Beginning Have children choose a pair of rhyming words and illustrate each word. Have them tell their rhyming words.

Intermediate Guide children in choosing new rhyming words to make an original poem. Remind children that they can use the word patterns to create a variety of rhyming words.

Advanced/Advanced-High Have children create their own poem. Have them write and illustrate the poem. Have them share the poem with the class.

Objectives
- Write using content-based grade-level vocabulary. • Spell familiar English words with increasing accuracy.
- Write using a variety of grade-appropriate sentence lengths in increasingly accurate ways as more English is acquired.

Customize Literacy in Your Classroom

Table of Contents
for Customize Literacy

Customize Literacy is organized into different sections, each one designed to help you organize and carry out an effective literacy program. Each section contains strategies and support for teaching comprehension skills and strategies. *Customize Literacy* also shows how to use weekly text sets of readers in your literacy program.

Weekly Text Sets
to Customize Literacy

The following readers can be used to enhance your literacy instruction.

	Decodable Reader	Concept Literacy Reader	Below-Level Reader	On-Level Reader	Advanced Reader
Unit 2 WEEK 4	My Cap	The Bear	Meet Cam the Cow	Winter Fun	Skip and Run
Unit 2 WEEK 5	Tip and Pat	Animal Homes	The Iguana	A House for Pip	A Winter Home
Unit 2 WEEK 6	Tim and Sam	In the Garden	All About Me!	For Tim	A Yard for All

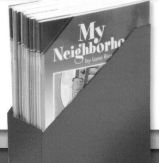

Customize Literacy in Your Classroom

Instruction in comprehension skills and strategies provides readers with avenues to understanding a text. Through teacher modeling and guided, collaborative, and independent practice, children become independent thinkers who employ a variety of skills and strategies to help them make meaning as they read.

Mini-Lessons for Comprehension Skills and Strategies

Envision It!
A Comprehension Handbook

Unit 1	Character, Setting, Sequence, Classify and Categorize, Predict and Set Purpose, Recall and Retell
Unit 2	Compare and Contrast, Setting, Main Idea, Realism and Fantasy, Sequence, Predict and Set Purpose, Recall and Retell
Unit 3	Compare and Contrast, Plot, Cause and Effect, Draw Conclusions, Main Idea, Predict and Set Purpose, Recall and Retell
Unit 4	Sequence, Cause and Effect, Character, Classify and Categorize, Setting, Predict and Set Purpose, Recall and Retell
Unit 5	Realism and Fantasy, Cause and Effect, Compare and Contrast, Plot, Main Idea, Draw Conclusions, Predict and Set Purpose, Recall and Retell
Unit 6	Compare and Contrast, Character, Main Idea, Plot, Setting, Draw Conclusions, Predict and Set Purpose, Recall and Retell

Envision It! Visual Skills Handbook

Author's Purpose
Categorize and Classify
Cause and Effect
Compare and Contrast
Draw Conclusions
Fact and Opinion
Generalize
Graphic Sources
Literary Elements
Main Idea and Details
Sequence

Envision It! Visual Strategies Handbook

Background Knowledge
Important Ideas
Inferring
Monitor and Clarify
Predict and Set Purpose
Questioning
Story Structure
Summarize
Text Structure
Visualize

Anchor Chart Anchor charts are provided with each strategy lesson. These charts incorporate the language of strategic thinkers. They help students make their thinking visible and permanent and provide students with a means to clarify their thinking about how and when to use each strategy. As children gain more experience with a strategy, the chart may undergo revision.

See pages 97–113 in the *First Stop on Reading Street* Teacher's Edition for additional support as you customize literacy in your classroom.

Good Readers DRA2 users will find additional resources in the *First Stop on Reading Street* Teacher's Edition on pages 100–102.

Contents

Pacing Guide

This chart shows the instructional sequence from *Scott Foresman Reading Street* for Grade K. You can use this pacing guide as is to ensure you are following a comprehensive scope and sequence. Or, you can adjust the sequence to match your calendar, curriculum map, or testing schedule.

Grade K

LANGUAGE ARTS

UNIT 1

	Week 1	Week 2	Week 3	Week 4	Week 5	Week 6
Phonological/ Phonemic Awareness	Rhyming Words	Syllables Sound Discrimination	Discriminate Sounds Segment Syllables	Discriminate Sounds	Isolate /m/ Discriminate Sounds	Isolate /t/ Discriminate Sounds Rhyme
Phonics	Letter Recognition: *Aa, Bb, Cc, Dd, Ee*	Letter Recognition: *Ff, Gg, Hh, Ii, Jj, Kk, Ll, Mm, Nn*	Letter Recognition: *Oo, Pp, Qq, Rr, Ss*	Letter Recognition: *Tt, Uu, Vv, Ww, Xx, Yy, Zz*	/m/ Spelled *Mm*	/t/ Spelled *Tt*
High-Frequency Words	*I, am*	*I, am*	*the, little*	*the, little*	*a, to*	*a, to*
Listening Comprehension	Character	Setting	Sequence	Classify and Categorize	Character	Classify and Categorize
Comprehension Strategies	Preview and Predict, Recall and Retell					

UNIT 2

	Week 1	Week 2
Phonological/ Phonemic Awareness	Isolate /a/ Oral Blending	Isolate /s/ Oral Blending
Phonics	/a/ Spelled *Aa*	/s/ Spelled *Ss*
High-Frequency Words	*have, is*	*have, is*
Listening Comprehension	Compare and Contrast	Setting

UNIT 4

	Week 1	Week 2	Week 3	Week 4	Week 5	Week 6
Phonemic Awareness	Isolate /h/ Oral Blending Segment Phonemes	Isolate /l/ Oral Blending Segment Phonemes	Isolate Blends Discriminate Phonemes Segment Phonemes	Isolate /g/ Segment Phonemes	Isolate /e/ Segment Phonemes Discriminate Phonemes	Isolate /e/ Segment Phonemes Discriminate Phonemes
Phonics	/h/ Spelled *Hh*	/l/ Spelled *Ll*	Consonant Blends	/g/ Spelled *Gg*	/e/ Spelled *Ee*	/e/ Spelled *Ee*
High-Frequency Words	*are, that, do*	*are, that, do*	*one, two, three, four, five*	*one, two, three, four, five*	*here, go, from*	*here, go, from*
Listening Comprehension	Sequence	Cause and Effect	Sequence	Character	Classify and Categorize	Setting
Comprehension Strategies	Preview and Predict, Retell					

UNIT 5

	Week 1	Week 2
Phonemic Awareness	Isolate /j/, /w/ Oral Blending Segment Phonemes	Isolate /ks/ Oral Blending Segment Phonemes
Phonics	/j/ Spelled *Jj* and /w/ Spelled *Ww*	/ks/ Spelled *Xx*
High-Frequency Words	*yellow, blue, green*	*yellow, blue, green*
Listening Comprehension	Realism and Fantasy	Cause and Effect

> *Are you the adventurous type? Want to use some of your own ideas and materials in your teaching? But you worry you might be leaving out some critical instruction kids need?* **Customize Literacy** *can help.*

(continued)

Week 3	Week 4	Week 5	Week 6
Isolate /p/ Oral Blending	Isolate /k/ Oral Blending	Isolate /i/ Discriminate Sounds Oral Blending	Isolate /i/ Discriminate Sounds Oral Blending
/p/ Spelled *Pp*	/k/ Spelled *Cc*	/i/ Spelled *Ii*	/i/ Spelled *Ii*
we, my, like	*we, my, like*	*he, for*	*he, for*
Main Idea	Realism and Fantasy	Sequence	Realism and Fantasy

Preview and Predict, Retell

UNIT 3

Week 1	Week 2	Week 3	Week 4	Week 5	Week 6
Isolate /n/, /b/ Oral Blending Segment Phonemes	Isolate /r/ Oral Blending Segment Phonemes	Isolate /d/, /k/ Oral Blending Segment Phonemes	Isolate /f/ Oral Blending Segment Phonemes	Isolate /o/ Oral Blending Segment Phonemes	Isolate /o/ Oral Blending Segment Phonemes
/n/ Spelled *Nn* and /b/ Spelled *Bb*	/r/ Spelled *Rr*	/d/ Spelled *Dd* and /k/ Spelled *Kk*	/f/ Spelled *Ff*	/o/ Spelled *Oo*	/o/ Spelled *Oo*
me, with, she	*me, with, she*	*see, look*	*see, look*	*they, you, of*	*they, you, of*
Compare and Contrast	Plot	Cause and Effect	Plot	Draw Conclusions	Main Idea

Preview and Predict, Retell

(continued)

Week 3	Week 4	Week 5	Week 6
Isolate /u/ Oral Blending Segment Phonemes	Isolate /u/ Oral Blending Segment Phonemes	Isolate /v/, /z/ Oral Blending Segment Phonemes	Isolate /y/, /kw/ Oral Blending Segment Phonemes
/u/ Spelled *Uu*	/u/ Spelled *Uu*	/v/ Spelled *Vv* and /z/ Spelled *Zz*	/y/ Spelled *Yy* and /kw/ Spelled *qu*
what, said, was	*what, said, was*	*where, come*	*where, come*
Compare and Contrast	Plot	Main Idea	Draw Conclusions

Preview and Predict, Retell

UNIT 6

Week 1	Week 2	Week 3	Week 4	Week 5	Week 6
Isolate /a/ and /i/ Blend Phonemes Segment Phonemes	Isolate /o/ Blend Phonemes Segment Phonemes	Isolate /e/ Blend Phonemes Segment Phonemes	Isolate /u/ Blend Phonemes Segment Phonemes	Consonant and Vowel Sounds	Consonant and Vowel Sounds
/a/ Spelled *Aa* and /i/ Spelled *Ii*	/o/ Spelled *Oo*	/e/ Spelled *Ee*	/u/ Spelled *Uu*	Consonants and Short Vowels	Consonants and Short Vowels
Review *here, do, little, with, what*	Review *where, is, go, that, come*	Review *the, was, to, like, from*	Review *for, of, my, we, yellow*	Review *have, they, four, two, blue*	Review *you, said, see, look, three*
Compare and Contrast	Character	Main Idea	Plot	Setting	Draw Conclusions

Preview and Predict, Retell

Pacing Guide

Grade K

LANGUAGE ARTS — UNIT 1

	Week 1	Week 2	Week 3	Week 4	Week 5	Week 6
Speaking and Listening	Follow Directions	Drama—Respond to Literature	Listen for Rhyme and Rhythm	Talk About Me	Announce-ments and Messages	Drama—Respond to Literature
Grammar/ Conventions	Say Our Names	Write Our Names	What We Look Like	What We Can Do	Nouns for People and Animals	Nouns for Places and Things
Writing	Song	Invitation	Poem	Instructions	Caption	Personal Narrative

UNIT 2

	Week 1	Week 2
Speaking and Listening	Listen for Sequence	Listen for Directions
Grammar/ Conventions	Nouns for More Than One	Proper Nouns
Writing	Label	List

UNIT 4

	Week 1	Week 2	Week 3	Week 4	Week 5	Week 6
Speaking and Listening	Give Directions	Compare and Contrast	Listen for Sequence	Discuss Authors and Illustrators	Listen for Story Elements: Character	Listen to Poems
Grammar/ Conventions	Subjects (Naming Parts)	Predicates (Action Parts)	Complete Sentences	Telling Sentences	Capital Letters and Periods	Pronouns *I* and *me*
Writing	Directions	Poem	Description	List	Informal Letter	List

UNIT 5

	Week 1	Week 2
Speaking and Listening	Ask and Answer Questions	Drama—Respond to Literature
Grammar/ Conventions	Questions	Question Marks and Capital Letters
Writing	Caption	Rhyme

Week 3	Week 4	Week 5	Week 6
Discussions	Listen for Setting	Give a Description	Listen for Plot
Adjectives: Colors and Shapes	Adjectives: Sizes and Numbers	Adjectives: Opposites	Adjectives
Notes	Poem	Caption	Story

UNIT 3

Week 1	Week 2	Week 3	Week 4	Week 5	Week 6
Respond to Literature	Sequence	Recite Rhymes	Oral Presentation	Messages and Letters	Ask and Answer Questions
Verbs	Verbs for Now and the Past	Verbs That Add -s	Verbs for Now and the Future	Meaningful Word Groups	Sentences
Summary	Invitation	Persuasive Statement	Caption	List	Poem

Week 3	Week 4	Week 5	Week 6
Discuss Literature	Sequence	Oral Presentation —Description	Discuss Literary Elements: Plot
Prepositions	Nouns	Nouns in Sentences	Verbs
Poem	Formal Letter	Invitation	How-to Report

UNIT 6

Week 1	Week 2	Week 3	Week 4	Week 5	Week 6
Recite Language	Discuss Fact and Opinion	Interpret Information	Discuss Literary Elements: Character	Oral Presentation —Book Report	Discuss Literary Elements: Setting
Pronouns I and me	Prepositional Phrases	Telling Sentences	Questions	Exclamations	Complete Sentences
List	Song	Rhyme	Rhyme	Poem	Report

Teaching Record Chart

This chart shows the critical comprehension skills and strategies you need to cover. Check off each one as you provide instruction.

Reading/Comprehension	DATES OF INSTRUCTION		
Predict what might happen next in text based on the cover, title, and illustrations.			
Ask and respond to questions about texts read aloud.			
Identify elements of a story including setting, character, and key events.			
Discuss the big idea (theme) of a well-known folk tale or fable and connect it to personal experience.			
Recognize sensory details.			
Recognize recurring phrases and characters in traditional fairy tales, lullabies, and folk tales from various cultures.			
Respond to rhythm and rhyme in poetry through identifying a regular beat and similarities in word sounds.			
Retell a main event from a story read aloud.			
Describe characters in a story and the reasons for their actions.			
Identify the topic of an informational text heard.			

Tired of using slips of paper or stickies to make sure you teach everything you need to? Need an easier way to keep track of what you have taught, and what you still need to cover? **Customize Literacy** *can help.*

Reading/Comprehension	DATES OF INSTRUCTION		
Identify the topic and details in expository text heard or read, referring to the words and/or illustrations.			
Retell important facts in a text, heard or read.			
Discuss the ways authors group information in text.			
Use titles and illustrations to make predictions about text.			
Follow pictorial directions (e.g., recipes, science experiments).			
Identify the meaning of specific signs (e.g., traffic signs, warning signs).			
Discuss the purposes for reading and listening to various texts (e.g., to become involved in real and imagined events, settings, actions, and to enjoy language).			
Ask and respond to questions about text.			
Monitor and adjust comprehension (e.g., using background knowledge, creating sensory images, re-reading a portion aloud).			
Make inferences based on the cover, title, illustrations, and plot.			
Retell or act out important events in stories.			
Make connections to own experiences, to ideas in other texts, and to the larger community and discuss textual evidence.			

Realism and Fantasy

Mini-Lesson

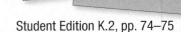

Objectives:
- Children determine if a story they hear or read could really happen.
- Children identify why they think a story could really happen or not.

Texts for Teaching
- *Bear Snores On*
- *Jack and the Beanstalk*
- *Max Takes the Train*

Leveled Readers
- See pages 16–17 for a list of Leveled Readers.

Understand the Skill

Student Edition K.2, pp. 74–75

Distinguishing **realism and fantasy** means to figure out whether a story could happen in real life. Children use clues about the characters, setting, and plot—along with their own experiences—to determine if it is realistic (could happen in real life) or fantastic (could not happen in real life).

Teach

Use the **Envision It!** lesson on K.2, pages 74–75 to visually teach realism and fantasy. Help children decide which fish is realistic and why.

Tell children that authors write different kinds of stories. One kind of story could happen in real life, and the other could not. Think aloud to model determining whether a story could happen in real life.

This story is about a bear and his friends. They all go outside to play, but something makes a noise. In the end they find a new friend. I can think about the book to find out if it could happen in real life. In real life, I don't think animals can talk like I do. In real life, I don't think a bear would play with an owl. I think this story would not happen in real life.

Practice

Show children a familiar story. Recall the story with children. Ask questions to help children decide whether a story could happen in real life, such as: Do animals talk in the story? Are there things in the story that could not happen in real life? How do you know? Talk with children about clues they see in the pictures and hear in the story that help them determine if a story could happen in real life or not.

If... students have difficulty identifying whether a story could happen,

then... point to specific parts of the story and ask pointed questions to connect prior knowledge to what happens in books, such as *Do you know animals who drive trucks?*

Apply

Tell children to listen carefully as you read a story and think about whether or not a story could happen in real life. As you read to children, pause to ask questions to help children think about whether the events, characters, and settings could happen in real life and how they know.

Writing

Children can draw and label two characters, one that could be in a realistic story, and one that could be in a fantasy. They can label each character. Post the characters in a two column chart under the headings *Realism* and *Fantasy*.

Texts for Teaching
- *Plaidypus Lost*
- *A Bed for the Winter*
- *Rooster's Off to See the World*
- *One Little Mouse*

Leveled Readers
- See pages 16–17 for a list of Leveled Readers.

Sequence

Student Edition K.2, pp. 94–95

Understand the Skill

Sequence means the order in which things happen. Sequence can also mean the steps we follow to make or do something. Understanding sequence is the first simple way to comprehend a story.

Teach

Use the **Envision It!** lesson on K.2, pages 94–95 to visually teach sequence. Using the pictures, retell what happens first, next, and last.

Tell children that they know lots of things that happen in order. Use a simple example, such as making a snack, and have children say what they do first, next, and last.

Practice

Read aloud the following passage and have children listen for what happens first, next, and last.

Three pigs built three houses. First, the wolf blew down the house made of straw. Then the wolf blew down the house made of sticks. Last, the wolf tried to blow down the house made of bricks. He couldn't blow that house down. The pigs were safe.

If... children have difficulty recognizing sequence,

then... retell the story and insert phrases such as *that's the first thing that happens, the next thing that happens is that . . .*

Apply

Ask children to listen carefully when you read stories to them. Have them ask questions: *What happened first in this story? What happened next? What happened last?* Then have them draw or write to show what happened in the story, in sequence. They can use a graphic organizer like this one.

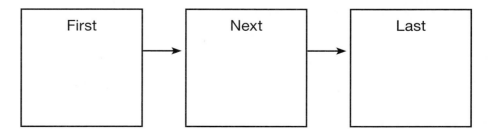

Writing

Together with children write what happens first, next, and last in a familiar story. Children can illustrate the events. They can label their pictures with *first, next, last.*

Student Edition K.1, pp. 74–75

Objectives:
- Children tell how things in a group are alike.
- Children sort items into groups of like objects.

Texts for Teaching
- *Miss Bindergarten Takes a Field Trip*
- *Dig Dig Digging*
- *If You Could Go to Antarctica*

Leveled Readers
- See pages 16–17 for a list of Leveled Readers.

Classify and Categorize

Understand the Skill

Classify and categorize means to put things that are alike into groups. Children can also describe groups by talking about what all the things in that group share.

Teach

Use the **Envision It!** lesson on K.1, pages 74–75 to visually teach classify and categorize.

Tell children that books often group things that are alike. Think aloud as you model looking at books. This book is all about trucks. This one is all about animals. I can look through the truck book and see different kinds of trucks, but they are all alike in some ways. How are the animals alike and different?

Practice

Explain that children can put things in groups. Draw a two-column chart for children like the one shown. Show children pictures of animals that live in the water and on land. Have children name each animal and tell where it lives. Ask: Which group does this animal belong in? How do you know?

Animals That Live on Land	Animals That Live in Water

If... children have difficulty putting objects in groups,
then... have them name what else they see in the picture with the animal. Ask: *Would you find that on land or in the water?*

Apply

Show children a familiar non-fiction book about one thing, such as flowers, seeds, or food. Together decide on a way to classify things in the book. Create a two-column chart to list the groups and things that belong in each group.

Writing

Children can write something that belongs in one of the groups listed in the chart.

Objectives:
- Children identify important ideas in a story.
- Children recall facts and details in a book.
- Children retell story events in their own words.

Texts for Teaching

- *Recall/Retell is a strategy that can be applied to any selection. Encourage children to recall and retell after they read.*

Recall/Retell

Mini-Lesson

Understand the Strategy

Recall/retell is related to summarizing, which children begin in Grade 1. This strategy means picking out the important ideas in a story or an article and restating them in one's own words. Being able to recall/retell enables readers to organize information and evaluate the importance of what they read.

Teach

Tell children that they can retell what happens in a book. They should not tell everything that happened. They should think about the important ideas. They should put the important ideas in their own words. Using a familiar fiction or nonfiction book, model asking questions to help determine the important ideas. (Use a fiction book one day, and a nonfiction book another.) Then summarize in a sentence or two.

This book is about winter and how animals get ready for it. Some animals hibernate during winter and some go where it's warmer.

The main character wants to earn money to buy his Mom a gift. Instead of buying something, he ends up baking cookies for her with his Dad.

Questions for Fiction
• What happened first in this book?
• What did the main character want to do?
• Did he or she do it? How?
• What happened at the end of this book?

Questions for Nonfiction
• What is this book mostly about?
• What is one thing you learned in this book?

Practice and Apply

Read a story together and use the questions to talk about the story. Then use pictures and have children retell the story.

If... children have difficulty retelling,

then... talk about what happened first, next, and last.

Anchor Chart

Anchor charts help children make their thinking visible and permanent. With an anchor chart, the group can clarify their thinking about how to use a strategy. You might make a chart of the questions to help children recall and retell and hang it in the classroom.

Glossary of Literacy Terms

This glossary lists academic language terms that are related to literacy.
They are provided for your information and professional use.

A

alliteration	the repetition of a consonant sound in a group of words, especially in poetry
animal fantasy	a story about animals that talk and act like people
antonym	a word that means the opposite of another word
author's purpose	the reason the author wrote the text
autobiography	the story of a real person's life written by that person

B

background knowledge	the information and experience that a reader brings to a text
biography	the story of a real person's life written by another person

C

cause	why something happens
character	a person, an animal, or a personified object in a story
classify and categorize	put things, such as pictures or words, into groups
compare and contrast	tell how things are the same and different
comprehension	understanding of text being read—the ultimate goal of reading
comprehension strategy	a conscious plan used by a reader to gain understanding of text. Comprehension strategies may be used before, during, or after reading.
context clue	the words, phrases, or sentences near an unknown word that give the reader clues to the word's meaning

D

details	small pieces of information
dialogue	written conversation
draw conclusions	arrive at decisions or opinions after thinking about facts and details and using prior knowledge

E

effect	what happens as the result of a cause
expository text	text that contains facts and information. Also called *informational text*.

F

fable	a story, usually with animal characters, that is written to teach a moral, or lesson
fact	piece of information that can be proved to be true
fairy tale	a folk story with magical characters and events
fantasy	a story that could not really happen
fiction	writing that tells about imaginary people, things, and events
folk tale	a story that has been passed down by word of mouth
foreshadowing	the use of hints or clues about what will happen later in a story

generalize make a broad statement or rule after examining particular facts

graphic organizer a drawing, chart, or web that illustrates concepts or shows how ideas relate to each other. Readers use graphic organizers to help them keep track of and understand important information and ideas as they read. Story maps, word webs, Venn diagrams, and KWL charts are graphic organizers.

graphic source a chart, diagram, or map within a text that adds to readers' understanding of the text

G

historical fiction realistic fiction that takes place in the past. It is an imaginary story based on historical events and characters.

humor writing or speech that has a funny or amusing quality

H

idiom a phrase whose meaning differs from the ordinary meaning of the words. *A stone's throw* is an idiom meaning "a short distance."

imagery the use of language to create beautiful or forceful pictures in the reader's mind

inference conclusion reached on the basis of evidence and reasoning

inform give knowledge, facts, or news to someone

informational text writing that contains facts and information. Also called *expository text*.

interview a face-to-face conversation in which someone responds to questions

I

legend a story coming down from the past about the great deeds of a hero. Although a legend may be based on historical people and events, it is not regarded as historically true.

literary elements the characters, setting, plot, and theme of a narrative text

L

main idea the big idea that tells what a paragraph or a selection is mainly about; the most important idea of a text

metacognition an awareness of one's own thinking processes and the ability to monitor and direct them to a desired goal. Good readers use metacognition to monitor their reading and adjust their reading strategies.

monitor and clarify a comprehension strategy by which readers actively think about understanding their reading and know when they understand and when they do not. Readers use appropriate strategies to make sense of difficult words, ideas, or passages.

M

Instruction

M

moral	the lesson or teaching of a fable or story
mystery	a story about mysterious events that are not explained until the end, so as to keep the reader in suspense
myth	a story that attempts to explain something in nature

N

narrative	a story, made up or true, that someone tells or narrates
narrator	the character in a selection who tells the story
nonfiction	writing that tells about real things, real people, and real events

O

onomatopoeia	the use of words that sound like their meanings, such as *buzz* and *hum*
opinion	someone's judgment, belief, or way of thinking
oral vocabulary	the words needed for speaking and listening

P

personification	a figure of speech in which human traits or actions are given to animals or inanimate objects, as in *The sunbeam danced on the waves.*
persuade	convince someone to do or to believe something
play	a story that is written to be acted out for an audience
plot	a series of related events at the beginning, middle, and end of a story; the action of a story
poem	an expressive, imaginative piece of writing often arranged in lines having rhythm and rhyme. In a poem, the patterns made by the sounds of the words have special importance.
pourquoi tale	a type of folk story that explains why things in nature came to be. *Pourquoi* is a French word meaning "why."
predict	tell what a selection might be about or what might happen in a text. Readers use text features and information to predict. They confirm or revise their predictions as they read.
preview	look over a text before reading it

Q

questioning	a reading strategy in which readers ask and answer questions to help make sense of what they read

R

reading vocabulary	the words we recognize or use in print
realistic fiction	a story about imaginary people and events that could happen in real life

repetition	the repeated use of some aspect of language	**R**
rhyme	to end in the same sound(s)	
rhythm	a pattern of strong beats in speech or writing, especially poetry	

science fiction	a story based on science that often tells what life in the future might be like	**S**
semantic map	a graphic organizer, often a web, used to display words or concepts that are meaningfully related	
sequence	the order of events in a selection or the order of the steps in which something is completed	
sequence words	clue words such as *first*, *next*, *then*, and *finally* that signal the order of events in a selection	
setting	where and when a story takes place	
stanza	a group of lines in a poem	
steps in a process	the order of the steps in which something is completed	
story map	a graphic organizer used to record the literary elements and the sequence of events in a narrative text	
story structure	how the characters, setting, and events of a story are organized into a plot	
summarize	give the most important ideas of what was read. Readers summarize important information in the selection to keep track of what they are reading.	
supporting detail	piece of information that tells about the main idea	

tall tale	a humorous story that uses exaggeration to describe impossible happenings	**T**
text structure	the organization of a piece of nonfiction writing. Text structures of informational text include cause/effect, chronological, compare/contrast, description, problem/solution, proposition/support, and ask/answer questions.	
theme	the big idea or author's message in a story	
think aloud	an instructional strategy in which a teacher verbalizes his or her thinking to model the process of comprehension or the application of a skill	
topic	the subject of a discussion, conversation, or piece of text	

visualize	picture in one's mind what is happening in the text. Visualizing helps readers imagine the things they read about.	**V**

Leveled Readers Skills Chart

Scott Foresman Reading Street provides more than six hundred leveled readers. Each one is designed to:

- Practice critical skills and strategies
- Build fluency
- Build vocabulary and concepts
- Develop a lifelong love of reading

Grade K

Title	Level*	DRA Level	Genre
Max the Duck	A	1	Fantasy
Fun for Us	B	2	Informational Text
Nick the Fix-It Man	B	2	Informational Text
Red and Blue	B	2	Realistic Fiction
We Have Fun Together	B	2	Fantasy
Two or Three?	B	2	Realistic Fiction
Buds for Mom	B	2	Realistic Fiction
A Walk in the Forest	B	2	Realistic Fiction
Looking for Animals	B	2	Realistic Fiction
Skip and Run	C	3	Fantasy
A Winter Home	C	3	Informational Text
A Yard for All	C	3	Fantasy
The Fawn	C	3	Realistic Fiction
We Can Do It!	C	3	Realistic Fiction
Fun With Gram	C	3	Realistic Fiction
They Will Grow	C	3	Realistic Fiction
What Can You Do?	C	3	Informational Text
Sad and Glad	C	3	Realistic Fiction
The Trip	C	3	Informational Text
Pigs	C	3	Informational Text
Frog's New Home	C	3	Informational Text
Five Bears	C	3	Fantasy
My Walk in Antarctica	C	3	Realistic Fiction
A Trip to Washington, D.C.	C	3	Informational Text
The Bus Ride	C	3	Realistic Fiction
The Boat Ride	C	3	Realistic Fiction
Ming on the Job	C	3	Realistic Fiction
The Big Train	D	4	Realistic Fiction
Get On the Bus!	D	4	Realistic Fiction
Catch the Ball!	D	4	Realistic Fiction
Homes	D	4	Informational Text
The Best Club Hut	D	4	Realistic Fiction
A Small Trip	D	4	Informational Text
The Box	D	4	Informational Text
Our Camping Trip	D	4	Realistic Fiction
Safe Places for Animals	D	4	Informational Text

* Suggested Guided Reading Level. Use your knowledge of children's abilities to adjust levels as needed.

This chart lists titles of leveled readers appropriate for students in Kindergarten. Use the chart to find titles that meet your students' interest and instructional needs. The books in this list were leveled using the criteria suggested in *Matching Books to Readers: Using Leveled Books in Guided Reading, Grades K–3* by Irene C. Fountas and Gay Su Pinnell. For more on leveling, see the *Reading Street Leveled Readers Leveling Guide.*

Comprehension Strategy	Target Comprehension Skill	Additional Comprehension Instruction	Vocabulary
Recall/Retell	Character	N/A	N/A
Recall/Retell	Setting	N/A	N/A
Recall/Retell	Sequence	N/A	N/A
Recall/Retell	Classify and Categorize	N/A	N/A
Recall/Retell	Character	N/A	N/A
Recall/Retell	Classify and Categorize	N/A	N/A
Recall/Retell	Compare and Contrast	N/A	N/A
Recall/Retell	Setting	N/A	N/A
Recall/Retell	Main Idea	N/A	N/A
Recall/Retell	Realism and Fantasy	N/A	N/A
Recall/Retell	Sequence	N/A	N/A
Recall/Retell	Realism and Fantasy	N/A	N/A
Recall/Retell	Compare and Contrast	N/A	N/A
Recall/Retell	Plot	N/A	N/A
Recall/Retell	Cause and Effect	N/A	N/A
Recall/Retell	Plot	N/A	N/A
Recall/Retell	Draw Conclusions	N/A	N/A
Recall/Retell	Main Idea	N/A	N/A
Recall/Retell	Sequence	N/A	N/A
Recall/Retell	Cause and Effect	N/A	N/A
Recall/Retell	Sequence	N/A	N/A
Recall/Retell	Character	N/A	N/A
Recall/Retell	Classify and Categorize	N/A	N/A
Recall/Retell	Setting	N/A	N/A
Recall/Retell	Realism and Fantasy	N/A	N/A
Recall/Retell	Cause and Effect	N/A	N/A
Recall/Retell	Compare and Contrast	N/A	N/A
Recall/Retell	Plot	N/A	N/A
Recall/Retell	Main Idea	N/A	N/A
Recall/Retell	Draw Conclusions	N/A	N/A
Recall/Retell	Compare and Contrast	N/A	N/A
Recall/Retell	Character	N/A	N/A
Recall/Retell	Main Idea	N/A	N/A
Recall/Retell	Plot	N/A	N/A
Recall/Retell	Setting	N/A	N/A
Recall/Retell	Draw Conclusions	N/A	N/A

Section 3 Matching Books and Readers

What Good Readers Do

You can use the characteristics and behaviors of good readers to help all your students read better. But what are these characteristics and behaviors? And how can you use them to foster good reading behaviors for all your students? Here are some helpful tips.

Good Readers enjoy reading! They have favorite books, authors, and genres. Good readers often have a preference about where and when they read. They talk about books and recommend their favorites.

Develop this behavior by giving students opportunities to respond in different ways to what they read. Get them talking about what they read, and why they like or dislike it.

This behavior is important because book sharing alerts you to students who are somewhat passive about reading or have limited literacy experiences. Book sharing also helps you when you select books for the class.

Good Readers select books they can read.

Develop this behavior by providing a range of three or four texts appropriate for the student and then letting the student choose.

This behavior is important because students gain control over reading when they can choose from books they can read. This helps them become more independent in the classroom.

Good Readers use text features to help them preview and set purposes.

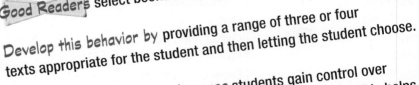

Develop this behavior by having students use the title and illustrations in fiction texts or the title, contents, headings, and other graphic features in nonfiction texts to make predictions about what they will be reading.

This behavior is important because previewing actually makes reading easier! Looking at features and sampling the text enables readers to predict and set expectations for reading.

Good Readers predict and ask questions before and while they read.

Develop this behavior by asking questions. After reading a passage, ask students what they think will happen next in a fiction text. Have them ask a question they think will be answered in a nonfiction text and read on to see if it is.

This behavior is important because when students predict and ask questions as they read, they are engaged. They have a purpose for reading and a basis for monitoring their comprehension.

> 66 Want to improve your students' performance by fostering good reading behaviors? **Customize Literacy can help.** 99

Good Readers use effective strategies and sources of information to figure out unknown words.

Develop this behavior by teaching specific strategies for figuring out unknown words, such as sounding out clusters of letters, using context, reading on, and using references.

This behavior is important because when readers have a variety of strategies to use, they are more able to decode and self-correct quickly. Readers who do these things view themselves as good readers.

CH-
QU-
ST-

Matching Books & Readers

Good Readers construct meaning as they read and then share or demonstrate their understanding.

Develop this behavior by having students retell what they read or write a summary of what they read in their own words.

This behavior is important because the ability to retell or write a summary is essential for success in reading. It shows how well a student has constructed meaning.

Good Readers make connections.

Develop this behavior by asking questions to help students make connections: *What does this remind you of? Have you ever read or experienced anything like this?*

This behavior is important because making connections helps readers understand and appreciate a text. Making connections to self, the world, and other texts supports high-level thinking.

Conversation Starters

Asking Good Questions Children want to read and listen to interesting and thought-provoking books! You can help them talk about these books. Use questions such as the following to assess listening comprehension and help children think about books. As you read longer books, pause often to ask questions about past and future events.

Cause and Effect

- What happens in this story?

- Why does it happen?

Classify and Categorize

- How are these things alike?

- Do these things belong in the same group?

- Is this thing like the others? Does it belong in the group?

- How do you know that it is like/not like the others?

- How would you group these things?

Character

- Who is in this story?

- What does this character like to do?

- How did the character feel in this part of the book?

- What does this character think about what happens in the book?

- Does this character seem real or made-up? What makes you think so?

- What character would you like to be? Why?

Compare and Contrast

- How are these things/characters/stories alike?

- How are these things/characters/stories different?

Draw Conclusions

- What happens in the story?

- What did the characters do to show you that they are kind/mean/strong?

- Which character do you like best? Why?

- Do you like this story? What makes you like it or dislike it?

Main Idea

- What is this story all about?

- What is the big idea of this story?

- What clues help you know what the story is about?

Plot

- In the story, what happens at the beginning? in the middle? at the end?

- What are other important things that happen in a story?

- What do you think is the most exciting/important thing that happens?

- What is the problem that the character has to solve/fix?

- How is that problem solved or fixed?

Realism and Fantasy

- Could this story happen in real life? Why do you think as you do?

- What things in the story could happen in real life?

- Do the people in this story act like people you know?

- How do you know if a story is make-believe or could really happen?

Sequence

- In this story, what happened first? next? last?

Setting

- What do the pictures tell me about when and where this story happened?

- What is this place like? What do you think it would be like?

- Does the place seem real or made-up? How can you tell?

- Do you want to visit this place? Why?

Connecting Science and Social Studies

Scott Foresman Reading Street Leveled Readers are perfect for covering, supporting, or enriching science and social studies content. Using these books ensures that all students can access important concepts.

Grade K Leveled Readers

Science

Earth and Space Science

Fiction Books
- *We Can Do It!*

Life Science

Nonfiction Books
- *A Winter Home*
- *What Can You Do?*
- *The Trip*
- *Pigs*
- *Frog's New Home*
- *A Small Trip*
- *Safe Places for Animals*

Fiction Books
- *A Walk in the Forest*
- *Looking for Animals*
- *Skip and Run*
- *Big Cats*
- *My Pal Fran*
- *Fun with Gram*
- *They Will Grow*
- *Sad and Glad*

Physical Science

Fiction Books
- *Catch the Ball!*
- *The Best Club Hut*

Grade K Leveled Readers

Social Studies

Citizenship

Nonfiction Books
- *Fun for Us*
- *Nick the Fix-It Man*
- *The Box*

Fiction Books
- *Red and Blue*
- *We Have Fun Together*
- *Two or Three?*
- *Buds for Mom*
- *Ming on the Job*

Culture

Nonfiction Books
- *Homes*

Fiction Books
- *Max the Duck*
- *Five Bears*
- *My Walk in Antarctica*
- *The Bus Ride*
- *The Boat Ride*
- *Get On the Bus!*
- *Our Camping Trip*

History

Fiction Books
- *The Big Train*

Geography

Nonfiction Books
- *A Trip to Washington, D.C.*

Matching Books & Readers

Connecting Science and Social Studies

Grade 1 Leveled Readers

Science

Earth and Space Science

Nonfiction Books

- *All About the Weather*
- *The Communication Story*
- *Over the Years*
- *Ready for Winter?*
- *Using the Telephone*

Fiction Books

- *Cody's Adventure*
- *Marla's Good Idea*
- *What a Detective Does*

Life Science

Nonfiction Books

- *All About Food Chains*
- *Animals Change and Grow*
- *Around the Forest*
- *Around the World*
- *Baby Animals in the Rain Forest*
- *Bees and Beekeepers*
- *The Dinosaur Detectives*
- *The Dinosaur Herds*
- *Fun in the Sun*
- *Honey*
- *In My Room*
- *Learn About Butterflies*
- *Learn About Worker Bees*
- *Let's Go to the Zoo*
- *Let's Visit a Butterfly Greenhouse*
- *Look at Dinosaurs*
- *A Mighty Oak Tree*
- *Monarchs Migrate South*
- *People Help the Forest*
- *The Seasons Change*
- *Seasons Come and Go*
- *What Animals Can You See?*

Life Science

Fiction Books

- *Bix the Dog*
- *Britton Finds a Kitten*
- *Carlos Picks a Pet*
- *Cary and the Wildlife Shelter*
- *Mac Can Do It!*
- *Mack and Zack*
- *Plans Change*
- *Sam*
- *The Sick Pets*
- *Time for Dinner*
- *What Brown Saw*
- *Which Animals Will We See?*
- *Which Fox?*

Physical Science

Nonfiction Books

- *The Inclined Plane*
- *Simple Machines at Work*
- *Simple Machines in Compound Machines*

Grade 1 Leveled Readers

Social Studies

Citizenship

Nonfiction Books
- *A Class*
- *A Garden for All*
- *Great Scientists: Detectives at Work*
- *Here in My Neighborhood*
- *A New Library*
- *Puppy Raiser*
- *The Story of the Kids Care Club*
- *Ways to Be a Good Citizen*

Fiction Books
- *The Art Show*
- *At Your Vet*
- *Big Wishes and Her Baby*
- *Double Trouble Twins*
- *Fly Away Owl!*
- *Grasshopper and Ant*
- *Hank's Song*
- *Let's Build a Park!*
- *Look at My Neighborhood*
- *My Little Brother Drew*
- *On the Farm*
- *Paul's Bed*
- *A Play*
- *Rules at School*
- *Space Star*
- *Squirrel and Bear*
- *That Cat Needs Help!*

Culture

Nonfiction Books
- *Cascarones Are for Fun*
- *My Babysitter*
- *Special Days, Special Food*
- *We Are a Family*
- *What Makes Buildings Special?*

Fiction Books
- *Go West!*
- *Grandma's Farm*
- *Gus the Pup*
- *Jamie's Jumble of Junk*
- *A New Baby Brother*
- *A Party for Pedro*
- *A Visit to the Ranch*
- *Where They Live*

History

Nonfiction Books
- *School: Then and Now*
- *Treasures of Our Country*

Fiction Books
- *Loni's Town*

Government

Nonfiction Books
- *America's Home*
- *Our Leaders*

Fiction Books
- *Mom the Mayor*

Matching Books & Readers

Planning Teacher Study Groups

Adventurous teachers often have good ideas for lessons. A teacher study group is a great way to share ideas and get feedback on the best way to connect content and students. Working with other teachers can provide you with the support and motivation you need to implement new teaching strategies. A teacher study group offers many opportunities to collaborate, support each other's work, share insights, and get feedback.

Think About It

A weekly or monthly teacher study group can help support you in developing your expertise in the classroom. You and a group of like-minded teachers can form your own study group. What can this group accomplish?

- Read and discuss professional articles by researchers in the field of education.

- Meet to share teaching tips, collaborate on multi-grade lessons, and share resources.

- Develop lessons to try out new teaching strategies. Meet to share experiences and discuss how to further improve your teaching approach.

Let's Meet!

Forming a study group is easy. Just follow these four steps:

1. **Decide on the size of the group.** A small group has the advantage of making each member feel accountable, but make sure that all people can make the same commitment!

2. **Choose teachers to invite to join your group.** Think about whom you want to invite. Should they all teach the same grade? Can you invite teachers from other schools? Remember that the more diverse the group, the more it benefits from new perspectives.

3. **Set goals for the group.** In order to succeed, know what you want the group to do. Meet to set goals. Rank goals in order of importance and refer often to the goals to keep the group on track.

4. **Make logistical decisions.** This is often the most difficult. Decide where and when you will meet. Consider an online meeting place where group members can post discussion questions and replies if people are not able to meet.

What Will We Study? Use the goals you set to help determine what your group will study. Consider what materials are needed to reach your goals, and how long you think you will need to prepare for each meeting.

How Will It Work? Think about how you structure groups in your classroom. Use some of the same strategies.

- **Assign a group facilitator.** This person is responsible for guiding the meeting. This person comes prepared with discussion questions and leads the meeting. This could be a rotating responsibility dependent on experience with various topics. This person might be responsible for providing the materials.

- **Assign a recorder.** Have someone take notes during the meeting and record group decisions.

- **Use the jigsaw method.** Not everyone has time to be a facilitator. In this case, divide the text and assign each portion to a different person. Each person is responsible for leading the discussion on that particular part.

Meet Again Make a commitment to meet for a minimum number of times. After that, the group can reevaluate and decide whether or not to continue.

> "Have some great teaching tips to share? Want to exchange ideas with your colleagues? Build your own professional community of teachers. **Customize Literacy** gets you started."

Trial Lessons

Use your colleagues' experiences to help as you think about new ways to connect content and students. Use the following plan to create a mini-lesson. It should last twenty minutes. Get the support of your colleagues as you try something new and then reflect on what happened.

Be Creative! As you develop a plan for a mini-lesson, use these four words to guide planning: *purpose*, *text*, *resources*, and *routine*.

- **Purpose:** Decide on a skill or strategy to cover. Define your purpose for teaching the lesson.

- **Text:** Develop a list of the materials you could use. Ask your colleagues for suggestions.

- **Resources:** Make a list of the available resources, and consider how to use those resources most effectively. Consider using the leveled readers listed on pages CL16–CL17 and CL22–CL25 of Customize Literacy.

- **Routine:** Choose an instructional routine to structure your mini-lesson. See the mini-lessons in Customize Literacy for suggestions.

Try It! Try out your lesson! Consider audio- or videotaping the lesson for later review. You may wish to invite a colleague to sit in as you teach. Make notes on how the lesson went.

How Did It Go? Use the self-evaluation checklist on page CL29 as you reflect on your trial lesson. This provides a framework for later discussion.

Discuss, Reflect, Repeat Solicit feedback from your teacher study group. Explain the lesson and share your reflections. Ask for suggestions on ways to improve the lesson. Take some time to reflect on the feedback. Modify your lesson to reflect what you have learned. Then try teaching the lesson again.

Checklist for Teacher Self-Evaluation

How Well Did I ...	Very Well	Satisfactory	Not Very Well
Plan the lesson?			
Select the appropriate level of text?			
Introduce the lesson and explain its objectives?			
Review previously taught skills?			
Directly explain the new skills being taught?			
Model the new skills?			
Break the material down into small steps?			
Integrate guided practice into the lesson?			
Monitor guided practice for student understanding?			
Provide feedback on independent practice?			
Maintain an appropriate pace?			
Assess student understanding of the material?			
Stress the importance of applying the skill as they read?			
Maintain students' interest?			
Ask questions?			
Handle student questions and responses?			
Respond to the range of abilities?			

Building Community

Books for Teachers

Children aren't the only ones who need to read to grow. Here is a brief list of books that you may find useful to fill your reading teacher basket and learn new things.

A Professional Bibliography

Adams, M. J. "Alphabetic Anxiety and Explicit, Systematic Phonics Instruction: A Cognitive Science Perspective." *Handbook of Early Literacy Research.* The Guilford Press, 2001.

Adams, M. J. *Beginning to Read: Thinking and Learning About Print.* The MIT Press, 1990.

Afflerbach, P. "The Influence of Prior Knowledge and Text Genre on Readers' Prediction Strategies." *Journal of Reading Behavior,* vol. XXII, no. 2 (1990).

Armbruster, B. B., F. Lehr, and J. Osborn. *Put Reading First: The Research Building Blocks for Teaching Children to Read.* Partnership for Reading, Washington, D.C., 2001.

Bear, D. R., M. Invernizzi, S. Templeton, and F. Johnston. *Words Their Way.* Merrill Prentice Hall, 2004.

Beck, I., M. G. McKeown, and L. Kucan. *Bringing Words to Life: Robust Vocabulary Instruction.* The Guilford Press, 2002.

Biemiller, A. "Teaching Vocabulary in the Primary Grades: Vocabulary Instruction Needed." *Vocabulary Instruction Research to Practice.* The Guilford Press, 2004.

Blachowicz, C. and P. Fisher. "Vocabulary Instruction." *Handbook of Reading Research,* vol. III. Lawrence Erlbaum Associates, 2000.

Cunningham, P. M. and J. W. Cunningham. "What We Know About How to Teach Phonics." *What Research Says About Reading Instruction,* 3rd ed. International Reading Association, 2002.

Daniels, H. *Literature Circles.* 2nd ed. Stenhouse Publishers, 2002.

Dickson, S. V., D. C. Simmons, and E. J. Kame'enui. "Text Organization: Instructional and Curricular Basics and Implications." *What Reading Research Tells Us About Children with Diverse Learning Needs: Bases and Basics.* Lawrence Erlbaum Associates, 1998.

Diller, D. *Making the Most of Small Groups: Differentiation for All.* Stenhouse Publishers, 2007.

Duke, N. K., V. S. Bennett-Armistead, and E. M. Roberts. "Bridging the Gap Between Learning to Read and Reading to Learn." *Literacy and Young Children: Research-Based Practices.* The Guilford Press, 2003.

Duke, N. K. and C. Tower. "Nonfiction Texts for Young Readers." *The Texts in Elementary Classrooms.* Lawrence Erlbaum Associates, 2004.

Ehri, L. C. and S. R. Nunes. "The Role of Phonemic Awareness in Learning to Read." *What Research Has to Say About Reading Instruction.* 3rd ed. International Reading Association, 2002.

Fountas, I. C. and G. S. Pinnell. *Guided Reading: Good First Teaching for All Children.* Heinemann, 1996.

Fountas, I. C. and G. S. Pinnell. *Matching Books to Readers: Using Leveled Books in Guided Reading, K-3.* Heinemann, 1999.

Harvey, S. and A. Goudvis. *Strategies That Work: Teaching Comprehension to Enhance Understanding.* 2nd ed. Stenhouse Publishers, 2007.

Hiebert, E. H. and L. A. Martin. "The Texts of Beginning Reading Instruction." *Handbook of Early Literacy Research.* The Guilford Press, 2001.

Indrisano, R. and J. R. Paratore. *Learning to Write, Writing to Learn. Theory and Research in Practice.* International Reading Association, 2005.

Juel, C., G. Biancarosa, D. Coker, and R. Deffes. "Walking with Rosie: A Cautionary Tale of Early Reading Instruction." *Educational Leadership* (April 2003).

National Reading Panel. *Teaching Children to Read.* National Institute of Child Health and Human Development, 1999.

Pressley, M. *Reading Instruction That Works: The Case for Balanced Teaching,* 3rd ed. The Guilford Press, 2005.

Smith, S., D. C. Simmons, and E. J. Kame'enui. "Word Recognition: Research Bases." *What Reading Research Tells Us About Children with Diverse Learning Needs: Bases and Basics.* Lawrence Erlbaum Associates, 1998.

Snow, C., S. Burns, and P. Griffin, eds. *Preventing Reading Difficulties in Young Children.* National Academy Press, 1998.

Vaughn, S., P. G. Mathes, S. Linan-Thompson, and D. J. Francis. "Teaching English Language Learners at Risk for Reading Disabilities to Read: Putting Research into Practice." *Learning Disabilities Research & Practice,* vol. 20, issue 1 (February 2006).

Building Community

UNIT 2

Acknowledgments

Acknowledgments

Illustrations

Cover: Rob Hefferan
12 Natalia Vasquez
28, 32, 48, 69, 88–89, 108–109 Mick Reid
50–51 Paul Meisel
50–51 Colleen Madden
52 Carolyn Croll
58–65 Maria Mola
70–71 Carolina Farias
72 Susan Mitchell
78–85 Wednesday Kirwan
90–93 David Austin Clar
92 Anthony Lewis
99–105 Cale Atkinson
110–111 Remy Simard
112 Jannie Ho
119–125 Robbie Short.

Photographs

Every effort has been made to secure permission and provide appropriate credit for photographic material. The publisher deeply regrets any omission and pledges to correct errors called to its attention in subsequent editions.

Unless otherwise acknowledged, all photographs are the property of Pearson Education, Inc.

Photo locators denoted as follows: Top (T), Center (C), Bottom (B), Left (L), Right (R), Background (Bkgd)

10 (B) ©William Leaman/Alamy
49 Cyril Laubacher/©DK Images, Dave King/©DK Images, Geoff Brightling/©DK Images, Mike Dunning/©DK Images
68 ©DK Images, Jane Burton/©DK Images
130 (T) ©DK Images
131 (T, B) ©DK Images

144

Teacher Editions

KWL Strategy: The KWL Interactive Reading Strategy was developed and is used by permission of Donna Ogle, National-Louis University, Skokie, Illinois, co-author of *Reading Today and Tomorrow*, Holt, Rinehart & Winston Publishers, 1988. (See also the *Reading Teacher*, February 1986, pp. 564–570.)

Understanding by Design quotes: Wiggins, G. & McTighe, J. (2005). *Understanding by Design*. Alexandria, VA: Association for Supervision and Curriculum Development.

Illustrations

Cover Rob Hefferan

Running Header Steven Mach

Photos

Every effort has been made to secure permission and provide appropriate credit for photographic material. The publisher deeply regrets any omission and pledges to correct errors called to its attention in subsequent editions.

Unless otherwise acknowledged, all photographs are the property of Pearson Education, Inc.

Teacher Notes

Teacher Notes

Teacher Notes

Teacher Notes

Teacher Resources

Looking for Teacher Resources and other important information?

In the **First Stop** on Reading Street

- **Dear Kindergarten Teacher**
- **Research into Practice on Reading Street**
- **Guide to Reading Street**
- **Assessment on Reading Street**
- **Writing on Reading Street**
- **Differentiate Instruction on Reading Street**

- **ELL on Reading Street**
- **Customize Literacy on Reading Street**
- **Digital Products on Reading Street**
- **Teacher Resources for Kindergarten**
- **Index**

Teacher Resources

Looking for Teacher Resources and other important information?

In the **First Stop** on Reading Street

- **Dear Kindergarten Teacher**
- **Research into Practice on Reading Street**
- **Guide to Reading Street**
- **Assessment on Reading Street**
- **Writing on Reading Street**
- **Differentiate Instruction on Reading Street**

- **ELL on Reading Street**
- **Customize Literacy on Reading Street**
- **Digital Products on Reading Street**
- **Teacher Resources for Kindergarten**
- **Index**